# Time Out
# 1000
## things to do in Britain
timeout.com

**Time Out Guides**

**Published by Time Out Guides Ltd,** a wholly owned subsidiary of Time Out Group Ltd.
Time Out and the Time Out logo are trademarks of Time Out Group Ltd.

© Time Out Group Ltd 2008

10 9 8 7 6 5 4 3 2 1

**This edition first published in Great Britain in 2008 by Ebury Publishing**
A Random House Group Company
20 Vauxhall Bridge Road, London SW1V 2SA

**Random House Australia Pty Limited** 20 Alfred Street, Milsons Point, Sydney, New South Wales 2061, Australia
**Random House New Zealand Limited** 18 Poland Road, Glenfield, Auckland 10, New Zealand
**Random House South Africa (Pty) Limited** Isle of Houghton, Corner Boundary
Road & Carse O'Gowrie, Houghton 2198, South Africa

Random House UK Limited Reg. No. 954009

**Distributed in USA by Publishers Group West**
1700 Fourth Street, Berkeley, California 94710

**Distributed in Canada by Publishers Group Canada**
250A Carlton Street, Toronto, Ontario M5A 2L1

**For further distribution details, see www.timeout.com**

ISBN: 978-1-84670-081-1

A CIP catalogue record for this book is available from the British Library

Printed and bound by Firmengruppe APPL, aprinta druck, Wemding, Germany

The Random House Group Limited supports The Forest Stewardship Council (FSC), the leading international forest certification organisation. All our titles that are printed on Greenpeace approved FSC certified paper carry the FSC logo. Our paper procurement policy can be found at http://www.rbooks.co.uk/environment.

All rights reserved. No part of this publication may be reproduced, stored in a retrieval system, or transmitted in any form or by any means, electronic, mechanical, photocopying, recording or otherwise, without prior permission from the copyright owners.

**Time Out Guides Limited**
Universal House
251 Tottenham Court Road
London W1T 7AB
Tel + 44 (0)20 7813 3000
Fax + 44 (0)20 7813 6001
Email guides@timeout.com
www.timeout.com

### Editorial
**Editor** Elizabeth Winding
**Deputy Editor** Sarah Thorowgood
**Listings Editor** Cathy Limb
**Researchers** Alex Brown, Gemma Pritchard
**Proofreader** Tamsin Shelton
**Indexer** Jackie Brind

**Managing Director** Peter Fiennes
**Financial Director** Gareth Garner
**Editorial Director** Sarah Guy
**Series Editor** Cath Phillips
**Editorial Manager** Holly Pick
**Assistant Management Accountant** Ija Krasnikova

### Design
**Art Director** Scott Moore
**Art Editor** Pinelope Kourmouzoglou
**Senior Designer** Henry Elphick
**Graphic Designer** Gemma Doyle, Kei Ishimaru
**Digital Imaging** Simon Foster
**Ad Designer** Jodi Sher

### Picture Desk
**Picture Editor** Jael Marschner
**Deputy Picture Editor** Katie Morris
**Picture Researcher** Gemma Walters

### Advertising
**Commercial Director** Mark Phillips
**Sales Manager** Alison Wallen
**Advertising Sales** Ben Holt, Alex Matthews, Jason Trotman
**Advertising Assistant** Kate Staddon
**Copy Controller** Declan Symington

### Marketing
**Head of Marketing** Catherine Demajo
**Marketing Manager** Yvonne Poon
**Sales & Marketing Director North America** Lisa Levinson

### Production
**Group Production Director** Mark Lamond
**Production Manager** Brendan McKeown
**Production Controller** Caroline Bradford
**Production Coordinator** Julie Pallot

### Time Out Group
**Chairman** Tony Elliott
**Financial Director** Richard Waterlow
**Group General Manager/Director** Nichola Coulthard
**Time Out Magazine Ltd MD** Richard Waterlow
**TO Communications Ltd MD** David Pepper
**Managing Director, Time Out International** Cathy Runciman
**Group IT Director** Simon Chappell

---

**Contributors** Sonya Barber, Gareth Buckell, Nuala Calvi, Femke Colborne, Simon Coppock, Peterjon Cresswell, Rob Crossan, Keith Davidson, Jonathan Derbyshire, Marcus Gipps, Charlie Godfrey-Faussett, Will Fulford-Jones, Hugh Graham, Sarah Guy, Malcolm Hay, Derek Hammond, Ronnie Haydon, Phil Harriss, Emma Howarth, Richard Jones, Carol Klein, Tom Lamont, Cathy Limb, Kate Mossman, Cath Phillips, Kate Rew, Nick Rider, Sam Le Quesne, Rachel Ragg, Kate Riordan, Mark Robertson, Robin Sales, Ros Sales, Cyrus Shahrad, Andrew Shields, Daniel Smith, Caroline Stacey, Matt Thorne, Sarah Thorowgood, Ben Tobias, Maisie Tomlinson, Yolanda Zappaterra.

**Interviews by** Nuala Calvi, Jonathan Derbyshire, Kevin Hill, Elizabeth Winding, Yolanda Zappaterra.

**The Editor would like to thank** all contributors to *Time Out* guides and *Time Out* magazine (whose work forms the basis for parts of this book), as well as the following for their inspired suggestions and invaluable assistance: Liam Bailey, Nuala Calvi, Cloth of Gold Field Archery Club, Simon Coppock, Gemma Doyle, Sarah Guy, Derek Hammond, Mike Hardwick, Emma Howarth, Cathy Limb, Eleanor Mayfield, Cath Philips, Martin Pirongs, Cyrus Shahrad, Christina Thiesen, Sarah Thorowgood, Maisie Tomlinson.

**Cover photography by** Liam Bailey; Heloise Bergman; Tove K Breitstein; Bristol Balloon Fiestas Ltd; Scott Chasserot; John Coutts; Crown Copyright (2007) Visit Wales; English Heritage Photo Library; Britta Jaschinski; Gillian Hutchinson; IOM Department of Tourism and Leisure; Longleat Enterprises Ltd; Jael Marschner; John Oakey; Jonathan Perugia; Olivia Rutherford; Jonty Wilde; Mike P Witby; Sandy Young; other featured establishments.

**Photography** see p320.

**Illustrations** Ian Keltie – www.keltiecochrane.com.

© Copyright Time Out Group Ltd
All rights reserved

# Contents

| | |
|---|---|
| *About the guide* | 7 |
| *Introduction* | 9 |
| *1000 things* | 10-303 |

## Features

| | |
|---|---|
| Brave a cave | 20 |
| Telling tales | 40 |
| Pitch perfect | 62 |
| Spin city | 80 |
| It's a small world | 96 |
| Club class | 112 |
| A bird in the hand | 132 |
| Walk on the wild side | 152 |
| The first cut | 174 |
| Flower power | 190 |
| Surfin' UK | 210 |
| Take the plunge | 234 |
| Super markets | 256 |
| Literary landscape | 278 |
| Joking aside… | 290 |

## A few of my favourite things

| | |
|---|---|
| Maggie O'Farrell | 12 |
| Matthew Bourne | 32 |
| Fergus Henderson | 56 |
| Stella Vine | 84 |
| Katharine Hamnett | 136 |
| Martin Parr | 157 |
| Julie Myerson | 196 |
| David Starkey | 218 |
| Ekow Eshun | 261 |
| Julie Verhoeven | 270 |

| | |
|---|---|
| *Advertisers' index* | 304 |
| *County index* | 305 |
| *Theme index* | 309 |
| *A-Z index* | 315 |

### Jane Austen's House Museum
Chawton, Alton, Hants
tel: 01420-83262
e-mail: enquiries@jahmusm.org.uk
www.jane-austens-house-museum.org.uk
Open : Daily 1Mar – 31Dec & 1 Jan
10.30 am – 4.30 pm
Admission fee charged
Refreshments opposite

17th century house where Jane Austen lived from 1809 to 1817. Here she wrote and revised her 6 novels, including Pride and Prejudice and Sense and Sensibility. Book & souvenir shop, pleasant garden. Major plans for 2009 to mark 200th anniversary of Jane's arrival in Chawton.

---

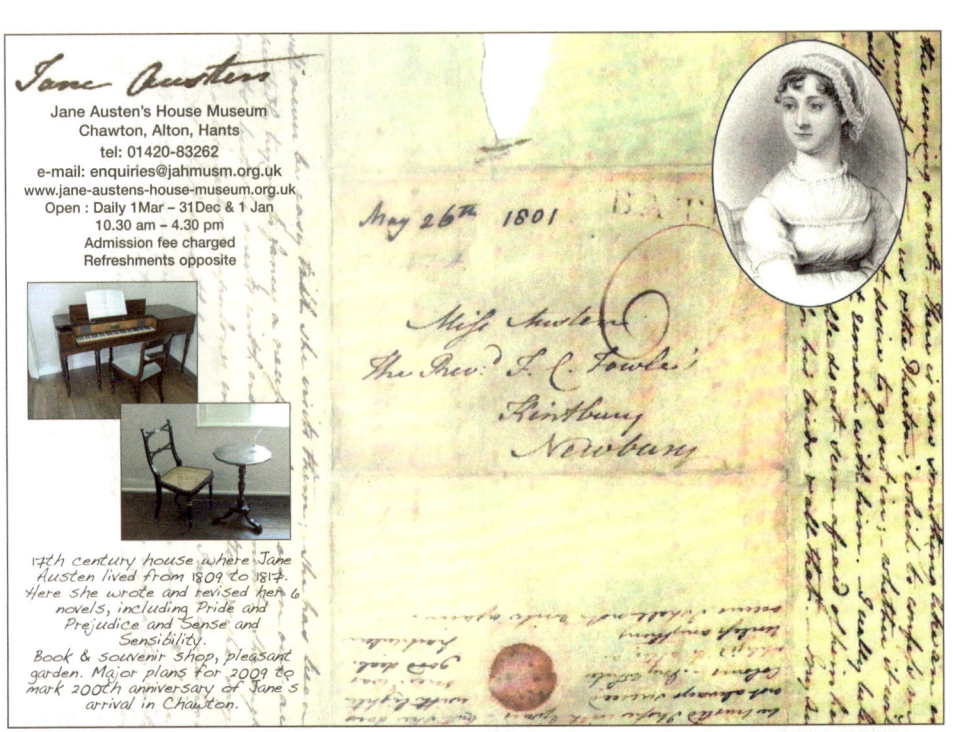

## Entertain your brain!

With ten galleries, fantastic Planetarium, tours and special events, there's something for everyone at Thinktank, Birmingham's interactive science museum. Combine your visit with a show at the IMAX® Cinema.

**Open daily from 10am - 5pm (last entry 4pm)**

### thinktank IMAX CINEMA
Birmingham science museum

**Call 0121 202 2222 or visit www.thinktank.ac**
**Thinktank, Millennium Point, Curzon Street, Birmingham B4 7XG**

# About the guide

## Telephone numbers
All phone numbers listed in this guide assume that you are calling from within Britain. If you are calling from abroad, dial your international access code, then 44 for the UK; follow that with the phone number, dropping the first zero of the area code.

## Disclaimer
While every effort has been made to ensure the accuracy of information within this guide, the publishers cannot accept responsibility for any errors it may contain. Businesses can change their arrangements at any time so, before you go out of your way, we strongly advise you to phone ahead to check opening times, prices and other particulars.

## Advertisers
The recommendations in *1000 Things to do in Britain* are based on the experiences of Time Out journalists. No payment or PR invitation of any kind has secured inclusion or influenced content. The editors select which venues and activities are listed in this guide, and the list of 1,000 was compiled before any advertising space was sold. Advertising has no effect on editorial content.

## Let us know what you think
Did we miss anything? We welcome tips for 'things' you consider we should include in future editions and take note of your criticism of our choices. You can email us at guides@timeout.com.

# wagamama

### number 214, visit wagamama

## delicious noodles | rice dishes
## freshly squeezed juices | salads
## wine | sake | japanese beers

positive eating + positive living

### wagamama.com

uk | ireland | holland | australia | uae | belgium | new zealand | denmark | turkey | usa | cyprus

# Introduction

As you'll soon discover within these pages, every corner of the country yields its own – often unexpected – delights. They range from the sublime to the surreal: world-class art in tiny churches; a cricket match held in the sea; a campsite in the treetops; the azure-lapped white sands of a remote Scottish beach. Forget flying halfway across the world in search of adventure: there's opportunity enough to hike, bike and climb your way across Britain, not to mention go caving, coasteering, surfing and snorkelling – through a dense Welsh peat bog, should the fancy take you.

Then there are the quieter, quintessentially British pleasures: steam trains, cream teas, stately homes and cider orchards. Playing Poohsticks on the bridge where AA Milne and Christopher Robin once stood, attending the Proms or devouring a proper Devon cream tea all have a timeless appeal – and that's before we even start on the great British seaside, or the joys of wild camping on the sun-dappled flanks of Dartmoor.

Suggestions of what to include in the book came from all kinds of sources. Jo Brand, Lee Mack and Jack Dee were among the stand-ups who chose their all-favourite comedy venues, while a stellar array of DJs revealed the clubs they really rate. Carol Klein led us through Britain's great gardens; author Matt Thorne, meanwhile, proved deliciously indiscreet when it came to the literary festivals scene. Fashion designers, photographers, rollercoaster addicts, chefs, artists and authors all contributed their ideas, and the list soon took shape.

One book can't hope to cover everything, of course, but we hope it inspires you on your own exploration of Britain. Our 1,000 things aren't set out in order of merit, or carved up into counties (although there are thematic and by-area indexes on *p309* and *p305*). Instead, rather like a journey around Britain, we hope this book has unexpected discoveries at every turn, opening up new vistas across a landscape that may not be quite so familiar as it seemed.

*Elizabeth Winding, Editor*

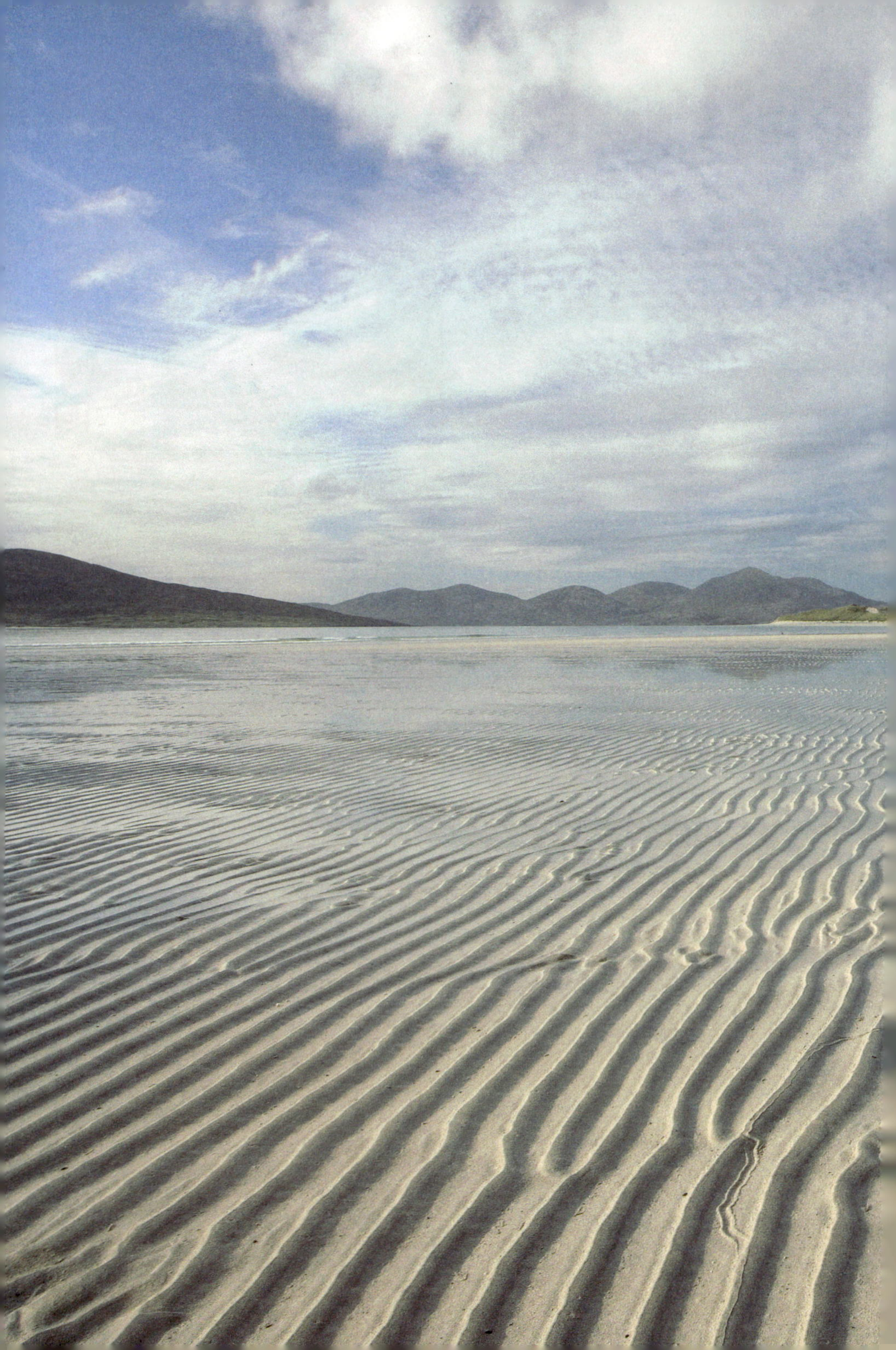

# 1
### Adopt a beach
Feel like being beside the seaside and getting a warm glow from providing some much-needed TLC for your favourite beach? The Marine Conservation Society runs a nationwide clean-up operation (www.adoptabeach.org.uk) to help clear Britain's beaches of the tons of plastic bottles, crisp packets and assorted rubbish that threaten to choke our coastline. Visit the website, sign up to your beach of choice – and don't forget the bin-liners.

## A few of my favourite things

# 2-7

## Maggie O'Farrell, writer

There's an extraordinary shop just off Princes Street in Edinburgh, called the Repository for Distressed Gentlefolk (23A Castle Street, Edinburgh EH3 2DN, 0131 220 1187). I was walking past one day, and the name fascinated me. Inside it's full of handicrafts made by the elderly ladies of Edinburgh, all for charity: patchwork, baby shawls, pyjamas, balaclavas... even knitted nativity sets at Christmas. My mum ordered an haute couture Arran coat for her dog. It's like going back 60 years, to a Britain that doesn't really exist any more: utility clothing and make do and mend. Blink and you miss it – it's very small. I really don't know what it's doing there, or how it affords the rent.

**As a child, I went on bucket-and-spade holidays to Dunraven Bay in South Wales. It's an incredibly beautiful beach – and up on the headland were the ruins of an old stately home, Dunraven House. There was a walled garden, high on the cliffs, that had run completely wild. It had tumbledown greenhouses and a fishpond, and the remains of a kitchen garden; it was like** *The Secret Garden*, **which was one of my favourite books. I went back recently, and it had all been tidied up; it's still beautiful, but I missed the ramshackle secret garden. It's still one of my favourite places, though, and I go there whenever I can.**

My favourite second-hand bookshop is the Bookshop in Lyme Regis (Marine Parade, The Cobb, Lyme Regis, Dorset DT7 3JF, 01297 444820). It's about the size of a broom cupboard, and stuffed with hundreds and hundreds of books. My husband and I spend about £100 every time we go in there, and come back from Lyme Regis with a car laden with ancient, slightly mildewed paperbacks. It's got amazing stock – I feel like a child in a sweet shop. I almost feel worried about talking about it, in case other people go there and buy everything.

**Lancrigg Country House is a vegetarian hotel, set in a rambling Victorian house just outside Grasmere (Easedale, Grasmere, Cumbria LA22 9QN, 015394 35317, www.lancrigg.co.uk). I worked there as a student, and it's one of those places that's really got under my skin. It's in a beautiful valley – you can walk though the gardens and carry on up the valley to a tarn right at the top. It's very unusual to find a vegetarian hotel, and the food's fantastic. The room above the dining room is my favourite, because of the view; I set an important scene from my first novel in there. I think it's one of my favourite rooms in the world.**

The Hunterian Museum (Royal College of Surgeons, 35-43 Lincoln's Inn Fields, London WC2A 3PE, 020 7869 6560, www.rcseng.ac.uk/museums) displays the collections of the 18th-century anatomist John Hunter. I first heard about him when I read about the giant O'Brien, an incredibly tall Irish man who used to tour the circuses. He was terrified of Hunter, because he knew Hunter wanted to dissect him – and when he died, Hunter pursued him and bribed the pallbearers. I went to the Hunterian to see his skeleton, and found the museum was extraordinary. There are lots of specimens and skeletons, and foetuses of children who had weird birth defects. There's a cyclops child with one eye, and a set of sextuplets, suspended in formaldehyde. It's astonishing; there's just a tiny bit of glass between you and these 200-year-old sextuplets, who were miscarried by the wife of a shoemaker. I've taken friends to see it, and a lot of people think it's very gruesome – but I think it's fascinating.

**The Caledonian sleeper train (0845 601 5929, www.firstgroup.com/scotrail) is the overnight train from Euston to Inverness. It's one of my favourite journeys in the world. There's something very seductive about going to bed in filthy Euston, then waking up in the mountains and snow, with deer outside. The train's like British Rail, but with beds – very no-nonsense. I don't always sleep brilliantly, but I don't mind: you're being pulled sideways the length of the country, and there's something quite exciting about that.**

*Maggie O'Farrell's latest novel is* The Vanishing Act of Esme Lennox *(Headline Review, £14.99).*

# 8 Visit the island beneath the waves

Tiree is a small, outlying Hebridean island, around four hours by ferry from Oban in Argyll (www.isleoftiree.com). Often sunny and very windy, with stunningly beautiful white sand beaches, it attracts everyone from windsurfers and surfers to visitors who just want peace, quiet and pristine surroundings. On its north coast, between Vaul Bay and Balephetrish Bay, stands a glacial boulder known as the Ringing Stone, deposited as the last Ice Age was in retreat. Legend has it that if the Ringing Stone ever breaks, Tiree will sink into the sea. When approaching the island by boat, that doesn't seem as far-fetched as it sounds; so much of the terrain is low-lying that it often vanishes behind the wave tops.

# 9 Sort your street out

Make like Tom Hanks in *The Burbs* and take the future of fly-tipping into your own hands, with the revolutionary www.fixmystreet.com. Over 300 problems a month are being sorted out by councils across Britain thanks to the service, which lets you report neighbourhood nuisances, then passes them on to the relevant authorities. Pictures posted on the site of freezers abandoned in freaky places and mysterious crater-like pot holes appearing make strangely compelling viewing. Pity the poor person who complained to Lambeth Council about an aptly named shitzu being allowed to 'deposit poo at will' outside their house, and the Barnsley resident whose neighbours have started digging a trench in the middle of their road.

# 10 *See a quagga and a zebroid in Tring*

The remarkable collection at Tring, little sister to London's mighty Natural History Museum, was assembled by the eccentric Walter Rothschild. Born into the celebrated banking dynasty, the baron was a lifelong collector of wildlife, both stuffed and alive; in his day, the grounds at Tring Park were home to kangaroos, giant tortoises and a tame wolf – along with the zebras that sometimes drew his carriage. These days, the display cases at Tring are a veritable Noah's Ark of animals, including species that have long since become extinct such as the South African quagga (a subspecies of zebra), and sweet-looking stripey Tasmanian wolf. An enormous elephant and two rhinos dominate gallery 3, but the oddest exhibit of all is on a far smaller scale, housed in one of the specimen cupboards: a pair of fleas dressed in Mexican dancer's costumes – one of the most surreal sights your eyes will ever behold.

**Natural History Museum at Tring** *Walter Rothschild Building, Akeman Street, Tring, Hertfordshire HP23 6AP (020 7942 6171/ www.nhm.ac.uk/tring).*

# WWT LONDON Wetland CENTRE

# DISCOVER THE WILDER SIDE OF LONDON

Explore the London Wetland Centre and discover the beautiful wildlife that lives here. Centre includes lakeside restaurant, discovery centre, gift shop and adventure area for children.

**Open 7 days a week from 9.30am to 6pm**
**T: 020 8409 4400    Visit wwt.org.uk/london**

WWT London Wetland Centre, Queen Elizabeth's Walk, Barnes, SW13 9WT
Alight at Barnes Station or take the no. 283 Duck Bus from Hammersmith Tube

Registered charity no. 1030884

## 11 Walk a fell with Wainwright

The irascible, obsessive Alfred Wainwright – author and illustrator of seven indispensable fell-walking guides to the Lake District in the 1950s – has made an unlikely appearance in a distinctly 21st-century medium. A Cumbrian Tourism podcast (www.golakes.co.uk) now enables you to trudge the 1,100 feet up the Lion and the Lamb with your headphones full of the stubborn poetry of the pipe-smoking loner. The voice is that of actor Nik Wood-Jones, but his narration – using Wainwright's original 1958 account of the climb – has the approval of the Wainwright Estate.

## 12 Run to the sun in Newquay

This 'custom car, VW and dance festival' was launched in 1987, in homage to the unique love that exists between a surfer-dude and his VW Beetle. Nowadays, Run to the Sun (01637 851851, www.runtothesun.co.uk) draws 80,000 custom car enthusiasts to Newquay, where they compare wheels, soak up the surf and dance the night away. Held over three days in May, the event starts with a 'cruise', as hundreds of cars drive to the event in convoy; then, at the festival proper, there are DJs, laser shows and stand-up comics, as well as shine-your-car competitions and other auto-related events. Bodacious.

## 13 Visit Kew's country outpost

As well as gardens galore, Kew's lesser-known West Sussex site, Wakehurst Place, is home to the amazing Millennium Seed Bank. Its objective? To collect seeds and specimens from over 24,000 different plant species, guarding them against extinction. Learn why and how the seeds are stored in underground vaults, and check out the world's largest seed – the rather saucily shaped Coco de Mer.
**Wakehurst Place** *Ardingly, near Haywards Heath, West Sussex RH17 6TN (01444 894000/ www.kew.org).*

## 14 Get a prime view of the Proms – for a fiver

Prommers are the rabble of picnic-wielding hardcore classical music fans who pile into the standing room-only areas in the stalls and gallery of the Albert Hall during the Proms – and you can be one too. If you're prepared to spend up to half an afternoon queuing, you can Prom for a fiver and get an unparalleled opportunity to get close to some of the world's best classical music performers. So close, in fact, that you can smell the conductor's sweat, if you nab a spot in the front row or two.

If that sounds a bit too intense, leave the hardcore Prommers to it and head for a space slightly further back; in longer concerts people tend to sit down for the second half, so there's no danger of your view being obscured.
**BBC Proms** *Royal Albert Hall, Kensington Gore, London SW7 2AP (020 7589 8212/ www.bbc.co.uk/proms).*

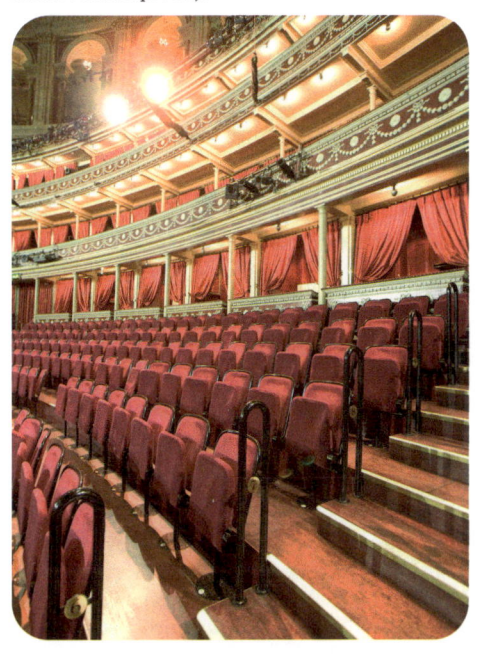

# 15-24 *Support an independent cinema*

In this era of shiny multiplexes and predictable Hollywood plots, flying the flag for independent films is ever more important. Superb indie cinemas dot the country; here are our favourites.

## BFI Southbank, London
The British Film Institute is known for its splendid retrospectives and themed seasons, paying tribute to cinema's great and good – and its forgotten stars. After the screening, head to its café for a beer-fuelled dissection of the action.
**BFI Southbank** *Belvedere Road, London SE1 8XT (020 7928 3232/www.bfi.org.uk).*

## Broadway, Nottingham
Last time we dropped by, cinematic gems on offer here ran from well-chosen oldies (*Love on the Dole*, *Secrets and Lies*) to the pick of the big-budget releases. Paul Smith's a regular – and designed the dapper striped seat covers.
**Broadway** *14-18 Broad Street, Nottingham NG1 3AL (0115 952 6611/www.broadway.org.uk).*

## Chapter, Cardiff
The Chapter boasts a gallery space, a café and three theatres as well as two cinema screens; no wonder it's got its own loyalty card.
**Chapter** *Market Road, Cardiff CF5 1QE (029 2030 4400/www.chapter.org).*

## Cornerhouse, Manchester
The fortnightly Breakfast Club here is hungry cinephile heaven: a traditional English plus a classic film (*The Big Lebowski*, say, or Robert Bresson's *Pickpocket*), for under a tenner.
**Cornerhouse** *70 Oxford Street, Manchester M1 5NH (0161 200 1500/www.cornerhouse.org).*

## Edinburgh Filmhouse
In business for over 30 years, the Filmhouse is rightly beloved of film aficionados north of the border. Don't miss the annual Dead by Dawn festival – a gory treat for horror-lovers.
**Filmhouse** *88 Lothian Road, Edinburgh EH3 9BZ (0131 228 2688/www.filmhousecinema.com).*

## Glasgow Film Theatre
An art deco beauty, Glasgow Film Theatre's events range from the monthly Monorail Film Club (where speakers have included Franz Ferdinand's Alex Kapranos) to the friendly screenwriters' discussions and workshops.
**Glasgow Film Theatre** *12 Rose Street, Glasgow G3 6RB (0141 332 8128/www.gft.org.uk).*

## Riverside Studios, London
This west London repertory cinema makes the cut thanks to its enticing double bills – Werner Herzog's *Grizzly Man*, say, followed by *Rescue Dawn*, or a Billy Wilder film duo. There's also an excellent on-site theatre, a café and bar.
**Riverside Studios** *Crisp Road, London W6 9RL (020 8237 1111/www.riversidestudios.co.uk).*

## Showroom, Sheffield
With four screens, there's generally something to suit most tastes at Sheffield's Showroom. And a night at the cinema doesn't mean a staid evening: the bar's open until 1am on Friday and Saturday for a post-screening tipple.
**Showroom** *Paternoster Row, Sheffield S1 2BX (0114 275 7727/www.showroom.org.uk).*

## Side Cinema, Newcastle
Run by Amber Films, which has been producing social documentaries about the area since 1968, the Side Cinema shows independent international films as well as some of Amber's own works in its 48-seater cinema.
**Side Cinema** *5-9 Side, Newcastle-upon-Tyne NE1 3JE (0191 232 2208/www.amber-online.com).*

## Watershed, Bristol
Housed in two converted Victorian warehouses, amid a stretch of raucous riverside bars and clubs, the Watershed offers welcome respite. Best of all, it doesn't sell popcorn – so your neighbour can't ruin an arthouse masterpiece with an ill-timed crunch.
**Watershed** *1 Canon's Road, Harbourside, Bristol BS1 5TX (0117 927 5100/www.watershed.co.uk).*

## 25 Make tracks at Silverstone

Fancy yourself the new Lewis Hamilton (or the old Nigel Mansell, or the very old Jackie Stewart)? For £155 you can burn rubber at Silverstone, home of the British Grand Prix, in a single-seater F1-style car. The day includes a briefing on safety and driving techniques, two sessions on the track (with and without a pace car) and an assessment from the instructors at the end. If something less technical appeals, sign up to learn the art of the power-slide in Silverstone's specially adapted skid cars (think Audis with bicycle-style stabilisers); a session costs £99. For both activities, you need to have held a full driving licence for at least a year.
**Silverstone Circuit** *Silverstone, Northamptonshire NN12 8TN (0870 458 8270/www.silverstone.co.uk).*

## 26 Pig out at Judges Bakery

Judges is no ordinary high-street bakery: every product on its shelves is made from organically certified ingredients, from the jam doughnuts to the deliciously dense rye bread. Artificial additives are a no-no – even the pink meringue pigs are dyed with raspberry and beetroot juice.
**Judges Bakery** *51 High Street, Hastings, East Sussex TN34 3EN (01424 722588/www.judges bakery.com).*

## 27 Get up close and personal with Stonehenge...

In high season, when the day-trippers descend in force, the roads leading to Stonehenge are hellish – and it's tempting to turn around and head back home. Yet while it may have become a horribly commercialised experience, there's no denying the wonder of Stonehenge. Dodge the hordes by going on a pre-opening or post-closing 'access' visit to the site (01722 343834, www.english-heritage.org.uk). Only 26 people are admitted at a time, and you'll be able to go right inside the stone circle, bathed in morning or evening light. Book well in advance.

## 28 ...or escape the tourist trappings at Avebury

There's more to Wiltshire's prehistoric landscape than the 'S' word. Avebury, little sister to Stonehenge, is a quieter spot where wandering among the ancient stones can be a far more spiritual and peaceful experience. What's more, it's free (though there is a charge for the car park). Close by, you'll also find Silbury Hill and West Kennett Long Barrow, plus giant hill carvings of white horses at Manton and Cherhill.
**Avebury** *on the A361/A4361, near Marlborough, Wiltshire SN8 1RF (01672 539250/www.national trust.org.uk).*

# 100% PURE COMEDY

## THE COMEDY STORE

DON WARD PRESENTS

# A SERIOUS NIGHT OUT!

www.thecomedystore.co.uk

Tickets and Information:

**LONDON**
0844 847 1728

**MANCHESTER**
0844 826 0001

## 29 Relive the Routemaster days

Having done the unthinkable a couple of years back and phased out these iconic gas guzzlers, Transport for London – following public outcry – realised the error of its ways and brought a few back into circulation on what it describes as 'heritage routes' (www.tfl.gov.uk). These are, in fact, the perfectly ordinary routes 9 and 15, but which between them take in most of central London's sights. Buses are scheduled to run every 15 minutes daily until 6.30pm.

## 30-34 See stars

Cloud coverage and poor viewing conditions can make star-gazing in the real night sky challenging for novices – so planetariums (to find your nearest, see www.planetarium.org.uk), which project the sky on to a giant dome, are the perfect solution. If you messed about too much to learn anything during school planetarium trips of yesteryear, go again and see if you can still spot the Big Dipper (extra points for identifying a zodiacal constellation). Arguably the country's best new planetarium is at the Royal Observatory in Greenwich (020 8312 8565, www.rog.nmm.ac.uk). Focusing on time, astronomy and the art of navigating by the stars, it uses an impressive 'digistar' projector, so your celestial viewing is like visiting a 360-degree cinema. Birmingham's Think Tank (0121 202 2222, www.thinktank.ac) and Leicester's National Space Centre (0116 261 0261, www.spacecentre.co.uk) use similar projectors and also have talks and loads of children's activities. Liverpool's World Museum (0151 478 4393, www.liverpoolmuseums.org.uk/wml) has a 62-seater planetarium with 30-minute shows; entrance is free, though you need to nab a ticket from the ground-floor information desk. At the South Downs Planetarium in Chichester (01243 774400, www.southdowns.org.uk) there's an ever-changing line-up of shows – from tours of Mars to spectacular re-creations of the Northern Lights.

## 35 Lunch with cheese-lovers

Lovers of fine fromage take note: cheese nirvana awaits in Lincoln, in the shape of the Cheese Society's café. As you'd expect, cheese of all descriptions plays a starring role on the menu: staple dishes include a rich double-baked gruyère soufflé, fondue for two and a classic cheddar rarebit; specials might include Thai green curry with Indian paneer cheese, or tartiflette, an Alpine dish concocted from potato, double cream and reblochon cheese, which tastes just as delicious in the flatlands of Lincolnshire as it does on the slopes. If you can't make it to the café, the society also offers a mail-order service.

**Cheese Society Café** *1 St Martin's Lane, Lincoln LN2 1HY (01522 511003/www.thecheesesociety.co.uk).*

## 36 Get creative at the Roald Dahl Museum

Before JK, Roald Dahl was the ubiquitous favourite of young British bookworms. This museum and activity centre in the village of Great Missenden, home to the author for 36 years until his death in 1990, boasts an archive of Dahl's manuscripts and letters, as well as objects from his writing hut and mementoes from his life. The big draw is the organised storytelling sessions: Dahl's tales are read out throughout the summer holidays. If it's sunny, readings take place in the Wundercrump courtyard, named after the BFG's exclamation of joy; if it's rainy, they're held in Miss Honey's classroom, where Mathilda terrorised the evil Mrs Trunchbull with a piece of chalk. Other activities include chocolate decorating (for budding Willy Wonkas), 'marvellous experiment' workshops (for fans of George) and an annual celebration of the author's birthday on 13 September, now officially 'Roald Dahl Day'.

**Roald Dahl Museum & Story Centre** *81-83 High Street, Great Missenden, Buckinghamshire HP16 0AL (01494 892192/www.roalddahlmuseum.org).*

# 37 *Head underground*

# Brave a cave

**Cyrus Shahrad** *discovers Derbyshire's hidden depths.*

Having a fear of being trapped in a cave is no more irrational than being scared of great white sharks, or finding bird-eating spiders in your breakfast cereal. That said, I'm genuinely bad in tight spaces; not clinically claustrophobic, perhaps, but scarred for life by a childhood mishap involving a duvet cover that still brings on cold sweats in cramped tube carriages and overcrowded nightclubs.

Thank heavens, then, for Betti. As our team splashes ever further down the dark gullet of the unfortunately named Giant's Hole – as the wet walls close in on all sides and the framed shard of overcast Derbyshire sky fades and finally flickers out behind us – it's a fellow caving novice's sociable stream of chatter that keeps me rooted in reality and stops me turning into one of the hyperventilating refuseniks who so regularly cut expeditions short. Not that I'm taking any chances: those rare occasions when I dare to look up reveal a line of red and yellow boiler suits snaking eerily into the blackness; for the most part, however, I keep my headlamp trained on my Wellington boots, only too aware that taking a tumble and breaking a leg deep in the cave system could mean the difference between my next meal being a cosy dinner back at the hotel or a hospital breakfast following a night of protracted rescue efforts.

It's one of a number of harsh insights into the intricacies of caving given less than an hour earlier by Duncan and Daryl of Acclimbatize, the former a gruff giant with a shaved head and a knack for unnerving anecdotes, the latter a softly spoken Northerner with a wool hat and a reassuring smile. Their office is little more than a walk-in wardrobe in a disused mill outside Matlock, its walls hung with shelves of battered helmets, coils of once-colourful rope and framed pictures of erstwhile Acclimbatizers up to their bug eyes in torrents of muddy water. On one side of the room, a series of buckets mark how many hours are left on the battery packs of various headlamps; on the other is a rack of barely wearable bin-end fleeces and an unnatural crush of those red and yellow boiler suits.

Through the front door, the lowering sky promises another deluge of rain. I make a nervous joke about how at least caving is one sport that the great British weather can't ruin; Duncan, calmly stroking his beard, informs me that this isn't the case: 'active stream caves' are notorious for flooding in heavy weather, so we won't be going into one of those today.

'Actually,' says Daryl, scrutinising his computer screen, 'it says here that the sun should be coming out later this afternoon. I think we should risk it.'

It sounds like a sick joke to me, but before I can protest the scene is stolen by a gaggle of giggling students from Nottingham University, who tumble out of their cars and, introductions over, begin rifling through piles of wellingtons and striking amused fashion poses in their oversized boiler suits. I smile and play along, while surreptitiously sizing up my companions as you might on an aeroplane you're convinced is going to crash: who will freak out first; who will display a surprising capacity for leadership; who will provide the most meat should we be forced to resort to cannibalism.

This sense of pre-destined doom colours everything up to and including our descent into the hell mouth itself, from the funereal procession of our cars as we wind our way through the lonely limestone escarpments of the Peak District, to the obvious futility of Duncan's safety instructions as we double-check harnesses, test headlights and don helmets.

All of this changes, however, after five minutes in the cave system itself, when the initial smothering panic is replaced with an expeditionary sense of adventure. Unlike rock climbing, in which the majority of routes can be pre-emptively scrutinised over tea and biscuits – which foot goes where, which ledges look most likely to support your weight – there's something about caving that defies planning. Who knows what lies around the next blind corner, or which tunnels will lead into cavernous chambers and which dwindle into nothing? Having guides who could navigate the caves with their eyes closed is all well and good, but there's still something otherworldly about the experience – a feeling that's enhanced by the unexpected beauty of the caves and their bizarre geological formations, from the barnacle-like accumulations of 'cave popcorn' to the roofs studded with fossilised marine life. The further we descend, the harder it is to believe that this landscape has existed all along – that we were, in fact, driving over it less than half an hour earlier.

At no point does our caving trip inspire the stomach-tumbling terror feared by those fed on horror stories and half-remembered episodes of *999* – there are no submerged tunnels or suddenly collapsing ceilings to negotiate – but nor is it a walk in the park. Several passages are tight enough to necessitate crawling on our hands and knees, while the 'active stream' itself is deep and rapid enough to demand the regular emptying of squelching wellies. At one point, our team abseils one by one down a three-storey overhanging rock face; later on, we're clipped on to a running line and made to traverse a perilous shelf. With a 30-foot drop on one side, some abandon the search for slippery handholds and simply cling on to the rope for dear life, legs flailing gracelessly over the abyss as they slide down.

It's the final flourish, however, that provides the most powerful adrenalin rush. Emerging grazed and muddied from one of the tighter tunnels, we find ourselves in an enormous chamber dominated by a deafening waterfall, on top of which Daryl has fixed a wire ladder with all the rigidity of a ship's rigging. Another caving group emerges from a separate tunnel, and stands waiting in the cold as one by one we climb blindly, Daryl's shouted instructions drowned out by the raging cascade of water.

The second party, increasingly impatient, begins to sing – *I Vow to Thee My Country, Dancing Queen, Angels* – the echo of their chorus lending the scene a bizarrely symbolic gravity, like that legendary orchestra playing on as the *Titanic* began her slow submergence.

Reason clouded by the surrealism of my surroundings, I leave the team assembling above the waterfall and wander alone down an arterial side passage, before turning off my headlamp for a moment. Sure enough, the darkness that descends is like nothing I've ever known – I pass a hand in front of my face and convince myself that I can see it, only to then witness exactly the same thing with my eyes clamped shut. It's a deeply unsettling sensation, and one that makes the sky seem all the more heartbreakingly welcome when we finally emerge blinking into the open air some ten minutes later – not least because the clouds have parted and, as Daryl promised, the sun is streaming down across the Peaks.

And what a gorgeous, glorious thing the sun is. I'll never make a joke about the great British weather again.

**Acclimbatize** *01629 820268/www.acclimbatize. co.uk. Prices start from £15 per person.*

# 38-39
## Play Poohsticks

Pooh may have been a Bear of Very Little Brain, but the game he accidentally invented in *The House at Pooh Corner* is sheer genius. True aficionados make a pilgrimage to a humble wooden bridge in Posington Wood, there to indulge in the time-honoured pursuit. Now officially known as Poohsticks Bridge, it's the spot where AA Milne used to play the game with his son Christopher. Follow the footpath (signposted, if a trifle muddy) from the Pooh car park just off the B2026 – and keep a sharp eye out for likely sticks along the half-mile walk. For more Pooh-related sights in the forest, pick up a special map from the Ashdown Forest Centre. Those with a real flair for stick-dropping should also consider competing in the World Poohsticks Championships, an annual charity fundraiser held at Days Lock in Oxfordshire (www.pooh-sticks.com).

**Ashdown Forest Centre** *Wych Cross, Forest Row, East Sussex RH18 5JP (01342 823583/ www.ashdownforest.org).*

## 40 Laugh out loud at Bristol's Silent Comedy Festival

Fed up with seeing sub-standard prints of his favourite silent movies, screened at the wrong speeds and with dodgy musical accompaniment, film fan Chris Daniels founded the Slapstick Silent Comedy Festival (www.slapstick.org.uk) in 2005. Comedian Paul Merton came on board, and the four-day event now attracts several thousand people to the Watershed Media Centre and other venues across Bristol each January. The line-up for 2008 included a gala screening, hosted by Merton, of Charlie Chaplin's 1925 classic *The Gold Rush*, with a live 15-piece band playing a new orchestration of the original film score, plus former 'Goodies' Tim Brooke-Taylor and Graeme Garden picking their favourite Buster Keaton shorts, screened with accompaniment from a three-piece improv band.

## 41 Eat herrings in Hemsby

Back in the 19th century, the village of Hemsby on the Norfolk coast was an important fishing community – and if you turn up for the annual Longshore Herring Festival, held in late August or early September, the villagers and members of Hemsby Lifeboat Station are keen not to let you forget it (www.hemsbyinshorerescue.org). The 'silver darlings' are cooked up on the beach for the delectation of visitors, in the traditional rolled oats and beef dripping. Other attractions include donkeys rides along the beach (not recommended after a herring splurge) and postmodern views of the wind turbines of Scroby Sands wind farm, churning away out in the slate-hued North Sea.

## 42 Learn to fence at the Royal Armouries

Forget the monotony of jogging or the gym and get in touch with your swashbuckling side at the Royal Armouries Museum in Leeds. Open sessions during spring half-term give members of the public a taster of fencing; if you enjoy it, you can join the fencing club, which meets at the museum every Friday evening. Open to fencers of all abilities (over-eights only), it's a bargain £3 per session, while six-week beginners' courses are a mere £25. With all that lunging, parrying and thrusting, you'll soon be fighting fit.

**The Royal Armouries** *Armouries Drive, Leeds LS10 1LT (0113 220916/www.royalarmouries.org).*

## THE ROALD DAHL MUSEUM AND STORY CENTRE

**Enter the chocolate doors of this great little museum and**

- delve into Roald Dahl's archive on our touch-screen monitors
- create your own gobblefunk words and stories
- pick up writing tips from Roald Dahl and other top writers
- visit our shop and the delumptious Café Twit

GREAT MISSENDEN · ROALD DAHL · THE HOME OF

www.roalddahlmuseum.org
01494 892192

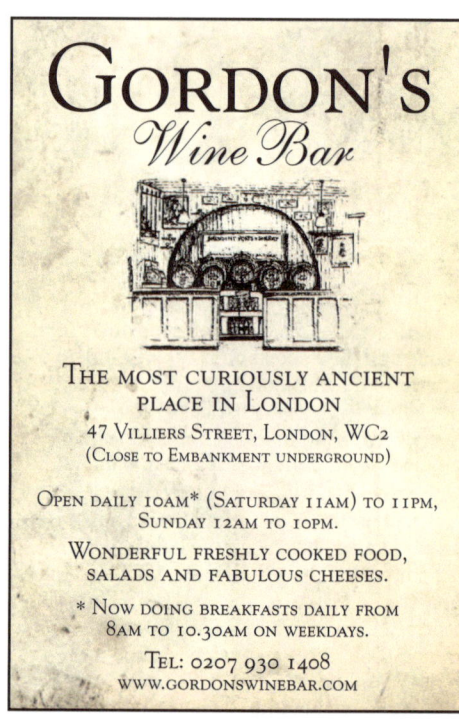

---

## GORDON'S Wine Bar

THE MOST CURIOUSLY ANCIENT PLACE IN LONDON
47 VILLIERS STREET, LONDON, WC2
(CLOSE TO EMBANKMENT UNDERGROUND)

OPEN DAILY 10AM* (SATURDAY 11AM) TO 11PM,
SUNDAY 12AM TO 10PM.

WONDERFUL FRESHLY COOKED FOOD,
SALADS AND FABULOUS CHEESES.

*NOW DOING BREAKFASTS DAILY FROM
8AM TO 10.30AM ON WEEKDAYS.

TEL: 0207 930 1408
WWW.GORDONSWINEBAR.COM

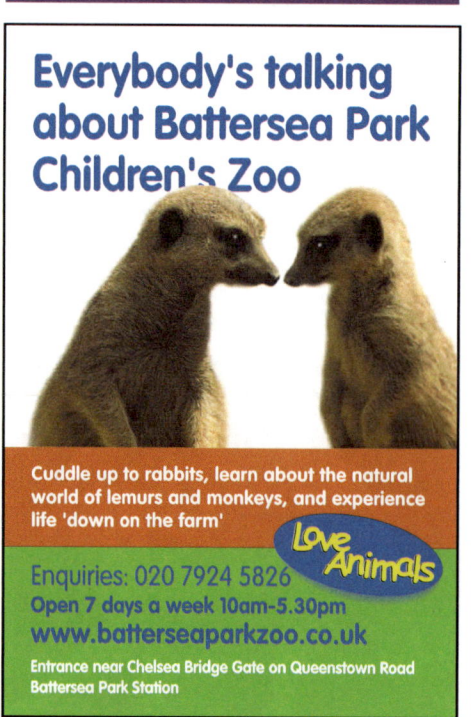

---

## Everybody's talking about Battersea Park Children's Zoo

Cuddle up to rabbits, learn about the natural world of lemurs and monkeys, and experience life 'down on the farm'

*Love Animals*

Enquiries: 020 7924 5826
Open 7 days a week 10am-5.30pm
www.batterseaparkzoo.co.uk

Entrance near Chelsea Bridge Gate on Queenstown Road
Battersea Park Station

---

Airline flights are one of the biggest producers of the global warming gas $CO_2$. But with **The CarbonNeutral Company** you can make your travel a little greener.

Go to **www.carbonneutral.com** to calculate your flight emissions then 'neutralise' them through international projects which save exactly the same amount of carbon dioxide.

Contact us at **shop@carbonneutral.com** or call into the office on **0870 199 99 88** for more details.

CarbonNeutral® flights

## 43 Tackle a mountain bike trail in Dalby

With its 34 miles of scenic trails weaving through the trees, Dalby Forest in North Yorkshire really is a pedal pusher's paradise. Experienced cyclists should head for the red-graded circular trail, with its steep inclines, steps and adrenalin-packed jumps, but there are also plenty of more gentle rides for novices. The visitors' centre can provide you with a map of all the trails (01751 460295, www.forestry.gov.uk), and it is possible to hire bikes and organise trips from the Purple Mountain Bike Centre (01751 460011, www.purplemountain.co.uk).

## 44 Unlock the 29 at Caen

Just west of Devizes, the Kennet & Avon Canal (01452 318000, www.visitkanda.com) descends 237 feet in two and a half miles through the 29 Caen Hill locks, like a gigantic flight of stairs. Designed by John Rennie in 1810, they were the crowning engineering achievement on the canal, which linked southern England's east-to-west waterways. The main flight of 16 consecutive locks running up a one-in-30 gradient is the most impressive sight, each lock with its own side pool. They're a short stroll along the towpath, but boats can take up to five or six hours to work their way over the hill.

## 45 Enjoy local art in Cornwall

The quality of light, colourful local life and lovely landscapes around Newlyn have long made this Cornish harbour town a mecca for artistic types. Its art gallery was founded back in 1895 to exhibit the work of the Newlyn School – a group of artists that included Edwin Harris, Walter Langley and Norman Garstin, whose work often depicted everyday life in the small fishing community.

The gallery's commitment to showcasing local artists may be undimmed, but its premises have undergone some radical changes, thanks to a massive refurbishment in 2007. Now, the gallery boasts an impressive sister art space in Penzance, the Exchange. Once a '50s telephone exchange, it has changing light displays along the length of its undulating glass façade; a salient contrast to Newlyn's Victorian premises. Both sites warrant a visit, but the original outpost remains our favourite. Its new extension, with lovely sea views and Cornish slate-clad exterior, allows the exhibits within to take centre stage.

**Newlyn Art Gallery** *New Road, Newlyn, Cornwall TR18 5PZ (01736 363715/ www.newlynartgallery.co.uk).*
**The Exchange** *Princes Street, Penzance, Cornwall TR18 2NL (01736 363715/www.nsanewlyn.com).*

# 46-49 Take a llama for a stroll

It may sound peculiar, but this is a wonderful way to chill out. Your pace becomes slower when leading a llama, so the walk is as much about taking in and enjoying your surroundings as appreciating the therapeutic qualities of being with an animal companion. And the spitting? According to Linda Johnson of the Ashdown Forest Llama Park in East Sussex (01825 712040, www.llamapark.co.uk), 'llamas do spit, but rarely at people. It tends to be at each other – arguing over food, or the girls trying to get rid of unwanted attention from the boys. A faceful is quite effective.' Llama walks take place all over the country, including in the gently rolling hills of Surrey (0845 600 9484, www.surrey-hills-llamas.co.uk), the Forest of Dean (01594 528 482, www.severnwyellamatrekking.co.uk) and in Nottinghamshire (01636 629 051, www.llamatreks.co.uk).

# 50 Find a fossil

Known as the Jurassic Coast, the 95-mile stretch of coastline from Dorset to east Devon was awarded UNESCO Natural World Heritage status in 2001, in recognition of its unique geological 'walk through time', spanning the Triassic, Jurassic and Cretaceous periods. Archaeological treasures aside, the area is dotted with holiday hotspots; it's not all rock hammer-wielding science geeks hunting fossils along the beach (though you'll find some fantastic specimens – of both – at Lyme Regis's Philpot Museum). You probably won't randomly discover an ichthyosaurus skull, but at the base of the cliffs at Chippel Bay and further west ammonites are everywhere; some monsters are large enough to sit on and look out to sea. Don't even *think* about trying to remove them. Visit www.jurassiccoast.com or www.discoveringfossils.co.uk to find out about fossil hunts, and respect the National Fossil Collecting Code (yes, there is one): Plan, Safety, Patience, Respect, Report, Protect, Leave.

# 51 Climb a block of ice

Fancy scaling a wall of ice? The world's biggest indoor ice wall can be found at Ice Factor in Lochaber in the Scottish Highlands. Beginners are welcome for instruction on the techniques and kit that you'll need to tackle the sheer – and slippery – surface. Once you've mastered the wall, join one of the outdoor expeditions organised by the centre, and put your skills to the test at Ben Nevis or Glencoe.
**Ice Factor** *Leven Road, Kinlochleven, Lochaber PH50 4SF (01855 831100/www.ice-factor.co.uk).*

# 52 Make fairs magical again

Go back in time at this beautiful collection of Edwardian steam-driven fairground rides. The attractions are a real treat: there's a wooden helter skelter (the Lighthouse Slip), the Razzle Dazzle (a spinning, tilting device regarded as the world's first white-knuckle ride) and a big wheel. The setting is idyllic too – there are great views of the Sussex Weald from some of the rides. There are also steam railways (one of them miniature) and traction engine-hauled rides, plus a farm and woodland gardens. Once you've paid the entrance fee, all rides are free. For a truly magical time, go in the evening.
**Hollycombe Steam Fair** *Iron Hill, Liphook, Hampshire GU30 7LP (01428 724900/ www.hollycombe.co.uk).*

# 53 Catch an event at the National Library of Wales

Holding the largest collection of works about Wales and other Celtic nations in the world, the Llyfrgell Genedlaethol Cymru (National Library of Wales, to non-Welsh speakers) proudly celebrated its centenary in 2007. Join a tour of the imposing building, take in a lecture or exhibition, or watch the films that helped define Welsh culture in the 100-seat auditorium.
**National Library of Wales** *Aberystwyth, Ceredigion SY23 3BU (01970 632800/ www.llgc.org.uk).*

## 54 Skate the fens at Welney

There's something magical about gliding across the still, beautiful Cambridgeshire countryside, bundled up in woolly jumpers and with your breath freezing in the air – it's a world away from the noise and bustle of a commercial ice rink. Fen-skating has been a proud tradition at Welney since Victorian times, when thousands gathered to watch the annual championships – and even today, as soon as the ground freezes over, a dedicated band of skaters strap their skates on and take to the ice (www.welney.org.uk/skating_club.htm). After a session's skating, stalwarts retire to the Lamb & Flag Inn (Main Street, Welney, Wisbech, Cambridgeshire PE14 9RB, 01354 610242) to enjoy a fortifying pint and survey the evidence of Welney's glory – the walls are covered with photographs of past and present champions.

Time Out 1000 Things to do in Britain 27

# 55 Meet a pink pigeon in Jersey

If proof were needed that the era of formal zoos, with their connotations of frock-coated Victorians and pacing, captive animals, is coming to an end, then the Durrell Wildlife Conservation Trust provides it in spades. Devoted entirely to the preservation and propagation of endangered species, this beautiful, rambling facility belongs to an altogether more enlightened age.

Here, cute, cuddly, creepy and crawling victims of poachers, pestilence and dwindling habitats are granted asylum in spacious, elaborately landscaped enclosures, with specialist staff topping up food supplies (grown on a parcel of the Trust's organic farmland) and giving amusing talks on the resident fauna. And while the late naturalist and author Gerald Durrell may no longer be headquartered here, his pragmatic, upbeat approach to conservation is still at the heart of everything that goes on at the facility.

As a result of the Trust's focus on threatened species, many of the animals at Durrell are somewhat out of the ordinary. One moment you might find yourself watching a pair of giant jumping rats leaping about their forest-floor habitat, the next, you could be face to beak with a pink pigeon or gazing into the perpetually flabbergasted countenance of a Madagascan aye aye. Elsewhere, clusters of bald ibises chatter like deranged Oxford dons, Livingstone's fruitbats skulk like Transylvanian counts, and Andean bears sit atop massive upended tree trunks, sniffing the breeze with the kind of haughty curiosity that leaves you in no doubt that it is they who are watching you.

But despite the rainbow of unusual species in residence, it is those old crowd-pleasers, the primates, whose enclosures are perennially surrounded by fascinated onlookers. There is something undeniably compelling about observing gorillas or orang-utans close up, and Durrell offers the opportunity to get a glimpse of them operating in natural family groups. The enclosures are vast, with all manner of simulated terrains, yet it is possible to find yourself just metres away from a giant silver-back, his shovel-like hands delicately peeling an orange, or enjoying some slapstick monkey business courtesy of a troupe of deadpan Sumatran orang-utan adults and their crazy-haired offspring.

Naturally, the Trust makes a marvellous family day out, but its size and layout also mean that shady nooks and quiet corners are in abundant supply for adults who feel they've earned a read of the paper or a snooze under a tree. And there are opportunities aplenty to sponsor animals, join the staff on a ship bound for Mauritius or simply buy an eco-friendly souvenir from the gift shop.

**Durrell Wildlife Conservation Trust** *Les Augrès Manor, La Profonde Rue, Trinity, Jersey JE3 5BP (01534 860000/www.durrellwildlife.org).*

## 56 Venture off-menu at L'Enclume

Housed in an elegantly appointed stone blacksmith's forge ('enclume' means 'anvil' in French), Michelin-starred L'Enclume is not quite the hearty pub lunch you might expect in a sleepy Lakes village such as Cartmel. Instead, chef-proprietor and chief experimenter Simon Rogan champions his own brand of molecular gastronomy, using innovative combinations of locally sourced ingredients.

The set menus are adventurous enough, but for those who really want to go gastronomically off-piste there is the 'Underground Menu'. Consisting of 26 'no holds barred' (but thankfully tiny) courses, it requires 24 hours' notice, as well as serious stamina and a healthy wallet. Dishes change nightly and are occasionally invented on the spot, but one established favourite is the 'Razor Role Reversal', where the contents of a razor clam are mixed with chestnuts and served in an eggshell, while creamy chicken (once from an egg) is served in the clam shell. Another is the 'Experamenthol Frappe' – a punning, fragrant pre-pudding that melds pear jelly, espresso snow crystals and eucalyptus mousse.

You might well finish with what has become one of the signature dishes, the futuristic 'Stiffy Tacky Pudding' – a deconstructed version of the traditional sticky toffee pudding that Cartmel claims as its own. In L'Enclume's alternative take, each element of the pudding is formed into isolated bubbles. To get the full effect, pile them all into your mouth and get popping.

**L'Enclume Restaurant & Rooms** *Cavendish Street, Cartmel, near Grange-over-Sands, Cumbria LA11 6PZ (015395 36362/www.lenclume.co.uk).*

## 57 Take paintball to new levels in Leicestershire

Paintball itself may be old news, but the version practised at Southfields Farm takes it one step beyond, featuring heavy weapons, full-scale tank battles and D-Day-style landing craft.
**Chaos Paintball** *Southfields Farm, Husbands Bosworth, Leicestershire LE17 6NW (01858 880239/www.chaospaintball.co.uk).*

## 58 Warm up your vocal chords

For those of us not naturally talented enough to be paid to perform on Britain's top concert platforms, there is another way. Singlive UK (01609 780315, www.singliveuk.com) organises around ten large-scale concerts a year for amateur singers, in major venues that include Birmingham's Symphony Hall, Leeds Town Hall and the Bridgewater Hall in Manchester. No previous experience is required and there are no auditions – so no *X-Factor*-type showdown to choke up in. Simply book your place, show up for around 12 weekly rehearsals, and prepare to share the stage with up to 300 other singers in a bumper choral extravaganza.

## 59 Play a round at St Andrews

Playing the Old Course at St Andrews is the fulfilment of a dream for many golfers. Demand is understandably high – more than 42,000 rounds are completed each year – so thwackers and hackers will need to brush up their skills before being let loose on the sacred sward. Men must have a handicap below 24, women 36, and a certificate to prove it. Playing a round here costs £61-£130 depending on the time of year and you can hire clubs and shoes – which come with a complimentary pair of socks.

Most people apply in advance, though around half of all starting times over the year are put into a daily ballot; your chance of success depends on how busy the course is and the weather. If you're on your own, get up early, find the starter and hope to be joined up with a two or three ball.

Failing that, you could always play one of the other six courses at St Andrews – but it's not the same as treading in Tiger's footsteps, is it?
**St Andrews Links Trust** *Pilmour House, St Andrews, Fife KY16 9SF (01334 466666/ www.standrews.org.uk).*

# 60

### Step inside the Insect Circus

Roll up, roll up, ladies and gents! Gasp at the audacity of the wasp-tamer, marvel at the trained butterflies and admire the worm charmer's wiles! All this excitement and more is on offer when ringmaster Ronald McPeake and his Insect Circus and Museum come to a town (or more likely festival) near you. As well as the acts, which walk a sublime, er, tightrope between good old-fashioned family entertainment and surreal comedy, there are the bizarre ephemera, housed in a lovingly decorated Bedford lorry that tours the country. For details of its itinerary, visit www.insectcircus.co.uk.

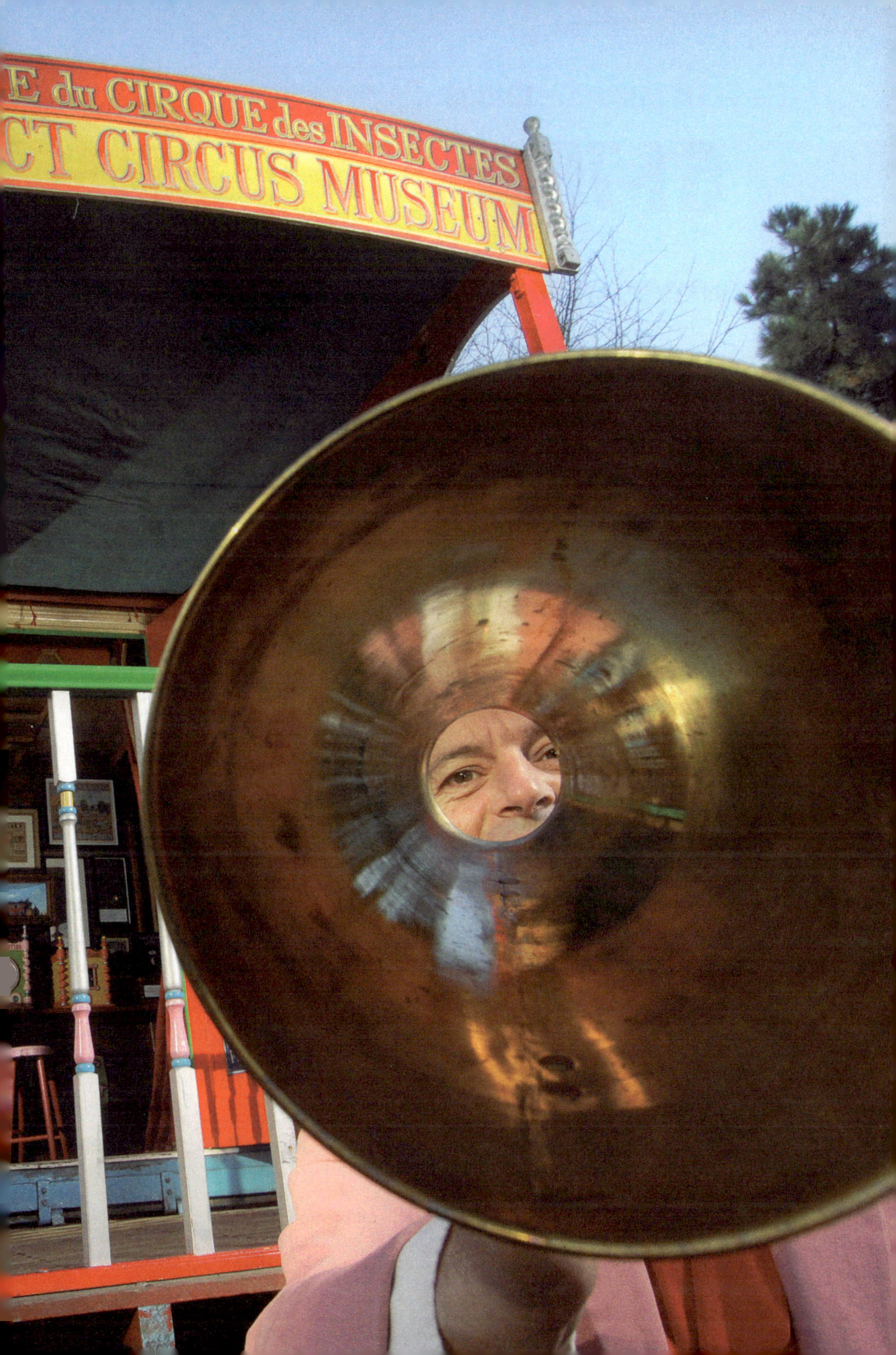
E du CIRQUE des INSECTES
CT CIRCUS MUSEUM

## A few of my favourite things

# 61-70

## *Matthew Bourne, choreographer*

Aside from being one of the oldest dance venues in the country, Sadler's Wells (Rosebery Avenue, London EC1R 4TN, 0844 412 4300, www.sadlerswells.com) is doing incredible things in terms of bringing new choreographers to the fore. It used to just programme big visiting companies, but now there's a whole host of associate artists in the building all the time, planning new projects.
**The Lowry in Manchester (Pier 8, Salford Quays, Manchester M50 3AZ, 0870 787 5780, www.thelowry.com) is an amazing modern building that has built up a wonderful dance audience. It feels like even the people furthest back in the auditorium are really close to the stage.**
It's the hardest thing in the world to get a venue to present your work when you're an up-and-coming choreographer, but probably the best resource is the Place (17 Duke's Road, London WC1H 9PY, 020 7121 1100, www.theplace.org.uk). It's the venue to go to see new talent. Any name in contemporary dance you can think of has started out there: Russell Maliphant, Wayne McGregor, Lea Anderson. It has an enormous amount of performances on throughout the year.

The Linbury Studio Theatre (Royal Opera House, Bow Street, London WC2E 9DD, 020 7304 4000, www.roh.org.uk) gives people the possibility of presenting mid- to small-scale work at the Royal Opera House, which is – dare I say it – probably a lot more interesting than what's going on in the main house.
I've got a great affection for old theatres, but as places to work and visit they're often not great. Two exceptions are the Birmingham Hippodrome (Hurst Street, Birmingham B5 4TB, 0870 730 1234, www.birminghamhippodrome.com) and the Edinburgh Festival Theatre (13-29 Nicolson Street, Edinburgh EH8 9FT, 0131 529 6000, www.eft.co.uk). They still have their old auditoria, but have surrounded them with modern facilities.
**I'm a big fan of old cinemas as well. There's a good place in Brighton, the Duke of York's Picturehouse (Preston Circus, Brighton BN1 4NA, 0871 704 2056, www.picturehouses.co.uk). It was built in 1910 and is one of the oldest cinemas in the world. It screens alternative movies and has homemade cakes in the foyer.**
I also like the Screen on the Green (83 Upper Street, London N1 0NP, 020 7226 3520, www.screencinemas.co.uk) because it's my local and has an old-world charm.
I enjoy visiting graveyards for inspiration. Hampstead Churchyard (Church Row, London NW3 6UU, 020 7794 5808, www.hampsteadparishchurch.org.uk) is where the Llewelyn Davies boys, on whom *Peter Pan* was based, are buried, along with the artist John Constable. Highgate Cemetery (Swain's Lane, Highgate, London N6 6PJ, 020 8340 1834, www.highgate-cemetery.org) is amazing too – it's where Karl Marx, George Eliot and Ralph Richardson's graves are. It's the ultimate spooky graveyard – and the one that was used for all the old British Hammer Horror films.

## 71 *Get square eyes at the National Media Museum*

There's nothing like the heady whiff of nostalgia – something Bradford's National Media Museum has cleverly cottoned on to. The archive of old kids' TV programmes is guaranteed to transport you straight back to your childhood, and those enthralling afternoons spent glued to the telly – only now, your mum's not here to tell you to sit further away and harp on about getting your homework done. We'd advise ringing ahead to book one of the museum's private viewing booths, so you can follow Mr Spoon back to Button Moon and sing along with the Wombles without an audience of sniggering small children to distract you.
**National Media Museum** *Bradford, West Yorkshire BD1 1NQ (0870 701 0200/ www.nationalmediamuseum.org.uk).*

## 72 Become a cocoa bean connoisseur

Scottish chocolatier Coco has made it its mission in life to create a nation of chocolate connoisseurs – and what sweeter subject could there be to study? Its eagerly-attended tasting evenings teach you the essential five sensory tests with which to determine a superior chocolate bar – one with a high cocoa content – while the one-day chocolate school shows you how to become a master chocolatier. And since good quality chocolate reportedly contains only a tenth of the calories of the usual corner shop fare, you won't even have to feel guilty about eating your creations. Don't miss the deliciously rich hot chocolate either – made of pure cocoa and hand-flaked chocolate, with no added sugar.
**Coco** *174 Bruntsfield Place, Edinburgh EH10 4ER (0131 228 4526/www.cocochocolate.co.uk).*

## 73 Follow a snorkelling trail in Dorset

Part of the Purbeck Marine Wildlife Reserve on the Jurassic Coast, Kimmeridge Bay is a snorkelling paradise. The clear water in the shallow bay resembles a giant rock pool, with reefs and ledges of black shale, varied species of weed and kelp, and an abundance of unusual sealife such as trigger fish, rays, John Dory, cuckoo wrasse and the rare black-faced blenny. If you're a confident snorkeller, you can follow a 400-metre-long trail beginning on the beach and moving through five different seabed habitats. A waterproof guide is available from the Marine Information Centre; conditions are best during neap tides.
**Purbeck Marine Wildlife Reserve** *Kimmeridge, Wareham, Dorset BH20 5PF (01929 481044/ www.dorsetwildlife.co.uk).*

## 74 Get back to the land on Open Farm Sunday

Kids who think spuds and sausages magically spring into being at the supermarket would do well to swap their Wiis for wellies for a day on their local farm. That's where the annual Open Farm Sunday event (www.farmsunday.org), founded in 2006, comes in. Hundreds of farms across the country throw open their gates to visitors, offering activities such as trailer rides, guided farm walks, nature trails and milking and sheep shearing demonstrations – not forgetting sheepdogs and fluffy baby animals to pet, all set against the muted cacophony of clucking, quacking, mooing, honks and oinks.

# wellcome collection

"London's brave venue where science, art and culture converge"
NATURE

"unexpectedly elating"
TIME OUT

**FREE**
EXHIBITIONS AND EVENTS

GALLERIES OPEN TUESDAY–SUNDAY
OPEN UNTIL 22.00 THURSDAY
WWW.WELLCOMECOLLECTION.ORG

183 EUSTON ROAD, LONDON NW1
⊖ EUSTON, WARREN STREET

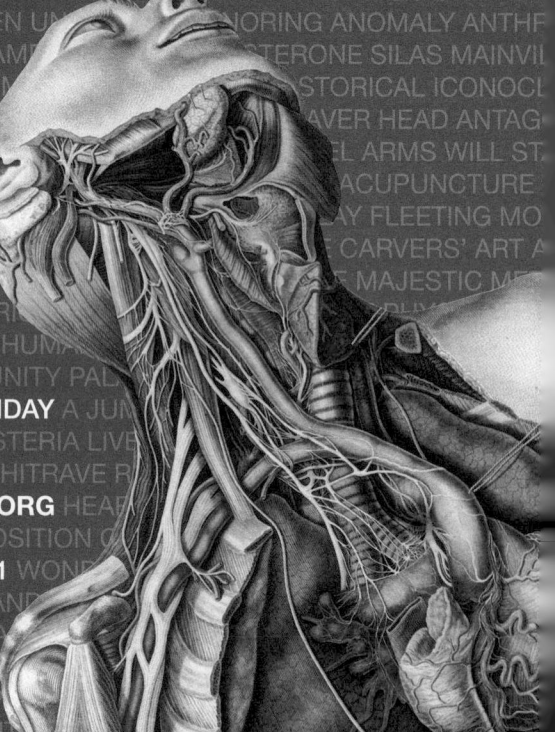

# 75 Take to the water at Wakestock

It may not have suffered the crippling overexposure of surfing or skateboarding, but wakeboarding (a cross between freestyle snowboarding and waterskiing) is a big deal – popular enough to claim over three million participants globally. And as the sport has grown, so too has Wakestock (01758 710000, www.wakestock2007.co.uk), which started out back in 2000 in Abersoch, North Wales, as a diminutive competition followed by a party in a car park. Today it's the single largest wakeboarding-cum-music festival in Europe, drawing a crowd and competitors from across the world; artists, meanwhile, range from Mark Ronson and Jack Penate to Kosheen and Carl Cox. Wakestock happens on the Llyn Peninsula: competitive events are split between Pwllheli Marina (ramps and rails) and Abersoch Beach (the Big Air Classic), while the main festival site is at Penrhos, with views over Cardigan Bay and the distant mountains of Snowdonia. For 2008, however, the organisers will also be staging a second three-day event in the sprawling grounds of Blenheim Palace in Oxfordshire, with riders tearing across Capability Brown's tranquil lake and enough blistering bands and DJs to shake the Duke of Marlborough's serene country pile to its foundations. Tickets cost from £40 per day.

# 76 Ride the diggers at Diggerland

Budding Bob the Builders, *Scrapheap Challenge* fans and anyone who digs diggers and dumpers, take note: excavation heaven is here. Gouge enormous holes out of the ground (and fill them in again), drive construction machinery, race JCBs, or watch, bemused, as formation diggers dance to music. Kids can drive bulldozers and dumper trucks, or zoom off on the Young Driver Experience – if they're not swinging in a giant JCB scoop or digging for buried treasure. There are also sites in Devon, Durham and Yorkshire.
**Diggerland** *Roman Way, Medway Valley Leisure Park, Strood, Kent ME2 2NU (0870 034 4437/ www.diggerland.com).*

# 77 Snap up a modern masterpiece at the Art Car Boot Fair

This cross between a car boot sale and a burlesque club (www.artcarbootfair.com) has been up and running sporadically since 2003. Sponsored, rather incongruously, by Vauxhall and organised by an optimistic bunch of YBAs, there's a carnival atmosphere around east London's Truman Brewery when the ACBF comes to town (usually on a Sunday in June). In the past, stallholders have included the likes of the Chapman Brothers, Sarah Lucas and Gavin Turk, the snack vans were courtesy of Fergus Henderson of St John restaurant fame, and the free massages provided by one Tracey Emin. Those heady days may be over now, but you can still pick up some splendid art bargains, the like of which would never be seen at the Affordable Art Fair, plus some cheeky little numbers that could well be worth a fortune one day like matching T-shirt and mug combos from rising stars Gareth Pugh and David David, and cavort with the beautiful crowd in the Routemaster roller disco bus.

Time Out 1000 Things to do in Britain 35

# 78-88 Lose yourself in Britain's best mazes

The best thing about mazes, according to Britain's leading maze designer, Adrian Fisher, is that there's nothing practical about them. 'They're completely over the top,' he says. 'Purely for fun.' Fisher should know: he's designed mazes all over the world, including one for horse-drawn carriages in Florida. Britain boasts hundreds of quirky mazes of its own, made out of everything from hedges or mirrors to water; below is a list of our favourite year-round options.

## Blenheim Palace
The expansive Marlborough Maze at this Oxfordshire country house covers over an acre and encompasses various attractions, including putting greens and a giant chess set. Climb one of the bridges for an aerial view of its design.
**Blenheim Palace** *Woodstock, Oxfordshire OX20 1PX (01993 811091/www.blenheimpalace.com).*

## Chatsworth
Planted in 1962, the yew maze at this country house in Derbyshire is a relatively recent addition to the grounds. Though compact, it presents quite a challenge.
**Chatsworth** *Bakewell, Derbyshire DE45 1PP (01246 565300/www.chatsworth.org).*

## Crystal Palace Park
London's largest, this circular 'tea maze' is so called because of its appropriateness for a tea-time stroll. Pour yourself a cuppa then try to conquer it.
**Crystal Palace Park** *London SE20 8DT (020 7357 6894/www.crystalpalacepark.net).*

## Glendurgan Garden
Laid out in 1833 by Alfred Fox, the laurel maze at this subtropical Cornish garden is dotted with palm trees and is less angular than the other mazes on our list, in keeping with the garden's sense of controlled wildness.
**Glendurgan Garden** *Mawnan Smith, Falmouth, Cornwall TR11 5JZ (01872 862090/www.national trust.org.uk).*

## Hampton Court Palace
Designed in the late 17th century, the maze at Hampton Court contains half a mile of pathway. Despite Jerome K Jerome's hysterical account of its hazards, the route is relatively tame – but, 'as the oldest hedge maze in the world, it's worth seeing out of curiosity,' says Fisher.
**Hampton Court Palace** *West Molesley, Surrey KT8 8AU (0844 482 7777/http://hrp.org.uk/HamptonCourtPalace).*

Longleat Maze

## Hever Castle
As well as a yew maze dating back to 1904, this castle in Kent also boasts a water maze. Weighted paving slabs control the flow of the fountains, to the inevitable delight of children.
**Hever Castle** *Hever, Edenbridge, Kent TN8 7NG (01732 865224/www.hever-castle.co.uk).*

## Julian's Bower
The origins of this turf labyrinth are lost in the mists of time, but it is thought to date back to the medieval period. Set on a hill, the spot overlooks the rivers Ouze, Trent and Humber.
**Julian's Bower** *Alkborough, North Lincolnshire. OS map ref: SE879217.*

## Leeds Castle
The gorgeous yew maze at Leeds Castle was planted in 1988. Explorers make their escape via a 90-foot underground tunnel in the centre, decorated with sculptures of mythical beasts.
**Leeds Castle** *Maidstone, Kent ME17 1PL (01622 765400/www.leeds-castle.com).*

## Longleat
Laid out in 1975, Longleat's maze paths run for almost two miles. Bridges and observation towers add another dimension, allowing you to see the maze's stunning pattern from above. 'Very big and very nice,' is Fisher's verdict.
**Longleat** *Warminster, Wiltshire BA12 7NW (01985 844400/www.longleat.co.uk).*

## Saffron Walden
This ancient turf maze on Saffon Walden Common is of uncertain origin, dating back to at least 1699. It is thought to be the largest of its kind in the world and has been restored a number of times, most recently in 1979.
**Saffron Walden Common** *Common Road, Saffron Walden, Essex CB10 2XE (01799 510444/ www.uttlesford.gov.uk/tourism/mazes.htm).*

## Wookey Hole
This indoor 'magical mirror maze' in Somerset's Wookey Hole Caves is ideal for maze fiends looking for a challenge in the colder months. Comprised of 40 mirrors, it boasts plenty of distortion tricks and false passages.
**Wookey Hole Caves** *Wookey Hole, Wells, Somerset BA5 1BB (01749 672243/ www.wookey.co.uk).*

## 89 Plunge into Harrogate's Turkish Baths...
One of only three Victorian Turkish baths remaining in England, Harrogate's is the most historically complete – and in fine fettle after a full restoration in 2004. The Moorish design is extraordinary, with fabulous Islamic arches and screens, walls of vibrant glazed brickwork and arabesque painted ceilings. After a shower, visit the eucalyptus-scented steam room, where the high humidity opens pores and eases tense muscles. Then have another shower, before taking a bracing dip in the plunge pool. Towel down and work your way up through the three interconnecting hot room chambers: the tepidarium (warm – a mere 45°), calidarium (hot – 55°) and laconium (a roasting 60°). When you've finished, spend half an hour cooling down in the elegant frigidarium, before returning to real life. Fresh fluffy towels are provided, so all you need are personal toiletries. Those who fancy some full-on pampering can also book themselves in for a variety of health and beauty treatments, from reiki to Swedish massage or a Monticelli mud detox. Prices range from £11 for an off-peak session in the Baths to £510 for you and 59 friends to have the place to yourselves on a Saturday night.
**Harrogate Turkish Baths** *Parliament Street, Harrogate, North Yorkshire HG1 2WH (01423 556746/www.harrogate.gov.uk/turkishbaths).*

## 90 ...or sample its sulphurous spring water
Harrogate's Royal Pump Room Museum is the site of Europe's strongest sulphur well. Tasting like a cross between seawater and rotten eggs, thanks to its mix of sodium chloride and hydrogen sulphide, this potent blend was considered by the Victorians to be 'highly beneficial for most forms of indigestion, including constipation, flatulence and acidity'. In fact, it just goes to prove that anything that's good for you is likely to taste revolting. Luckily, Betty's famous tea shop is just up the road.
**Royal Pump Room Museum** *Crown Place, Harrogate, North Yorkshire HG1 2RY (01423 556188/www.harrogate.gov.uk/museums).*

# 1000 things to do in London

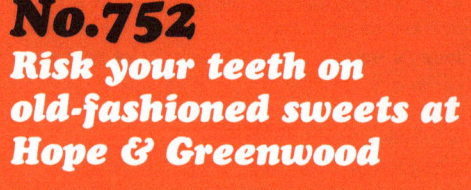

## No.752
### Risk your teeth on old-fashioned sweets at Hope & Greenwood

If it's sweets you're after then this is the place for you. Teeming with rosy apples, sherbert pips, cola cubes and more, Hope & Greenwood is one centre of sweetie excellence not to be missed.

**Hope & Greenwood**
20 North Cross Rd, SE22 9EU
(0208 613 1777/
hopeandgreenwood.co.uk

*Alys Tomlinson*

### For hundreds more great ideas...

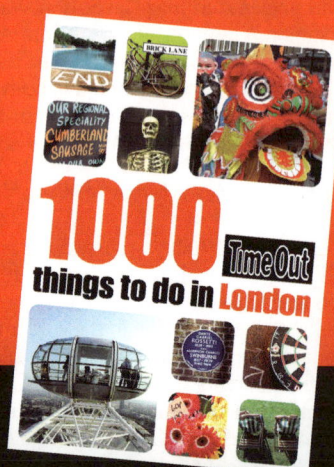

**Time Out Guides**

Available at all major bookshops at only £12.99/$19.95 and from timeout.com/shop

# 91 Visit Victoria and Albert

Tranquil Frogmore House, in the grounds of Windsor Castle, was one of Queen Victoria's favourite retreats – a place where, she wrote, 'all is peace and quiet, and you only hear the hum of the bees, the singing of the birds'. When her beloved Albert died in 1861, she commissioned a magnificent mausoleum in its grounds, and was buried there alongside him in 1901. Its lavish interior, inlaid with precious marbles, is a paean to Victorian opulence: in the centre, marble effigies of the queen and her consort recline on an immense granite sarcophagus. The mausoleum is open to the public for just six days every year in May and August, and on the Wednesday closest to her majesty's birthday (24 May).
**Frogmore House** *Windsor Home Park, Windsor, Berkshire SL4 2JG (020 7766 7305/www.royal collection.org.uk).*

# 92 Explore England's oldest gin distillery

Mother's Ruin? Not the way we drink it. Plymouth Gin was documented back in 1896 as the original base for the first dry martini, and over the years it has been enjoyed by Churchill, Franklin D Roosevelt, Ian Fleming and Alfred Hitchcock. Where better to taste the noble brew than among the historic buildings of Plymouth's Barbican district in Black Friars, England's oldest gin distillery? Since 1793, this place has been knocking out Plymouth Gin according to a unique recipe that combines a special blend of botanicals with soft Dartmoor water. The site has a varied history; originally a Dominican monastery, established in 1431, it also provided final lodging on English soil for the Pilgrim Fathers. After an audio-visual presentation on the Barbican area and the history of gin, you'll be shown the 155-year-old copper pot in which the gin is still made and, in the weighing room, get to touch and smell the botanicals used – before sampling the finished product.
**Black Friars Distillery** *60 Southside Street, Plymouth, Devon PL1 2LQ (01752 665292/ www.plymouthgin.com).*

# 93 Go bog snorkelling

In Wales, they know that snorkelling in the sea is for wimps. Here, brave contenders' mettle is tested by the annual World Bog Snorkelling Championship (http://llanwrtyd-wells.powys.org.uk/bog.html), held on the August Bank Holiday in the dense Waen Rhydd peat bog south of Llanwrtyd Wells in Powys – Britain's smallest town.

Armed with their own snorkel and flippers (the organisers don't provide for part-timers – wetsuits are 'optional but advisable'), plucky competitors swim two 60-yard lengths through a muddy trench cut into the bog, with separate categories for Men, Ladies and Juniors. And if that wasn't difficult enough, conventional swimming strokes are banned.

**94-101** *Hang out with the literati*

# Telling tales

*Author **Matt Thorne** goes behind the scenes at Britain's literary festivals.*

The best British literary festivals manage to create an atmosphere in which everyone feels privileged. Authors experience the thrill of meeting readers who are knowledgeable about their books; readers get the opportunity to meet authors they've long admired and ask them the questions they've always wanted to discuss. At the most successful festivals a party atmosphere reigns, as writers listen in on other authors and readers get to experience the literary world at close quarters – before heading off for a pint.

Deciding which literary festival is for you depends on what you want. The Guardian Hay festival (0870 990 1299, www.hayfestival.com) has done a tremendous job of publicising itself, but is no longer the first port of call for the discerning reader. The literary element has lost out to chefs, politicians and musicians, and while a few big-name authors still appear, the serious festival-goer is better off with Edinburgh (0131 473 2000, www.eif.co.uk) and Cheltenham (01242 227979, www.cheltenhamfestivals.co.uk). Two of the oldest literary festivals in the country, they nonetheless retain the adventurous spirit that inspired their inception. Visitors to either festival will see a bill that brings together the authors of the best books of any given year, and allows them to mix and match between household names and lesser-known but equally interesting new literary talents.

Most authors heading to Edinburgh stick around for a couple of days, and a competitive spirit sometimes emerges in the writers' backstage yurt. Certain authors, particularly those with a Scottish connection (Irvine Welsh, Ian Rankin) are always going to sell out, but most writers draw a healthy audience. Still, with so much on there's always the possibility that you might end up like one unlucky multiple award-winning author who showed up to his event to discover even the proverbial one man and his dog had stayed at home. And any author catching sight of the millions of people in Jacqueline Wilson's all-day signing queue is bound to feel a twinge of envy.

*'A sexagenarian author informed me, "Festivals always go with more of a swing when you bring a hooker along".'*

I've always had a great time at Edinburgh, but perhaps the most memorable occasion was when I shared the bill with Tibor Fischer and Dan Rhodes. Rhodes, later to be included in the *Granta Book of Best Young British Novelists*, was going through a difficult time with his then publisher and agent, and decided to let rip. As chick-lit novelist Jenny Colgan later commented in the *Independent on Sunday*, 'He was being extraordinarily rude about publishing in general and his publishers in particular. I couldn't believe it. He was calmly telling people that all publishers are bastards and, by the way, here are their names.' It's this kind of reckless behaviour that makes a performance memorable, and inspired by Dan's example, when an audience member asked me what kind of readers Tibor and I attracted, I responded, 'Weirdos, mostly.' This immediately cut our signing queue in half, and Tibor still hasn't forgiven me.

The always enjoyable Cheltenham festival was the location of one of the most legendary literary events of all time. 'Sex in Literature' is the sort of panel discussion that you might find at any festival, but in 1962 the organisers brought together a dream bill of Carson McCullers, Norman Mailer and Kingsley Amis. After the debate, and the subsequent night's drunken conversation, an overexcited Amis ended up leaving his wife for the event's organiser, Elizabeth Jane Howard. Similar couplings have happened countless times since, but this is the one that's entered literary history. This sort of thing goes on at literary festivals all the time, and organisers have learned to be sensitive about not asking whether an author is bringing a spouse or a secret partner, but I still couldn't help feeling shocked when a sexagenarian author noticed I was attending alone and informed me, 'These festivals always go with more of a swing when you bring a hooker along.'

**Guardian Hay Festival**

**Time Out** 1000 Things to do in Britain **41**

*'For writers and guests at King's Lynn, it's less like attending a literary festival than taking a walk-on part in some strange soap opera.'*

Perhaps the most convivial literary gatherings of all are Norfolk's King's Lynn fiction and poetry festivals (01553 691661, www.lynnlitfests.com). Most of the authors who attend are put up in the homes of the town's inhabitants, and for writers and guests alike it's less like attending a literary festival than taking a walk-on part in a strange soap opera.

Each weekend begins with a bagpiper greeting the arriving authors on the train station platform, then becomes increasingly surreal. Last year the opening night party ended in chaos after a drunken author tripped a fire alarm, and at the end of my reading an audience member approached me and asked if I could sign his book with the message 'Dear Charlotte, fuck you.' The festival's patron saint is Beryl Bainbridge, who headlines every year – and seeing a writer of her calibre opening up and exposing her wicked sense of humour is worth the price of admission alone. But be careful of the licentious atmosphere if you don't want to have some explaining to do when you get home: author Toby Litt once found himself the recipient of a letter from two audience members who had so enjoyed his performance the previous year that they invited him for a threesome (an offer he politely declined).

Port Eliot (01503 232 783, www.porteliotlitfest.com), the Cornwall-based festival run by Peregrine and Catherine St Germans, Simon Prosser of Hamish Hamilton and actor and musician Rick Worthy is taking a year off in 2008, but promises to return in 2009. The premise is that it offers the chance to see writers doing something other than reading – so you might find Hari Kunzru DJing, Alain de Botton acting as an agony uncle, Geoff Dyer juggling fire or Louis de Bernières playing with his mandolin band. I'm not a man of many talents, and when I attended Simon suggested that as I had no musical, sporting or comic ability, I could just read an explicit story I'd written for an anthology Zadie Smith had edited for the ICA. Helen Walsh would read the dirty bits from her book *Brass*, and they'd bill it as an 'XXX' performance. Alas, as the festival is so family-friendly, much of the audience were underage. Not wanting to offend, I explained this was an adult event, and parents might wish

**Edinburgh Literary Festival**

**Guardian Hay Festival**

to remove their offspring before we started. As Geoff Dyer later observed, 'Liberal mums and dads scoffed at the idea and refused to budge. Five minutes later, they were shooing their confused progeny out of the tent as if it were the *Titanic* and only a single lifeboat remained.'

While Port Eliot offers music alongside literature, some of the more alternative summer music festivals have started to catch on to the appeal of catering to the audience's literary tastes. Southwold's Latitude festival (www.latitudefestival.co.uk) offers a weekend bill that is the equal of many solely literary events, offering mainstream favourites such as Esther Freud and Will Fiennes alongside alternative icons like Howard Marks and Lydia Lunch. Latitude isn't the only music festival with an literary component: the Green Man festival (www.thegreenmanfestival.co.uk) in the Brecon Beacons in South Wales also offers Man Booker-nominated authors alongside contemporary folk music.

Anyone looking for the liveliest of the newer arrivals should head down to the Laugharne Festival (01994 427 689, www.laugharne festival.org), located in the Welsh town where Dylan Thomas spent the last few years of his life. Focusing on the 'edgier side of literature', with a bias towards Welsh and Celtic authors, the festival has already attracted the likes of Patrick McCabe, Niall Griffiths and Owen Sheers, and in 2008 will feature Patti Smith, Roger McGough and Will Self.

Although reading may be a private act, readers are getting increasingly public about their passions: no matter where you live, there's bound to be a literary gathering somewhere not too far away. New festivals are springing up every year, and if you wanted to you could probably attend one every weekend – an encouraging sign that the grassroots appeal of literature is still as strong as ever.

*A list of every UK festival can be found on the British Council's website at www.britishcouncil.org.*

## 102 Hop on a helicopter to Scilly

One of the few scheduled helicopter services in Britain, the flight from Penzance to St Mary's or Tresco isn't the cheapest way to get to the Isles of Scilly – but it's surely the best. After the thrill of vertical take-off and a gravity-defying hover above the bay, your red-and-blue Sikorsky S61 zips along far lower than fixed-wing commercial aircraft. Only a couple of dozen fellow passengers will be with you, and the large windows, which start at hip-height, make the experience of flying far more intense: watch the cliff edge drop away as you barrel out from the peninsula, then follow the 'copter's shadow as it skims over the waves below. The flight only lasts 20 minutes and currently costs from £77 to £154, but it's worth every penny.

**British International** *Heliport, Penzance, Cornwall TR18 3AP (01736 363871/www.islesofscilly helicopter.com).*

## 103 Pay your respects at Eyam's churchyard

At first glance Eyam is just another handsome Peak District village, but in the 17th century it was the site of a notable act of collective self-sacrifice. The plague came to Eyam from London by way of fleas, in cloth sent to the village tailor, George Vicars. He died on 7 September 1665 and, realising the danger, rector William Mompesson, with fellow clergyman Thomas Stanley, persuaded the villagers into voluntary quarantine; food and other supplies were left on the outskirts of the village. Between September 1665 and October 1666 almost 260 people died – at least a third of the community.

The tranquil churchyard bears testament to their bravery; Catherine Mompesson, wife of the vicar, is among the plague victims buried there. A remembrance service is held every Plague Sunday (the last Sunday in August). For more information, visit Eyam Museum – noting its rat-shaped weathervane.

**Eyam Museum** *Hawkhill Road, Eyam, Derbyshire S32 5QP (01433 631371/www.eyammuseum. demon.co.uk).*

## 104 Orbit the earth at the National Space Centre

Parents take note: Leicester's Space Centre, opened in 2001, is educational *and* entertaining. Geeky kids zoom around the audio-visual displays and interactive exhibits (although intoning 'Leicester, we have a problem' just doesn't have the same ring) and are wowed by the rockets in the Rocket Tower. Budding Buzz Aldrins can watch space shows beamed up in the multimedia Space Theatre, experience life on a lunar base camp or boldly embark on a 3D mission through the solar system.

**National Space Centre** *Exploration Drive, Leicester LE4 5NS (0116 261 0261/ www.spacecentre.co.uk).*

## 105 Slip into Austen-world

Never mind the endless TV and film adaptations, visit the home of Jane Austen to get a real feel for how life was then. The author lived in this red-brick 17th-century house for the last eight years of her life (1809-17), with her mother and sister. It's not action-packed, but it is atmospheric – and *Mansfield Park*, *Emma* and *Persuasion* were all penned here.

**Jane Austen's House Museum** *Chawton, Alton, Hampshire GU34 1SD (01420 83262/www.jane-austens-house-museum.org.uk).*

## 106 Steam along on the Gloucestershire Warwickshire line

Ten miles of line between Toddington and Cheltenham Racecourse has been beautifully restored by volunteers over the past 30-odd years: today, the railway looks like an old-fashioned train set, with its well-kept stations, dinky tearooms and awesome shiny engines. Special events include *Thomas the Tank Engine* days, fish and chips evenings, and Cheltenham race-meeting specials – but the GWR is best enjoyed on a quiet summer's evening.

**Gloucestershire Warwickshire Steam Railway** *Railway Station, Toddington, Gloucestershire GL54 5DT (01242 621405/www.gwsr.com).*

# 107
## See thousands of scooters ride through Ryde

Come August bank holiday weekend, scooter enthusiasts from all over the country flock across the Solent to the Isle of Wight, there to attend its ever-growing annual rally (www.vfmscoot.co.uk). The normally sedate streets of Ryde are filled with the sound of revving two-stroke engines as polished-up Vespas and Lambrettas growl into action, and admiring crowds gather to gawp at resplendent vintage rarities.

The three-day event culminates in Sunday's eagerly awaited mass ride-out, which sees thousands of scooters roar past the esplanade in the August sunshine. A glorious jumble of ageing mods, cool kids in Converse on gleaming 1960s scooters and proud collectors on expensively customised classics, the parade's a sight to behold – just watch out for the heady trail of exhaust fumes left in its wake.

# 108
## Take a seat in the Devil's Chair

Travelling across England with an apronful of rocks is clearly hard work; the prospect of then filling in a valley with them is enough to make even Old Nick take a breather. The story goes that he rested on the highest outcrop of the spooky Stiperstones hills in Shropshire, to take in the stunning views of the heather-covered moors. As he rose to continue his journey, the apron strings snapped and out tumbled the rocks. Being the Prince of Darkness, he naturally didn't bother to gather them up, and simply left them strewn all over the ridge. It's certainly one explanation for the valley's name – Hell's Gutter – and the local legend that the rocks smell of brimstone in hot weather. We've no idea why the Cloven One chose an apron over a far more serviceable wheelbarrow, but come here on the longest night of the year and you might get an answer – he's said to revisit his throne and summon local followers to preside over their choosing of the next year's king (www.shropshiretourism.info).

# bodyflight BEDFORD

## Learn to fly!

Learn to fly in the world's largest indoor skydiving wind tunnel. No experience is needed and no jumping or heights are involved, just simulated freefall on a vertical column of air. You can really fly at Bodyflight Bedford! Prices start from as little at £39.

**www.bodyflight.co.uk**
T: 0845 200 2924

Building 36, Twinwoods Business Park, Twinwoods Rd,
Clapham, Bedfordshire MK41 6AE

# 109 Go skydiving – indoors

You'd be hard-pushed to find something weirder to do of a weekend (that doesn't involve the privacy of your own home) than taking a body flight. Offering the ultimate in armchair skydiving, the Bodyflight centre has a vertical wind tunnel that simulates the experience of freefalling at 170mph. After a tuition session, you leap into the jet of air and feel the adrenaline rush – safe in the knowledge that parachute failure won't be an issue.
**Bodyflight** *Building 36, Twinwoods Business Park, Twinwoods Road, Clapham, Bedford, Bedfordshire MK41 6AE (0845 200 2960/www.bodyflight.co.uk).*

# 110 Dance with the pagans at Beltane

Edinburgh's Beltane Festival (www.beltane.org) is – officially – the modern revival of a pre-Christian celebration to welcome in the spring. To the casual observer, though, it looks more like an excuse to bang drums, paint your body, dance around the firelight and generally go a bit pagan-crazy with iconic figures like the May Queen, the Green Man and their ilk. It's a tightly organised event, however, taking place on top of Calton Hill every year on 30 April and entailing elaborate costumes, pagan rituals and a dramatic torch-lit procession.

# 111 See a tenor for a tenner

The Buxton Festival (01298 70395, www.buxtonfestival.co.uk), an annual two-week summer opera festival in the Peak District spa town, relies on public funding for just ten per cent of its income. Which is great news for you, the punter, because it has to sell tickets – even if that means flogging them at bargain-basement prices. Performances take place in the picturesque Buxton Opera House and include renditions of around half a dozen operas each season, often with appearances from top young operatic talents. Tickets for side seats start at £7, with top-price dress circle seats at only £45.

# 112 Visit Legoland backwards

Legoland's grounds occupy 150 acres and there are over 50 rides and attractions: a lot to cover in a day, especially if you're under a metre tall. Standing an hour in line for that three-minute thrill seriously eats into your day out – so to avoid tantrums, study a site map and plan your hit list, then get there as soon as it opens. Once you're in, head straight for the rear of the site then visit each attraction in reverse order to cut through the crowds and queues. It seems obvious, yet surprisingly few visitors do it.

Don't bother with the Hill Train at the entrance – walking is faster – and don't get distracted along the way; you'll only have a ten-minute wait for a Wave Surfer soaking. Now, either hit the Jungle Coaster or whizz round to Pirate Falls for more watery fun; the latter's right next to the Dragon and Dragon's Apprentice rollercoasters. Keep going round; if you're already wet, a spin on the Viking's River Splash won't hurt, and that's the last of the main queue-heavy rides before it's time for lunch.

For tinies, the Carousel, Chairoplane and Ferris Wheel queues are usually pretty fast-moving; older kids will find Driving School and Balloon School worth the wait. Dozens of other attractions await: Sky Rider, Space Tower, 4D movie shows and Duplo Play Town. Don't miss Miniland, with its scaled-down landmarks from Europe and the US, created from nearly 40 million Lego bricks. Can you spot the Dalek?
**Legoland Windsor Park** *Winkfield Road, Windsor, Berkshire SL4 4AY (0870 504 0404/www.legoland.co.uk).*

# 113-123 Search for Nicholas Owen's ingenious priest-holes

It was a dangerous business being a Catholic priest in the 16th century. Under the Protestant Elizabeth I, administering to Catholics was a capital offence. The nation's priests were forced into hiding, often receiving aid from sympathetic families who risked severe punishment if they were caught.

How to hide a priest? Enter Nicholas Owen, master builder of what became known as priest-holes. Beginning his work in the 1580s, Owen created hundreds of cunning hideaways across the country – some large enough to contain a dozen men, most with just enough space for one priest to stow away, often in great discomfort.

It was a torrid time for priests, despite Owen's efforts. While most of 14th-century Scotney Castle (Lamberhurst, Tunbridge Wells, Kent TN3 8JN, 01892 893868, www.nationaltrust.org.uk) is now in ruins, you can still see the priest-hole in which Father Richard Blount evaded capture in the 1590s. He escaped the priest-hunters on two separate occasions, each time staying hidden in squalid conditions for over a week.

Owen's hides couldn't save Edmund and John Campion, however. They were discovered at Samlesbury Hall (Preston New Road, Samlesbury, Preston, Lancashire PR5 0UP, 01254 812010, www.samlesburyhall.co.uk) in 1581. Edmund is said to have been offered the chance to save John's life if he gave up information about Owen. Edmund refused and was transported to London for execution; John was killed on the spot. Ironically, Owen gave himself up at Edmund's hanging, bursting forward to protest the injustice and being arrested for his troubles. Though tortured, he convinced his credulous captors he was someone else, and was released.

He couldn't evade capture indefinitely, though. A priest-hole of his in Coughton Court (near Alcester, Warwickshire B49 5JA, 01789 400777, www.coughtoncourt.co.uk) had successfully sheltered Father Henry Garnet, wanted for suspected involvement in the Gunpowder Plot – but Owen himself was not so lucky. Thought, falsely, to be a plotter, Owen was starved out of one of his own hides. Taken to the Tower of London, Owen was tortured for days – racked so severely that his stomach eventually burst open, killing him He died never having given up details of the hundred or so hideaways he had built. In recognition of his labours, the Catholic Church declared him a saint in the 1970s.

Due to the astonishing ingenuity of Owen's constructions, their discovery has been slow. Some fascinating examples have been unearthed though – including the four hides secreted around the Great Staircase at Harvington Hall (Harvington Hall Lane, Harvington, Kidderminster, Worcestershire DY10 4LR, 01562 777846, www.harvingtonhall.com), and one discovered by chance in the 1960s at Ripley Castle (Harrogate, North Yorkshire HG3 3AY, 01423 770152, www.ripleycastle.co.uk). At Baddesley Clinton (Rising Lane, Baddesley Clinton Village, Knowle, Solihull, West Midlands B93 0DQ, 01564 783294, www.nationaltrust.org.uk), a hide extends down a kitchen drain, while at Sawston Hall there's one carved from stone and fitted with a peephole (Sawston, Cambridge CB2 4JR, 01223 832888). The priest-hiding trapdoor at Oxburgh Hall (Oxborough, King's Lynn, Norfolk PE33 9PS, 01366 328258, www.nationaltrust.org.uk) blends in seamlessly with the surrounding tiled floor; Speke Hall (The Walk, Liverpool L24 1XD, 0151 427 7231, www.nationaltrust.org.uk) has a special mirror built into a chimney that allowed the inhabitants to spot approaching priest-hunters.

The two hides discovered at Ingatestone Hall (Hall Lane, Ingatestone, Essex CM4 9NR, 01277 353010) represent a remarkable double bluff on the part of the owners, as Elizabeth I is said to have spent several nights here on her royal progress of 1561. At Moseley Old Hall (Moseley Old Hall Lane, Fordhouses, Wolverhampton, Staffordshire WV10 7HY, 01902 782808, www.nationaltrust.org.uk), meanwhile, the priest-hole is said to have actually housed royalty, hiding the Catholic Charles II for two days as he made his way into European exile in 1651.

# 124 *Pull over at Tebay Services*

Fed up with soulless motorway service stations with monosyllabic staff, serving overpriced, nutrition-free fare? Opened in 1972 by two local families, Tebay Services on the M6 (Old Tebay, Penrith, Cumbria CA10 3SS, 01396 24505, www.westmorland.com) provides a welcome change from the usual cheerless refuelling; here, drivers sit at the outdoor eating area tucking into fresh, own-made mozzarella-topped field mushrooms, while children throw bread for the lake's feathered residents. To think that junction 38 could be home to such a haven. This could well be the only place you'll find tattooed HGV drivers skipping the full English coronary, breakfasting instead at the fresh fruit bar and then buying local specialities such as pork and apple burgers or Hawkshead relish from the farm shops for later.

# 125 *See the Sphinx at Brimham Rocks...*

...then pick out the dancing bear and the blacksmith's anvil while you're picnicking among the 300-million-year-old rock formations. Set within the Nidderdale Area of Outstanding Natural Beauty, midway between Ripon and Harrogate, Brimham Rocks is a great place for hide-and-seek – or, for the well-equipped, some serious climbing. Access is via scenic routes, so pack your binoculars and take in the fabulous Dales countryside. Choose a nice day, as the rocks may be closed in bad weather; otherwise, they're open daily from 8am to dusk. If you're going in winter, take a flask: the kiosk doesn't operate between December and March.

**Brimham Rocks** *Summerbridge, Harrogate, North Yorkshire HG3 4DW (01423 780688/www.brimhamrocks.co.uk/ www.nationaltrust.org.uk).*

# 126 *Watch a wicket in the Solent*

Take one sailing club on the mainland side of the Solent and another over on the Isle of Wight, then add a sandbank midway that only appears for an hour every year. What do you get? Why, an annual cricket match in the middle of the sea, of course! Every August, the tide charts are studied closely to discover when players and spectators can land in dozens of yachts on the Brambles sandbank – there's even a temporary pub to provide liquid refreshment. Crews of passing oil tankers goggle at the surreal sight of men in whites, seemingly walking on water, and stumps are only pulled when the sea reclaims the crease for another year. Contact the Royal Southern Yacht Club (www.royal-southern.co.uk) or the Island Sailing Club (www.islandsc.org.uk) to find out when to get rowing…

# 127

## Have an argument at Speakers' Corner

If you feel like slinging a bit of mud, you'll feel right at home at Speakers' Corner in London's Hyde Park (www.speakerscorner.net). You have two options: bring a stepladder and say your piece, or have a good heckle at other people's rantings and ravings from down below. Either way, this bastion of free speech is a great place to get things off your chest of a Sunday morning. George Orwell, Karl Marx and Friedrich Engels are among the mighty intellects to have held forth on the hallowed patch – though not all of the speakers who step up are quite as coherent.

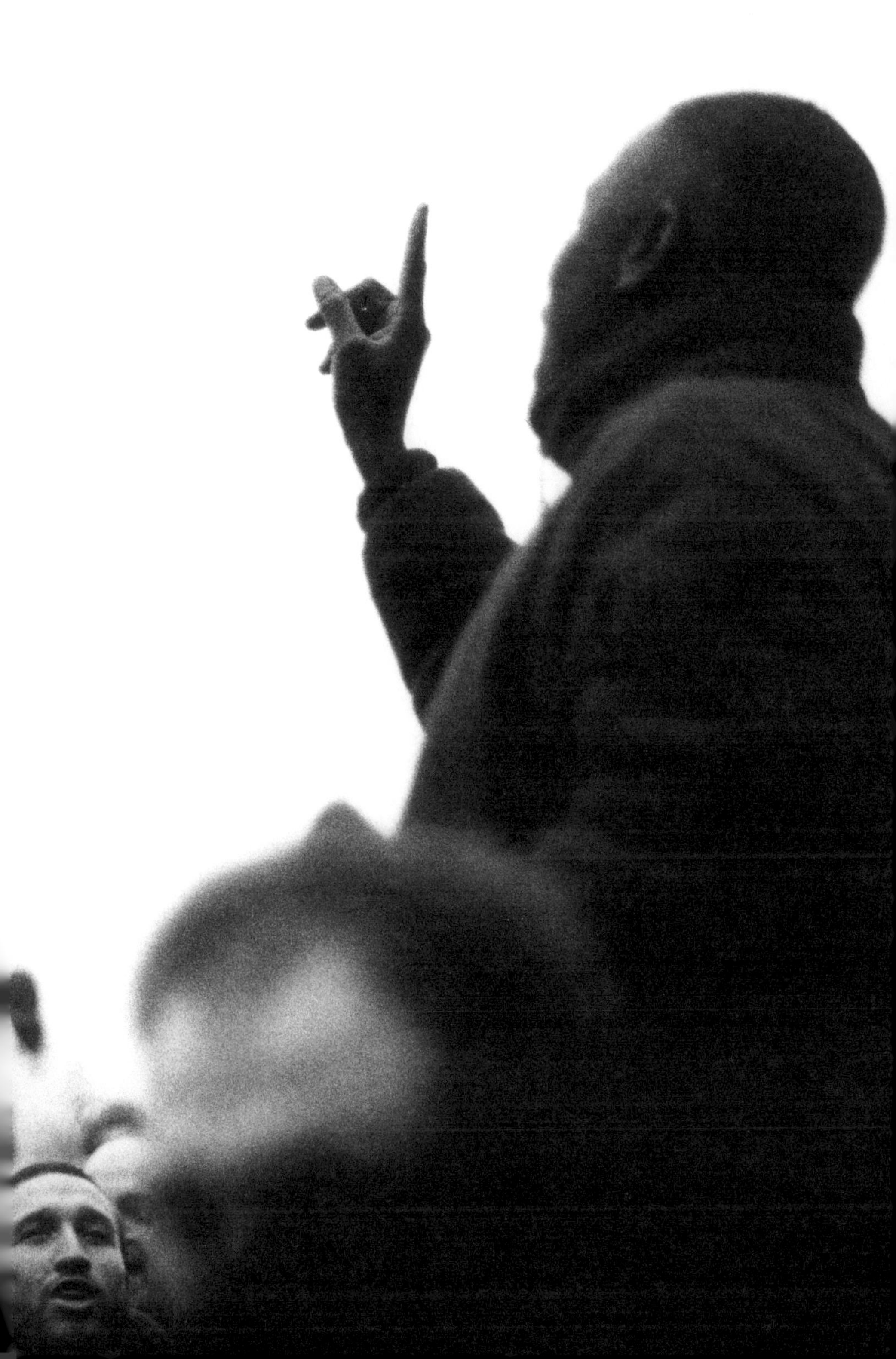

# 128 Escape to Portmeirion

Built up over 50 years by Sir Clough Williams-Ellis, this private wonderland of rescued follies and agreeably warped Italianate architecture sits on its own peninsula on the North Wales coast. Of course, Portmeirion is best known for its links with cult spy-sci-fi series *The Prisoner*, filmed here in the 1960s. Though long gone from our screens, it's far from forgotten – as the Prisoner Appreciation Society's convention, held here every year, attests.
**Portmeirion** *Gwynedd LL48 6ET (01766 770000/ www.portmeirion-village.com).*

# 129 Sample brezeln and butterkuchen

Hailing from Germany, Falko's eponymous owner is a fully qualified *konditormeister* – a master of all things sugary. Sweet confections abound at his Edinburgh bakery, from almond-topped *butterkuchen* (butter cake) to gooey rhubarb and custard tarts. Savoury tooths will prefer a salty *brezel* – like an oversized pretzel.
**Falko** *7 Bruntsfield Place, Edinburgh EH10 4HN (0131 656 0763/www.falko.co.uk).*

# 130 See modern masters in Walsall

Monet, Van Gogh, Renoir and Turner are among the artists featured in the Garman Ryan Collection at the New Art Gallery in Walsall, purpose-built for £21.5 million in 2000. The 365 artworks were donated by Lady Kathleen Epstein, third wife of sculptor Sir Jacob Epstein – whose pieces are also on display. Lady Kathleen, a racy figure in the Bloomsbury Set between the wars, was shot and wounded by the sculptor's first wife Margaret; when Sir Jacob died, she became his sole beneficiary. The gallery also has a lively programme of temporary exhibitions and artists' residencies.
**New Art Gallery Walsall** *Gallery Square, Walsall, West Midlands WS2 8LG (01922 654400/ www.artatwalsall.org.uk).*

# 131 Discover the dark arts in Cornwall

Exhibits at this one-of-a-kind Cornish museum range from fascinating 17th-century cartoons and propaganda to brutal scold's bridles – iron muzzles, used to keep suspected witches quiet. While part of its remit is to put the hysterical persecution of herbalists, midwives, gypsies and women who did not toe the line into context, there's also plenty of eerie material among the 7,000 exhibits. As well as divination mirrors, fortune-telling tea cups, spells and charms, there are some deeply creepy curses (a stuffed toad, a doll with a dagger embedded in its stomach), human skulls strapped to pentacle-shaped stands and – most bizarrely – a dead sparrow in an old red slingback shoe. Possibly not the ideal rainy day refuge for families with impressionable young 'uns.
**Museum of Witchcraft** *The Harbour, Boscastle, Cornwall PL35 0HD (01840 250111/www.museum ofwitchcraft.com).*

# 132 Learn to grow your own veg with the experts

Concerned about the provenance of your veg? Then get growing at RHS Harlow Carr gardens. Urban gardeners can see for themselves what can be done with a mere ten-by-ten-foot plot, or marvel at the bountiful produce in the kitchen garden. Special events include talks and demonstrations by the gardeners (free entry makes them particularly popular, so arrive early to nab a parking space) and tasting events. There's also a range of courses, covering everything from ground preparation to growing vegetables in containers – perfect for yards and roof terraces. Run by top horticulturalist, writer and broadcaster Joe Maiden, courses take place throughout the year; costs vary, but RHS members receive a discount. When you've finished, recuperate with a Fat Rascal in the on-site Betty's Café.
**RHS Garden Harlow Carr** *Crag Lane, Harrogate, North Yorkshire HG3 1QB (01423 724666/www.rhs.org.uk).*

# 133
## Fly on Scotland's Falkirk Wheel...

A populist engineering marvel, the Falkirk Wheel is the crowning glory of the Millennium Link. The project involved reopening the old Union Canal (Edinburgh to Falkirk) and the Forth & Clyde Canal (Falkirk to Glasgow), allowing boats to travel right across central Scotland. The big (35-metre) height difference between the canals at Falkirk called for a huge boat lift, and the Wheel – modern, powerful and surprisingly elegant – was opened by the Queen in 2002. Day-trippers can 'fly' on the Wheel by joining one of the hour-long boat trips from the visitor's centre.
**Falkirk Wheel** *Lime Road, Tamfourhill, Falkirk FK1 4RS (0870 050 0208/ www.thefalkirkwheel.co.uk).*

# 134
## ...or admire its Victorian forefather

A masterpiece of Victorian engineering, the Anderton Boat Lift was built in 1875 to transport boats between the Trent & Mersey Canal and the River Weave below. After a 2002 restoration, the 60-foot hydraulic lift is once again in tip-top working order; to experience the so-called 'Cathedral of Canals' in action, take a one-way boat trip through the lift.
**Anderton Boat Lift** *Lift Lane, Anderton, Northwich, Cheshire CW9 6FW (01606 786777/ www.andertonboatlift.co.uk).*

# 135
## Go badger-watching in Dorset

Evenings in the countryside don't have to be spent downing cider in the local pub. Old Henley Farm near Dorchester has two well-equipped hides (heating, carpets and comfy seats) from which you can spy on a dozen local badgers going about their nocturnal foraging, as well as getting a peek at a menagerie of bats, rabbits, foxes and owls. While badgers are famously shy, the farm claims a 100 per cent sighting rate.
**Old Henley Farm** *Buckland Newton, Dorchester, Dorset DT2 7BL (01300 345293/www.badger watchdorset.co.uk).*

# 136
## Take a summer tour of Parliament

The Houses of Parliament shut for the summer recess in August and September, so once MPs and Lords have safely decamped to Tuscany and Provence, the corridors of power are free to be stalked by members of the public. Tours take about 75 minutes and are led by a trained guide, who will show you the two debating chambers – the House of Commons and the House of Lords – and the Queen's Robing Room, used by Her Majesty at the annual State Opening of Parliament.
**Houses of Parliament** *London SW1A 0AA (0870 906 3773/www.parliament.uk).*

Advertisement

# Will you dine with a
# Blonde or Brune tonight?

At last, Speciality Beers such as Leffe are finding their rightful place at the dinner table

## A beer with dinner?

It's not such a strange question. The parallels between Speciality Beers and wine are plenty. Both have a rich tradition stretching back through generations and can be favourably paired with many culinary delights. But with such a tempting array of beers to choose from, how can you recognise a brew that's really special?

The clue is in the name. Speciality Beers really are special. Brewed in their country of origin, these authentic beers are made from age-old recipes. Each has its own unique taste and style, enhanced by the flavours of natural ingredients such as coriander, curaçao, roasted barley or morello cherries. They are brewed rather differently to your average lager, too. Abbots, at the Abbey de Leffe in Belgium, have been brewing Leffe for almost 800 years.

The beer is fermented at a higher temperature, producing the aromatic qualities. Any beer brewed with such care and attention deserves to be savoured and enjoyed. Drinking it is a ritual, never to be rushed. The perfect Leffe should be served in the unique Leffe Chalice glass, crafted to heighten the drinking experience. Master Beer Sommelier and Belgian Beer Ambassador, Marc Stroobandt says, "Speciality Beers such as Leffe are full of tantalising flavours and stimulating aromas. They are great with food and enjoyed by wine and beer drinkers alike." Similar to wine pairing, Speciality Beers can add a whole new depth to the gastronomic experience.

Leffe Blonde and Leffe Brune each have their own distinct character. Blonde has a well-balanced, fruity flavour, while Brune is a darker and maltier brew. Whichever brew you choose, Leffe is an ideal introduction to the world of Speciality Beers. So why not discover Leffe with your dinner tonight?

For more information on Leffe and other Speciality Beers visit: **www.specialitybeerselection.com**

## Discover Life. Discover Leffe

© InBev UK Limited, 2008. Please Drink Responsibly. www.drinkaware.co.uk

## 137 Ski on real snow – whatever the weather

It's no coincidence that so many members of the British ski and snowboard teams hail from Milton Keynes. This was the location of the UK's first indoor snow slope, which allowed riders to perfect tricks too dangerous for dryslope, launching countless careers and raising the game of a nation previously considered something of a dodo on the international winter sports circuit. Industry leader Xscape (www.xscape.co.uk) owns installations in Milton Keynes, Castleford in Leeds and Glasgow's Braehead, all of which appease the freestyle contingent with dedicated ramp and rail nights every Thursday and Friday from 7-11pm. But it's not all bent metal and aerial bravado: the rewards of 170-metre slopes with mellow gradients are best reaped by beginners, who can avoid rude awakenings in the Alps with pre-emptive group or private tuition (group lessons from £15 per hour adults, £10 children), while snow-starved tots can enjoy sliding around on toboggans, snow-trikes or rubber rings. OK, so the sterile lighting and oversized refrigerator ambience may not constitute a winter wonderland in the traditional sense, but it remains a close second for as long as the soft stuff refuses to settle in the great outdoors.

## 138 Learn the art of fly fishing

The Arundell Arms in Lifton, on the northern edge of Dartmoor, has the rights to 20 miles of wild river on the Tamar and four of its tributaries. In the hands of the same family for the last 45 years, this small village hotel has been organising fishing holidays since the early 1930s and continues to provide tuition at all levels in salmon and trout fly fishing. Courses for beginners last four days or a weekend, and include the basic casts, knot-tying techniques, choice of tackle and flies, and induction into some of the all-important mysteries of river fishing lore.
**Arundell Arms Hotel** *Lifton, Devon PL16 0AA (01566 784666/www.arundellarms.com).*

## 139 Take the Smiths tour

Want to reel around the very fountain that Morrissey sang about? Well, Phill Gatenby may not be able to arrange that precise stunt, but he'll surely take you to every other spot linked to Manchester's premier indie-jangle moaners. During the tour, he'll drive you from the Salford Lads Club to Strangeways Prison, from the Morrissey mosaic to Whalley Range, for a mere £10 a head. And if Morrissey himself is in town, you get to enjoy it from the upholstered comfort of the MozBus (in reality, a coach). For details, email Phill at mozbus@aol.com – and don't forget your gladioli.

## 140 Make like Spider-Man on Honister's Via Ferrata

Even trumping the guided tours through the awesome subterranean world of the old slate mines in Honister, the new Via Ferrata (Italian for 'iron way') system of iron rungs and a super-safe fixed climbing cable enables you to hook up and scale the original miners' hair-raising shortcut home, up the mountainous quarry walls. Don't even think about looking down.
**Honister Slate Mine** *Honister Pass, Borrowdale, Keswick, Cumbria CA12 5XN (01768 777714/www.honister-slate-mine.co.uk).*

## 141 See open-air theatre in Regent's Park

Each June, the alfresco theatre that has been at the heart of London's Regent's Park since 1932 throws open its gates for the season (www.openairtheatre.org). Shakespeare's *A Midsummer Night's Dream* is the signature play on the annual repertoire, and performances taking place as dusk descends on a balmy evening make the park feel as enchanted and timeless as Oberon's forest. Book early, and pack a picnic hamper.

## A few of my favourite things

# 142-146

## *Fergus Henderson, chef*

Any lunchtime at Sweeting's restaurant in the City (39 Queen Victoria Street, London EC4N 4SA, 020 7248 3062) is brilliantly British. It used to be a wet fish shop, so it has these amazing surfaces for things to drip off. They have a bizarre system by which you order your food – the waiters, who seem to be pinned behind counters, yell your order to runners and then your fish appears as if from nowhere. The whole place is pretty fishy, but no one seems to mind, even though they're in suits. I always think restaurants that only open for lunch have a certain sense of place about them, and the whole ritual becomes much more focused.

**One of the great joys of running your own restaurant is buying food from amazing farms around the country. Among my favourites is Credenhill Snail Farm (Credenhill, Hereford HR4 7DN, 01432 760218). It's run by a very eccentric British sort of chap, who's been breeding snails in this country for years. I only know him as Tony the snail man. I can't** remember how I met him, but I think he just emerged offering snails. Luckily, they turn up dead, cooked and out of their shells. They're great in a stew with sausages and chickpeas, or popped in a nettle soup.

My old head chef, Paul Hughes, runs a fantastic butchers' shop called the Ginger Pig, which has a stall in Borough Market and a shop in Marylebone (8 & 10 Moxon Street, London W1U 4EW, 020 7935 7788, www.thegingerpig.co.uk). Paul's got a way with all things piggy, and will sort you out with anything from ears and spleen to heart and brain. He also really understands a pork pie, which is such an amazingly comforting, reassuring thing. You know where you are with a pork pie.

**For a treat, there's a butcher in the Hebrides called MacLeans (Scarinish, Isle of Tiree PA77 6UH, 01879 220342), which I think is a miracle. Because they're on a little island, they're allowed to slaughter the animals themselves. It's perfect – you see these happy sheep chomping away, and then suddenly a lovely chop emerges. The lamb almost seems to be self-marinating, because of all the herbs the animals eat and the salt wind that comes in from the sea.**

At home, we live on Italian food. I Camisa & Son (61 Old Compton Street, London W1D 6HS, 020 7437 7610), which is run by a wonderful lady called Gaby, is the only nice Italian shop in the centre of town. It's tiny, but it's extraordinary what they manage to pack into it; we're trying to eat our way round the whole place for a bit of variety. It's also the only shop I know that does really good garlic sausages and stuffed pigs' trotters.

# 147 *Watch lacrosse in Stockport*

Despite its popular association with girls' public schools, men's lacrosse is a rough-and-ready pursuit. Skilful and physical (shoulder-charging is permitted, and rapped knuckles are a hazard), it's at its strongest in the north-west, where Stockport is home to the oldest club in England. Legend has it that in 1876 a group of rugby players were on the train home from a match in which a fellow team member had been seriously injured when, through the carriage window, they spotted a bizarre-looking game in which players were waving strange sticks around their heads. The match, it transpired, was between the Canadian Montreal Club and Caughnawaga Native Americans – on a tour to promote the little-known North American sport. The rugby club disbanded and its players instead took up this odd pursuit, employing sticks shaped like a bishop's crosier (hence the name 'la crosse').

**Stockport Lacrosse Club** *Stockport Cricket Club, Beech Road, Cale Green, Stockport SK3 8HD (0161 480 2766/www.stockportlacrosse.co.uk).*

# 148 See eye-to-eye with a giraffe

Up close, most people won't have seen much more of live giraffes than their extraordinary supermodel-esque long legs. The giraffe paddock at Marwell gets around the animals' 18-foot height and associated visitors' problems with an elevated walkway; from here, you can not only check out the giraffes' fluttery long eyelashes and get a sense of their viewpoint, but see the cheetahs, hippos, flamingoes and buffalo in the neighbouring enclosures too.
**Marwell Zoological Park** *Colden Common, Winchester, Hampshire SO21 1JH (01962 777407/www.marwell.org.uk).*

# 149 Hone your aim with Bisley's clay pigeons

As opposed to its more bellicose American counterpart, the NRA (National Rifle Association) of the United Kingdom is a benign bunch of enthusiasts, whose clay shooting centre at Bisley is steeped in 120 years of sporting history. Set in 3,000 acres of prime Surrey heathland, Bisley offers tuition at all levels four days a week, and Olympic-standard facilities for accomplished riflemen. Indeed, the centre will host the Olympic event in 2012.
**National Clay Shooting Centre** *Bisley Camp, Brookwood, Woking, Surrey GU24 0PB (01483 797666/www.nsc-clays.co.uk).*

# 150 *Hear arias outdoors*

When Leonard and Rosalind Ingrams moved into their new pad in rural Oxfordshire in 1989, they made a happy discovery: the terrace of Garsington Manor lent itself surprisingly well to opera performances. Twenty years on, Garsington hosts a summer season of intimate opera in its fabulously quaint gardens, to rival anything you'll hear in the UK's best opera houses. Its productions have been well received not only at home but also on tour in some of the world's top venues, including the Met in New York. The performances have a deliberately long interval, during which it is customary (à la Glyndebourne) to go for a walk around the gardens, open a bottle of something fizzy and consume one's picnic (in evening dress) on one's picnic rug. Lovely.
**Garsington Opera** *Garsington Manor, Garsington, Oxford OX44 9DH (01865 361636/www.garsingtonopera.org).*

# Time Out Travel Guides

## Worldwide

All our guides are written by a team of local experts with a unique and stylish insider perspective. We offer essential tips, trusted advice and honest reviews for everything you need to know in the city.

Over 50 destinations available at all good bookshops and at timeout.com/shop

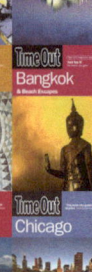

**Time Out Guides**

# 151 See the Speedway Grand Prix roar by

With the arresting motto 'No brakes, no gear, no fear', the British leg of the Speedway World Championship (www.british-speedway.co.uk), first held in 1995, has found a permanent home at Cardiff's Millennium Stadium. Usually held in June, the British Grand Prix features 15 fearless riders on gear-less, brake-less 500cc bikes, tearing round the track at up to 70mph.
**Cardiff Millennium Stadium** *Westgate Street, Cardiff CF10 1NS (0870 013 8600/www.millenniumstadium.com).*

# 152 Count the stones at Long Meg (twice)

Legend has it this Cumbrian stone circle was formed when a local witch and her daughters were caught celebrating a witches' Sabbath out on the moor, and turned to stone. Long Meg became an imposing, 12-foot-high block of red sandstone, while her daughters form a vast circle nearby. It's said to be impossible to count the stones and arrive at the same number twice – but if you do, the spell will be broken and Meg and her daughters will finally be released. A tourist draw for centuries, the Bronze Age stones certainly made an impression on Wordsworth, who declared, 'next to Stonehenge, it is beyond dispute the most notable relick that this or probably any other country contains'. For more on the folklore surrounding the stones, check out www.themodernantiquarian.com.

# 153 Cross Shropshire's Iron Bridge

Several British towns and cities lay claim to the title 'birthplace of the Industrial Revolution', but none is as bucolic as Ironbridge. Nestling in a gorge on the River Severn, the town takes its name from the world's first iron bridge, opened in 1781. The gorge is now a World Heritage Site, and home to ten award-winning museums (01952 884391, www.ironbridge.org.uk): don a hard hat to walk through the dark, oozing tar tunnel, or explore a recreated Victorian town at Blists Hill.

# 154 Sup sarsaparilla at Britain's last temperance bar

When the temperance movement was at its 19th-century peak, there were booze-free pubs in many a Northern town – hoping to wean the working class off the gin and on to more wholesome refreshments, like a nice half of dandelion and burdock. The only temperance bar that's still open is Fitzpatrick's, little changed since it opened in 1890. Amid the herbal remedies for flu, childhood fears and PMT, stocked in a bizarre array of flagons, urns and jars, stands the keynote sarsaparilla, an age-old 'cure' for syphilis concocted from the eponymous spiky vine from the Americas. It's a cordial, so diluted to taste – perhaps, given the bitter smell, quite heavily.
**Fitzpatrick's** *5 Bank Street, Rawtenstall, Rossendale, Lancashire BB4 6QS (01706 231836/www.fitzpatricks1890.co.uk).*

# 155
## Experience Armageddon at Hack Green...

This decommissioned RAF bunker once helped protect the UK from nuclear attack – or at least gave us the option to fire off some retaliatory missiles before the country was utterly annihilated. These days, threat diminished, the underground space exhibits military ephemera, including (mercifully dud) missiles and the console from which a PM might have given the order to launch a nuke. Part of the tour involves a simulation of an attack; pretty nervy, by all accounts. But military nuts will love it, as will anyone with an interest in WMDs and their terrible capacity for destruction.

**Hack Green Nuclear Bunker** *off the A530 Whitchurch Road, near Nantwich, Cheshire CW5 8AL (01270 629219/www.hackgreen.co.uk).*

# 156-159
## ...then discover Britain's other Cold War bunkers

**Kelvedon Hatch Secret Nuclear Bunker**
*Crown Buildings, Kelvedon Hall Lane, Brentwood, Essex CM14 5TL (01277 364883/www.secretnuclearbunker.co.uk).*
Built for the RAF in 1953, Kelvedon became a Regional Government HQ in the late '60s.

**RAF Holmpton**
*Rysome Lane, Withernsea, East Yorkshire HU19 2QR (01964 630208/www.rafholmpton.com).*
Until it was redesignated as an Emergency War HQ in the 1980s, Holmpton was a radar station.

**Scotland's Secret Bunker**
*Crown Buildings, Troywood, Fife KY16 8QH (01333 310301/www.secretbunker.co.uk).*
Hidden beneath a farmhouse, the bunker could sleep 300 survivors – and even has a chapel.

**York Cold War Bunker**
*Monument Close, York, North Yorkshire YO24 4HT (01904 646940/www.english-heritage.org.uk).*
Opened in 1961, this bunker was HQ of Number 20 Group, Royal Observation Corps.

# 160
## Visit Milton Keynes' Peace Pagoda

Milton Keynes may be more associated with identikit retail parks and regimented grid roads in many people's minds, but it's also home to the western hemisphere's first peace pagoda, built by the nuns and monks of the Nipponzan Myohoji order. A thousand cedars and cherry blossom trees were donated to the garden by the people of the Japanese town of Yoshino – so time your visit for spring, when the ranks of cherry blossom erupt in a blaze of crimson, white and pink.

**Peace Pagoda** *Willen Park (access from Brickhill Street), Willen Road, Milton Keynes, Buckinghamshire MK15 0BA (01908 663652/ www.mkbuddhism.org.uk).*

# 161
## Lead the way at the Cumberland Pencil Museum

Get misty-eyed over extracts from Raymond Briggs's much-loved *Snowman*, admire the world's longest pencil (almost 26 feet long), then drop into one of the regular artist-led workshops. Topics range from the art of the caricature to sessions on sketching wildlife.

**Cumberland Pencil Company** *Southey Works, Greta Bridge, Keswick, Cumbria CA12 5NG (017687 80898/www.pencilmuseum.co.uk).*

# 162
## Discover Homotopia

Ever wondered what Liverpool through Brian Epstein's eyes would look like? Or had a penchant to be part of an international pansy-planting art project? If so, drag yourself along to Homotopia (www.homotopia.net), an annual Liverpool celebration of LGBT creativity and culture. Last year radio broadcasts included Peter Tatchell on 'Pink Iraq', Stella Duffy and Patrick Gale spoke at the Queer Literature Gala, while a 'drag lip-synch musical about the alleged slutty one from Buck's Fizz' ensured a few pert bottoms on seats.

# 163-164

## Take a punt on the Cam or Cherwell

Come summertime, there's no easier way to feel like a character from *Brideshead Revisited* than by whiling away an afternoon on a punt – a 24-foot flat-bottomed boat, piloted by standing on the rear platform and propelling the thing along with a 16-foot pole. Just bear in mind that punting isn't as easy as it looks – and it's not just the tendency to lubricate journeys with lukewarm champagne that sees people so regularly lose their poles or slip and fall in. To avoid collisions, skip overly congested sections (passing King's College in Cambridge, or beneath Magdalen Bridge in Oxford), and instead head away from the city on a more rural retreat. Punts can be hired from Scudamore's in Cambridge (01223 359750, www.scudamores.com) and the Cherwell Boat House in Oxford (01865 515978, www.cherwellboathouse.co.uk).

## 165 *Go wild camping*

# Pitch perfect

*With stout walking boots and some serious misgivings, Maisie Tomlinson heads into the great outdoors.*

The last time I slept under canvas, I was crammed between the bins and the shower block in a field with 200 others, and I still slept with one hand on the mallet. In my city-dweller's psyche, the countryside is teeming with the most disturbed sort of killer, and a thin layer of nylon (door zipped fast or no) offers laughable protection.

Nevertheless, since hooking up with a Devonshire lad born and bred, it has been his single-minded quest to get me back to nature. Not for him the canvas suburbia of organised campsites, with their rows of neatly marshalled tents, chemical toilets and trappings of civilisation: instead, we're off wild camping.

In most parts of England and Wales, you have to ask the landowner's permission before pitching your tent. In practice, many turn a blind eye if you're only there for a night and are discreet, or don't even notice you're there (the golden rule being 'pitch late, leave early'). In Scotland, it's legal to camp wild, so long as you follow the rules: leave the flora and fauna as you found it (party animals and budding Ray Mears take note), avoid farmland and camp well out of sight of any houses and roads. After that, it's simply a question of remembering to pack the essentials – an Ordnance Survey map, compass, torch, plenty of food and water, and a sturdy tent and sleeping bag.

Our destination is Dartmoor, England's last great wilderness, and a place where camping is encouraged. Nonetheless, I'm a little nervous. According to folklore, Dartmoor is rife with strange apparitions – from a pair of disembodied throttling hands to the pack of demon hounds that inspired the *Hound of the Baskervilles*. It's also home to a notorious prison – a dour, forbidding cluster of grey stone buildings, which Martin blithely points out as we drive past.

**Time Out** 1000 Things to do in Britain 63

> *'I take a silent note of the landmarks, should a hasty, hound-pursued retreat be in order.'*

But on this sunny afternoon in late August the moors look gentle and inviting, and after a glorious day sampling cream teas and cider and swimming in the River Dart, it's time to leave society behind and choose our spot before sundown. As we puff through the purple heather and startled sheep with our backpacks, I take a silent note of the landmarks, should a hasty, hound-pursued retreat be in order. We settle on a hilltop tor; high enough for a decent view, but with shelter from the wind among the boulders. Then, cracking open a couple of beers, we climb the crags to watch the sun go down.

The views are astonishing. Sprawling impossibly far in every direction, with not a house in sight, the hills roll away beneath us. As the sun sets and the moors give off a ruddy glow, distant figures start to pour down the hillsides, back to cars and pubs and hotels before nightfall. It's a peculiar feeling, resisting the instinct to join them – but before long we're alone, and vast shadows begin to pool across the landscape.

With the tent hastily assembled and supper simmering on a disposable barbecue, we wrap ourselves in blankets and perch on the highest rock with a bottle of champagne. A mile or so to the south we spot our only neighbours through the gathering dusk, setting up camp in the centre of an ancient, unpleasantly eerie-looking stone circle.

As a thick cloud of fog drifts across the peaks towards our camp, we decide to take cover – along with the wild ponies, making their way uphill to the shelter of the tor. It's thrilling to be alone with the elements as the skyline darkens and the wind picks up, although in a few minutes we're completely enveloped in swirling mist – this really is the Dartmoor of Conan Doyle's imagination. We grope blindly towards bed, before anything can even think about looming out of the mist. The tent, though snug enough, is rattling and howling as loudly as if we were parked on an Andean glacier rather than the English countryside.

An hour passes, and at last there is quiet. We open the zip to find the mists have cleared and the grass is soaked with dew. It's a beautiful night, the black canvas of the sky dotted with innumerable stars – and before I can protest, Martin has grabbed my hand and is striding away for a midnight walk. We switch off the torch, as he insists that night vision will kick in after half an hour without one. (Note: I don't know if this is true. Although after seeing the first pair of eyes glint in the torch's beam, I am happy to comply.) Being utterly alone in the darkness is intoxicating and strangely liberating, as we clamber up a tor, lie back and count the occasional shooting star.

And then I hear it. The distant yet distinct chorus of a pack of baying dogs. The red-eyed demon hounds hunting down the souls of wandering travellers? Prison bloodhounds on the trail of a dangerous escapee?

A moment of trying to be brave, then I'm skidding down the rocks and tripping back to the tent as fast as my legs can carry me, Martin laughing all the way behind me.

*For information on wild camping in Dartmoor, see www.dartmoor-npa.gov.uk.*
*For more on wild camping in Scotland, visit www.mountaineering-scotland.org.uk/leaflets/wildcamp.html.*

# 166-180
## Tackle the National Trails

The 15 National Trails in England and Wales provide over 2,500 miles of well-managed footpaths across some of our most glorious and varied countryside. Lengths vary: the South West Coast Path runs for a challenging 630 miles, while the Yorkshire Wolds Way is a more manageable 79 miles. Some, such as the Pennine Bridleway and the South Downs Way, are suitable for horses and mountain bikes as well as walkers; others have sections that accommodate wheelchair-users, children and buggies. Serious hikers may enjoy the challenge of completing entire trails, but equally you can just hop on a train (many routes are accessible by public transport) and walk a section for a day trip. Visit the National Trails website (www.nationaltrail.co.uk) to pick and plan your path. Hadrian's Wall, at 84 miles, takes on average seven days to complete, passing farmland, salt marshes and Tyne bridges. Local associations run the gamut from Roman history to railway heritage (George and Robert Stephenson), literature (Sir Walter Scott) and football (Shearer! Shearer!).

# 181
## Crunch a clove at the Garlic Festival

While it's a less-than-ideal premise for a first date, the Isle of Wight's garlic festival has nevertheless grown into the island's biggest and most popular event, attracting some 25,000 people over a weekend in August (01983 863566, www.garlic-festival.co.uk). Fact fans will be intrigued to know that the Isle of Wight is the UK's premier garlic-growing region – something the festival, which has been held since 1983, won't let you forget in a hurry, with pungent, garlic-infused beers and ice-creams for sale, as well as the more conventional breads and mussels. In addition to the piles of food and drink, entertainment is also provided, in past years by the eclectic likes of Chas & Dave, a troupe of Middle Eastern dancers, strongman John Evans and Mungo Jerry.

# 182
## Hide out in the Plantation Garden

Lying hidden deep in the heart of Norwich (and notoriously difficult to find) is the tranquil idyll of the Plantation Garden. Set in three acres, this 'secret garden' is an excellent example of how to make a silk purse out of a sow's ear; once a chalk quarry, the site was bought by a wealthy local businessman in 1856, who spent the next 40 years transforming it into a magical garden. After World War II it was left to run wild – but a sterling restoration effort in recent years has returned it to its former glory.

**Plantation Garden** *Earlham Road, Norwich, Norfolk NR2 3DB (www.plantationgarden.co.uk).*

# 183
## Check out the Cholmondeleys

Forget tutu-clad ballerinas and prepare to be amazed: contemporary dance performances by the all-female Cholmondeleys (pronounced Chumlees) and their male counterparts, the Featherstonehaughs (Fanshaws), will blow your mind. Often created in collaboration with artists, designers and film makers, each show is a sensory treat of original, enchanting and occasionally hilarious dance (020 7378 8800, www.thecholmondeleys.org).

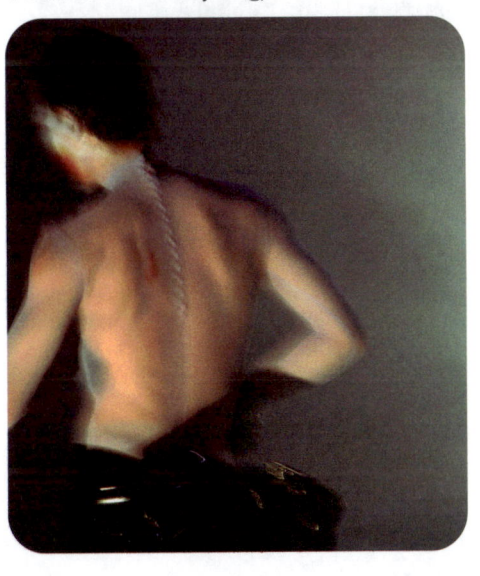

## 184-187 Cross the millennium bridges

Early visitors to London's Millennium Footbridge, linking St Paul's Cathedral to Tate Modern, experienced its famous 'wobble' on its opening in June 2000. The sway was caused by the synchronised footfall effect of hundreds of people stepping in unison; 'walking tests' and the installation of dampers subsequently reduced the movement of the 1,150-foot-long bridge. Spoilsports. To cross the three other millennial bridges – also wobble-free, alas – visit the Manchester Ship Canal, the River Lune in Lancaster, and Glasgow – the latter featuring two spans that lift impressively over the Clyde.

## 188 Uncover the secrets of real ale at the Hook Norton Brewery

Old Hooky, Hooky Gold and Hooky Dark; names to gladden the heart of any real ale aficionado. Their creator, the Hook Norton Brewery, is still part-powered by an impressive steam engine, installed in 1899, and runs two-hour tours taking in the brewery and a museum. Tours culminate in a spot of sampling; under-12s aren't admitted. Never mind; they can look out for Nelson, Major and Consul, the brewery's shaggy shire horses – still used for local deliveries.

**Hook Norton Brewery** *Brewery Lane, Hook Norton, Oxfordshire OX15 5NY (01608 730384/www.hooknortonbrewery.co.uk).*

## 189 Meet the thoroughbreds at Lambourn

The downs around the small Berkshire market town of Lambourn are known as the Valley of the Racehorse for good reason: thousands of thoroughbreds are trained here every year. Every Good Friday, dozens of trainers open their yards to the public to reveal some of their training techniques first hand (www.lambourn.info). Once you've watched potential champions being put through their paces, the rest of the day is given over to equine demonstrations, children's games and a country show.

## 190 Admire Lalique's angels in Jersey

Unremarkable from the outside, St Matthew's Church hides an enchanting secret. Inside, the font, altar cross and a row of exquisitely carved angels were all sculpted from glass in the 1930s by renowned glass designer René Lalique, best known for his stunning perfume bottles and art nouveau jewellery. The glass used in the church is 'verre blanc moule presse' – a slightly opaque, milky variety that casts a suitably ethereal light throughout this ecclesiastical oddity.

**St Matthew's Church** *Millbrook, St Lawrence, Jersey JE3 1LN (01534 502864).*

## 191 Visit Hawkstone Park…

The tourist board bills Hawkstone as the 'first theme park in the country', but don't expect thrill rides and sprawling queues. In their stead you'll discover a lovely 100-acre site, dotted with fantastical grottoes, tunnels, towers and bridges, constructed in the 18th and early 19th centuries. Grotto Hill is topped with a ruined Gothic arch; the perilously narrow Swiss Bridge crosses a rocky chasm; the Cleft narrows into a creepy tunnel; and the 100-foot Monument offers amazing views. Allow at least half a day to ramble the circular route, and take a torch.

**Hawkstone Park** *Weston-under-Redcastle, Shrewsbury, Shropshire SY4 5UY (01939 200611/www.hawkstone.co.uk).*

# 192-199
## ...then take in some other famous follies

### Faringdon Tower
*14 Beech Close, Faringdon, Oxfordshire SN7 7EN (01367 241142/www.faringdonfolly.org.uk).*
Built in 1935, this understated tower stands in the middle of a hill fort. Pay £1 and climb 100 feet to the top; on a clear day, the views over the Vale of the White Horse are exceptional.

### House in the Clouds
*Uplands, Thorpeness, Suffolk IP6 4NQ (020 7224 3615/www.houseintheclouds.co.uk).*
This famed folly was erected in 1923 as the new water tower for nearby Thorpeness. The water tank was cunningly 'disguised' as a quaint little cottage – now a highly unusual holiday let.

### King Alfred's Tower
*Stourhead Estate Office, Stourton, Warminster, Wiltshire BA12 6QD (01747 841152/www.alfredstower.info).*
The most dramatic of the 18th-century follies on the Stourhead Estate is the 160-foot King Alfred's Tower, erected in 1772 to commemorate a Saxon victory of 871.

### Painshill Park
*Portsmouth Road, Cobham, Surrey KT11 1JE (01932 868113/www.painshill.co.uk).*
Extravagant follies abound at this romantic 160-acre garden, laid out by the brilliant 18th-century amateur landscape architect Charles Hamilton. A ruined abbey, giant waterwheel, mausoleum, hermitage, Chinese bridge, Turkish tent, Gothic tower and Crystal grotto are among Hamilton's decorative flourishes.

### Quex House
*Birchington, Kent CT7 0BH (01843 842168/www.quexmuseum.org).*
In the late 19th century, Major Powell-Cotton hunted down all manner of exotic animals – then stuffed and put on display at Quex House. After gawping at the surreal dioramas, take a woodland walk to Waterloo Tower, with its peal of 12 bells. Call to check opening times.

### Ruined Castle at Mow Cop
*Mow Cop is about 6 miles north of Stoke-on-Trent (www.mowcop.info). OS map ref: SJ855573.*
The picturesque ruined castle is not all it seems – in fact, the artfully tumbledown ruins were built in 1754 to provide a suitably romantic view from nearby Rode Hall.

### Rushton Triangular Lodge
*Near Rushton, Kettering, Northamptonshire NN14 1RP (01536 710761/www.english-heritage.org.uk).*
Recusant Catholic Sir Thomas Tresham built the tower as a coded celebration of the Holy Trinity. Everything is in threes, with three 33-foot walls, each with three windows, and triangles galore; even the chimney is triangular.

### Wainhouse's Tower
*Skircoat Moor Road, Halifax, North Yorkshire (01422 357257).*
This 275-foot tower was planned as a factory chimney, designed to comply with the Smoke Abatement Act of 1870, then converted by eccentric industrialist Edward Wainhouse into 'an astronomical and physical observatory'.

**Rushton Triangular Lodge**

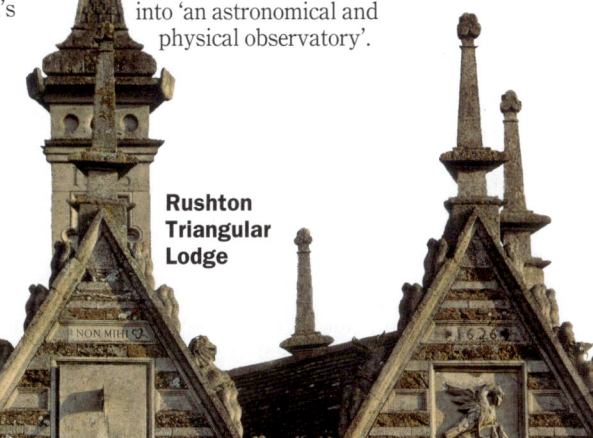

# 200 Embrace the alternative in Powys

**Ronnie Haydon** discovers an eco-friendly clifftop haven.

A visit to the Centre for Alternative Technology begins with a delightful ascent to the moral high ground. Set on a wooded clifftop, high above the Dulas Valley, you reach it via an ingenious water powered funicular railway. At the top of the 80-foot cliff, the views stretch to Tarren-y-Gesail, the southernmost peak in Snowdonia. From here on in, your ecological education – and the fun – begins in earnest, as you explore the centre's seven acres of buildings, landscapes, gardens and interactive displays, designed to demonstrate the power of wind, water and sun, and show visitors how, through environmentally responsible buildings, energy conservation, organic growing and waste management, our impact on the environment can be tempered.

An introductory video describes CAT's beginnings, founded by Gerard Morgan-Grenville in 1974, in the disused Llwyngwern slate quarry near Machynlleth. After three decades of unsuccessful attempts at power-generation through water, wind and sun, enough money was raised to invest in a huge wind turbine; now the centre is not only self-powered, but sells power back to the National Grid. Water is provided by an existing man-made reservoir in a former slate quarry, and sewage is processed in reedbeds.

The low-energy house, originally built as an experimental prototype by Wates Homes in 1976, shows how energy-saving measures have come on in intervening decades – we're not sure quadruple-glazed windows would ever really have caught on. If you're a DIY buff, you might be more interested in the timber frame self-build display, in all its energy-saving glory, which explains how you can build your own sustainable residence from a flat pack.

A series of organic gardens aims to inspire visitors to go green, as well as eat up (and compost) their greens, and there's loads of information about growing your own veg. The busiest area, however, is all about recycling, composting and exploring renewable energy: here, competitive dads test their muscle power, attempting to light up bulbs by pedalling on a bike-generator, while kids slide merrily into the composting area, indulge in splashy water play or explore the giant underground mole hole.

Even going to the loo here is an eco-friendly exercise, thanks to the flush-free compost toilet. (Take our word for it, it smells no worse than a bog-standard, water-wasting loo.) Your business goes into a mysterious place where it stays for two years, until it turns into sweet-smelling compost.

Beyond the composting area is the animals' enclosure, with its chickens, ducks, geese and goats. They provide manure for the garden and eggs and milk for the excellent quiches and pies sold in the café. There's a pleasantly landscaped lake whose hungry carp are partial to leftovers – but when the food in the café is fair trade, vegetarian and strong on wholesome homebakes and salads, there's usually little left for them.

It all combines to give kids and eco-conscious adults some powerful food for thought before they make their water-powered descent back to a 'civilisation' that seems a lot less civilised after a visit to CAT.

**Centre for Alternative Technology**
Machynlleth, Powys SY20 9AZ (01654 705950/www.cat.org.uk).

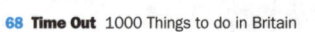

## 201 Order pie 'n' mash at Manze's

South of Tower Bridge stands the oldest pie 'n' masherie still in business – it's about the same age as Tower Bridge itself. At one time there were 14 Manze family shops dolloping gloopy parsley liquor on to eels and pies, but the tiled walls and marble tables, mirrors and metal serving pots at this branch were the first. Ordering is easy: 'Pie and double mash, loads of liquor, please.' 'Double pie and mash.' 'Triple eels, double mash, hold the liquor.' Sorted.
**M Manze** *87 Tower Bridge Road, London SE1 4TW (020 7407 2985/www.manze.co.uk).*

## 202 Catch an Ayckbourn play in Scarborough

Arguably Britain's most successful living dramatist, Alan Ayckbourn has written more than 70 plays during his prolific theatrical career. Almost all of them have had their first outing at the Stephen Joseph Theatre, where Ayckbourn has been artistic director since 1971. Although set to retire from the post in 2008, he's expected to continue premièring work at the venue for some time to come.
**Stephen Joseph Theatre** *Westborough, Scarborough, North Yorkshire YO11 1JW (01723 370541/www.sjt.uk.com).*

## 203 Go river-bugging in Perthshire

'We don't expect prior experience, just a basic level of water confidence. You don't even have to be able to swim.' Reassuring words from Kate Mason-Strang of Nae Limits, but this sport is not for potamophobes. River-buggers are strapped into an inflatable seat that looks like a giant ladybird (the bug – geddit?) and must manoeuvre through a series of cascading 'staircase' rapids and pools, using only paddle and flipper. It's a far more intimate experience than conventional white water rafting, says Mason-Strang: 'There are guides in the water too, of course, but basically you're on your own, so it's a much higher adrenaline rush'. Aside from the buzz of bouncing off rocks down nature's own crazy waterslide, you're surrounded by glorious Scottish scenery – not that you'll see too much of it as you slalom past. Intrigued and undeterred by how daft you'll look? A half-day introduction (over-14s only, weight restriction 16 stone) can be had for £50 from www.naelimits.co.uk.

**Time Out** 1000 Things to do in Britain **69**

# 204

**Squeeze into a corset at the Fashion Museum**

*There are over 3,000 pieces on display at Bath's Fashion Museum (01225 477173, www.fashionmuseum.co.uk), from haute couture glad rags to quirky 1940s swimming costumes.* Check out the impossibly voluminous 19th-century dresses, for ladies who didn't (and couldn't) do much more than glide about or sit and sew in stuffy drawing rooms, or try on reproduction Victorian-era corsets and crinolines and see if you can beat Scarlett O'Hara's famed 'handspan' waist – a quite literally breathtaking 17 inches.

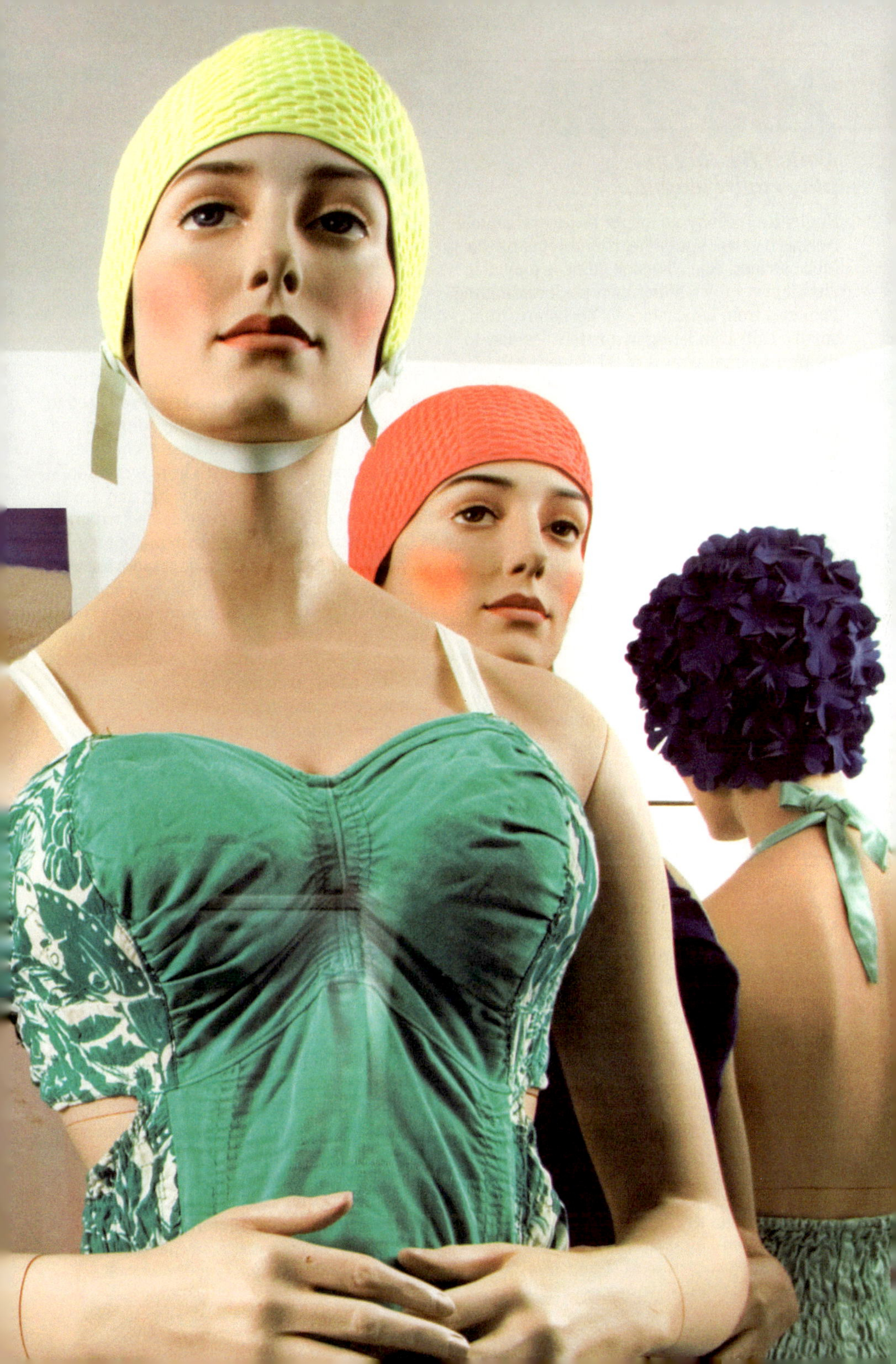

# 205-208
## Watch the 'big four' play rugby league...

Rugby league may no longer be an exclusively Northern game, but its heartland remains the M62 corridor. The 13-a-side game is played in almost every town along its route, crossing the Pennines from Lancashire to Yorkshire: from small outfits competing in amateur leagues to the professional set-ups of the Super League. Four clubs – Bradford (www.bradfordbulls.co.uk), Leeds (www.leedsrugby.com), St Helens (www.saintsrlfc.com) and Wigan (www.wiganwarriors.com) – are the dominant forces on the domestic scene, and going to a game remains an earthy, passionately tribal experience.

# 209
## ...or enjoy some village rugby union in Wales

When rugby split into two factions in 1895, rugby league essentially became the preserve of the working class in the north-west, while rugby union was adopted by middle- and upper-class Southerners. The exception to the rule was South Wales, where rugby union had laid deep roots in its pit villages and towns. While the scene has changed dramatically over the years, not least with the advent of professionalism, its strength as a unifying force in sometimes troubled communities remains. Watch a match in the Rhondda, say, and you're reminded of the power of sport as a tool for social cohesion. Crowds are small, but humorous and knowledgeable, and there are no airs and graces about the players, who'll often join you for a post-match pint in the clubhouse.

**Mountain Ash RFC** *Oxford Street, Mountain Ash, Rhondda-Cynon-Taff, Mid Glamorgan CF45 3PL (01443 472918/www.mountainashrfc.co.uk).*
**Senghenydd RFC** *The Welfare Ground, Senghenydd, Mid Glamorgan CF83 4FW (029 2083 0467/www.senghenyddrfc.com).*
**Tredegar RFC** *Park Hill, Tredegar, Gwent NP22 3NN (01495 722879/www.tredegar-rfc.co.uk).*
**Ystrad Rhondda RFC** *73 William Street, Ystrad, Rhondda-Cynon-Taff, Mid Glamorgan CF41 7QY (www.ystradrhonddarfc.co.uk/01443 435621).*

# 210
## Pan for gold

Lead was mined in the wilds of Wanlockhead, Dumfries, until the 1950s – but more precious metal also runs through its veins. There's gold in them thar moors, and some of it is about as pure as it gets: 23 carats, to be precise. Fancy your prospects? It's not just a case of getting tooled up with a pick-axe and pan; you need to know where to look, and digging, dipping and sifting all have their own special techniques. You'll probably just unearth iron pyrite (fool's gold), but if you strike it lucky you may find a few flakes or even a tiny nugget. It's hard graft and the elements can be punishing, but it's exciting stuff; practitioners do it more for the addictive rush of discovery than any real hope of financial reward (though some prospectors have found enough gold over the years to have rings made). The Museum of Lead Mining runs one-day panning courses at £65; well worth trying before heading for the hills.
**Museum of Lead Mining** *Wanlockhead, Biggar, Lanarkshire ML12 6UT (01659 74387/www.leadminingmuseum.co.uk).*

# 211
## Travel back in time at Avoncroft

Avoncroft Museum has provided a haven for 25 historic buildings spanning seven centuries, all painstakingly rebuilt after being rescued from developers' bulldozers. There's a Tudor boozer and an Edwardian showman's wagon, a cruck barn from Warwickshire and an ancient local cider mill – all peopled by re-enactors, who don't just climb inside the bricks and mortar, but the very skin of long-extinct communities. The National Telephone Kiosk Collection is curiously enthralling, including every GPO and BT model from the 1920s to the present day. And, sure enough, there's also a Tardis.
**Avoncroft Museum of Historic Buildings** *Stoke Heath, Bromsgrove, Worcestershire B60 4JR (01527 831363/www.avoncroft.org.uk).*

## 212 Learn new moves at Dancebase

As well as hosting performances from a whole host of professional dance companies, Dancebase offers classes in over 40 different forms of dance. Learn the routines from your favourite musicals, try a spot of barefoot ballet, get down to hip hop or take to the floor for a waltz. One-off workshops cover everything from can can to cheerleading and skanking – the dance of choice for dedicated ska and reggae fans.
**Dancebase** *National Centre for Dance, 14-16 Grassmarket, Edinburgh EH1 2JU (0131 225 5525/www.dancebase.co.uk).*

## 213 See your speedometer soar – without breaking the law

Ever idly wondered exactly how fast your humble hatchback could go if you really put your foot down? Find out at Run What Ya Brung (www.rwyb.co.uk), a regular fixture at Northamptonshire's Santa Pod raceway. You can take any car you like along to the event, and race it over the quarter-mile drag strip – be it a souped-up Subaru or your gran's Ford Fiesta (though best ask her first).
**Santa Pod Raceway** *Airfield Road, Podington, Wellingborough, Northamptonshire NN29 7XA (01234 782828/www.santapod.co.uk).*

## 214 Enjoy abstract art in the open air

Along with her husband Ben Nicholson, Dame Barbara Hepworth was one of Britain's leading 20th-century abstract artists. At the outbreak of war in 1939, she moved with her young family to St Ives, building a studio and sculpture garden where she lived and worked until her death in a studio fire in 1975. The following year saw the public opening of the site, in accordance with her wishes. The pieces here were among Hepworth's favourites, and most still occupy the positions in which she placed them. Wandering the little gravel pathways and finding the organic bronze, stone and wood sculptures emerging from behind exotic plants, with St Ives' church tower peeking out beyond, is nothing short of joyous on a summer's afternoon.
**Barbara Hepworth Museum & Sculpture Garden** *Barnoon Hill, St Ives, Cornwall TR26 1AD (01736 796226/www.tate.org.uk/stives/hepworth).*

**OUR CLIMATE NEEDS
A HELPING HAND TODAY**

Be a smart traveller. Help to offset your carbon emissions from your trip by pledging Carbon Trees with Trees for Cities.

All the Carbon Trees that you donate through Trees for Cities are genuinely planted as additional trees in our projects.

Trees for Cities is an independent charity working with local communities on tree planting projects.

www.treesforcities.org    Tel 020 7587 1320

**Trees for Cities**
Charity registration number 1032154

# 215 Visit Liverpool in its Capital of Culture year

As European Capital of Culture 2008, Liverpool will be hosting over 350 events – many of them free (0151 233 2008, www.liverpool08.com). Among the offerings, which encompass theatre, art, dance, music and sport, unexpected delights include the International Shanty Festival, to be held in the rejuvenated Albert and Wellington Docks in July, October's Liverpool is Burning, billed as 'the Ultimate Dance Off', and December's Labyrinth of Light – when St George's Hall will flicker with the flames of 800 candles. Celebrated Scousers will also be descending on their hometown, from Sir Paul McCartney to Sir Simon Rattle, who'll be making a triumphant return to his roots to conduct at the Philharmonic Hall.

# 216-217 Look out to sea at Land's End or the Lizard

Britain's most westerly and southerly points, Land's End and the Lizard battle it out for the tourists with differing displays of rugged brawn. The dramatic rocky outcrop of Land's End is home to a theme park that peddles crystals, model dragons and fudge – but thankfully it's little more than a pimple on the beautiful face of Cornwall. Bypass the tourist tat and the bloke who takes your photo next to the corny signpost (New York 3,000 miles) and walk south-east along three miles of springy footpath over the cliffs to Porthcurno. You'll be spellbound by the scale of it all, and the foamy violence below.

Lizard Point is a very different beast. It's tamer to look at (although a tiny café on the edge of the cliff provides a steamy, welcoming refuge), but the forces of nature wink at you from hidden nooks. The lighthouse, now a youth hostel, sweeps the bay with its warning beacon. A footpath from Rosenithon leads to the Manacles – a rocky 'graveyard of ships' lurking at sea – and the little bays are full of quicksand. But don't forsake one Cornish coast for the other; visit both, and see where you feel more alive (www.cornwalltouristboard.co.uk).

# 218 Prepare the catch of the day at Billingsgate

Where better to learn seafood skills than east London's famed fish market? Billingsgate Seafood Training School runs courses for almost everyone: knife skills and fish preparation for enthusiastic amateurs and chefs (don't forget to bring a cool bag to take your handiwork away in), dedicated parent-and-child sessions (gutting a mackerel and struggling with squid can be an oddly bonding experience), and free 'Get into Fish Frying!' seminars for would-be chippie owners.

**Billingsgate Seafood Training School** *Office 30, Billingsgate Market, Trafalgar Way, London E14 5ST (020 7517 3548/www.seafoodtraining.org).*

# 219 Play a game of real tennis

People argue about the history of all sorts of sports ad infinitum – which country first played football, whether rugby was really invented at Rugby – but everyone who knows about such things acknowledges that real tennis is the oldest racket sport in the world. The game played by Roger Federer and co is a product of evolution rather than pure invention – and it all started with medieval monks using their hands to knock a rudimentary ball around monastery cloisters. Players began to use a glove, until someone had the bright idea of stitching cord to create a web around the fingers. Then, thanks to the attachment of a frame and handle, a racket emerged.

Remarkably, the modern game of real tennis is indistinguishable from that of five centuries ago. The court that Charles I built at Hampton Court in 1625 is still used for championship play today (www.realtennis.gbrit.com), while newly built courts are all designed to represent the layout of those monastery cloisters. The court floor is still made of stone, and the ball, though similar in appearance to a lawn tennis ball, is made with a core of cork, bound in cloth, tightly tied with string then covered in felt and hand-stitched.

The 'real' part of the name is often thought to be a corruption of 'royal', reflecting the game's regal connections during its 16th- and 17th-century heyday in England and France. Louis X caught a chill from playing on a cold stone floor and died soon afterwards, while Charles VIII followed him after banging his head on a court's doorway. Henry VIII was an ardent player; Anne Boleyn was watching a game when she was arrested, while Henry was on court when news arrived of her execution. In 1600, Paris had more courts than churches. However, the truth of the 'real' genesis is more prosaic. 'Real' became used in the 19th century to distinguish the game from the lawn version, which grew in popularity when the pneumatic rubber ball was invented – the craze for which contributed to the steady decline of the sport's progenitor. Real tennis retreated to country houses, public schools, universities and institutions, where it became increasingly elitist and inaccessible.

Only in the last 20 years has the sport enjoyed a resurgence. Although there are still just 26 courts in the UK (and only a further 19 in the rest of the world), there are more opportunities for beginners than ever before. I learned how to play in Leamington (Leamington Tennis Court Club, 50 Bedford Street, Leamington Spa, Warwickshire CV32 5DT, 01926 424 977). I quickly discovered that the low bounce of the ball on the stone floor renders top-spun lawn tennis shots redundant, and that a cut stroke is the way to get the ball over the net. As for serving – well, it's not just toss and whack. The railroad, bobble and giraffe are just three of the myriad serves that take years to master. The basic principles of scoring (15-30-40-Deuce-Advantage-Game) are familiar, but real tennis has yet one more twist. You don't automatically lose a rally if the ball bounces twice at your end of the court. Instead, you change ends and replay the point, with the person who failed to return the ball then trying to make a shot that bounces twice closer to the back wall than the original shot. It's called a 'chase', and it explains why real tennis is said to demand stealth, subtlety and a degree in applied mathematics.

Indeed, raw power and athleticism are less important than skill and application, which is why you can keep playing into comparative old age. Real tennis has also managed to retain its sportsmanlike reputation. The age-old points of etiquette – owning up to a ball that's 'down', giving the player from the receiving side of the court right of way when changing ends, acknowledging a good shot from an opponent – are still observed.

Fancy a go? Most real tennis clubs (see www.irtpa.com for a list) around the UK offer trial sessions for beginners, and coaching is always available from the club pro. One satisfying swipe into the winning gallery, and you may well find yourself hooked.

## 220 Watch penguins on parade in Edinburgh

Edinburgh Zoo (Corstorphine Road, Edinburgh EH12 6TS, 0131 334 9171, www.edinburghzoo.org.uk) has one very special penguin: Nils Olav, mascot for the Norwegian army, with his own rank (currently Commander-in-Chief). Every few years, the zoo is treated to the spectacle of the visiting troops standing in line to be inspected by Nils. Not to be outdone, his companions have masterminded their own daily parade (2.15pm): an event begun when a keeper accidentally left the penguin enclosure open, and was followed around the zoo by a posse of curious escapees.

Best Industrial Museum in Europe 2007

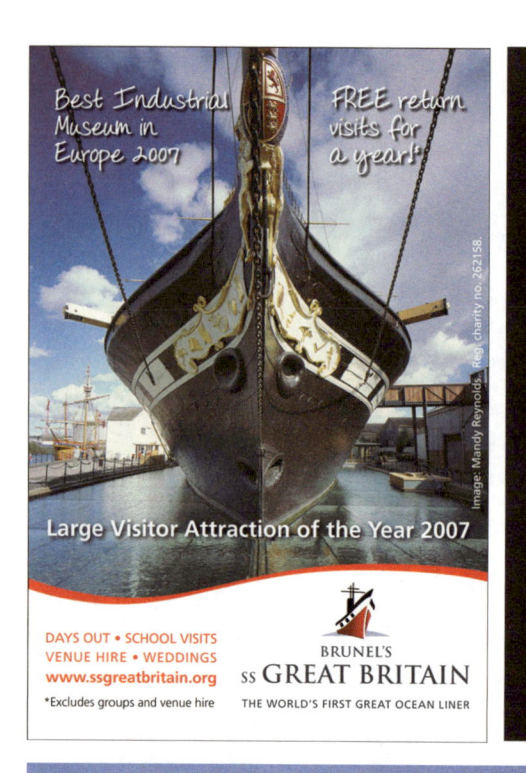

FREE return visits for a year!

Large Visitor Attraction of the Year 2007

DAYS OUT • SCHOOL VISITS
VENUE HIRE • WEDDINGS
www.ssgreatbritain.org
*Excludes groups and venue hire

BRUNEL'S
SS GREAT BRITAIN
THE WORLD'S FIRST GREAT OCEAN LINER

# timeout.com
The hippest online guide to over 50 of the world's greatest cities

Time Out Online

## Make it a day of discovery
Exhibitions and events at historic sites across Sussex all year

Exciting museums, historic houses, gardens and even a castle! Call for details or see our website: www.sussexpast.co.uk for special events, such as Roman Gladiators, Game & Country Fair, Celtic Festival, Medieval Fair and Tudor Day.

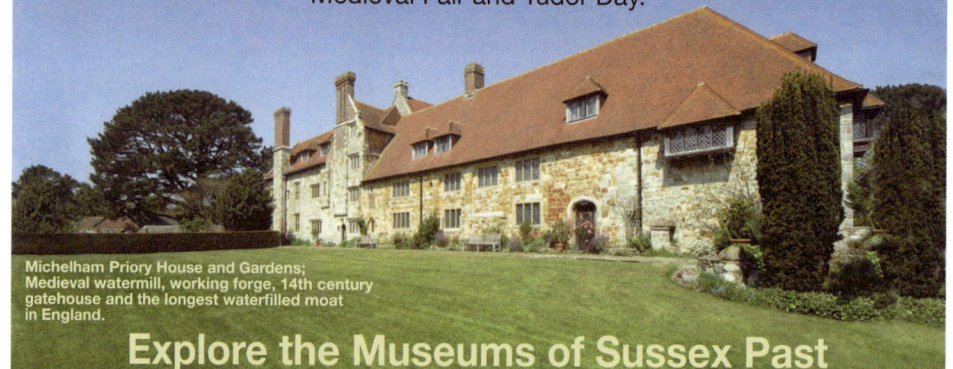

Michelham Priory House and Gardens; Medieval watermill, working forge, 14th century gatehouse and the longest waterfilled moat in England.

### Explore the Museums of Sussex Past

Anne of Cleves House, Lewes
01273 474610

Priest House, West Hoathly
01342 810479

Michelham Priory, Nr Hailsham
01323 844224

Fishbourne Roman Palace, Nr Chichester
01243 785859

Lewes Castle & Barbican House Museum
01272 486290

Marlipins Museum, Shoreham-by-Sea
01273 462994

SUSSEX PAST

## 221 Salute James Bond at Beaulieu

There are 250 record-breaking, gas-guzzling reasons to visit the National Motor Museum, but the collection of James Bond's original boy's toys is enough to convince most blokes to set the SatNav for the New Forest. Here are skidoos, serious motorcycles, missile-toting Jags and the world's first ever jet ski – straddled by Roger Moore in 1977's *The Spy Who Loved Me* – not to mention the periscope-topped Lotus Submarine car. All this and one of Jaws' huge shirts too.

**National Motor Museum** *Beaulieu, Brockenhurst, Hampshire SO42 7ZN (01590 612345/ www.beaulieu.co.uk).*

## 222 Come, see and conquer Fishbourne Roman Palace

Only unearthed in the 1960s, as workmen dug a new water main, Fishbourne was once home to an extravagant Roman palace. Last year saw the opening of a new £3.5 million building over the spectacular mosaic floors (you'll know the iconic image of Cupid riding a dolphin) – plus now there are 3D reconstructions, a formal garden to explore, and the chance to fumble priceless remains. Call for details of ceramics and mosaic-making workshops (adults only).

**Fishbourne Roman Palace** *Salthill Road, Fishbourne, Chichester, West Sussex PO19 3QR (01243 785859/www.sussexpast.co.uk).*

## 223 Marvel at Orkney's Italian Chapel

On one of Orkney's smaller islands, Lamb Holm, stands an exquisite chapel of 1940s vintage, constructed from two wartime Nissen huts and any odds and ends that its makers could lay their hands on (01856 872856, www.visitorkney.com). This was no mean feat, since the builders were Italian prisoners of war, captured in North Africa and interned on Orkney to construct a series of causeways down the south-east side of the island group. Beyond the simple façade lies an astonishingly detailed interior and magnificent altarpiece – largely the work of one prisoner, Domenico Chiocchetti, who returned to the island in the 1960s as the guest of honour at a special service in the chapel. Entirely anomalous in the low, windswept landscape, the Italian Chapel remains a profoundly beautiful oddity.

**Time Out** 1000 Things to do in Britain **79**

## 224 *Run away to join the circus*

# Spin city

*A nervous* **Kate Mossman** *takes to the flying trapeze.*

Early morning in London's Circus Space, and I'm already feeling waves of apprehension. Buoyant instructors lead a gentle warm-up, but I can't take my eyes off the hoops, girders, nooses and bouncy things hung around the converted Hoxton warehouse – the dreadful paraphernalia of organised fun. By the end of the day, after six hours of rotational workshops in everything from juggling to flying trapeze, I'll have had my hands on all of it.

My fellow participants are a mixed bag of couples, have-a-go students and competitive dads. Some have dabbled in gymnastics in the past and fancy taking it to the next level; others were given circus vouchers as comedy birthday presents, and have only just worked up the guts to use them. The latter look pale – glancing at one another over star-jumps and shoulder rolls – and I register their fear with a degree of relief.

If one thing's going to break the ice, it's a couple of loose cannons. And here they are – two boys, wild and fearless, throwing themselves at the equipment before the first class has begun. We are warned that the tame-looking wire trapeze (just two feet off the ground) can act as a 'cheese grater' if treated roughly – so you need to keep your head straight, and step off calmly if you start to fall. In boy-language, this means show the damn wire who's boss: 'Hey – quick – let's do it now when she's not looking'; shoes off, skidding across the serrated metal, they lurch to the other side before they've had the chance to give in to gravity's pull.

The rest of us obediently begin with the acrobatics class, staring at the sprung floor and trying in vain to remember the moves that once wowed the playground. Which hand do you put down first for a cartwheel? (You lead with your weaker arm, and come down on the stronger.) The biggest shock for me is the amount of muscle-wastage I've generated by doing nothing with my arms for ten years, other than working a computer and lifting a cup to my lips. My cartwheels are strangely reminiscent of those sticky rubber frogs that kids throw against windows – peeling off tentatively, legs over head in a drooping semi-arc, again and again in limp determination till gravity leaves me belly-up on the floor.

The group relationship is surprisingly supportive. Those who came out of the womb as natural gymnasts effortlessly cartwheel across the room, but pause to cheer on the loose shapes I'm throwing. Dignity has no place here: I was four feet tall the last time I attempted a backwards roll, and now I am trapped upside down *in medias res*, knees over head, neck cricked and knickers exposed.

One day at the circus, and my whole concept of 'A Challenge' is realigned. It's no longer an unwieldy abstract (a job, a relationship); it's keeping a coloured plastic top in the air long enough to toss it skyward. The silence is pin-drop during the spinning workshop – and woe betide anyone who dares to call the diabolo a 'giant yo-yo' by the end of the session.

> '**I am Ariel in The Tempest, descending with a nymph on either side. I've achieved something I gave up striving for at the age of 13 – a state of grace.**'

Next comes a lesson in stilt-walking, explained by the trainers with forensic detail. We must think of the 20-inch metal splints velcroed to our legs as 'an exoskeleton', and train our 'muscle memory' to support this new ankle-to-calf relationship.

Sadly, my muscle memory seems forgetful. I just can't master stilts – even with the help of Andy. Just 17 years old and a first-time circus genius, with black eyes flashing and the veins in his forearms standing out like electricity cables, he leads me teetering onwards with gentle encouragement: 'head up – focus on the far wall'. But I'm already staring at my wobbling peg legs in horror, and teeter ten feet to the crash-mat and collapse.

From there, I survey the scene. Teachers and project managers are stuck on the ground like slippery newborn foals. Watching them rising to their modest new height with faces beaming, the whole thing becomes a moving celebration of the smallest of human endeavours.

The wire trapeze, just 15 feet long and raised two feet off the ground, is another wonderfully pointless exercise. The rules of balance are by now familiar: flatten your diaphragm (starting to ache) as you tiptoe forward, and don't look down. Seconds later, I'm unexpectedly at the other side. And suddenly it doesn't matter that outside in London the traffic rages, and the air is wet and greasy, because at this moment – delicately placing one ballet pump in front of the other, with two cohorts taking my finger tips – I am Ariel in *The Tempest*, descending with a nymph on either side. I've achieved something I gave up striving for when I hit 13 – a state of grace.

But grace is fleeting and the flying trapeze awaits, saved for the end of the day (by which time we're told, somewhat ominously, our wrists will be 'strong enough to take on the challenge'. My eye makes a rapid risk assessment. Hooks in the ceiling – a tangle of wires – red crash-mat 20 feet below. But the trapeze men are reassuringly familiar, like caricatures from the Moulin Rouge days – a vision of fin-de-siècle macho splendour, bear-like and boisterous with rock-hard thighs packed into stripy leggings. Taking pity on me, they explain how to crouch down to lower the take-off as they hook my harness up.

I've never felt such raw, physically arresting fear before. My feet lock themselves to the platform and the smallest move – namely, placing my second hand on the bar, the sign that I'm ready to jump – is momentarily impossible. I am very scared. If I'm scared, it's possible that I will faint. If I faint, I will let go of the trapeze and fall – and die.

I can hear my mother's voice imploring in my ear. The onlookers below wear the haunted faces of my nearest and dearest, attending a certain sad ceremony. But I find myself feeding from the fright – and suddenly I'm off, marking my first exhilarating arc with a long, drawn-out expletive.

I'm shaking – not with fear but with the purest of adrenalin rushes. With ropes to keep you aloft should your withered arms somehow let you down, the trapeze is a powerful but perfect transgression of the boundary between Safe and Stupid – and all without the need for major insurance policies.

We scatter at 5.30pm, heading off for fish and chips and three days of wholesome muscular agony in unforeseen nether regions, stomachs and palms. In retrospect, the whole circus experience works rather like that turn on the flying trapeze. It's a controlled climax of sensory impressions – terror, elation, brief invincibility – then a drop-kick sending you back where you came from, spluttering with pride and mild hysteria.

**Circus Space** *Coronet Street, London N1 6HD (020 7613 4141/www.thecircusspace.co.uk). Circus Skills courses £55-£99 per person.*

# 225-231
## Run a marathon

The annual 26.2-miler through London (www.london-marathon.co.uk) may grab all the publicity, but there are plenty of lower-key events if going the distance is more important to you than the experience of running across Tower Bridge – and they all have their own appeal. March's Steyning Stinger Marathon in West Sussex (www.steyningac.co.uk) offers fantastic views over the South Downs – when you're not too busy tramping through mud and climbing gates. If you need the thought of sustenance to keep you going, Redruth's Duchy Marathon (www.duchymarathon.org.uk), also in March, hands out a Cornish pasty as well as the usual medal to every finisher, while haggis is a pre-race alternative to pasta at Edinburgh's Marathon (www.edinburgh-marathon.com) in May. If hungry hordes leave you cold, consider the Tresco Marathon (www.tresco.co.uk) in April; with a limit of 125 runners, it's one of the smallest in the world, and you have to run laps, Tresco being just two miles across. Back on the mainland, you can take in ancient ruins at May's Neolithic Marathon (www.wiltshirewildlife.org) – it starts off at Avebury and finishes at Stonehenge. For masochists, the Great Langdale Marathon (www.greatlangdaleraces.org.uk) in September is reckoned to be the toughest going – the magnificent Lake District scenery is the only (partial) compensation. For further inspiration, the *Runner's World* site (www.runnersworld.co.uk) lists more than 40 UK marathons.

# 232 Go zorbing in Dorset

Basically, this involves being strapped inside a ten-foot inflatable sphere-within-a-sphere, then launched some 650 feet down a Dorset hill. The latest twist is 'hydro-zorbing', where a couple of buckets of water are chucked into the sphere with you – good for a hangover, or so the organisers say.
**Zorb South UK** *Pine Lodge Farm, Bockhampton, Dorset DT2 8QL (01929 426595/www.zorbsouth.co.uk).*

# 233 Buy a bloom at Mottisfont Abbey

The old-fashioned roses collection at Mottisfont is a glorious sight from late May to June, as the lush blooms entwine pergolas, cling to walls and archways and line the pathways. Take advantage of June's extended opening hours and visit at dusk, when the worst of the crowds have gone home: as the heady scent of roses drifts across the walled garden, you'd be hard-pressed to find a more romantic spot. The gardeners hold rose sales from Easter to June, with some 150 varieties on offer – including the pink-and-white striped Rosa Mundi, and wonderfully fragrant Constance Spry.
**Mottisfont Abbey Garden, House & Estate**
*Mottisfont, near Romsey, Hampshire SO51 0LP (01794 340757/www.nationaltrust.org.uk).*

# 234 Sample the deep south in Glasgow

The Grand Ole Opry is an institution for Glasgow's legions of country music fans, who gather in the tacky hall, decorated with Confederate memorabilia, there to imbibe cheap liquor, line dance, witness the fake shoot-out and – yee haw – play bingo. It's like nowhere else in Britain, and all the better for it.
**Grand Ole Opry** *2-4 Govan Road, Kenning Park, Glasgow G51 1HS (0141 429 5396).*

# 235 Eat 'sparrer grass' in the Vale of Evesham

To taste the first of the asparagus crop fresh from the farm gate, head for Worcestershire in early summer. There are countless country pubs serving up perfect aromatic tips with bread and butter and a pint in these parts, such as the Round of Gras (Bretforton Road, Badsey, Evesham, Worcestershire WR11 7XQ, 01386 830206, www.roundofgras.co.uk). The annual Asparagus Festival (www.british-asparagus.co.uk), held in Bretforton in late May, marks the rush to get asparagus into the shops – but aficionados reckon the fast-growing crop only hits perfection once the warmer weather arrives.

## A few of my favourite things

# 236-241
## Stella Vine, artist

Thomas Hardy's Cottage in Dorset (Higher Bockhampton, near Dorchester, Dorset DT2 8QJ, 01297 561900, www.nationaltrust.org.uk) is a joy to visit. The atmosphere is really inspiring; Hardy wrote *Far from the Madding Crowd* there. It's tricky to find, but once you have, park the car and walk up through the woods, then full circle back past the miniature ponies.

**The Georgian Theatre Royal (Victoria Road, Richmond, North Yorkshire DL10 4DW, 01748 825252, www.georgiantheatreroyal.co.uk) is the tiniest, cutest theatre I've ever seen. It was built in 1788 and the furthest seat is only 35 feet from the stage. I once played Little Nell in *The Old Curiosity Shop* there, but it's just as nice to sit in as it is to perform in.**

One of the best walks in England is from the Rumbling Kern at Howick to Dunstanburgh Castle (Craster, Alnwick, Northumberland NE66 3TT, 01665 576231, www.nationaltrust.org.uk). For a long walk, follow the coast from Alnmouth, passing Seaton Point, Boulmer, the Rumbling Kern and Craster before the stunning walk up to the castle. Or park at Howick to explore the great rock formations of the Kern, and walk from there. If you want a much shorter, simpler walk, start from Craster – my granny, who's in her nineties, recently managed it. Stay at the White Swan in Alnwick (Bondgate Within, Alnwick, Northumberland NE66 1TD, 01665 602109, www.classiclodges.co.uk).

**Wells-Next-the-Sea (www.wells-guide.co.uk) on the north Norfolk coast is famous and deserves to be; park at Holkham beach and walk the coast to Wells, passing the higgledy-piggledy beach huts on the way.** *Shakespeare in Love* was filmed here, on the windswept coastline. Buy some fish and chips and watch the fishing boats, then head back through the fairytale pine woods.

Possibly my favourite place in Britain is the Uffington White Horse, an elegant chalk horse carved into the Berkshire Downs. The best way to experience it is to walk up to the site of Uffington Castle, now an atmospheric circular ridge, and walk down to the horse. From there it's a sweep down further to Dragon Hill and the bottom of the Manger, a strange valley, then a steep walk back up to the car park. It's a wonderful trip with friends or alone, and is blissful on a rainy or windy day. It's fairly well signposted from the village of Uffington, a mile and a half away, and there's a nice campsite nearby too.

**In London, one of my favourite ways to spend a Wednesday or Sunday night is to watch the Comedy Store Players (www.comedystoreplayers.com), a hearty gang of improvisers that includes Paul Merton and Josie Lawrence, though all the players are brilliant. Get there really early to get good seats and munch on the bar snacks, which are pretty good value.**

# 242 *Escape modern life with monks*

If you're serious about wanting peace and quiet on your holidays, then get thee to a monastery. Mount Saint Bernard Abbey in Charnwood Forest, Leicestershire, is home to the brothers of the Cistercian Order, founded in 1098 by French monks intent on following the sixth-century creed of solitude and silence laid down by St Benedict. Luckily for you, the saint's 53rd rule states that guests should never be lacking in a monastery. The monks are already kept pretty busy running a 200-acre dairy farm, shop, orchard and beehive, but their guesthouse will accommodate you for up to five nights and won't charge a penny (although offerings towards the upkeep of the house might be a nice gesture).
**Mount Saint Bernard Abbey** *Coalville, Leicester LE67 5UL (01530 839162/www.mountsaintbernard.org).*

# 243 Conquer at conkers

The annual World Conker Championships, held in the village of Ashton in Northamptonshire (www.worldconkerchampionships.com), is no laughing matter to the conker nuts that take part. Competitors play atop podiums on the village green; a loss is recorded once a conker has been reduced to tatters (for, as the rules clearly state, 'a small piece of nut or skin remaining shall be judged out; it must be enough to mount an attack'). Launched in 1965, the event attracts more and more people each year, some attending from increasingly diverse locations (who'll forget the year the grand prize was won by a visiting Mexican?), and there are now separate men's, women's and junior competitions. Places in the October event are limited and fill up quickly, but spectators can attend the nut-bashing for an entrance fee of £2.

# 244 Let romance blossom in Oxford's Botanic Garden

When Tolkien worked at Merton College, he used to come to these gardens for a spot of quiet contemplation; the giant 200-year-old black pine he sat beneath (now known as Tolkien's Tree) could well have inspired *The Lord of the Rings'* Treebeard. Another favourite spot for literary types is the simple wooden bench in the Lower Garden – found under a witch-hazel tree, across the bridge over the water garden. This was the setting for Will and Lyra's parting in Philip Pullman's *Amber Spyglass*, and the gardeners often find messages and love tokens left here.

Bookish connections aside, these are Britain's oldest botanic gardens. Look for the garden's oldest tree (an English yew planted in 1645); visit the verdant glasshouses, where cacti, water lilies and exotic fruit trees flourish; and check out the rock, water and bog gardens and the 1648 Collection – plants grown when the venerable garden was first founded.

**University of Oxford Botanic Garden**
*Rose Lane, Oxford OX1 4AZ (01865 286690/ www.botanic-garden.ox.ac.uk).*

# 245-250 Go back to university (for a public lecture)

It's not just the bearded student contingent who can reap the benefits of the world's finest minds – most universities put on talks, lectures and discussions that anyone can attend.

## Cardiff University
It isn't just literary giant Ian Rankin who's wowed audiences at Cardiff (029 2087 6935, http://events.cardiff.ac.uk): poet Paul Muldoon, consumer champion Marin Lewis and cabinet secretary Hilary Benn have all expounded in this Welsh academy's lecture halls. One of Cardiff's most notable ventures is the PUSH (Public Understanding of Science and Health) series, featuring leading minds from the world of test tubes.

## Gifford Lectures
Don't let the rather exclusive-sounding subject matter – 'natural theology' – put you off: the Gifford Lectures (www.giffordlectures.org) invite hugely distinguished thinkers to blend history, literature, science, philosophy and religion in wild and wonderful ways. Noam Chomsky, Simon Blackburn, Mary Midgley and Iris Murdoch have all taken part in the past. Lectures are delivered at St Andrews, Glasgow, Edinburgh and Aberdeen universities.

## London School of Economics and Political Science (LSE)
As you might expect from the country's foremost school of political and economic thought (020 7955 6043, www.lse.ac.uk/events), speakers here tend to be big names from the world of politics, business and social sciences – Bill Clinton, Kofi Annan, virtually every UK cabinet minister and numerous Nobel Prize winners have held forth here. Almost all lectures are free, and are also published as podcasts.

## Oxford University
The highlights of Oxford University's public lecture offerings are usually the Oxonia Distinguished Speaker Events (01865 270000, www.oxonia.org). But, as you'd expect, the calendar (be it Michaelmas, Trinity or Hilary term) is full of top-notch highbrow musings in gorgeous collegiate surroundings. Visiting and internal lecturers have included the critic Christopher Ricks, comedian Armando Iannucci, LSE chief Sir Howard Davies and Tony Blair.

## University of Cambridge
Cambridge (01223 332300, www.talks.cam.ac.uk) is said to be the top university in the country for public lectures, attracting big names like Sebastian Faulks and Jack Straw on a regular basis. The university's rightly lauded Darwin lectures can attract up to 700 people, eager to listen to Professor Lord Robert Winston, Kate Adie or Cherie Booth. The university union also plays host to impressive speakers, though some are for students only.

## University College London (UCL)
Why did Marcel Proust use the phrase 'le cup of tea'? What happens when husband and wife scientist teams collaborate? And just what is the mathematical problem known as 'the Monster'? Find out in less than an hour at this ongoing lecture series given by academics from University College London (020 7679 2000, www.ucl.ac.uk/lhl), in the Darwin Lecture Theatre on Gower Street. It all makes for a much more stimulating backdrop to your sandwich than the tills at Pret, that's for sure.

# 251-253
## Celebrate Chinese New Year

The biggest event in the Chinese calendar, the New Year or Spring Festival takes place in either late January or early February, depending on when the new moon falls. Central to the celebrations are the traditional lion and dragon dances, which parade through the streets bringing good luck to homes and businesses, and noisily warding off evil with drums and cymbals. In the capital, festivities are organised by the London Chinatown Chinese Association (www.chinatownchinese.co.uk) and begin with the lighting of Chinese lanterns in Oxford Street. They continue with a parade through the Strand to Rupert Street, with further performances, stalls, food and fireworks in and around Trafalgar Square. In Liverpool (www.visitliverpool.com), which has one of the oldest Chinese communities in Europe, the New Year is welcomed in at the Chinese Arch on Nelson Street with firecracker performances and t'ai chi demonstrations. And in Manchester (www.visitmanchester.com), celebrations include an impressive Golden Dragon Parade from Albert Square to Faulkner Street.

# 254
## See an orchestra on the beach

The Aldeburgh Festival centres around a series of concerts at Snape Maltings Concert Hall, a converted 19th-century malthouse that stands among the rivers and marshes of rural Suffolk. For two weeks in June, music fans flock to this rural retreat to take in some world-class chamber music in idyllic surrounds. If you can't decide between going to a concert and catching some rays on the region's splendid beaches, there's even a series of free events held on the sands. Performances include opera from members of Aldeburgh's Jerwood Opera Writing Programme and concerts from the Britten-Pears Orchestra, the festival's training orchestra for talented young musicians.
**Aldeburgh Festival** *Snape Maltings Concert Hall, Snape, Suffolk IP17 1SP (01728 687110/ www.aldeburgh.co.uk).*

# 255
## Cross the Highlands in luxury

Ah, the romance of a scenic train journey. But who needs the Orient Express when you've got Scotland? The luxury Royal Scotsman's route across the Highlands (0845 077 2222, www.royalscotsman.com) is staggeringly gorgeous, whooshing past fathoms-deep lochs, bruised-looking crags and remote glens. The Edwardian Observation Car, with its armchairs and open-air veranda, is the last word in old-fashioned gentility. A tumbler of Scotch is all you need to complete the picture.

# 256

### Let the kids run riot at Bewilderwood

Set in 50 acres of unspoilt woodland near the Norfolk Broads and built from sustainably sourced wood, this adventure park is a paradise for kids – with no plastic tat, flashing lights or headache-inducing computer wizardry in sight (01603 783900, www.bewilderwood.co.uk). Instead, children can shoot down zip wires, explore the treetop village, build dens and launch themselves down the vertiginously steep Slippery Slope slide. Once the small fry have scrambled and slid to their hearts' content, hitch a ride back into the real world in the BewilderBoat – a reclaimed lifeboat, converted to run on electricity.

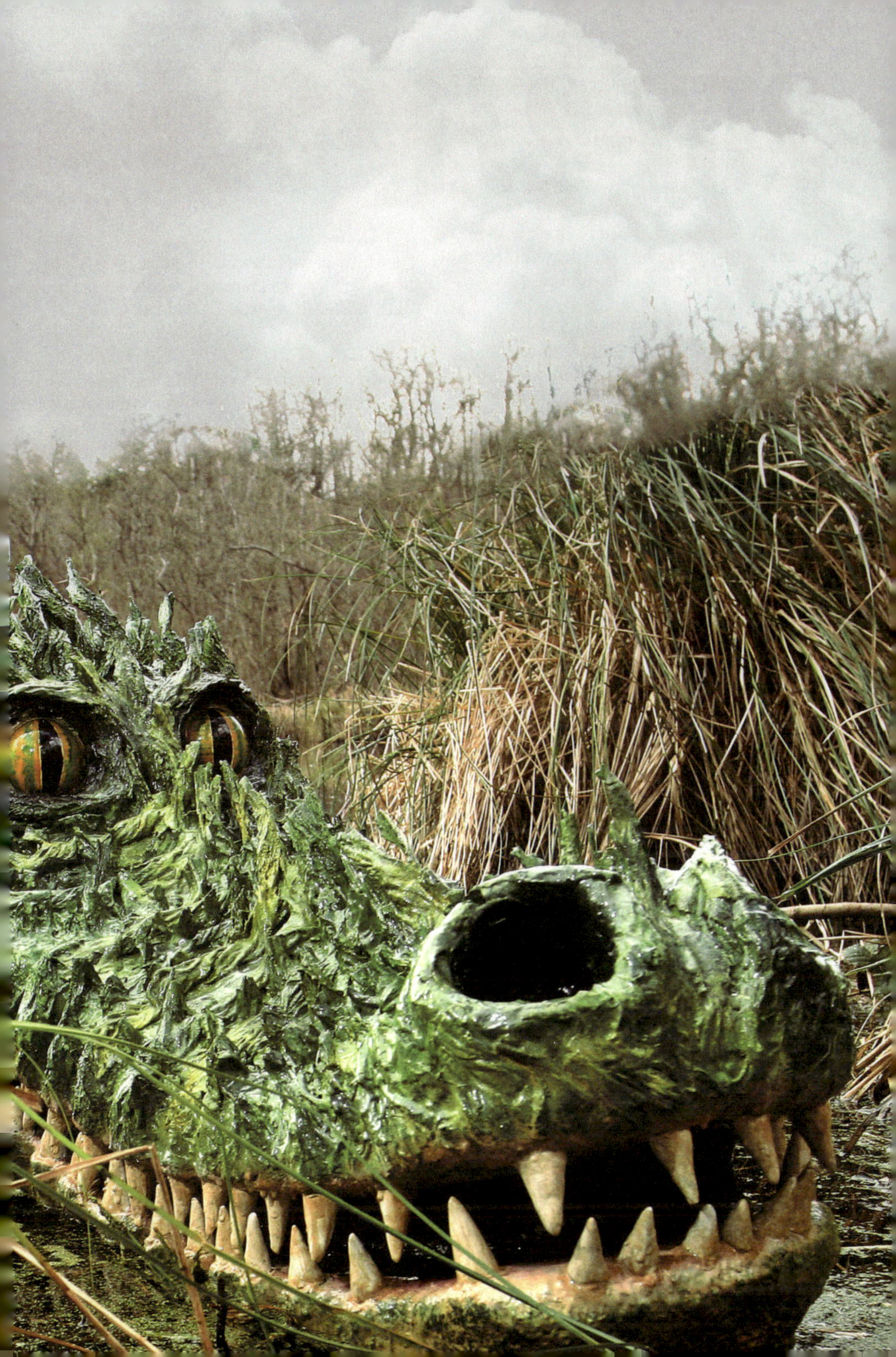

# 257-271 Take to the ice outdoors

Most outdoor rinks are open from early to mid November to mid January, until around 10pm – but call ahead to check dates and times.

## Bristol Zoo Gardens
Skate amid gorillas, penguins, seals and 400 other exotic species at Bristol's outdoor rink (0117 974 7399, www.bristolzoo.org.uk).

## Cardiff Winter Wonderland
As well as an rink, Cardiff's ice-fest (029 2023 0130, www.cardiffswinterwonderland.com) includes Christmas shows at the New Theatre, a Santa's Grotto and a rollicking New Year's party.

## Chester Zoo Frost Fair
Glide around Chester's frost fair (01244 650240, www.chesterzoo.org/frostfair) before taking a 'visit to Lapland' (a Santa's Grotto) and meeting some Indian elephants.

## Eden Project, St Austell
In a surreal twist, the world's largest greenhouse becomes a skating arena, complete with lantern processions, Cornish choirs and mulled wine (01726 811911, www.edenproject.com).

## Edinburgh Winter Wonderland
Below the looming Edinburgh Castle, Princes Street is lit up on midwinter evenings with a couple of ice rinks (one exclusively for kids) and a Christmas market (0131 622 6555, www.gildedballoon.co.uk).

## Exeter Castle
The 18th-century courtyard of Exeter Castle (01392 665082, www.exeter.gov.uk) is turned into a giant ice rink, with a 50-foot Christmas tree and lights.

## Forum, Norwich
The Forum (01603 727950, www.theforum norwich.co.uk) offers outdoor skating for eight weeks: there's also a week-long Christmas fair, with 80 stalls selling festive foods and crafts.

## Ice Cube, Leeds
The shiny new Millennium Square is the setting for Britain's largest temporary outdoor ice rink (0113 395 0891, www.leeds.gov.uk).

## Ice Factor, York
In the shadow of medieval Clifford's Tower, the Ice Factor (01653 619169, www.theicefactor.co.uk) is one of the cosiest outdoor skating experiences, with its rink surrounding an illuminated oak tree.

## Natural History Museum, London
Museum-goers can cool down at the 1,000-square-metre ice rink in the gardens (020 7942 5000, www.nhm.ac.uk), then warm up again at the Christmas fair.

## On Ice at Piccadilly, Manchester
Manchester's rejuvenated Piccadilly Gardens undergo another (temporary) overhaul each winter, providing a rink in the heart of the city (0870 066 6845, www.onicepiccadilly.com).

## Somerset House, London
London's original outdoor skating venue, Somerset House (020 7845 4600, www.somerset houseicerink.org.uk) is still one of the best, thanks to its magnificent 18th-century environs.

## Times Square, Newcastle
Times Square becomes a 4,800-square-metre skating rink (0191 243 8210, www.life.org.uk), and is open until late February.

## Tower of London
Ironically, one of the Tower's warmest-ever welcomes is its frozen moat ice rink (0870 602 1100, www.toweroflondonicerink.com).

## Warwick Castle
The skate trail (0870 442 2372, www.eventsat thecastle.co.uk) allows you to whizz round the castle's Peacock Gardens and forms part of a Victorian Christmas package, with a music hall, a steam fair and Ebenezer's Haunted House.

Somerset House

# THE SHORTLIST

## WHAT'S NEW | WHAT'S ON | WHAT'S BEST

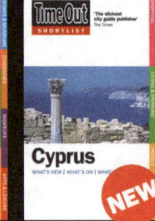

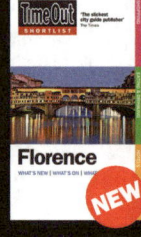

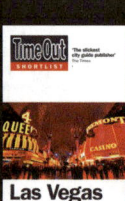

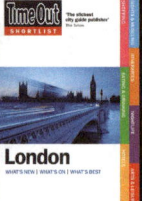

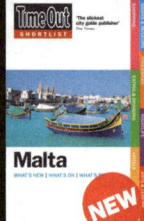

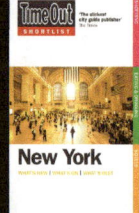

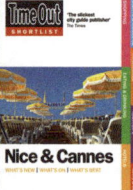

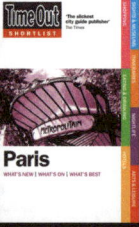

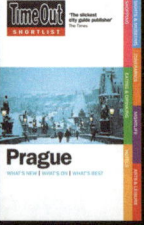

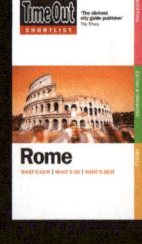

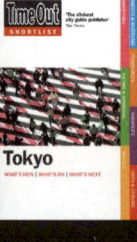

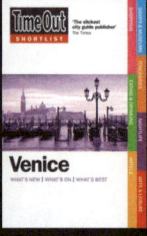

- POCKET-SIZE GUIDES
- WRITTEN BY LOCAL EXPERTS
- KEY VENUES PINPOINTED ON MAPS

Available at all major bookshops from only £6.99/$11.95 and from timeout.com/shop

**Time Out SHORTLIST**

## 272 Race round Manchester Velodrome

The steeply banked velodrome track looks like a daunting prospect on your first encounter – and the news that track bikes have neither gears nor brakes provides little consolation. But once you start pedalling, the buzz is addictive. The Olympic team is based at Manchester, but you don't have to be a pro to take to the track: there are taster sessions for novices of all ages, with bike and helmet hire included.
**National Cycling Centre** *Stuart Street, Manchester M11 4DQ (0161 223 2244/www.manchester velodrome.com).*

## 273 Explore Kew Gardens by night

If you don't have kids, you'll want to borrow someone else's for this: if you can gather a group of four or five, Kew Gardens is yours to explore in the dead of night. Aimed at eight- to 11-year-olds, the Midnight Ramble usually involves an exploration of the tropical houses and a search for nocturnal creatures like owls, bats and badgers, before retiring to the campfire for stories and a sleepover. Tickets cost £40 for adults and kids: book well ahead.
**Royal Botanic Gardens** *Kew, Richmond, Surrey TW9 3AB (020 8332 5655/www.kew.org).*

## 274 Meet Alfred the gorilla at Bristol's City Museum

Bought by Bristol Zoo in the 1930s, Alfred was one of the first gorillas to be successfully kept in captivity. He was an instant hit, throwing snowballs at visiting Bristolians, who took him to their hearts (and, poor thing, on walks around the zoo on a lead, dressed in woolly jumpers). He became an icon for Bristol and something of a star; visiting GIs sent home postcards of Alfred, and his presence grew stateside. Sadly, his health deteriorated after World War II. In 1948, reported the *Daily Mail*, he fled into his cage and collapsed as a plane flew overhead (planes were one of his pet hates, along with bearded men and double-decker buses). But his memory lives on; those who saw Alfred at the zoo visit him again with grandchildren – now as a stuffed exhibit in the City Museum.
**Bristol's City Museum & Art Gallery** *Queen's Road, Bristol BS8 1RL (0117 922 3571/ www.bristol.gov.uk/museums)*

# 275-282 *Make a gastronomic pilgrimage*

**Caroline Stacey** *kneels before some Epicurean altars.*

A meal at the crucible of contemporary gastronomy, the Fat Duck (High Street, Bray, Berkshire SL6 2AQ, 01628 580333, www.thefatduck.co.uk), guarantees an informed opinion about how fabulous taste combinations like caviar and white chocolate really can be. Heston Blumenthal famously applies science to trigger surprise and pleasure in all the senses, and the experience of feeling green tea and lime mousse chilled by liquid nitrogen vanish on the tongue in a puff of steam is like nothing else. Though dishes can be challenging – snail porridge with Joselito ham and shaved fennel – classics such as sole veronique with pont neuf potatoes are there for the cautious. Book well ahead if you wish to surrender yourself to Blumenthal's genius.

Everyone's heard of Raymond Blanc, chef de cuisine from central casting, and a meal at his exquisitely manicured Manoir aux Quat' Saisons (Church Road, Great Milton, Oxfordshire OX44 7PD, 01844 278881, www.manoir.com), is de rigueur as a reminder of why French food should be revered. Book at least three months ahead for Saturday night.

While David Everitt-Matthias may be unknown to TV viewers, Le Champignon Sauvage (24-28 Suffolk Road, Cheltenham, Gloucestershire GL50 2AQ, 01242 573449, www.lechampignonsauvage.co.uk) is adored by seasoned critics. His French cooking is notable for the meticulous craftsmanship evident in dishes like seared scallops with cauliflower purée, cumin velouté and a caramel flavoured with *ras el hanout*.

The Walnut Tree Inn (Llanddewi Skirrid, Abergavenny, Monmouthshire NP7 8AW, 01873 852797, www.thewalnuttreeinn.com) was legendary for 30-odd years, even before Shaun Hill, a quiet colossus among chefs, took over. Go for dishes like smoked haddock boudin with shrimps and dill, wild duck with morel mushrooms and game gravy, and buttermilk pudding with rhubarb and cardamom. Only half the tables are bookable in advance.

Rick Stein's Seafood Restaurant (Riverside, Padstow, Cornwall PL28 8BY, 01841 532700, www.rickstein.com) is responsible for a brand empire and a sea change in the local Padstow economy. Although Stein's no longer based there, the fishy cooking has his dabs all over it. Cornwall's newer kid on the block is the prodigiously talented Nathan Outlaw. He doesn't do frills, fancy menu descriptions or tablecloths – he just dazzles with the balance and refinement of his cooking. Catch his celebrated lobster risotto, brill with leeks, mustard and brown shrimps, and quince tart with stem ginger ice-cream at the unfussily soigné Restaurant Nathan Outlaw in the Marina Villa Hotel (Esplanade, Fowey, Cornwall PL23 1HY, 01726 833315, www.themarinahotel.co.uk).

Anthony Flinn, another precocious chef with an eponymous restaurant, successfully brings the avant-garde approach to Britain. Unlike his mentor Ferran Adrià's El Bulli, you don't need to book a year ahead at Anthony's (9 Boar Lane, Leeds LS1 6EA, 0113 245 5922, www.anthonysrestaurant.co.uk); two weeks' notice should secure a weekend table. The setting is minimalist but there's maximum skill and imagination at work in a kitchen that pulls together dishes like sous vide (slow vacuum-cooked) veal with Earl Grey mousse and pear purée, followed by a pudding of coconut timbal with black sesame seed and carrot foam.

The seafood in the north-west of Scotland is exceptional, and nowhere more so than at the Summer Isles Hotel (Achiltibuie, Ross-shire IV26 2YG, 01854 622282, www.summerisleshotel.co.uk). There are amazingly fresh ingredients on the doorstep and the flavours are as stunning and bright as the long summer evenings (though you'll have to book months ahead). Lunch or oysters in the bar are consolation if the hotel is booked up. Summer Isles may be far flung, but planning and going out of your way will always pay off if you're making a gastronomic pilgrimage.

# 283 Visit Appleby Horse Fair

Established in 1685, Appleby's horse fair is one of Europe's largest, with up to 900 traveller vehicles and colourful, horse-drawn caravans heading to the site each June. Although it's a riotous get-together, the fair's main purpose is horse-trading, with hundreds of steeds changing hands each day (and sometimes several times over the course of the week). Watch the animals being washed and groomed in the River Eden, before potential buyers check them out on the closed road between Appleby and Brampton. Harness racing takes place at Holme Farm Field, and there are plenty of stalls selling food and drink, crafts and equine equipment – not to mention fortune tellers – if you fancy a break from all the horseflesh. Wellies are a must.

**Appleby Tourist Information Centre** *Moot Hall, Boroughgate, Appleby-in-Westmorland, Cumbria CA16 6XE (01768 351177/www.applebytown.org.uk).*

# 284 Rent an Airstream

A bottle of cold beer, the opening harmonies of 'Good Vibrations' wafting through the air, the sunlight glinting off the chrome curves of an Airstream caravan; this is about as close as you can get to starring in your own American road movie. OK, so you're stationary in the middle of a working dairy farm in a field on the Isle of Wight, with a bank of cloud scudding across the sky, but the same spirit of freedom is most certainly present. Vintage Vacations (07802 758113, www.vintagevacations.co.uk) owns ten beautifully restored old caravans, most of them classic Airstreams from the 1950s and '60s, and they're available to hire for short breaks of up to a week (from £145 for a midweek two-night stay). All amenities are included in the reasonable tariff, and the caravans boast shower facilities (though you are asked to use the farm's loo block; vintage caravan loos are a step too retro).

# 285 Feel like a giant at Bekonscot

# It's a small world

*On the surface, life in Bekonscot Model Village looks idyllic – but is all as it seems?* **Elizabeth Winding** *investigates.*

Almost every day for a year, photographer Liam Bailey would take the train up to Beaconsfield from London, toting his camera and tripod, and step into a different universe. Towering over Bekonscot's well-ordered streets and houses, its 1930s aerodrome and neatly trimmed golf course, he'd carefully arrange the reflectors and remote flash, illuminating the village's inhabitants in their bright, hard glare, then begin shooting. As the project went on, he became more and more fascinated by the tiny figures whose frozen, static lives he was documenting; the ambiguities in their faces and actions, and the untold stories he imagined lay behind them.

Built in the 1930s by wealthy accountant Roland Callingham, Bekonscot model village is, by anyone's standards, a very peculiar place. Originally constructed to keep Callingham's dinner guests amused, it gradually grew and grew. Its realms encompass everything from a country club to rows of tiny shops (Dan D Lyon the florist; Chris P Lettis the greengrocer), and even a tiny beach, where model donkeys trudge along the sand. According to the official line, it's 'stuck firmly in an idyllic 1930s timewarp'; a miniaturised utopia where cricketers gather on the village green, the vicar greets the faithful at the church porch, and housewives dutifully hurry to the butcher's for a nice leg of lamb (no supermarkets here). Order prevails: one of the thatched cottages may be ablaze, but a diminutive fireman is at hand to put it out, while six old-fashioned coppers see that law and order is maintained.

But as Bailey came to realise, all may not be quite as it seems. 'When I got up close, I realised that the benevolence everyone associates with the village isn't necessarily reflected in the characters,' he says. Looking at his photos, the models' painted faces often have an unexpectedly unnerving quality: the father of the bride, for instance, with his gimlet blue eyes and twisted mouth, or the lolling, sinister figure on the top deck of a bus, coldly surveying the other passengers. 'Even though they're

**Time Out** 1000 Things to do in Britain 97

just painted models, the human brain's need to understand the relationships between the characters takes over,' says Bailey. 'It's all about what you read into their faces.'

As he photographed the village, Bailey became absorbed by the figures he encountered, and what he began to think of as their stories. 'My heart would start racing; the feeling of what was going on was so passionate. What's on that old woman's mind as she leaves the market square with her bag of shopping? Who's the man turning a corner sneaking after?' He also found that shooting a tableau from a slightly different angle could superimpose new – sometimes unsettling – levels of meaning. One particularly emotive shot, he says, was a close-up of a smartly dressed woman's back, one hand raised to knock on a door. 'A couple of women were visibly upset by it, and told me, "When I saw that, it sent a shudder down my spine. That's the thing my mum told me happened to her when she was 18, and had to have an abortion – a woman came knocking." It's the colours, and the bag in her right hand, just out of the frame; there's a real presence about her in that shot.'

An image of a man in a hat reaching out towards a little boy also invites alternative explanations. 'From the way it's photographed, the insinuation is that it's a pick-up. One of the guys in the studio is gay, and he said, "Oh god! That's how I started! Down at the fairground, a bloke in a hat… It was just like that for me."' If there are darker undercurrents to the sunny world of Bekonscot, it's not a line its current owners seem keen to pursue (the village has been run by the Church Army since 1978), and it's left to sharp-eyed visitors to make what they will of ambiguous figures like the three lithe sun-worshippers sprawling by the pool, sporting eye-wateringly tight trunks.

For a while, the village moved with the times, and as the century moved on it slowly acquired the trappings of modern-day Britain: pylons; housing estates; even a miniature Concorde. But in 1993 the decision was made to turn back time and restore it to an unblemished 1930s aesthetic – with a few new additions. Darker-skinned characters were added in, although the shades are often somewhat peculiar ('They never really got the colour palette of black or Asian skin'). This editing of the past fascinated Bailey. 'I'm not here to rip the village apart and be cynical about it, because I think it's a wonderful place, but from a sociological point of view it's very interesting to see how we view ourselves and our past – and, more importantly, how we want to portray it.' The village is also a subtle but telling reflection of the class system. 'Professional characters like the doctor and the nurse have been very well made, but they've been less delicate with, say, labourers working in the country; in effect, the quality of your model has been determined by your social standing,' says Bailey. 'So the priest is superbly done, but somebody hacking away in a forest might have one eye pointing to Kilkenny and the other to Cork.'

Shot in documentary style under bright lighting, the miniature world Bailey's shots capture is like a curiously skewed distillation of reality; a world whose vivid colours and characters seem larger than life, despite their tiny proportions. Inevitably, the real world sometimes intruded into the pictures – stray crisps packets the size of cars, or curious blackbirds stopping to investigate – but Bailey chose to edit those shots out, keeping the illusion intact. 'It's like when Hitchcock said the worst thing he ever did was to let the bomb go off on the bus [in *Sabotage*]. He had everybody gripped when the child was on the bus, with the box with a bomb in it; then he cut away, and four or five minutes later, bang! The explosion just released everyone in the cinema. With this project, I wanted to keep that tension.'

Tension is a word that Bailey often uses when he's talking about the village. First, there's the tension of not knowing what the characters might do next, the sense that they are forever poised on the brink of action. Then there's the tension – and frustration – induced by a lifetime of inertia, of being trapped in the same pose. For the man running away from the bull, the woman kneeling to scrub her front step, the boy poised to dive at the edge of a diving board, tantalisingly close to the sparkling blue water, life has stood still for almost half a century.

'There's a fuzzy picture of some people on a bus that really encapsulated that for me,' explains Bailey. 'They've been sitting on that bus for 40 years, and they've never got off it, never been outside it – never actually got to the point where they're at the end of their journey. For me, it's the most poignant image in the book.'

**Bekonscot Model Village** *Warwick Road, Beaconsfield, Buckinghamshire HP9 2PL (01494 672919/www.bekonscot.com).* Forever England *by Liam Bailey is published by Dewi Lewis (£9.99); for details of the project, and Liam Bailey's other work, see www.liambaileyprojects.com.*

# 286-290
## Marvel at a mystery play

It's hard to believe that a modern audience could be enthralled by the pared-down piety of medieval entertainments, but the enigmatic art of the mystery play continues to draw crowds around the country. Originally little more than basic representations of the better-known Bible stories performed in churches by the clergy, the plays evolved over the centuries: taken up by the guilds after the Pope forbade clerics from acting in 1210, they developed into a series of 'cycles' performed over several days and were enjoyed for 500 years, their popularity only waning with the rise of conventional theatre.

Several cities have now revived the tradition: Lincoln (01522 880674, www.lincolnmystery plays.co.uk) and Chester (01244 304618, www. chestermysteryplays.com) both have cycles scheduled for June 2008, alongside a wealth of related talks and exhibitions. The next cycle in Lichfield (www.lichfieldmysteries.co.uk) is scheduled for the May Bank Holiday weekend in 2009; in York (www.yorkmysteryplays.co.uk) it's 2010. In London, the Players of St Peter (www.theplayersofstpeter.org.uk) have been performing extracts from various mystery plays in the church of St Clement in Eastcheap every November for 60 years.

# 291
## Taste Victory on Nelson's poop deck

If you're visiting Portsmouth Historic Dockyard hoping to experience a personal Trafalgar, best go when the guided tours are running. Tour days come in oddly random clumps throughout the year – check the website – but are by far the best way to get inside the life and mind of a Georgian sailor – as well as his cramped living, working and fighting quarters. Feel the rigours of duty and discipline as you visit Nelson's Great Cabin where he prayed and planned, the quarterdeck where he was wounded, and the orlop deck where he uttered his last words.
**HMS Victory** *HM Naval Base, Portsmouth, Hampshire PO1 3NH (023 9283 9766/ www.hms-victory.com).*

# 292
## Swim the Isles of Scilly

The somewhat alarming mission statement of unique travel company Swimtrek (020 8696 6220, www.swimtrek.com) is 'ferries are for wimps, let's swim!' And it's dead serious: the island-hopping itineraries make full use of human hydropower, having you swim from one destination to another while staff keep an eye on you from a boat. One of Swimtrek's British-based trips (costing £645) is six days of swimming around the stunning Isles of Scilly, some 30 miles south-west off the coast of Cornwall. There are over 100 islands in these parts, but thankfully you're not expected to reach them all. In fact, while your fitness levels need to be good, you don't have to be a Duncan Goodhew-type Olympian: the average distance covered each day is around one-and-a-half miles, and the natural buoyancy of sea salt makes the going easier too. Still unsure? A two-day taster tour (£195) swimming the non-tidal part of the Thames (which is also the clean end) might help assuage any fears of a watery grave.

# 293
## Dig the crazy murals at Longleat

For most of us, the name 'Longleat' is synonymous with winding up car windows to avoid becoming lion food. But there's one little-vaunted corner of the Elizabethan stately home that's guaranteed to make up for having your aerial snapped off by a baboon: the mind-expanding murals painted throughout the private apartments. They are the brilliantly colourful and humorous life's work of Lord Bath, falling characteristically between classical and hippie influences. 'Cocoons, therapies and fantasies,' is how he describes them; 'keyhole glimpses into my psyche.'
**Longleat** *Warminster, Wiltshire BA12 7NW (01985 844400/www.longleat.co.uk).*

## 294 Go riding on Silecroft Beach

There's nothing like a ride on horseback along the sands to blow away the cobwebs – and this gorgeous beach, stretching for miles along the edge of the Lake District, is an idyllic spot. Murthwaite Green Trekking Centre is close to the beach (which means there aren't many roads to negotiate) and offers both experienced hackers and first-timers the opportunity for a gallop (or sedate trot) through the surf. Treks last from half an hour to a whole day; the centre also offers romantic riding holidays.
**Murthwaite Green Trekking Centre** *Millom, Silecroft, Cumbria LA18 5LP (01229 770876/ www.murthwaitegreen.co.uk).*

## 295 Hop on board the Bluebell Railway

The romance of the steam era lives on in Sussex, where the UK's first preserved standard gauge passenger railway can be found. Ride one of more than 30 locomotives, including the Golden Arrow Pullman, which recreates the glamorous dining train that once linked London with Paris. Open most Saturday evenings and Sunday lunchtimes, the train hosts 1940s and murder mystery themed dinners. Equally quaint is the 1920s Sussex Belle Pullman, which serves old-fashioned cream teas – call for this year's dates.
**Bluebell Railway** *Sheffield Park Station, East Sussex TN22 3QL (01825 720825/www.bluebell-railway.co.uk).*

## 296 Walk among Glasgow's forgotten dead

Set on a hill at the east end of Glasgow city centre, cheek by jowl with the cathedral, the Necropolis started life as parkland in the 17th and 18th centuries. In 1825, a major monument to Scottish religious reformer John Knox was added, and town planners realised the park would make a fine cemetery, modelled on Père Lachaise in Paris. Interdenomenational from the outset (the first burial was a Jewish jeweller, interred in 1832), the Necropolis housed the city's great and good in increasingly elaborate graves and mausoleums until it was full to bursting. These days, it has descended into an atmospheric and even Gothic state of decay – somewhere to walk, look at memorials dating back nearly 180 years, and reflect on the fleeting nature of posthumous regard.
**Glasgow Cathedral & Glasgow Necropolis** *Castle Street, Glasgow G4 0QZ (www.glasgow necropolis.org).*

# 297
## Salute a surfing hero at the National Maritime Museum

NMM Cornwall differs from its Greenwich cousin in that it concentrates on the south-west of England's maritime heritage. Proudly Cornish (and all the more interesting for its local emphasis), its programme is packed with talks, workshops, family activities and film screenings, alongside changing exhibitions and displays. It's not restricted to local artefacts; the Set Sail gallery features an Indian masulah surf boat, and you can see Shackleton's *James Caird* – the little wooden boat that survived its near-impossible mission to reach South Georgia for help after the *Endurance* was destroyed.

See an elaborately carved scrimshaw, a bathtub used to row across the Channel, Sir Ranulph Fiennes's socks, and tow-headed dudes exclaiming 'awesome!' in front of the 13-foot Tom Blake-designed hollow wooden surfboard, dating from the 1930s – they have him to thank for the fact that boards evolved from enormously heavy solid-wood affairs.

**National Maritime Museum Cornwall** *Discovery Quay, Falmouth, Cornwall TR11 3QY (01326 313388/www.nmmc.co.uk).*

# 298
## Go hound trailing in the Lake District

Somewhere in Cumbria, almost every day of the week from April to October, hounds are hot on a trail – and finding a meet is a great way to get into the spirit of the Lakes, and support a traditional local sport that has been enjoyed for at least 200 years (www.houndtrailing.org.uk). Superbly fit and strong, the dogs race over a pre-laid aniseed trail that can be anything up to ten miles long, tearing across steep fells, bounding over dry stone walls and deciding a few modest bets in the process. Descended from fox hounds, trail hounds are specially bred and trained to endure the most arduous courses through some of the country's most stunning scenery. It's always a stirring sight to see them way off in the distance on the hill, strung out at full speed and hunting their way home.

# 299
## Look to the skies at the RAF's biggest air show

As well as overhead feats of aerial derring-do, this huge Lincolnshire event has tents crammed with aviation memorabilia, helicopter pleasure flights, classic car, motorcycle and military vehicle shows and, for any truculent teenagers in the party, flight simulators and a funfair.

**Waddington Air Show** *Royal Air Force Station Waddington, Lincolnshire LN5 9NB (01522 726102/www.waddingtonairshow.co.uk).*

# 300
## Catch an event at Dartington Hall

Built in 1388 by Richard II's half brother, and later a sanctuary for two of Henry VIII's wives, the imposing Dartington Hall is now given over to more public-minded affairs. A year-round programme of music, dance, theatre and film has been running here for over three decades, and is as remarkable for its diversity of programming as it is for its illustrious setting. Visiting artists have ranged from world-class string quartet the Lindsays to Russian visual theatre troupe Derevo, while a ten-day literary festival takes place in July. There are also frequent opportunities to get creative, from an international summer school encompassing opera writing and African drumming to craft workshops in lithography and bookbinding.

**Dartington Hall** *Totnes, Devon TQ9 6DE (01803 847070/www.dartington.org/arts).*

# 301 Enjoy the view from 'Edinburgh's disgrace'

Though some might say the deep-fried pizza in local fish and chip shops is Edinburgh's disgrace, the name actually applies to the classical Greek-style monument on Calton Hill. Modelled on the Parthenon, it was begun in 1822 as a grand memorial for the dead of the Napoleonic Wars, but the city ran out of money. Left incomplete, the National Monument, as it's officially known, turned into a very visible embarrassment. Given its position, however, it does offer utterly fantastic views of the Old Town, Holyrood Park, the Firth of Forth and the rest of the city – easily worth the short walk from the east end of Princes Street.

# 302 Eat cockles at Leigh-on-Sea...

The cockle sheds at Leigh-on-Sea hold some of the freshest seafood in England. This, combined with the charm of the cobbled streets, clapboard houses and small sandy beach, makes a lovely day out – and it's all just a few minutes from the train station. Wander along the estuary, then have a plate of cockles from Osborne Bros (with a Guinness from the Crooked Billet next door). The range of seafood available here belies its size – the counter is packed with eels (smoked and jellied), oysters, mussels, prawns, shrimps, whelks, crab and sprats – and there are other sheds, fish and chip shops and tearooms too.

**Osborne Bros** *Billet Wharf, High Street, Leigh-on-Sea, Essex SS9 2ER (01702 477233/ www.osbornebros.co.uk).*

# 303 ...or drink an oyster-infused pint on Mersea Island

Another Essex institution, further up the coast, is Mersea Island's vineyard and brewery. While you're in these parts, make sure you sample its wares, including the unusual Oyster Ale: six local molluscs are added to each cask.

**Mersea Island Vineyard** *Rewsalls Lane, East Mersea, Colchester, Essex CO5 8SX (01206 385900/www.merseawine.com/brewery.htm).*

# 304 Monkey around at Go Ape

Go Ape's centres give you the chance to express your inner monkey, by swinging from tree to tree, using rope bridges, zip slides and Tarzan swings to take you up to the tree tops high above the forest floor. Happily, you're not expected to survive your aerial adventure by a powerful grip and monkey-like agility alone: you'll be fitted with a sturdy safety harness before setting off. Of the 16 Go Ape courses scattered across the UK (0845 643 9215, www.goape.co.uk) the largest is in the Delamere Forest, just east of Chester in Cheshire, with its extensive zip wires and beautiful views of Lake Linmere. Participants must be at least ten years old.

# 305
## Swim at Saltdean...

In the roaring '30s, lidos – an idea adoped from Venice's glamorous bathing spots – were all the rage, and art deco shrines to swimming and sun-worshipping sprang up across the land. The lido at Saltdean in Brighton (01273 888308, www.saltdean.info/lido.htm) is a particularly glorious example, with its elegant, curved lines – rather like a stately ocean liner.

# 306-317
## ...then take the plunge in some of Britains's other loveliest lidos

### Brockwell Lido, London
A recent £3 million restored this south London lido to its 1930s glory, but also brought some sparklingly modern additions: airy yoga and pilates studios, a small indoor pool and a gym (020 7274 3088, www.brockwell-lido.co.uk).

### Chagford Swimming Pool, Dartmoor
The river-fed pool at Chagford (01647 432929, www.roundash.com/pool.htm) is a great spot for a dip after a walk across the moors, with solar pool covers to make the water temperature a touch less bracing.

### Droitwich Spa Lido, Worcestershire
After a sterling local campaign, the 1930s lido at Droitwich (01905 799342, www.wychavon leisure.co.uk) was rescued from dereliction and reopened in 2007. The water has a high salt content, making swims delightfully buoyant.

### Guildford Lido, Surrey
With temperatures climbing up to 26 degrees, this heated Olympic-sized lido (01483 443322, www.guildfordspectrum.co.uk) is a welcoming prospect even on cloudy days.

### Ilkley Pool & Lido, Yorkshire
Ilkley's lido is a lovely spot – but for the faint of heart, there's always the heated indoor pool to retreat to (01943 600453, www.bradford.gov.uk).

### Jesus Green Pool, Cambridge
Set by the River Cam and surrounded by trees, the 100-yard lido at Jesus Green is one of Europe's longest outdoor pools, and a wonderfully tranquil spot for a length or two (01223 302579, www.cambridge.gov.uk).

### Jubilee Pool, Cornwall
Next to the harbour and promenade in Penzance, with glorious views across the bay, the triangular Jubilee Pool (01736 798090, www.jubileepool.co.uk) is a vision of art deco splendour, and deservedly Grade II listed.

### Parliament Hill, London
After a stroll on Hampstead Heath, there's nothing nicer than cooling off in the lido (020 7485 5757, www.cityoflondon.gov.uk/open spaces) – though on sunny days, everyone seems to have the same idea.

### Pells Pool, East Sussex
This spring-fed pool in the seaside town of Lewes is the oldest outside pool in the country (01273 472334, www.pellspool.org.uk). After a swim, tea and cakes await in the café.

### Sandford Parks, Cheltenham
With its paddling pool, children's pool and slides, Sandford's perfect for families (01242 524430, www.sandfordparkslido.org.uk) – though a couple of lanes are set aside for those planning some serious swimming.

### Stonehaven Pool, Aberdeenshire
This Olympic-sized pool is heated to a toasty 29 degrees – plus there are midnight swims beneath the stars on Wednesdays (01569 762134, www.stonehavenopenairpool.co.uk).

### Tinside Lido, Plymouth
The beauty contest hopefuls who paraded around the pool in Tinside's 1930s heyday may be a thing of the past, but the Grade II-listed pool's still a stunner (01752 261915, www.plymouth.gov.uk).

# 318
## Learn to fly a Tiger Moth

The Imperial War Museum Duxford has plenty to recommend it, not least its regular air shows and a building designed by Norman Foster – the neighbouring American Air Museum. If you're a dedicated wing-nut, though, what better way to learn more about our nation's aviation history than by taking to the skies? Flights are available for around £100 in a variety of classic planes, such as the 1930s Tiger Moth bi-plane, and include the loan of old-fashioned gear like leather jackets and goggles. And if you've always dreamed of being Biggles and flying the things yourself, introductory lessons are also available.
**Imperial War Museum Duxford** *Duxford, Cambridgeshire CB22 4QR (01223 835000/ www.iwm.org.uk).*

# 319-321
## Ramble through a firing range

Signs warning of unexploded ordinance are generally a good reason to avoid hiking in an area, however tempting the terrain. But the Ministry of Defence is now inviting ramblers on to its land, posting details on its website of a dozen walks across its 590,000 acres (0121 311 2140, www.access.mod.uk). MoD land doesn't suffer from the ravages of being farmed to within an inch of its life: tank tracks aside, the environment is as nature intended – a haven for wildlife. Enjoy heather moorland and views of the Firth of Forth at Castlelaw, Edinburgh (0131 310 4943); investigate long and round barrows on Salisbury Plain (01980 674763); or walk through the deserted village of Tyneham in Dorset (01929 404819), whose inhabitants were forced to leave after the valley became a firing range in the 1940s. Exercise caution: speak to an access officer before heading out, and note that red flags indicate live firing.

# 322-334
## Spend the night in Carisbrooke Castle – or another historic pile

English Heritage (www.english-heritage.org.uk) offers 13 holiday cottages and apartments on its properties, from castles and ruined abbeys to rambling grand estates. Each is unique, and all boast stylish, contemporary interiors; there's history enough when you step outside. If you opt for a stay in Carisbrooke Castle on the Isle of Wight, banish any images of a cold, dank dungeon: you'll be kipping in a swish second-floor apartment (sleeping a family of four), set within the castle's walls. Once the officers' barracks for the castle garrison, it offers commanding views over the ancient ramparts and main courtyard. Couples might prefer to cosy up in the snug Custodian's House at Henry VIII's Pendennis Castle in Cornwall, whereas Field Hall Lodge accommodates groups of up to six at Northumberland's Belsay Hall, a medieval castle and Greek Revival house; there are also loads of places to visit locally, including Hadrian's Wall, Durham Cathedral and Alnwick Castle. Our other favourites include the elegant Sergeant Major's House at Dover Castle, with its lovely views over the channel, and the Prior's Lodge at Mount Grace Priory in North Yorkshire – a single-storey stone cottage, nestled in the tranquil priory grounds.

# 335
## Punch and (hang and truncheon) Judy at Llandudno Pier

The Codman family has run a Punch and Judy pitch at Llandudno Pier since time immemorial – 1860, to be precise, when 'Professor' Bert Codman ran the show. Nowadays it's his great-granddaughter Jackie Millband-Codman who orchestrates the time-honoured anarchy, along with her husband Morris – using puppets carved from local driftwood by the Professor. Now that's the way to do it.

**Punch and Judy** *Promenade, Llandudno, Conwy LL30 2LP (www.visitconwy.org.uk).*

# 336
## Stand well back at the Hallaton bottle-kicking

Only once a symbolic hare pie has been tossed to the baying crowd can battle commence: make no mistake, this Easter Monday festival is all about high spirits and rising sap (www.hallaton.org/bottlekicking.html). Over the remains of a pagan shrine, a small barrel of beer appears, and 100 burly blokes collide. Anyone is free to join in the scrum for either side, Hallaton or Medbourne, two miles away. The aim is to score, by wrestling the bottle into the stream outside your home village. There's only one rule: no weapons. The ruck passes clean through bramble hedges, scattering the circling crowd when the 'bottle' breaks loose into the hilltop meadow full of ice-cream vans, pushchairs, picnics and ambulances. Ouch.

# 337
## Dare to do the downhill at Aonach Mor

In the same range as Ben Nevis, Aonach Mor is home to a snowsports centre with a gondola that carries skiers and snowboarders to a station high up the mountain. The facility also has a world championship-standard mountain bike downhill course, which drops nearly 2,000 feet in under two miles. You put your bike in the gondola, head up, then try to stay alive on the way down. Helmets are mandatory, while a full suspension mountain bike with disc brakes, body armour and insurance are recommended. Some of the descent really does have to be seen to be believed, although top riders complete it in around four minutes. (If you think chuntering around the woods near your house a few days every summer on that old machine with bouncy front forks qualifies you for this, think again.) The downhill is usually open May to September.

**Nevis Range Mountain Experience** *Torlundy, Fort William, Inverness-shire PH33 6SW (01397 705825/www.nevisrange.co.uk/summer).*

# 338 Meltdown at the RFH

That 'culture should be a stimulant not a sedative' is one of the main tenets of Meltdown, the annual summer week of convention-twisting music hosted by London's Royal Festival Hall, and directed by a different influential musician each year (Patti Smith and David Bowie have taken the reins in the past). The organisers like 'combining things that shouldn't be combined', which, in 2007, resulted in an extraordinary reinterpretation of Disney songs, masterminded by Jarvis Cocker and his unlikely collaborators: Pete Doherty, Nick Cave and Shane McGowan.
**Royal Festival Hall** *Southbank Centre, Belvedere Road, London SE1 8XX (0871 663 2501/ www.southbankcentre.co.uk/meltdown).*

# 339 Raise a toast to Tuckers Maltings

Based in the busy Devonshire market town of Newton Abbot for over 100 years, Tuckers produces enough malt in a year to make 15 million pints of beer. It's also the only working malthouse that's open to the public, allowing grateful beer-lovers to make the pilgrimage to pay their respects. The tour ends with a trip to Teignworthy Brewery for a pint – plus there's an in-house shop stocking over 200 bottled brews, ranging from apricot-infused fruity little numbers to no-nonsense stouts and ales.
**Tuckers Maltings** *Teign Road, Osborne Park, Newton Abbot, Devon TQ12 4AA (01626 334734/ www.tuckersmaltings.com).*

# 340 Explore Wisley's glittering glasshouse

The immense new glasshouse at the Royal Horticultural Society's garden at Wisley, built to celebrate the site's bicentenary and opened in 2007, has to be seen to be believed. The size of ten tennis courts, its three climate zones include a luscious tropical area, where giant tree ferns, palms and waterlilies bask in the humid heat.
**RHS Garden Wisley** *Wisley, Woking, Surrey GU23 6QB (0845 260 9000/www.rhs.org.uk).*

# 341 See Shakespeare under the stars

Performances at Cornwall's open-air Minack Theatre are only cancelled in horrendous storms, as the impossibly weatherbeaten stewards will testify. So take plenty of layers along with your picnic, then enjoy shows that range from *The Merry Wives of Windsor* to *The Pirates of Penzance* – and try not to be too distracted by the incredibly beautiful live-sea backdrop. (Imagine a *King Lear* in which Gloucester looks as if he really will throw himself off the cliff.) The seats and stage were hacked out of the granite in 1932, at the behest of bohemian eccentric Rowena Cade, and were originally lit by batteries and car headlights.

Off-season (October to May), the stunning seascape takes centre stage. You can view Porthcurno Bay from the coffee shop, through opera glasses kept next to the salt and pepper.
**The Minack Theatre** *Porthcurno, Penzance, Cornwall TR19 6JU (01736 810181/ www.minack.com).*

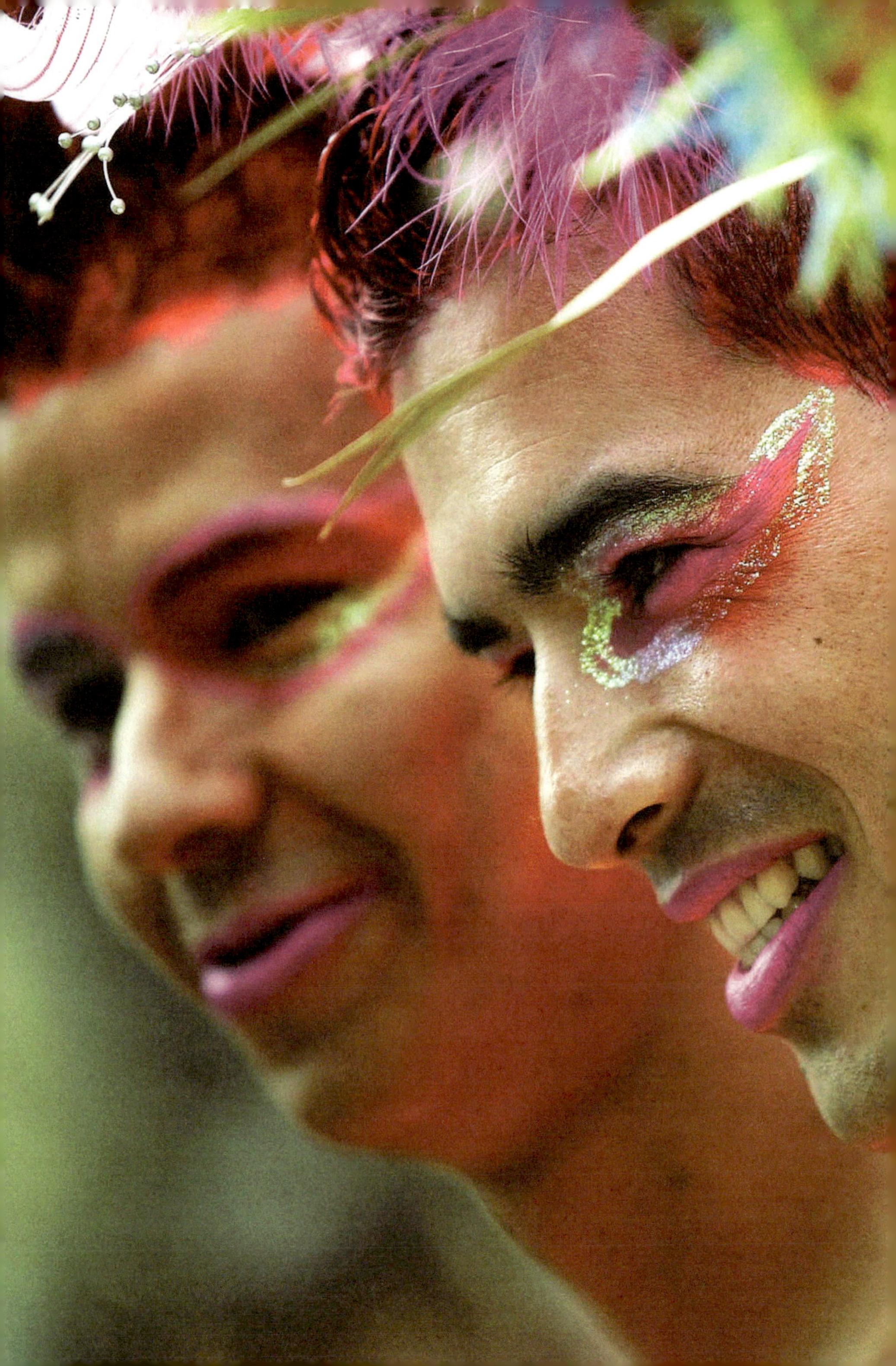

**342**

*Take pride*
After 18 years, Manchester's Gay Pride (www.manchesterpride.com) is still alive and high-kicking every August Bank Holiday. Hundreds of floats take part in the grand parade through the city, while Canal Street is the focus for the main music acts. Other Pride events are held across the country; for a list see www.gaytoz.com. Brighton Pride (www.brightonpride.org), on the first Saturday in August, is the UK's largest, culminating in a straight-friendly party in Preston Park; London's (www.pridelondon.org) is the country's oldest, upholding its Proud heritage in style on the first weekend in July every year.

# 343-344
## Follow in the footsteps of Stanley Spencer

Fans of the visionary English artist can take a pilgrimage to two sites in the Home Counties – both, fittingly enough for such a religious artist, inside chapels. The Thames Valley Berkshire village of Cookham – where Spencer was born and lived for much of his life, and where he's buried – is home to the Stanley Spencer Gallery (Kings Hall, High Street, Cookham, Berkshire SL6 9SJ, 01628 471885, www.stanleyspencer.org.uk). Opened in 1962 in the former Methodist chapel that Spencer visited as a child, the tiny gallery is sparkling after year-long renovations, completed in 2007. Afterwards, take a stroll round the village, the backdrop for many a heavenly visitation in his paintings.

Over in Hampshire, the Sandham Memorial Chapel (Harts Lane, Burghclere, Hampshire RG20 9JT, 01635 278294, www.nationaltrust.org.uk), is the setting for Spencer's most famous work: a series of 19 wall paintings depicting his World War I experiences as a hospital orderly in Bristol and overseas in Macedonia. Inspired by Giotto's Arena Chapel in Padua, the red-brick chapel was built specially to house the murals, which were completed in 1932; as is typical of Spencer's conflation of the domestic and the spiritual, they chart soldiers' everyday routines rather than the horrors of war.

# 345
## Take in the Broadway views

Somewhat more genteel than its Manhattan counterpart, Broadway in Worcestershire is a quaint Cotswold village where the claims to fame are its artistic heritage – Elgar, JM Barrie and Vaughan Williams all lived here – and the fact that it's home to a 65-foot Gothic folly. Standing behind the village on Fish Hill, Broadway Tower (01386 852390) commands views over no fewer than 13 counties on a clear day. It also houses the Morris room, where craftsman William worked in what he considered his country retreat.

# 346
## Sleep in the treetops

Embrace your inner scabby-kneed child while climbing trees with this Cornwall-based outfit (07890 698651, www.mighty-oak.co.uk). The concept is especially exciting because, now that you're a grown-up, you're also allowed to sleep up in the tree once you've climbed it, instead of being called in for tea by your mum when it gets dark.

Those who toss and turn as they slumber needn't worry about hurtling 50 feet down to the hard earth in the middle of the night – climbers sleep on a comfortable, four-cornered hammock called a 'tree boat', and are securely attached by rope and a harness. The back-to-nature vibe is rounded off in the morning, with breakfast up in the branches among the birds. The company will even come to a suitable tree near you if you don't want to trek down to one of its sites in Cornwall. The experience costs £200 for one person, or £140 per person for groups of two to five.

# 347
## Jet down the Thames

Every London guidebook ever written repeats the suggestion that the city is best approached, viewed and appreciated by boat from the river. And even though the guidebooks are all dead right, it's unlikely that many authors specifically had in mind the view from a Rigid Inflatable Boat. The RIB is the Royal Marines' preferred offshore raiding boat, with extreme powers of acceleration and manoeuvrability thanks to the Rolls-Royce jet engine wedged in its rear end. Tours from Chelsea to the Millennium Bridge and back last around an hour, taking in all the sights, but be warned; these Flying Fish Tours could do it in 23.7 seconds, if they wanted to go flat out.

**Flying Fish Tours** *Cadogan Pier, Chelsea Embankment, off Albert Bridge Road, London SW3 5RJ (08449 915050/www.flyingfishtous.co.uk).*

# 348 *Order a sundae in Scarborough*

Whatever the weather, to visit the Harbour Bar is to enter a world of eternal sunshine and sweetness. This 1945 milk bar and ice-cream parlour, run by the Alonzi family, gleams with chrome, lemon curd-yellow Formica and glacé cherry-red stools and banquettes. On the mirrored walls, slogans exhort you to 'Get your vitamins the easy way – eat ice-cream every day!' If only. Riotously coloured knickerbocker glories overflow from gigantic conical glasses, while banana splits, frothy milkshakes and sundaes are concocted with own-made ice-cream at the counter. All in all, a perfect retro joy – and a delicious sugar rush.

**Harbour Bar** *1-3 Sandside, Scarborough, North Yorkshire YO11 1PE (01723 373662).*

**349-367** *Hit Britain's best clubs*

# Club class

**Cyrus Shahrad** *discovers where Britain's top DJs like to party when they're off-duty.*

There are few things in music more regular or reliable than a four-to-the-floor house beat, nor are there many more regular or reliable sources of income. All a DJ has to do is keep the tunes in time and avoid any shocking transgressions of the tried and trusted formula, and everyone goes home happy. Or at least, they used to.

'The UK club scene is younger and more open-minded than it was ten years ago,' says Duncan Dick of *Mixmag*. 'The whole "nu rave" term is very nebulous and hard to pin down, but the live music element of bands like Klaxons and Hot Chip has brought a generation of under-20s back into clubs and injected them with a new intimacy and diversity – take Chibuku at the Barfly in Liverpool (0151 708 5051, www.chibuku.com) or the Plug in Sheffield (0114 241 3040, www.the-plug.com). That whole millennial idea of superstar DJs being helicoptered to and from the superclub is largely a thing of the past: people want something a bit more spontaneous, something they can feel a little closer to.'

Not that this has sounded the death knell for more conventional clubbing. In 2007, London's nightlife scene may have suffered the closure of the Cross, Canvas and the Key, but other of the capital's stalwarts continue to thrive, most notably the End (020 7419 9199, www.endclub.com) and Fabric (020 7336 8898, www.fabriclondon.com). Few can claim an affinity with both of these clubs like drum 'n' bass don and Ram Records honcho Andy C, host of bi-monthly Ram nights at the former and a long-standing resident at the latter.

'The End is amazing for so many reasons. You've got a tearing sound system, a space age interior and the underground feel of that basement descent – seriously exciting when you've been queuing in the cold for two hours. Best of all is the way the DJ booth is located in the middle of the dancefloor: I can be up there mixing records with people dancing on all sides, which helps me vibe off the crowd and makes me feel like I'm partying alongside them.'

Fabric, by comparison, is a cavernous place: a maze of labyrinthine corridors and sepulchral chambers that has been confusing clubbers since it opened in 1999, complete with groundbreaking bass speakers beneath its floorboards. 'People really lose themselves in Fabric,' says Andy. 'You could go there five weekends in a row and have a different night every time. It's a world away from the End in terms of scale, but works on exactly the same ethos when it comes to supporting underground music. Between the pair of them, Londoners are blessed with two of the best clubs in the world.'

Another big name that's still pulling them in is Heaven (020 7930 2020, www.heaven-london.com), which more than lives up to its name in the eyes of techno legend Carl Cox. 'Heaven has a raw, underground feel, yet its central location means that punters have no trouble finding it or getting home afterwards. Its popularity with gay clubbers means even straight nights have a mixed crowd and a uniquely open-minded vibe. I've lost track of how many times I've played there, but it's always been packed to the rafters, and the atmosphere goes through the roof.'

House DJ Tall Paul, meanwhile, had a real soft spot for Turnmills in London (020 7250 3409, www.turnmills.co.uk), known for its superlative sound system and wonderfully diverse programming. (Sadly, at the time of writing, the venue is due to close as a club). He is, however, equally partial to smaller clubs such as Motion in Inverness (01463 222713, www.motioninverness.co.uk), the Syndicate in Blackpool (01253 753222, www.thesyndicate.com) and Bedbug at the Crank Club in Bournemouth (www.bedbug-music.com).

'Clubbing still feels in a bit of a recovery stage after its post-millennial meltdown,' says Paul. 'Come summer, the big boys like Cream, Gatecrasher and Global Gathering are back in circulation with their annual events, but it seems as if the most progression is happening in more intimate venues, where promoters are really listening to the crowds and mixing things up. Nowadays people don't mind dancing to the Killers in one room, then going next door to hear Carl Cox spin records. And that's actually more of a return to the source than some people realise: back in the day, there was nothing unusual about dropping a hip hop record after a house record – it's only in the last few years that things have become so pigeon-holed.'

Even Paul Oakenfold, the undisputed heavyweight of stadium dance events, admits a fondness for the relative intimacy of nights like Gatecrasher Loves Nottingham (0115 910 1101, www.gatecrasher.co.uk/nottingham), which at 1,000 people feels like an oversized living room compared to his performances at Glastonbury's main stage, LA's Hollywood Bowl or the Great Wall of China. 'It's operated by Gatecrasher,' he says, 'so it's top notch in terms of production, sound and promotion. Plus the venue itself is fantastic: the DJ is in the centre of the stage with the audience rising in theatrical tiers, so everyone has a great view of the action and feels part of the night. Some clubs fragment the crowd up into separate rooms, and that's the worst thing you can do for the atmosphere.'

Nowhere is the shift towards a closer relationship between public and performer more evident than in hip hop – something that former DMC scratch champion Mr Thing sees as long overdue. 'Big hip hop nights can be terrible, packed with teenagers hassling you to play Soulja Boy or whatever the latest major label monstrosity is. Block parties aside, I think that hip hop has its roots in those smaller nights – places with an underground edge that you had to go out of your way to seek out. In London, that's still the case at Herbal (020 7613 4462, w2.herbaluk.com), a smaller club with an intense sound system and a great crowd of regulars. Outside of London, Birmingham has some excellent venues: my personal favourite is the Yardbird (www.myspace.com/theyardbird birmingham), a 150-capacity funk and breaks club where you really feel like everyone is on the same wavelength.'

Such sentiments resound with Thing's occasional collaborator, boundary-busting internationalist DJ Vadim, who passes up the big names in favour of Thekla (0117 929 3301, www.theklabristol.com), a diminutive club based in a boat moored on Bristol's mud dock. Several of Vadim's Ninja Tune labelmates feel the same way about small venues across London: rapper Ty loves treading the boards of the legendary Jazz Café (020 7688 8899, www.meanfiddler.com), with its up-close-and-personal ground-floor standing room and upmarket mezzanine dining area, while Robin Brunson of Hexstatic has a love-hate relationship with the after-hours sleaziness of 333 – which has 'just the right mix of trendies, geeks and bewildered Japanese businessmen' (020 7739 1800, www.333mother.com). Chris Vogado of Zero dB's personal favourite is Plastic People; 'Dark and dingy and small enough to feel friendly, yet boasting the best sound system this side of Tokyo's Yellow' (020 7739 6471, www.plasticpeople.co.uk).

For many, however, Brighton is as rich and rewarding a clubbing destination as London, something due in no small part to Robert Luis's Tru Thoughts label. 'There's something almost incestuous about clubbing in Brighton,' says Luis. 'The scene is small enough for you to bump into someone you know, which means you rarely end up hanging out exclusively with your own crew. Plus the seaside vibe lends something special, especially in summer, when everyone gets to regroup on the beach after being kicked out of a club – a far cry from being ejected on to the uncaring streets of London at 6am.'

Luis's favourite Brighton venue is Concorde 2 (01273 673311, www.concorde2.co.uk), erstwhile home of big beat and a bastion of mixing live bands with DJs long before the nu rave revolution, but his own nights will be taking a turn for the freeform in 2008 with the advent of Where's It At?, an attempt to recapture the excitement of clubbing's heyday by nomadically shifting from venue to venue, announcing locations just days before the event.

Meanwhile, Brighton's Beardyman, UK beatbox champion and You Tube sensation, is striving for that same sense of the unpredictable at his Battlejam nights in Brighton's Audio (01273 697775, www.audiobrighton.com) and London's Cargo (020 7749 7840, www.cargo-london.com), where he and collaborator JFB sample not only records but each other and the audience before mashing the lot together in a scratchfest of monumental proportions. Both nights satisfy club culture's new hunger for the unexpected in ways that no conventional DJ set ever could. 'We're keen to shift the emphasis away from the venues and back to the parties themselves,' says Luis. 'I think people really want something more ad-libbed and spontaneous, and that can only be a good thing from a musical point of view.'

## 368 *Embrace extreme sports*

To untrained eyes, most extreme sports competitions get pretty tiring pretty quickly: unless you're the sort of person who knows his barrel roll from his switch backside nine, one person launching themselves into the stratosphere is going to look rather like the next – great for ten minutes of shock and awe, but hardly a sustained day's entertainment.

Not so at the White Air festival, held in Sandown on the Isle of Wight (01983 813813, www.whiteair.co.uk). Now in its 11th year, the event brings together competitors in 26 separate sports – including skateboarding, wakeboarding, BMX and parkour – who thrash it out to a soundtrack of bands and DJs over the course of four beer-fuelled days.

So far, so familiar – except that at White Air, punters aren't limited to expressing their appreciation at the aerial acrobatics, but are encouraged to participate at every available opportunity. Last year, 5,000 people turned up to try their hand at a range of sports not available at their local gym – from more conventional disciplines like surfing and skating to niche practices involving such potentially baffling equipment as camtrikes, aquaskippers and indo boards.

## 369 *Find Europe's finest art – in Glasgow*

One of Europe's most important civic art collections, Kelvingrove opened in 1901. Works span the Scottish colourists (Fergusson, Peploe), Dutch masters (Rembrandt), Italian Renaissance greats (Botticelli), Impressionists (Monet, Degas) and more. On the museum side of things, there's a superb armoury – and a ruddy great Spitfire hanging from the ceiling.
**Kelvingrove Art Gallery & Museum** *Argyle Street, Glasgow G3 8AG (0141 276 9599/ www.glasgowmuseums.com).*

## 370 *Visit Richard Burton in a Bedouin tent*

There is a corner of England that is forever Arabia. In a quiet graveyard in Mortlake lies the elaborate final resting place of Sir Richard Burton, 19th-century polyglot, explorer, soldier, diplomat, and translator of the *Kama Sutra* and *One Thousand and One Nights*. The mausoleum, carved from stone in the shape of a Bedouin tent, has been here since 'Ruffian Dick' died in 1890.
**St Mary Magdalen's RC Church** *North Worple Way, London SW14 8PR (020 8876 1326/ www.stmarymags.org.uk).*

## 371 Descend into the depths of the Big Pit

For a genuine insight into a lost way of life, take an underground tour at the Big Pit. After strapping on a hard hat, you're locked in a steel cage and dropped 282 feet down the mine shaft, into a maze of dark, confined tunnels – fortunately, with a jovial Welsh ex-miner to act as your guide. For 120 years, until the pit's closure in 1980, thousands of men spent their working lives down here – a sobering thought, as you emerge into the daylight from the hour-long tour, gulping in the fresh air.
**Big Pit National Coal Museum** *Blaenafon, Torfaen NP4 9XP (01495 790311/ www.museumwales.ac.uk).*

## 372 Cycle the New Forest on a bicycle made for two

The great outdoors, wild ponies, cosy pubs – in fine weather, the New Forest is cyclists' heaven. Pick a route (maps are provided); the eight-mile Ornamental Loop, which takes around two hours (allowing time for a breather at one of several pubs), is 99 per cent off-road and passes an arboretum and deer sanctuary. Cycleexperience in Brockenhurst (01590 624204, www.cyclex. co.uk) has tandems for hire, as well as more conventional bikes and tag-a-longs for kids.

## 373 See the big cats at Colchester

Amur (or Siberian) tigers are the largest of the world's five remaining sub-species of tiger – and there are just 400 left. Fingers crossed, then, that Colchester Zoo's Anoushka and Igor hit it off. Visit them and Sasha the white tiger, then check out the cheetahs and lions. Not all the rare felines are quite so imposing: the spotted Geoffroy's Cat from South America only weighs about nine pounds (the black ones could pass for domestic moggies), while the Manuls resemble a cross between a grumpy Persian and a draft excluder.
**Colchester Zoo** *Maldon Road, Stanway, Colchester, Essex CO3 0SL (01206 331292/ www.colchester-zoo.co.uk).*

## 374 Don't get bitter at the Marmalade festival

From as far afield as darkest Peru and Australia, competitors flock to Cumbria to have their preserves put through the most rigorous of tests by the Women's Institute – as well as two Masters from the Worshipful Company of Fruiterers and Gardeners, and a Michelin-starred chef. Rigorous judging aside (there's a silver spoon in it for the winner), the three-day Festival of Marmalade promises cooking demos and lectures, tasting sessions and top-notch food from local producers. In 2008, visitors also got the chance to see (though, sadly, not sample) the world's most expensive pot of marmalade, worth £5,000 and made from vintage champagne, 60-year-old malt whisky and gold leaf. Paddington Bear, patron of the festival, generally puts in an appearance too.
**Festival of Marmalade** *Dalemain Historic House & Gardens, Dalemain, Penrith, Cumbria CA11 0HB (017684 86450/www.marmaladefestival.com).*

## 375 Play vintage slot machines in Brighton

A working museum, Mechanical Memories offers a charming diversion from the mass of seafront tack in the vicinity, paying homage to the automated entertainments of yesteryear. The vintage slot machines date from the early 1900s until around 1960; £1 gets you ten plays on the likes of fortune-tellers, horse racing games and One Armed Bandits. Kids can stamp their name (or anything else) on to aluminium strips (like dog tags) to take home for just 20p, and giggle at the saucy What the Butler Saw machines. Note that the museum only opens from noon until 6pm during school holidays and weekends from Easter to September, and the odd fine weekend the rest of the year.
**Mechanical Memories Museum** *250C Kings Road Arches, Lower Esplanade, Brighton, East Sussex BN1 1NB (01322 287025).*

# 376
## Get back to nature on Lundy

Thanks to its remoteness from mainland Britain, Lundy island has been a retreat for medieval rebels, Jacobean pirates and Hanoverian smugglers over the course of its long history – and now provides an escape for frazzled refugees of modern life. The unspoilt granite outcrop, located just where the Bristol Channel meets the Atlantic, was formed from an ancient volcano and is only three and a half miles long, but has 23 charmingly eclectic holiday lets. Stay in a 13th-century castle built by Henry III, a weatherboard-clad fisherman's cottage, or a Georgian gentleman's villa. You can stay here in caravans for nothing if you don't mind a spot of conservation work, which might include protecting the Lundy Cabbage – a species found only on the island. The surrounding waters are a marine nature reserve, and one of the best dive wreck sites in Britain, with 137 ghostly ships lurking beneath the waves. Snorkelling safaris and walks are conducted by an Island Warden, mostly free of charge, for those interested in discovering more about the island's wealth of flora and fauna.
**Lundy Shore Office** *The Quay, Bideford, Devon EX39 2LY (01271 863636/www.lundy island.co.uk).*

# 377
## Crack a code at Bletchley Park

It was only in the 1970s that the wartime activities at Bletchley Park, also known as Station X, came to light. The code-breaking centre, which famously broke the Nazi's Enigma cypher machine, remained shrouded in mystery until declassification after the Cold War; Churchill famously described its workers as 'the geese that laid the golden eggs – but never cackled'. Opened to the public in 1994, Bletchley's displays cover the story of its code-breakers and machines; there's also a model railway, 1940s cinema and computer museum.
**Bletchley Park National Codes Centre** *Bletchley Park, Milton Keynes, Buckinghamshire MK3 6EB (01908 640404/www.bletchleypark.org.uk).*

# 378
## Invest in a large-scale sculpture

In a bid to safeguard the future of British sculpture, the Cass Sculpture Foundation commissions large works from home-grown talents, which are then put on display amid the ancient woodland of the Goodwood Estate. Anyone's welcome to visit, though serious collectors should take their chequebooks: all 70 sculptures on display at any one time in this enormous, ever-evolving exhibition are for sale.
**Cass Sculpture Foundation** *Goodwood, near Chichester, West Sussex PO18 0QP (01243 538449/www.sculpture.org.uk).*

Cowshed, Babington House

# 379-388
## Be pampered

### Barnsley House, Gloucestershire
This exclusive and beautifully appointed hotel has a spa to match, where traditional Cotswold stone is juxtaposed with sleek glass and stylish fixtures and fittings to stunning effect. Facilities include a hydrotherapy pool and six treatment rooms. A day spa package is available for £89, which includes a treatment and a two-course lunch, but you can also just pop in for a facial.
**Barnsley House** *Barnsley, Gloucestershire GL7 5EE (01285 740000/www.barnsleyhouse.com).*

### Bliss Day Spa, London
Treatments at Bliss are consistently good: efficient, long-lasting and featuring its excellent own-brand products. While there are longer, more relaxing body treatments to be had, Bliss is best for double-quick pedicures and manicures. Sit in line in your lunch break, put on headphones and settle back to watch telly.
**Bliss London** *60 Sloane Avenue, London SW3 3DD (020 7590 6146/www.blisslondon.co.uk).*

### Cowley Manor, Gloucestershire
Cowley Manor is a delectable blend of modern innovation in a period setting. Its spa illustrates the contrast perfectly, with its indoor and outdoor pools, steam room and sauna, and aromatherapy-inspired treatments. The signature treatment is a swoon-inducing mixture of acupressure, aromatherapy and reflexology. Spa facilities are reserved for overnight guests over the (busy) weekend, but day-trippers are welcome in the week.
**Cowley Manor** *Cowley, near Cheltenham, Gloucestershire GL53 9NL (01242 870902/www.cowleymanor.com).*

### Cowshed, Babington House, Somerset
A private member's club and hotel, Babington naturally has its own spa (for overnight guests only). Housed in what was once the Georgian pile's cowshed, these days you'll find indoor and outdoor pools, steam, sauna and aroma rooms and nine lakeside treatment cabins, where lashings of the luscious in-house product range are administered.
**Babington House** *Babington, near Frome, Somerset BA11 3RW (01373 812266/www.babingtonhouse.co.uk).*

## One Spa, Edinburgh

You don't have to be a guest to visit One in Edinburgh's Sheraton Grand hotel. An ESPA spa (both in the products used, and the company that designed it), its marine algae and Oshadi clay body wraps are blissful; the pool complex and thermal suite are the real draws though. Cleopatra baths (minus the ass's milk), an infinity hydropool and 62-foot ozone swimming pool are complemented by the Celtic- and Roman-inspired laconium, tepidarium and aroma grotto.
**One Spa** *8 Conference Square, Edinburgh EH3 8AN (0131 221 7777/www.onespa.com).*

## Pennyhill Park, Surrey

Size is everything at this swish hotel spa, which extends over 45,000 square feet. There are eight pools, the largest of which, the 'ballroom pool', even has piped music underwater. 'Thermal heaven' doesn't stint either; its 11 rooms include a tepidarium and an ice cave (to boost your circulation). In the 21 treatment rooms, expect lengthy and blissful rituals to complete the cosseting. You can also sleep over if a day trip seems too energetic.
**Spa at Pennyhill Park** *London Road, Bagshot, Surrey GU19 5EU (01276 486100/www.thespa.uk.com).*

## Serenity Spa, Seaham Hall, County Durham

Seaham Hall is just 20 minutes from the bustle of Newcastle, although you'd never know it at the hotel's adjoining spa. Open to non-guests, it's an oasis of oriental calm and quietude. In addition to the 45-strong treatment menu is a limestone hammam and Canadian redwood sauna and, to cool off, an ozone-cleansed pool that boasts secluded woodland views.
**Serenity Spa** *Lord Byron's Walk, Seaham, County Durham SR7 7AG (0191 516 1400/www.seaham-serenityspa.com).*

## Sequoia, The Grove, Hertfordshire

Another faultless ESPA spa within a hotel, many of the luxurious treatments here are inspired by the ancient Indian principles of Ayurveda. Day visitors must book treatments for a minimum of two hours; arrive early if you want to take advantage of the various heat and relaxation facilities, which include a large pool, a crystal steam room and a jacuzzi.
**Sequoia** *The Grove, Chandler's Cross, Hertfordshire WD3 4TG (01923 807807/www.thegrove.co.uk).*

## The Spa, Chewton Glen, Hampshire

The famously plush spa at Chewton Glen has no shortage of facilities, including an ozone pool, hydrotherapy pool and ten treatment rooms. High-tech Linda Meredith treatments using collagen and oxygen feature on the skincare menu, while the body is buffed and polished with Molton Brown products. A wide array of 'spa day' packages are available, including an evening of pampering for those forced to work a nine to five. If you've got more time, check in to the hotel for the night.
**Chewton Glen** *New Milton, Hampshire BH25 6QS (01425 275341/www.chewtonglen.com).*

## The Spa, Mandarin Oriental, London

It's hardly a cheap option (rituals of 120mins start at £250), but the level of soothing luxury at the Mandarin Oriental's spa justifies the expense. Day guests must book ahead; staff recommend arriving 45 minutes before your treatment to make use of the heavenly heat and water features, including an amethyst crystal steam room and Zen colour therapy area.
**Mandarin Oriental** *66 Knightsbridge, London SW1X 7LA (020 7838 9888/www.mandarinoriental.com/london).*

*Chesterfield church*  *No. 389*

## 389 Climb the crooked spire at Chesterfield

It's hard to miss the curiously contorted 230-foot spire of St Mary & All Saints. The tallest in Derbyshire, it leans out over nine feet from its centre. Some say a local blacksmith agreed to shoe the devil, but drove a nail into his foot by mistake; as Lucifer leapt away, he kicked the spire and bent it out of shape. Others reckon the devil stopped to rest on the church, and gave an almighty sneeze as the incense from mass tickled his nose; wrapping his tail around the spire to keep his balance, he twisted it round. The third legend has it that a virgin was getting married here, and the astounded spire leaned over to gawp. In truth, the twist was caused by the weight of the lead tiles on the unseasoned timber – and a shortage of expert craftsmen in the wake of the Black Death. Ring the verger to arrange a tour up to the spire's base (though not on Sundays); a small charge applies.
**St Mary & All Saints** *28 Cromwell Road, Chesterfield, Derbyshire S40 4TH (01246 206506/www.chesterfieldparishchurch.org.uk).*

## 390 Explore Scotland's poetic heritage

Housed in an award-winning modern building in Edinburgh's Old Town, the Scottish Poetry Library welcomes casual browsers. All the big names of Scottish verse are here (Robert Burns, George Mackay Brown, Hugh MacDiarmid, and more) along with lower-profile poets who also deserve your attention (Meg Bateman, for instance). For talks, readings and performances, drop by on National Poetry Day – 4 October.
**Scottish Poetry Library** *Crichton's Close, Canongate, Edinburgh EH8 8DT (0131 557 2876/www.spl.org.uk).*

## 391 Walk in the treetops at Salcey

Take the giant step from the fast lane of the M1 in Northamptonshire into the peace and quiet of neighbouring Salcey Forest (www.forestry.gov.uk/salceyforest). There's more to this ancient woodland than rare flowers, birdsong and picnics: it isn't every former medieval hunting forest that offers a bird's-eye view of its canopy from a spectacular, winding treetop walk, 66 feet high at the uppermost lookout and 984 feet long. Take a detour to see the 1,600-year-old remains of the Salcey Oak – once England's greatest, with a circumference of over 49 feet.

## 392 Stroll the Whistling Sands

On the North Wales coast, near Aberdaron, Porthor (www.nationaltrust.org.uk) earned its nickname from the whistling sound the sand emits when it's walked on – and is one of only a handful of such beaches (your next nearest is the Singing Sands on Eigg in the Hebrides). Rather prosaically, it's all to do with the texture of the rounded grains. Kids won't quickly tire of the novelty; while they're tramping up and down making music, go for a paddle or get your wetsuit on – this is also a very pleasant crescent-shaped beach, nicely sheltered and backed by steep grassy cliffs, and popular with bodyboarders when the surf's up.

## 393 Get spooked at eerie Orford Ness

The River Ore may be all that separates the shingle spit of Orford Ness from the mainland, but for decades only the chosen few ventured across. Bought by the Ministry of Defence in 1913, the peninsula became a secret military test site, off limits to the public for most of the 20th century. Behind its barbed wire fences, researchers worked to develop radar and shot Allied aircraft to smithereens on its windswept firing ranges, testing their vulnerability; during the Cold War the focus shifted to atomic weapons, and security tightened even further.

Although Orford Ness became a National Trust nature reserve in 1995, the past still dominates the site. Instead of being demolished, its hangars and firing ranges have been left to slide into dereliction, slowly corroding in the sea air. Facilities are spartan – toilets and a cold water tap – and scouring winds sweep in across the North Sea. 'From the start, our take on it was that a visit to Orford Ness should be a safe one – but not necessarily a comfortable one,' says site manager Grant Lohoar.

What the site does offer is solitude. The ferry from Orford only takes 12 visitors across at a time, and you can walk around without seeing another soul. Bleak as it is, the landscape has a stark beauty. Yellow-flowered gorse creeps across the swathes of shingle; inland, flocks of lapwings rise from still, silent lagoons and herons stalk the mudflats. Jagged-edged, rusting pieces of machinery and concrete pipes litter the landscape like abandoned art installations.

It's not everyone's cup of tea – and unsuspecting tourists, more accustomed to Suffolk's sweet seaside resorts, are sometimes taken aback, Lohoar admits. ('You can see them getting off the boat thinking "What the bloody hell have we come to here?"') Treacherous estuarine mud, military detritus and overgrown, open pits mean visitors must keep to set trails – not to mention the possibility that the odd cache of unexploded ordinance still remains. But the landscape is also fragile; a single footprint in the coastal shingle, slowly deposited over the centuries, could cause irreversible damage.

There's a guarded, watchful quality about the site – presided over by the pagoda-like silhouettes of labs 4 and 5, where testing on atomic bombs was once carried out. Special tours (invariably sold out months in advance) take you round. Inside, as damp seeps through the buckling, stained concrete and dank pools gather in the pits where bombs were once tested, they are eerily atmospheric.

What really brings the history home is the lone exhibit in the former control room: a squat, gleaming WE177. A decommissioned nuclear bomb, it had ten to 20 times the potency of the bomb that obliterated Hiroshima. Walking out into the gathering dusk, the bleak landscape and empty skies seem imbued with new meaning. 'Frankly, the site's history was about killing people,' says Lohoar. 'We're not passing judgement on whether it was a good, bad or indifferent thing – we're just presenting the facts.'
**Orford Ness National Nature Reserve** *Orford Quay, Orford, Woodbridge, Suffolk IP12 2NU (01394 450900/www.nationaltrust.org.uk). Opening times are limited Oct-June.*

# 394
## Become a Mass Observation observer

Achieve Pepys-like immortality while helping future generations understand our times by becoming part of the Mass Observation project, set up in 1937. It collects jottings on everyday life and current events from 'normal' people – diaries, poems, sketches, photographs, news cuttings and assorted scribblings – and then releases them 50 years later to social historians, interested in both the kind of socks you got for Christmas and the machinations of political machinery. The archive is generally heavily oversubscribed with volunteers, but is currently after the musings of men aged between 16 and 44; apply online at www.massobs.org.uk.

# 395
## Hear conceptual-meets-classical music in Huddersfield

Any festival that has featured a piece of music called *Ha, Ha! Your Mushrooms Have Gone* ('an installation featuring bio-electric sounds, generated by live locally grown mushrooms') has got to be worth a visit. That was just one of dozens of out-there musical compositions performed in 2007 during the 30th anniversary year of the Huddersfield Contemporary Music Festival (01484 425082, www.hcmf.co.uk).

Held at the end of November, it's challenging stuff: you might encounter anything from a concerto for dustbins to a vegetable orchestra, or a conductor wired up to cables and laptops, doing an odd interpretive dance. But it's not all about headline-grabbing gimmicks. Performers in years gone by have included contemporary classical music scene stars such as Karlheinz Stockhausen, Terry Riley, Brian Eno and John Cage – whose most famous piece, *4'33"*, consists of a pianist refraining from hitting any keys for four minutes and 33 seconds.

# 396-399
## See pigs fly at a kite festival

Pretty much every weekend from March to September, you'll find a kite festival or flying demonstration taking place somewhere around Britain – including several large-scale annual spectaculars. To see stunt kites in action, head for Wirral Kite Festival in early June. Held at the Dips in New Brighton, a naturally windy spot, it attracts experts from all over the world: if you fancy having a go, kite-making workshops cost £1. Next up, in July, is Sunderland's Kite Festival – part of the International Friendship Festival. There are wind sculptures, aerobatic kite displays and a kite exhibition, plus music, street theatre and kids' activities.

Unusually shaped kites always abound at Portsmouth's International Kite Festival, held in late August – from giant squids to mermaid-shaped high flyers. Bristol's International Kite Festival is also in August; expect flying killer whales, kite-fighting competitions and kite-making workshops. Contact the Kite Society (01206 271489, www.thekitesociety.org.uk) for details of these and other festivals across the country – then pack a picnic and watch the skies fill with colourful cloudbusters.

# 400
## Lay flowers at Byron's grave

After the dashing and dissolute poet died of rheumatic fever in 1824, supporting the Greek struggle for independence, his heart was buried under a tree in Messolonghi. His embalmed body, though, was brought back to England for burial in Westminster Cathedral. The Dean, however, was unimpressed by Byron's libertine lifestyle, and flatly refused. Instead, the poet's remains had to be interred in the family vault in the tiny Nottinghamshire church of St Mary Magdalene; look for the marble plaque, donated by the King of Greece. Only in 1969 did the ecclesiastical authorities finally relent, and agree to erect a memorial in Westminster's Poets' Corner.

**St Mary Magdalene Church** *Hucknall Torkard, Nottinghamshire NG15 7AS (www.hucknall-parish-church.org.uk).*

## 401 Promenade along Clevedon Pier

Opened in 1869, this elegant, iron-wrought pier in north Somerset is a Victorian gem – and the only Grade I-listed pier in Britain still standing (01275 878846, www.clevedonpier.com). While it partially succumbed to the wind and waves in 1970, it was saved from demolition by a decade of tireless campaigning (poet laureate Sir John Betjeman declared it 'the most beautiful pier in England' at a public enquiry to decide its fate), and was reopened in 1989. Stroll around the art gallery in the Toll House, take a paddle steamer trip, or simply admire the magnificent views over the Severn Estuary and its bridges.

## 402 Join the Big Garden Birdwatch

You don't need to be a budding Bill Oddie or even have a garden to take part in the world's biggest bird survey (and help the Royal Society for the Protection of Birds to monitor bird numbers in the UK). All you need are a pen and paper and a spare hour. You could do it in your lunch break in a city square: just write down the highest number of each species that you see at one time, then submit the results online. If you're not convinced you can tell a starling from a sparrow, there's a handy top 20 birds guide on the RSPB's website (01767 693690, www.rspb.co.uk).

## 403 See art in the dark

An environmental arts charity, the NVA (0141 332 9911, www.nva.org.uk) sets up large-scale art installations in some of Scotland's quieter corners, with the aim of putting often-neglected spots back on the map. The hugely ambitious projects take place outdoors, often at the dead of night, setting massive light and sound installations against some of Scotland's most awesome landscapes. *The Storr: Unfolding Landscape*, for example, invited attendees to climb the otherwordly rock formations at the Old Man of Storr on the Isle of Skye at midnight, while light displays flickered and shifted across the peaks, and experimental soundscapes drifted through the trees: weird, but undeniably wonderful. The events generally last from two to seven weeks and take place in the spring or summer; check the NVA's website for details of forthcoming projects and ticket information.

# 404
## Tuck in to a real Devonshire cream tea

The traditional county dish may be copied all over the world, but it's only authentic if made in Devon, from locally produced ingredients. The search for the perfect Devonshire cream tea must start with a firm resolution neither to count calories nor to measure cholesterol: clotted cream, which is central to the whole experience, is the richest of all creams, containing 55 per cent butterfat. Skip breakfast and lunch if you must, but, at four o'clock or thereabouts, find a teashop or a farmhouse where the word 'homemade' features prominently on the menu.

Devonshire cream teas are easiest to define by stating what they are not. The jam is not served in a tiny impenetrable plastic box, nor in a mini-jar; the cream is neither white nor foamy; the scones are not perfectly symmetrical, shiny-topped cylinders. The real thing involves a bowl of lumpy, home-made strawberry or raspberry jam, a deep dollop of yellow clotted cream, with skeins of bubbled, golden crust on it, and warm, irregularly shaped scones whisked from the oven and dusted with flour. Then there's the tea, which should be brewed in a china pot, poured into a china cup and served without sugar to counteract the scone's sweetness.

Try to avoid getting into a heated debate with a local about the order in which to add the filling of your horizontally split scone. Allegedly, the Cornish favour butter, then jam and the cream on top. In Devon it's usually lashings of cream first, followed by jam. A lifetime's research will help you decide which method suits you best: to butter or not to butter is indeed the question.

Of course, you may be offered cheese scones or scones with fruit in them, but the purists insist on two plain scones for a cream tea. Any mention of cider cake or whortleberry pie, however, and you've truly arrived – be sure to order these local delicacies, even if you feel you couldn't possibly manage to fit them in.

# 405
## See snowdrops bloom at Chelsea Physic Garden

Chelsea Physic Garden is England's second oldest botanic garden, founded by the Society of Apothecaries in 1673 to study botany and the 'physic' (healing) arts. If you visit during the annual Winter Openings (the gardens are otherwise closed from November until mid March), don't miss the famed and fairytale-like snowdrop collection. Incredibly, there are around 75 varieties of these delicate-looking but hardy little blooms; from the 'common' garden species to variants with green-tipped petals and double-headed flowers.
**Chelsea Physic Garden** *66 Royal Hospital Road, London SW3 4HS (020 7352 5646/www.chelsea physicgarden.co.uk).*

# 406 Ride the Railway Children's line

The five-mile Keighley & Worth Valley Railway (01535 645214, www.kwvr.co.uk) opened in 1867 to serve West Yorkshire's textile industry, and ran for almost 100 years before British Rail closed it down. Trainspotters and locals united to save it, however, and it reopened for passenger traffic in 1968. Most services are operated by steam trains, although there is also a diesel fleet. As well as running through some of Britain's most stunning countryside, the line visits Haworth, home of Charlotte, Emily and Anne Brontë, and is recognisable from numerous films and television series. Most famously, the station at Oakworth was the setting for the 1970s adaptation of *The Railway Children*; cream teas are now served in the Old Gentleman's saloon car. Hop on board all year round at any one of six stations from Oxenhope to Keighley, where the line connects with the national rail network.

# 407 Gather round Magdalen Tower on May Day

At 6am each May Day, while the rest of the country sweetly slumbers, the good people of Oxford – and a crowd of bleary-eyed, dishevelled students, somewhat the worse for wear after the college balls the night before – gather round Magdalen Tower (www.visit oxford.org). As the sun rises, choirboys sing madrigals from the top of the tower to the silent crowds below. It's an ethereally beautiful moment – though the celebration of spring soon turns into a spot of May Day misbehaviour, as undergraduates in carnival costumes and tuxedos spill out of pubs to defy the barriers and hurl themselves into the river from Magdalen Bridge. Student shenanigans aside, head for the High Street and city centre, where the pubs are open for a hearty breakfast and traditional Morris dancers surround the maypole in Radcliffe Square; look out for the costumed 'tree', lecherously seeking its merry maiden – a take on ancient pagan fertility rituals.

# 408 Have a deco at the De La Warr Pavilion

Recently the subject of a cool £8 million 70th-birthday refurb, the De La Warr Pavilion is an art deco icon. The light! The lines! The superb twisty staircase! It now houses a small but splendid permanent collection of classic design drawings, twin gallery spaces and a theatre. While the rather shabby retirement mecca of Bexhill offers few supporting attractions, the prom and beach are timeless pleasures, and the view from the first-floor bar's sleek balcony is heavenly of an evening.
**De La Warr Pavilion** *Marina, Bexhill-on-Sea, East Sussex TN40 1DP (01424 229111/ www.dlwp.co.uk).*

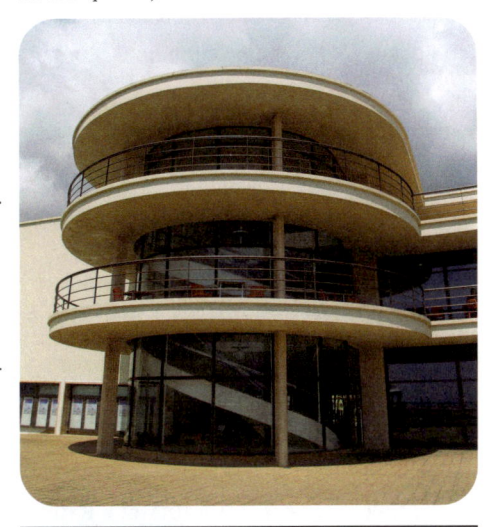

# 409 Make the St Helier's Day Pilgrimage

Each year, on the Sunday closest to St Helier's Day (16 July), a procession of robed officials, pilgrims and curious tourists meet at the parish church in St Helier, Jersey. They then cross the causeway to the rocky islet where the town's namesake lived from AD545, preaching to the islanders and mortifying his flesh by standing in pools of cold water – until an axe-wielding pirate chief took exception to his sermons and killed him. A wreath is laid in the saint's honour and an open-air service is held on the green.

# 410-414
## Choose your team at an alternative 'local derby'

Fiercely fought Derby matches are traditionally associated with football: Celtic v Rangers, say, or Liverpool v Everton. But they exist in other sports too – and though the crowds watching may be smaller in number, the passion aroused is no less intense. Here's a selection of the best.

**Cricket: Yorkshire v Lancashire**
Gone are the days when the 'Roses Match' would be watched by crowds of 25,000 and more, but the summer game's traditional rivalry still exists on both sides of the Pennines.
*www.lccc.co.uk; www.yorkshireccc.com.*

**Ice hockey: Billingham Bombers v Whitley Warriors**
Though these North-eastern clubs play in the comparatively modest English National League (North), the sense of competition between their well-padded players wielding large sticks has simmered nicely over the last three decades.
*www.billinghambombers.co.uk.*

**Rugby League: Hull FC v Hull KR**
One town, two clubs, with a rivalry that at times has turned from fierce to embittered. When Super League was created, it was suggested that the two should merge to form a new club, called 'Humberside'. The response from both quarters was, inevitably, unprintable.
*www.hullfc.com; www.hullkr.co.uk.*

**Rugby Union: Gloucester v Bristol v Bath**
The West Country is a stronghold of the 15-man game, and the rivalry between these three clubs dates back a century and more. The Shed at Gloucester's Kingsholm ground is the place to be, as its low tin roof amplifies the fans' roaring.
*www.gloucesterrugbyclub.com; www.bristolrugby.co.uk; www.bathrugby.com.*

**Volleyball: London Docklands v London Malory**
These two have been at the top of UK men's volleyball for a number of years. The crowds may be small, but the on-court action is always ultra-competitive.
*www.londondocklandsvc.com; www.hntc.co.uk/malory.*

# 415
## Hear world-class performers – in a church hall

East Neuk is a coastal region of Fife that, until quite recently, you might have been forgiven for not having heard of. But since 2005, the multi-genre East Neuk Festival (01334 475000, www.eastneukfestival.com) has done a remarkably good job of putting this rural Scottish fishing region on the cultural map – so much so that it won a prestigious Royal Philharmonic Society Award in 2007.

In the absence of any purpose-built venues, the festival makes creative use of various spaces around the region, including windswept churches, village halls and even hotel foyers. These secret venues make a refreshingly novel and intimate setting for classical music performances from the likes of the Scottish Chamber Orchestra, Alban Berg Quartet and many distinguished soloists.

# 416
## Walk Hadrian's Wall

It took Emperor Hadrian six years to build his wall from coast to coast, starting in AD 122, handily separating the Roman Empire from the barbarians for 250 years. Stretching from Ravenglass in the north-west to South Shields in the north-east, it's 85 miles long. Tackling the entire trail should take around seven days in total (www.nationaltrail.co.uk/hadrianswall); if you're not feeling up to the full monty, head for the wild and windswept outposts of the Northumberland National Park, where the stretches of wall are most dramatic.

Chesters is the single best-preserved Roman cavalry fort (and steam rooms), while Housesteads and Walltown boast settlements and top-class museums; the ancient fort town of Vindolanda has all this, plus full-scale repro Roman buildings.
**Vindolanda & the Roman Army Museum**
*Chesterholm Museum, Bardon Mill, Hexham, Northumberland NE47 7JN (01434 344277/ www.vindolanda.com).*

# 417 Crawl into a Neolithic burial chamber

From a distance it looks like nothing more than a bump on the hillside, but this fenced-off grassy mound in Somerset is Stoney Littleton Long Barrow (www.english-heritage.org.uk). Built around 5,000 years ago, it's one of the country's finest Neolithic tombs. Kids love exploring the multiple burial chambers – lure them out by offering a prize for the first to find the ammonite fossil on the tomb's exterior. For adults who don't mind the damp and cramped conditions, it's a wonderfully atmospheric relic of England's ancient past. It's located one mile south of Wellow off the A367; bring a torch.

# 418 See Lichfield's spires

Lichfield Cathedral is the only medieval church in the country with three spires – to admire their majesty at closer quarters, book a place on one of the roof tours. Built from striking red sandstone, the cathedral also contains some exceptional Georgian sculpture by Sir Francis Chantrey and fine 16th-century Flemish glass, along with the extraordinary Lichfield Angel – an early eighth-century Anglo-Saxon carving, unearthed during excavation work in 2003.
**Lichfield Cathedral** *19A The Close, Lichfield, Staffordshire WS13 7LD (01543 306100/ www.lichfield-cathedral.org).*

# 419 Go on safari in Kent

Forget Kenya: a safari experience can be yours for a fraction of the price in Kent, at the Port Lympne Wild Animal Park. Home to some 650 animals, including the largest breeding herd of black rhino outside Africa, the park's latest offering is an overnight safari package. After dinner around the communal campfire and a surprisingly cosy night under canvas (in commodious tents with with proper beds), you get to accompany the rangers on a magical dawn safari, getting up close and personal with the park's free-range zebra, giraffe, antelope and wildebeest.
**Port Lympne Wild Animal Park** *Lympne, near Hythe, Kent CT21 4PD (01303 264647/ www.totallywild.net).*

# 420

### Walk among the men at Crosby Beach

There's something eerily otherworldly about Antony Gormley's aptly titled art installation, Another Place, on Crosby Beach, Merseyside (www.sefton.gov.uk). Dotted along the shore, 100 life-sized cast-iron figures stand looking out to sea; some on the beach, others half-submerged by the slate-grey water, slowly corroding in the salty air and encrusted with barnacles. There's a tangible sense of loneliness and loss as each figure stands in isolation, scanning the empty horizon – though what they're waiting for is anyone's guess.

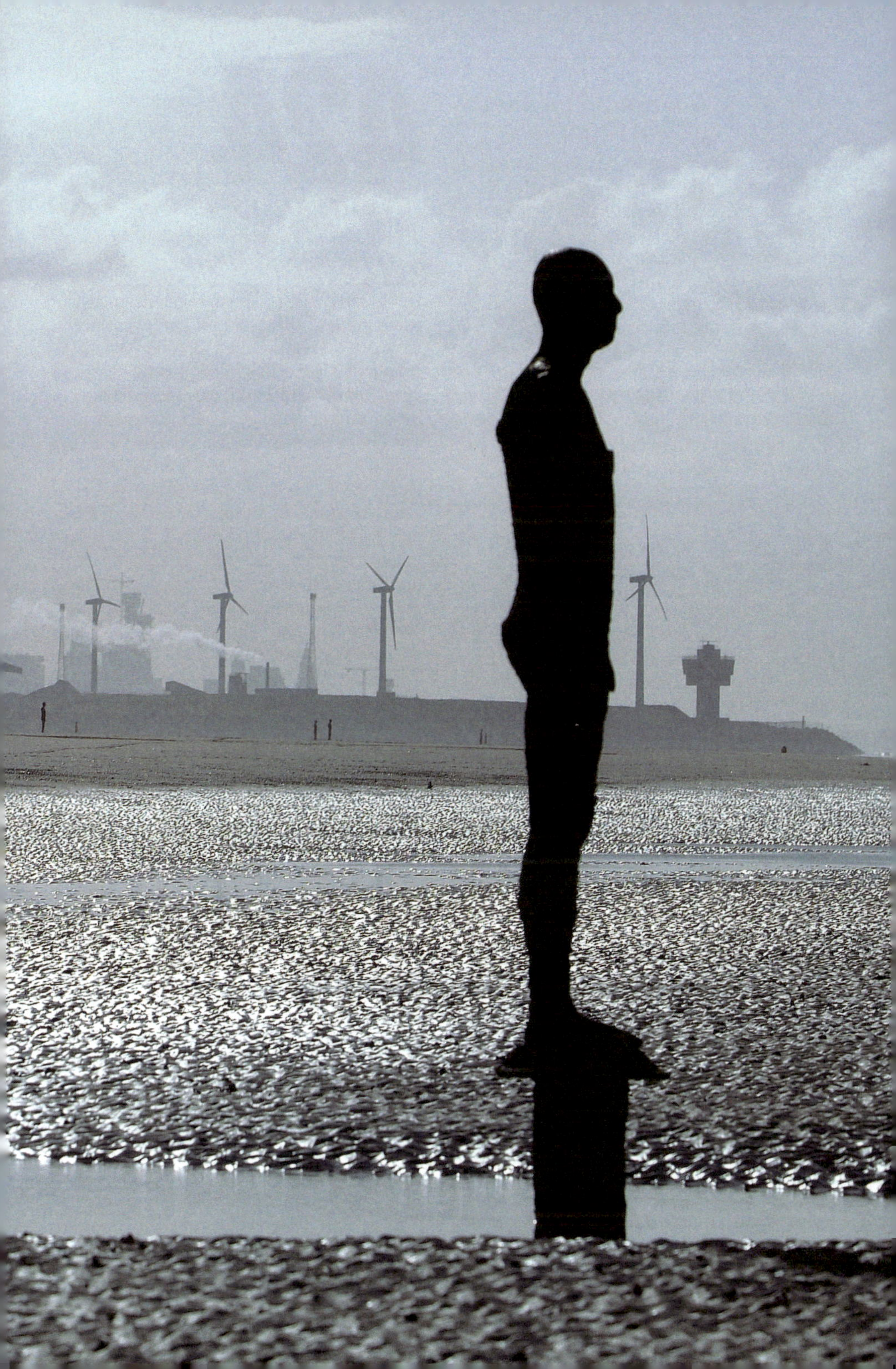

## 421 Go inside a mountain at Ben Cruachan

Soaring to a fairly hefty 3,695 feet above Loch Awe, on a clear day Ben Cruachan affords impressive views of the Highlands and islands. Lots of climbers regard it as a favourite, but it has one feature that truly distinguishes it from its peers: you can go inside. The mountain is home to an underground hydro-electric power station with a massive central turbine hall, built between 1959 and 1965. It's pure James-Bond-villain-lair fantasy on a grand scale – with added visitor centre and café. Arrive by bicycle or public transport and you'll get in for free.
**Cruachan Visitor Centre** *Dalmally, Argyll PA33 1AN (01866 822618/www.visitcruachan.co.uk).*

## 422 Take a tour of the Bodleian Library

The Bodleian holds about eight million items, including a Gutenberg Bible and Shakespeare first folio. While you can't get your paws on these leather-bound beauties, a library tour does take you through the wonderfully atmospheric 14th-century Divinity School, the Convocation House, where parliament was held during the Civil War, and Duke Humfrey's Library, a delightful medieval edifice. Extended tours for pre-booked groups (01865 277224) also take in the fascinating underground workings of the library, and emerge into the Radcliffe Camera.
**Bodleian Library** *Broad Street, Oxford OX1 3BG (01865 277000/www.bodley.ox.ac.uk).*

## 423 Follow the Coleridge Way

Opened in 2005, this 36-mile footpath stretches through Somerset's glorious countryside, from Porlock in the west, via Exmoor, the Brendon and Quantock Hills to Coleridge's old stamping ground of Nether Stowey. A keen walker, the poet once made it to Porlock in a day, drinking in nature along the way – although you might want to take it a little easier. An excellent and detailed route-planner can be found online at www.quantockonline.co.uk.

## 424 Stroll the deer park at Knole

Knole's imposing Kentish ragstone house and surrounding 1,000-acre deer park was once the Sackville ancestral home. Virginia Woolf's great friend Vita Sackville-West grew up here, and wrote fondly, 'it has the tone of England; it melts into the tawnier green of the park, into the blue of the pale English sky.' Sadly, 70 per cent of Knole's ancient trees were felled by the storm of 1987, but many hornbeam, oak and ash trees still stand resplendent. One of the last medieval deer parks in England, perhaps Knole's greatest charm is that it has remained virtually unchanged since then; the Sackvilles resisted the 18th-century fashion for Capability Brown-style landscaping, believing the grazing deer, now a 600-strong herd of fallow and sika deer, to be quite picturesque enough.
**Knole** *Sevenoaks, Kent TN15 0RP (01732 462100/www.nationaltrust.org.uk).*

## 425 Kip in Cley's windmill

Is this tranquil 18th-century windmill-turned-guesthouse the perfect romantic hideaway? It has the requisite four-posters, an atmospheric circular sitting room with roaring fire, and spectacular sea views. If you're weekending with friends, it's like being on a *Famous Five* adventure, with odd-shaped rooms, crannies and ladders that lead to lookouts – but crucial grown-ups' stuff such as quality linen on comfortable beds isn't sacrificed. Go for gentle ambles on the shingle beach, birdwatch, wander around Cley village's charming flint-walled cottages and stock up on local goodies before heading back for sunset views over the salt marshes and a top-notch dinner. The mill has six bedrooms; there are three more in the courtyard cottages.
**Cley Windmill** *Cley-next-the-Sea, Holt, Norfolk NR25 7RP (01263 740209/www.cleymill.co.uk).*

# 426-432 *Drink in the sights*

Taking in London's monuments from ground level can get tiring. Happily, a number of loftier drinking spots offer city panoramas – so you can survey them with a restorative cocktail in hand.

## 5th View
The website's promise of a 'sweeping view… towards Big Ben' from the refurbished café topping Waterstone's art deco flagship shop is pure hyperbole. Instead, drink cocktails or a bottled beer while you take in a wonderfully eccentric, *Mary Poppins*-style vista of London roofs, plus the tip of the Eye and the august spires and towers of Westminster.
**Waterstone's** *203-206 Piccadilly, London W1J 9HA (020 7851 2468/ www.5thview.co.uk).*

## Galvin at Windows
Windows is at the top of the Park Lane Hilton: the restaurant has the prime views (west over Hyde Park), but the bar offers you the rooftops of the West End – and drink prices that are decidedly high end.
**London Hilton** *22 Park Lane, London W1K 1BE (020 7208 4021/www.galvinatwindows.com).*

## Skylon
Yes, the bar-brasserie is beautifully designed, but forget that and feel the height and breadth of those Thames-side windows. Choose low sofas right beside the glass and sip from the bellini list, or slouch with a classic cocktail in one of the comfier swivel chairs, with your back to the bar and eyes on the prized riverscape.
**Royal Festival Hall** *Belvedere Road, South Bank, London SE1 8XX (020 7654 7800/www.dandd london.com).*

## Tate Modern Restaurant
The bar of Tate the Younger's restaurant has fabulous seventh-floor views and a wine list that borrows superb bottles from the illustrious list at Tate Britain's Rex Whistler restaurant. Members get access to the sixth-floor Members' Room, with full bar and eagles' eyrie terrace looking straight over the Millennium Bridge.
**Tate Modern** *Bankside, London SE1 9TG (020 7887 8888/www.tate.org.uk).*

## Tenth Bar
Due to be unveiled after a refurb in spring 2008, we'll stake our reputation on the panoramic view east over Hyde Park.
**Royal Garden Hotel** *2-24 Kensington High Street, London W8 4PT (020 7937 8000/ www.royalgarden hotel.co.uk).*

## Trafalgar Roof Garden
Bang on the corner of Trafalgar Square is a superbly located little champagne bar, hidden away on the roof of the Hilton. It only opens to the public in summer and at Christmas, and is frequently closed for corporate entertaining, but cocktails in the ground-floor Rockwell Bar are recompense should upstairs be off-limits.
**Trafalgar** *2 Spring Gardens, London SW1A 2TS (020 7870 2900/www.thetrafalgar.com).*

## Vertigo 42
Vertigo 42, on the 42nd floor of London's tallest building, makes you work for your view with a check-in process akin to that of an airport – but it's a genuine London must-do nonetheless.
**Tower 42** *25 Old Broad Street, London EC2N 1HQ (020 7877 7842/www.vertigo42.co.uk).*

*Trafalgar Roof Garden*

# 433 Be enraptored in Gloucestershire

# A bird in the hand

**Ronnie Haydon** *boldly takes up the gauntlet at the National Birds of Prey Centre.*

'People think owls are wise. That's a load of rubbish,' says Kellie Piper, one of the bird staff at the National Birds of Prey Centre, as she introduces us to an African spotted eagle owl called Kaiser. The young owl looks on amiably from his vantage point on the railing. 'He's as thick as two short planks.'

Kaiser turns his magnificent amber eyes to us, then flutters down to scuttle after Kellie as she walks to the demonstration area. His blank look as he steadies himself with elegant, outstretched wings suggests he's used to this routine, perhaps even to the uncharitable remarks being made about his intelligence. Kellie is Mummy, after all. Like many of the centre's feathered residents, he was raised on her tough love.

'We dupe them into thinking we're their parents,' Kellie goes on, taking a bedraggled yellow object from the bag slung over her hip, while Kaiser makes a graceful swoop to her fist. She offers the bird the titbit – a portion of day-old chick – and warms to her theme. 'We start handling them when they're very young so that we can teach them to follow us like this. Kaiser here is a crepuscular species, meaning he hunts at dawn and dusk; that's why he has orange eyes.'

Many of the birds that live here are owls. After Kaiser we're shown Hurricane, a ten-month-old adolescent great grey owl hailing from Scandinavia. Then there are African Magellan owls, burrowing owls, Abyssinian eagle owls, African spotted owls and, of course, the more familiar barns and snowies. All of them reserve a rather outraged expression for visitors passing their aviaries; we're obviously keeping them up. Diurnal residents include falcons, kites, eagles, ospreys, vultures, a highly amusing secretary bird called Tiger, of whom more later, and a whole load of guinea pigs.

The National Birds of Prey Centre has been here in deepest Gloucestershire for 40 years. It's owned by Keith and Jackie Beaven, who took it over in 2004. They're joined by a number of experienced handlers, each of whom look after their own team of raptors, flying about ten to 15 per day. Then there are any number of volunteers who help care for approximately 180 birds, from more than 50 different species. New clutches of chicks and wild, injured rescuees frequently swell the numbers. The 80-odd aviaries on view are inhabited by birds that are part of a flying team, or are used for breeding. The only classified areas round here are the moulting aviaries (where residents go to let their feathers down for a while, which they like to do in private) and the hospital area, often inhabited by wild birds that have been brought in for treatment.

The focal point of the centre is the Hawk Walk, where, on little lawns among rose-clad pergolas, trained flying birds are tethered during their flying sessions. Apart from letting out the occasional shriek when their gimlet eyes light on their handler, they're unnervingly still. When it's their turn to put on a show, a staff member dons a gauntlet and carries the star to the demonstration area, keeping a hold on the jesses (leather straps) attached to the bird's leg. Less excitable birds on the flying team, such as the owls and vultures, are simply let out of their pens when on duty.

Another barn-like building serves as a pet corner – a nod to the fact that some younger visitors might not be so enraptured by raptors as others. In here, children can hunker down with free-running guinea pigs and rabbits, and admire caged fancy mice and rats, chinchillas and chipmunks.

There's also a play area, a beautiful woodland walk that meanders around the centre's substantial acreage and numerous places to picnic.

Demonstrations take place daily, each one starring a different team of birds. A snowy owl, for example, prefers the 3pm winter gig, but his transatlantic burrowing cousin would rather perform in the spring and summer sessions.

The drama of the high-speed plummet on to prey is provided by the more athletic types, such as six-year-old Oman, a saker falcon. She positions herself in the trees around the flying grounds before taking off, turning on the wing and coming hell for leather at the chick Keith Beaven pulls from his bag. The speed and grace are astonishing but, we're told, birds of prey never fly for pleasure – only for food. A 'fed-up' bird will take itself off to a comfy roost and ignore its handlers, so part of the skill of falconry is keeping the bird at a keen weight, so that it's peckish enough to perform for us humans.

One of the most entertaining members of the team is 21-year-old secretary bird Tiger. He was brought here to breed with a female secretary 18 years ago, but sadly has not lived up to his name in the nest department – no pitter patter of little talons yet. Standing three feet high, he has the spindly legs of a heron, an orange face, a blue head crowned with sticky-up feathers that look like quills and a whole lot of attitude. He minces out of his pen after Kellie, one extravagantly lashed eye on the chick bag. He can fly, but chooses to walk around the grassland looking for food. His performance piece involves a dummy snake called Cedric. In the wild, secretary birds stamp snakes to death and Tiger can be called upon to do just that if there's a chick corpse in the offing. He's had Cedric's head off on many an occasion.

The centre's brief is sustained captive breeding, as well as education and training in falconry. Raptor chicks raised here either go on to be demonstration fliers, replacing retired ones, or are offered to a global network of zoos and parks. This is usually done on a bartering system – so no money changes hands.

Visitors keen to take up the gauntlet and learn to fly a raptor can book up for a falconry experience day. You're taught how to tie a falconer's knot, pick up the birds and – very excitingly – fly them to your fist. One of the most amiable feathered teachers in this art is saker falcon Gunther, who (along with his witty handler Marcus) soon puts rookie falconers at their ease. 'Gunther's named after the barman of dubious sexuality in *Friends*,' says Marcus. 'He has a lovely personality, and is completely bombproof. He's small, and only weighs just under one pound, but can tackle hares much bigger than himself.'

The reason eight-year-old Gunther is such an Experience Day stalwart is that he has an unusually soft spot for humankind. He'd been through five or six handlers before settling here and originally came for a short stay while his owner was away, but ended up being left at the centre indefinitely, during which time Marcus flew him every day and the pair bonded. When you hold him, you're struck by how light he feels, and flattered by his kindly interest in you. You can stroke his beautiful feathers, and he appears to enjoy the attention. And any aspersions cast on his sexuality should be quelled this season, when Gunther is due to be lined up with a ready and willing female partner to provide a couple more little Gunthers to continue his good work.

After the thrills of working both out in the fields and on site with the lure, and the extraordinarily uplifting feeling of having such powerful hunting birds coming to rest meekly on your fist, it's time for the centre staff to release the big guns. Experience Day customers are given the chance to hold the largest bird on demo duty at the time. This may be Ona or Nico, the splendid, fish-eating bald eagles.

Our visit coincided with young Serengeti, the beautiful bateleur eagle, being out and about. She's quite heavy, but still and quiet, her intelligent eyes scanning the middle distance for movement among the shrubs. In the wild, she'd be after snakes, small mammals and birds. Here she might take out a pigeon. Being only young, her feathers are delicately dappled, but will eventually turn black; her talons, clasping firmly to the gauntlet, are relatively short, but her scaly legs are long. When she opens her wings for balance, the span is impressive. When she's fully grown, they'll spread out six or seven feet (as a female, she grows larger than the male). Holding this

> '*Young Serengeti is a beautiful bateleur eagle, her intelligent eyes scanning the middle distance for movement among the shrubs.*'

creature may allow you briefly to connect with her, but the aloofness in that untamed eye precludes any petting or stroking – and in any case, we didn't like the look of that hooked, flesh-ripping beak.

**National Birds of Prey Centre** *Newent, Gloucestershire GL18 1JJ (0870 990 1992/ www.nbpc.co.uk). 1-, 3- and 5-day falconry courses cost from £125 to £450.*

## A few of my favourite things

# 434-451

## *Katharine Hamnett, fashion designer*

The loony seaside towns of Littlestone-on-Sea and Greatstone-on-Sea, near New Romney in Kent, have a melancholy Juergen Teller-like feel. We used to be driven down in one of our next-door neighbour's 1928 Rolls-Royces (he used to collect them, sometimes in bits). We would have barbecues on the beach wearing Maidstone market fur coats and Wellingtons – the only suitable clothes for the English seaside. **We had some mad picnics in Bedgebury Pinetum (Goudhurst, Cranbrook, Kent TN17 2SL, 01580 879820, www.bedgebury pinetum.org.uk), one of the largest collections of conifers in the UK.**
The Three Chimneys (Hareplain Road, Biddenden, Kent TN27 8LW, 01580 291472) is a tiny old pub with incredibly low ceilings. It's set on a crossroads that once marked the boundary of parole for the French Napoleonic prisoners of war from nearby Sissinghurst Castle.
**The Pitt Rivers Museum (South Parks Road, Oxford OX1 3PP, 01865 270927, www.prm.ox.ac.uk) is perfect, with its exhibitions of everything from Palaeolithic canoes to shrunken heads.**
I don't need to shop any more as I have my own online store, but I used to shop in vintage shops, Oxfam (www.oxfam.org.uk) and charity shops everywhere. Other favourites include Alexander McQueen (4-5 Old Bond Street, London W1S 4PD, 020 7355 0088, www.alexandermcqueen.com); Harvey Nichols (109-125 Knightsbridge, London SW1X 7RJ, 020 7235 5000, www.harveynichols.com); Liberty (Regent Street, London W1B 5AH, 020 7734 1234, www.liberty.co.uk); Diverse (294 Upper Street, London N1 2TU, 020 7359 8877, www.diverseclothing.com); Virginia (98 Portland Road, London W11 4LQ, 020 7727 9908); Hammersmith Town Hall vintage sales (Hammersmith Town Hall, King Street, W6 9JU, 020 8543 5075, www.pa-antiques.co.uk); and Portobello Road Market in Notting Hill, on a Friday (dealers' day).
**The Slimbridge Wetland Centre (Slimbridge, Gloucestershire GL2 7BT, 01453 891900, www.wwt.org.uk) is a great treat with its amazing diversity of water fowl.**
I love my old assistant Lionel Copley's beautiful, medieval, dog-friendly B&B, Swan House (1 Hill Street, Hastings, TN34 3HU, 01424 430014, www.swanhousehastings.co.uk), with its huge open fires.
**Knole Park (Sevenoaks, Kent TN15 0RP, 01732 450608, www.nationaltrust.org.uk) is an amazing, untouched Elizabethan palace that transports you back in time.**
Sir John Soane's Museum (13 Lincoln's Inn Fields, London WC2A 3BP, 020 7405 2107, www.soane.org) is an immaculately preserved house; I especially like the Piranesian basement and the secret panels in the print room.
**Camber Sands in East Sussex (www.east sussex.gov.uk) is a place that I return to time and time again. It's the nearest decent beach with sand dunes to London.**
I love spending time with my friends at Papageno restaurant and bar (29-31 Wellington Street, London WC2E 7DB, 020 7836 4444, www.papagenorestaurant.com). It has lunatic, hallucinogenically spectacular Ottoman/porno decor and fabulous service.

# 452 *Go on a Rebustour*

In Ian Rankin's detective fiction, Edinburgh is as much of a character as the celebrated Inspector Rebus himself. Rebustours (0131 553 7473, www.rebustours.com) now offers themed tours around relevant parts of the city centre. Walks feature readings from the novels, and often start and finish in favoured pubs like the Oxford Bar or the Royal Oak. Places fill up fast during the Edinburgh International Festival and Fringe in August, so book ahead.

# 453 Admire eerie carvings at Royston Cave

There's speculation that after their suppression, fugitive Knights Templar (a powerful Christian military order in the Middle Ages) used this man-made cave at Royston for their devotions or – more prosaically – for storage. The cave itself is swathed in mystery: believed to date from the 13th century, it's shaped like a beehive with a hole in the top for ventilation. Wall carvings show the crucifixion, the holy family and several saints, all revered by the Templars.
**Royston Cave** *Melbourn Street, Royston, Hertfordshire SG8 7BZ (01763 245484/ www.roystoncave.co.uk).*

# 454 Walk through the memorial gardens at Beth Shalom

In 1995, a non-denominational Christian conference centre in Nottingham became the UK's first Holocaust memorial centre. Set in landscaped memorial gardens on the edge of Sherwood Forest, Beth Shalom is a place of peace, memory and learning – the museum's aim is to help visitors learn *from* the horrific events of World War II, as well as about them.
**Holocaust Centre** *Beth Shalom, Laxton, Newark, Nottinghamshire NG22 0PA (01623 836627/ www.holocaustcentre.net).*

# 455 Go orienteering

Likened to tackling the *Times* crossword while undertaking a cross-country run, orienteering is the art of navigating a course in the shortest possible time, using a map and compass. If that sounds slightly onerous, don't be deterred – it's an extremely sociable sport, and local clubs work hard to cater to a range of different skill levels, including beginners and children. A good way to sample the sport is to tackle one of the 200 permanent courses that have been set up around the country. The British Orienteering governing body's website (01629 734042, www.britishorienteering.org.uk) has a complete list, as well as details of clubs.

# 456 Cross Telford's most audacious aqueduct

Designed by Thomas Telford, this slender aqueduct took ten years to build. Opened in 1805, it soars 125 feet above the River Dee valley and is over 1,000 feet long – though a mere 11 feet wide. Crossing by narrowboat is, quite frankly, terrifying: there's no barrier along the outer edge, so all that lies between you and the sheer drop is a thin, 3.5-foot-high lip of cast iron; little wonder children have to stay below deck during crossings. Walking across offers the same vertiginous views, but thankfully there's a barrier along the towpath. Best wait until you're safely across before reading up on its history: apparently, the mortar holding the whole thing together was made from oxen blood, lime and water. For further information, visit www.waterscape.com.

## 457 See chainsaw-wielding artists in action

The highlight of Tatton Park's Country Show, held over the August Bank Holiday weekend, is the extraordinary English Open Chainsaw Carving Competition. Spectators gawp as 25 competitors turn unpromising lumps of wood into extravagant sculptures, using humble chainsaws. It's an international affair: last year's main event – the classic three-day carve, judged by the entrants – was won jointly by American Bob King and Germany's Andreas Martin.

Contestants (who require a certificate of competence, to deter casuals) are assigned wood by lottery, then speedily get to work. Their admiring public must stand 16 feet back – apparently the maximum distance that stray woodchips are likely to fly – so the noise is little more than a background drone.

The truly fearless favour the speed carve: a half-hour carving orgy, where competitors bang out small sculptures amid a flurry of flying pine and a deafening wall of chainsaw noise.
**Tatton Park Country Show** *Tatton Park, Knutsford, Cheshire WA16 6QN (01625 374400/ www.englishopenchainsawcompetition.co.uk).*

## 458 Have some chamber music with your lunch

Next time the weather spoils your plans to spend lunchtime with the pigeons in Trafalgar Square, consider popping across to St Martin in the Fields for a spot of chamber music. The recently restored 18th-century church hosts free lunchtime concerts on Mondays, Tuesdays and Fridays, giving talented young musicians the opportunity to perform to an audience. The events have been happening in various guises for more than 60 years, and have an impressive track record for spotting top performers before they hit the big time; Benjamin Britten, Peter Pears, Adrian Boult, Robert Tear and Myra Hess all made appearances in the early years. Doors open at 12.30pm for a 1pm start, and there's a modest suggested donation of £3.50.
**St Martin in the Fields** *Trafalgar Square, London WC2N 4JJ (020 7766 1100/www.st martin-in-the-fields.org).*

## 459 Surf the Severn Bore

Surfing in Britain has always been a far remove from sunny California: wintersuits and booties in place of board shorts and bikinis; a post-surf pasty and a pint where the pina colada should be. Nowhere is this more the case than when surfing the Severn Bore (www.severn-bore. co.uk), a slow, fat wave formed as the moon's tide funnels the Severn into an increasingly narrow channel (the river goes from being five miles wide in Avonmouth to less than a hundred yards in Minsterworth), reaching up to six feet during spring tides, and rolling unbroken for miles at a time.

Surfers soon cottoned on to the potential of this freak freshwater wave (the first to surf it was one Colonel Churchill, a former commando, in 1955), with bore-riding quickly going from a niche sport to a cultural phenomenon that draws hundreds of wave-riders and bemused spectators. Online forums buzz with rumours as to the length of various rides – although some dispute Steve King's claim to an hour-and-a-quarter-long, seven-mile surf in 2006.

While there's no shortage of dedicated enthusiasts, anyone can enjoy this quirky waterborne beano, says local surf writer Mike Fordham. 'A lot of it's just luck of the draw: you can be the best surfer in the world and still be in the wrong place when the wave breaks, while complete amateurs may find themselves perfectly positioned for the longest ride of their lives. It's more *Swallows and Amazons* than *Big Wednesday*: no one should be put off from just turning up and having a go.'

Hopefuls can pick up the wave at a series of spots between Minsterworth and Lower Parting in Gloucester, although bear in mind that the best places soon become crowded, and serious surfers won't appreciate having their ride cut up short by first-timers floundering in the white water. The wave is slow enough and usually small enough to demand a heavy longboard, with trick-oriented shortboards struggling to pick it up.

# 460-464
## Catch top tennis seeds in action

If you didn't enter the Wimbledon ballot and don't fancy a night sleeping on the street outside the All-England Club in the hope of nabbing one of the few tickets sold on the day, fear not. A far easier way to see world-class tennis is to attend one of the tournaments held in early June, used as a pre-Wimbledon warm-up by the sport's star players.

The grass court season gets under way in Surrey with the Surbiton Trophy (020 8399 1594, www.thesurbitontrophy.com). Attended by players who aren't competing at the French Open, or have lost out in the early rounds, it's a good place to spot stars of the future.

As Wimbledon draws nearer, the sexes split. Female players head to the DFS Classic at the Edgbaston Priory Club (0870 909 3015, www.dfsclassic.com) in Birmingham, and the Eastbourne International Open (01323 412000, http://eastbourne.lta.org.uk). Meanwhile, the chaps battle it out at the Artois Championships at London's Queen's Club (0871 231 0829, www.artoischampionships.com) or the Nottingham Open (0870 909 3015, http://nottingham.lta.org.uk). Queen's, in particular, is an excellent indicator of Wimbledon success; 25 of the last 27 All-England champions have played there.

# 465
## See Chagall's stained glass at All Saints...

Tudeley's small, 12th-century church gained international recognition in 1967, when Marc Chagall designed its east window. Sir Henry and Lady d'Avigdor-Goldsmid commissioned the window as a memorial to their daughter Sarah, killed in a sailing accident at the age of 21; Chagall went on to design the rest of the church's stained glass, notable for its glowing, jewel-like hues and wonderfully alive, flowing lines. The chancel windows were the last to be installed, in 1985 – the year Chagall died. Call ahead before visiting.

**All Saints Church** *Church Lane, Tudeley, Tonbridge, Kent TN11 0NS (01732 357648/www.tudeley.org).*

# 466
## ...then admire his window at Chichester

In 1978, Chagall also designed a glorious stained-glass window for Chichester Cathedral – a joyous explosion of colour that was inspired by Psalm 150: 'Let everything that hath breath praise the Lord'.

**Chichester Cathedral** *Chichester, West Sussex PO19 1PX (01243 782595/www.chichestercathedral.org.uk).*

# 467 *Climb Blackpool Tower*

Ever since Victorian times, when the cotton mill workers of Lancashire first started to descend on Blackpool on rare days off from the dark satanic production line, Blackpool has stood for fun and frolics. With the coming of the railways it quickly grew into the biggest and best holiday resort in England – and arguably remains exactly that to this day. Not content with three piers, a Golden Mile of beautiful, safe sands, a giddying range of theatres, and annual illuminations bordering on the psychedelic, Blackpool also, of course, has its Tower – the ultimate backdrop for all the glitz, thrills, sensation and spectacle.

The entrance to Blackpool Tower leads into the cavernous aquarium, where sub-aquatic light and weird music set the mood for retro thrills. The Tower opened in 1893, when parts of 'Dr Cocker's Aquarium & Menagerie', which originally stood on the site, were built into its foundations, then slowly surmounted with 2,586 tons of steel and cast iron in an audacious, 518-foot remodelling of the Eiffel Tower. Each tank has a backdrop of luminous plastic coral, and 75 species of fish swim dozily among the miniaturised ruins of Atlantis.

At the ballroom level, you'll find a beautifully vaulted selection of the building's five million bricks, inset with jade-coloured Burmantoft tiles with images of birds, animals and angels. The ballroom is a faux-baroque masterpiece, with two ornate gilt balconies and a trompe l'oeil third balcony, which bleeds into a ceiling painted with allegorical figures. 'Bid me discourse and I will enchant thine ear' is emblazoned over the stage, with its backdrop of an Edwardian Amalfi coastline. The Wurlitzer organist hammers at his keys, grinning over his shoulder into the warm, twinkling ballroom, where, when the venue isn't the set for *Strictly Come Dancing*, hundreds of elderly dancers swoon and spin in unison as the beats blend seamlessly from cha-cha-cha to *Van der Valk*.

There's yet another timewarp in the form of the new 3D Jurassic Walk attraction, plus the opportunity to walk in steamy swamps (a blast of warm compressed air) and through the ice ages (a cold gust), taking in animatronic mammoths and hydraulic sabretooth tigers. A plummy, old-style BBC talkover is almost enough to convince you it's educational.

On Sea View Terrace level, the Heritage Trail's collection of old photos traces the evolution of the Tower and its long-faded stars. Little Emmie danced and sang with the Children's Ballet between 1908 and 1936; Reginald Dixon was organist from 1930 to 1970. Trapezes once hung from the ballroom ceiling, and long before Jungle Jim's Towering Adventureland, the space adjoining the family bar and food court was Ye Olde Englishe Village in Edwardian times. Next it was Chinatown Oriental Village then, in 1970, it was replaced with the Apollo Playground, the Tower Ascent lift rigged up as a rocket blast-off.

On a clear day you can see forever from the top of the Tower – or the Isle of Man, at least. You can also stand on a thick pane of glass set in the floor (encouragingly named 'The Walk of Faith') and picture yourself plummeting down to the Prom, 380 feet below. It's awesome. Winds permitting – the top is closed if they reach over 40mph – you should also take the time to send a postcard while you're up here. It's the highest post box in the UK, and your missive will be franked 'from the top of Blackpool Tower'.

But before you get too carried away at such dizzy heights, make sure you peel yourself away in time to file downstairs for the big finale (check with the box office for times): the big-top circus, set in the baroque gilt vault between the Tower's legs. No animals have been involved since 1990, but Mooky the Clown carries on the red-nosed tradition of Charlie Cairoli, and there's a showband and a real sense of glamour and excitement. The international line-up includes a German strongwoman, a Mongolian contortionist, an Italian balancing act, a Chinese acrobatic troupe, a Hungarian troupe who walk on giant balls and – kaboom! – the heroic American human cannonball. And for anyone, but especially kids, champing at the bit to run away to the circus themselves, the Tower will provide you with a head start: it is now running what have proved to be very popular circus workshops.

And as you emerge into the daylight, thine ear, eye and funny bone enchanted, thou too will agree with the billboards: Blackpool Tower's Too Big To Miss.

**Blackpool Tower** *Promenade, Blackpool, Lancashire FY1 4BJ (01253 622242/ www.theblackpooltower.co.uk).*

BLACKPOOL TOWER
SUPERHUMAN CANNONBALL
SUPERHUMAN CANNONBALL

# 468-470
## Hit the road in a camper van

Based in the surf mecca of Devon, O'Connors Campers (01837 659599, www.oconnors campers.co.uk) specialises in renovating authentic VWs, fitting them with new engines and interiors while retaining their classic boho look. There are 12 available for hire, from the 1960s splitscreen to '70s bay window models. 'A VW represents freedom and escape,' says O'Connors' Sam Money. 'They're not very big, so you can get them into a beach car park, but they've got everything you need inside. You can come straight out of the water, lean your surfboard up against the front and have a cup of tea – and if the waves aren't big enough, you just hop in and drive up the coast.'

Up in Oxfordshire, VW Camper Company (01295 812266, www.vwcamperco.com) has an eight-strong fleet of '70s Devon Moonraker conversions for hire – fitted with elevating roofs to accommodate full-size double beds.

Last but not least, Snail Trail in Bedfordshire (01767 600440, www.snailtrail.co.uk) ships in brand-new copies of original models from Brazil – so each of its fleet promises a smooth ride and gleaming good looks. Take your pick from the lovingly named Betty, Pearl, Flo, Elsie, Matilda, Nell, Pru, Dot, Sylvie and Ruby.

# 471
## Hide out at Gordon's

Handily located right by Charing Cross Station, Gordon's warren-like premises ooze history: Samuel Pepys lived here in the 17th century, and Rudyard Kipling was a tenant when vintner Arthur Gordon founded the wine bar in 1890. Laurence Olivier once wooed Vivien Leigh in its dim vaults – and it still feels like a cellar of naughty Londoners getting intimately frisky away from the stern torch of the ARP warden. Indeed, there's no better place to contemplate time's march over an amontillado or two.

**Gordon's Wine Bar** *47 Villiers Street, London WC2N 6NE (020 7930 1408/www.gordons winebar.com).*

# 472
## Beware the Bottomless Pit

Set at the foot of the spectacular Winnats Pass in the Peak District National Park, Speedwell Cavern takes you on an incredible journey. First, you descend 105 steps from the cave's entrance to the landing stage of an underground canal. Boarding the tour guide's boat, you glide quietly through the workings of a 200-year-old lead mine, then wend your way 656 feet below the surface of the hill to a magnificent, cathedral-like cavern containing the awesome Bottomless Pit – a huge subterranean lake.

**Speedwell Cavern** *Winnats Pass, Castleton, Hope Valley, Derbyshire S33 8WA (01433 620512/ www.speedwellcavern.co.uk).*

# 473
## Be glad you were born in modern times at the Thackray Museum

Severed legs, cholera-infested water pumps, stinky re-creations of Victorian Leeds and its somewhat unsavoury approach to personal hygiene: the Thackray Museum is a great reminder of why the modern health system is so marvellous. If you're still in any doubt, play doctors and nurses and make the choices that will either kill or cure the eight unfortunate characters who live among the rats, fleas and bedbugs in 'Living Health'. The truly hardy can then watch a video reconstruction of 11-year-old Hannah Dyson's anaesthetic-free leg amputation in the 1840s (the scary dentist's chair is a breeze by comparison). Once you've survived the 'Pain, Pus and Blood' gallery, you can follow the path of a pea through the digestive system in the 'Life Zone', learn why we all emit wind every day and discover how it feels to be pregnant by trying on the empathy belly in 'Having a Baby'.

**Thackray Museum** *Beckett Street, Leeds LS9 7LN (0113 244 4343/www.thackraymuseum.org).*

# 474
## Ride the ferry 'cross the Mersey

Was ever a journey so linked to a song? Pay your £1.40, hop on board and admire the cityscape before you. The ferry takes about ten minutes to cross between Seacombe on the Wirral and Pier Head in the city (0151 330 1444, www.merseyferries.co.uk), passing Liverpool's revived UNESCO World Heritage-status waterfront on the way. The Scouse experience is topped off by the delights of the Gerry and the Pacemakers 1964 hit, as you hove into port.

# 475
## Twist and go to the National Motorcycle Museum

For those with two-stroke oil coursing through their veins, the National Motorcycle Museum is a shrine, Solihull a place of pilgrimage. Boasting the world's biggest and best collection of road bikes and racers, you might think it a specialist pleasure for like-minded individuals who know their Nortons from their Beezers; but the hands-on history of the British bike is a delight anyone can share. Succumb to the thrill of the pre-war sidecar and the dashing heroes of the TT races: two wheels good, four wheels bad.
**National Motorcycle Museum** *Coventry Road, Bickenhill, Solihull, West Midlands B92 0EJ (01675 443311/www.nationalmotorcyclemuseum.co.uk).*

# 476
## Discover Exeter's underground scene

Accessed via Paris Street, Exeter boasts an intriguing network of underground passages. Built in the 14th century to carry fresh water from springs outside the city, the dark, narrow aqueducts can be visited on guided tours, which provide a unique view of the world beneath a town's paving stones. Tours last around 90 minutes. Be warned: it's a tight squeeze in places, and not for claustrophobics.
**Exeter Underground Passages** *2 Paris Street, Exeter EX1 1GA (01392 265887/ www.exeter.gov.uk/passages).*

**Glasgow School of Art**

# 477
## Admire Mackintosh's masterpiece

The prodigiously talented Charles Rennie Mackintosh was an unknown junior draughtsman in an architect's firm when he won a competition to design a new home for his former college, the Glasgow School of Art, in 1896. Despite being his first commission, the sandstone Mackintosh Building, with its wrought-iron railings and gates, is considered one of Britain's finest examples of art nouveau architecture. Financial constraints meant it was built in two phases: the East Wing from 1897 to 1899, the West Wing from 1907 to 1909 – hence the latter's more dramatic design. Still home to a working art school, the building can only be visited on guided tours, led by GSA students.
**Glasgow School of Art** *167 Renfrew Street, Glasgow G3 6RQ (0141 353 4526/ www.gsa.ac.uk).*

# 478-485 Sample Britain's finest cheeses

**Emma Howarth** *learns how to assemble the perfect cheeseboard.*

Cheese is having a moment. Blame it on Brit-popper-turned-cheesemaker Alex James or 'Wedginald' the webcam cheese (www.cheddarvision.tv) – watched by 1.6 million people as it matured in 2007 – but a limp slab of edam and pack of boursin no longer a respectable cheeseboard make.

If you want your dairy to impress, think small-scale, think artisan and think British. With over 500 types to choose from and at least 100 dairies making raw-milk varieties, today's British cheese can definitely hold its own. Chairman of the British Cheese Awards (www.thecheeseweb.com) Juliet Harbutt couldn't agree more. 'There's no way that a British focus could leave you with a poor man's board. In fact, it's quite the opposite,' she says.

So Britain's got the goods – but where should a best of British cheese quest begin? We picked the brains of Harbutt, Rhuaridh Buchanan of London's Paxton & Whitfield (www.paxtonandwhitfield.co.uk) and Kate O'Meara of the Cheese Society (www.thecheesesociety.co.uk) shop and café in Lincoln. All were firmly agreed on three essentials: keep it simple, local and interesting, mixing a combination of flavours, shapes and textures.

There are six main types: fresh (unripened, curd-style cheeses such as ricotta), soft (brie, camembert), semi-soft (edam, rind-washed cheeses), hard (parmesan, cheddar), blue (stilton, gorgonzola) and flavour-added (smoked cheese, cornish yarg); and three different sources of milk (goat, cow, sheep and mixtures of the three). For maximum interest and flavour, Harbutt suggests picking a cheese from each category for your board. But both Harbutt and Buchanan agree that it's better to serve one good cheese than several mediocre ones.

There's certainly no shortage of produce that makes the grade. Kate O'Meara plumps instantly for the British Cheese Award-winning tunworth (www.hampshirecheeses.co.uk), a rich, creamy soft cheese from Hampshire made with unpasteurised milk from Ayrshire cows. She also recommends a classic colston bassett stilton (www.colstonbassettdairy.com) and sparkenhoe (www.leicestershirecheese.co.uk), a traditional, handmade red leicester – the only one actually made in the county – that swiftly eradicates any memories of bland, day-glo orange supermarket cheese.

Harbutt, meanwhile, kicks things off with a touch of celebrity. She chooses little wallop (available from Paxton & Whitfield), the fresh goat's cheese washed in cider brandy and wrapped in vine leaves that she helped Alex James create. It's an unusual, punchy flavour that lives up to the hype. She also opts for old winchester (www.lyburnfarm.co.uk), a hard cow's milk cheese made in Wiltshire, and Scottish highland blue (widely available) made by Rhuaridh Stone of Highland Fine Cheeses in Tain.

Rhuaridh Buchanan also rates highland blue highly, along with a spicy, crumbly hard sheep's milk cheese from Kent called crockhamdale and a creamy, rind-washed (in honey mead) oxford isis.

Raring to get your taste buds round a few of these? Paxton & Whitfield, the Cheese Society, Neal's Yard Dairy (www.nealsyarddairy.co.uk) and Bath's Fine Cheese Company (www.finecheese.co.uk) are just a selection of quality cheesemongers that also offer excellent mail order services. Alternatively, hold out for the annual British Cheese Festival (www.thecheeseweb.com) and hand-pick a few favourites of your own.

## 486
## *Join the jet set in Shoreham*

The modern airport is, by and large, a pretty bleak proposition – but it wasn't always thus. Set in the South Downs, Shoreham's aerodrome captures the glamour of a bygone age. The Grade II-listed terminal, built in 1936, is an art deco gem; perfect for romantic, *Casablanca*-style farewells. Pack up your vintage Vuitton suitcase and hop on a scheduled flight across the channel to Alderney or France: even the destinations (Paris, Caen, Deauville and Le Touquet) ooze old-fashioned glamour. Pleasure flights and flying lessons are also available. If you're not catching a flight, take a tour of the visitors' centre: exhibits range from a World War II bomb to 'Archive Archie' – a touching tribute to the airport's unofficial pet rodent.
**Shoreham Airport** *Shoreham-by-Sea, West Sussex BN43 5FF (01273 467373/ www.shorehamairport.co.uk).*

## 487
## *Follow in Marx's footsteps at the British Museum*

Designed by the improbably named Sydney Smirke, the mightily impressive oval Reading Room at the British Museum has inspired the likes of Karl Marx, Mahatma Gandhi, George Orwell and Virginia Woolf, who felt like 'a thought in the huge bald forehead'. In 2000, its hallowed doors were thrown open to the public for the first time, rather than being restricted to library ticket holders. (Though note that temporary exhibitions are taking place in the Reading Room until early 2009, so there may be an entry charge). Another change since Marx's day is the magnificent Norman Foster-designed glass ceiling of the Great Court – creating Europe's largest public covered square.
**British Museum** *Great Russell Street, London, WC1B 3DG (020 7323 7323/ www.britishmuseum.org).*

## 488
## *See the white horse at Uffington...*

Galloping across the Berkshire Downs, Uffington's white horse is a 3,000-year-old enigma. Its unexpectedly abstract, stylised curves look more like a Matisse masterpiece than the handiwork of the Iron Age Britons, who laboriously hewed its 374-foot-long outline into the hillside, then filled the trenches with chalk blocks. If you fancy paying a visit, the site is near the Ridgeway, between Swindon and Wantage (OS grid ref SU301866). Don't get Uffington's ancient steed confused with the white horses of Wiltshire – they're much later additions to the landscape, carved in the 18th and 19th centuries.

## 489
## *...then visit the Cerne Abbas giant*

Cerne Abbas's giant, meanwhile, is the people of Dorset's scene-stealing 17th-century effort – stark naked, wielding a mighty club and in a state of apparent excitement. See him in all his glory, just off the A352 between Sherbourne and Dorchester (OS grid ref ST666017; www.cerneabbas.org).

## 490
## *Dive the scuppered German fleet at Scapa Flow*

At the end of World War I, 74 vessels from the German Imperial Navy's High Seas Fleet were held captive at Scapa Flow in Orkney, the Royal Navy's principal anchorage, while peace terms were worked out with Germany. As the talks dragged on, the local German commander, lacking up-to-date information, decided to scuttle the vessels the next time the British Navy was on exercise. So, on 21 June 1919, something like 400,000 tons of warship went straight to the bottom of Scapa Flow. Although many were later salvaged, three battleships and four light cruisers are still there. They now provide one of Britain's premier diving experiences, with companies like Scapa Scuba (www.scapascuba.co.uk) offering guided dives.

# 491
## Admire the autumn leaves at Westonbirt

One of the oldest and largest man-made 'tree gardens' in the world, Westonbirt Arboretum has over 3,000 species of tree and shrub from all corners of the globe, spread over 600 magical acres. The Japanese maples are particularly colourful in autumn, while a walk through the Enchanted Wood has become a Christmas tradition, with the branches strung with lights, and mulled wine and roast chestnuts to be quaffed. Free guided walks through the Arboretum take place at 2pm every Saturday and Sunday from Easter to October.

**Westonbirt National Arboretum** *near Tetbury, Gloucestershire GL8 8QS (01666 880220/ www.forestry.gov.uk/westonbirt).*

# 492
## Discover where the Olympic revival really kicked off

Those who think that the first modern Olympics took place in Athens in 1896 are sadly mistaken. In fact, that honour goes to the little-known Shropshire village of Much Wenlock. They were the brainchild of Victorian philanthropist William Penny Brookes, who worked as a GP and magistrate in the village. Perturbed by the amount of petty crime he saw, he campaigned tirelessly for the resurrection of the Olympic Games of ancient Greece, to promote 'moral, physical and intellectual improvement'. In 1850, he organised the very first 'Olympian Games' in the village – which, while including the obvious sports of football and cricket, also featured events such as a wheelbarrow race and the memorable 'Old Woman's Race for a Pound of Tea'. The games continue to be held every July (www.wenlock-olympian-society.org.uk). If you can't make the Olympic weekend, then an Olympian Trail takes you around the key local sites, and recounts the full story of Brookes and his little-documented Olympic revival.

# 493-499 *See seals*

There are some 120,000 seals around the British Isles: the common seal and the larger (and, ironically, more common) grey seal. The best time to see them is when they come to shore to breed and give birth. Common seals usually pup between June and August, grey seals from late October through December; the spring moult is another good time to catch them.

## Blakeney National Nature Reserve, Norfolk
Around 500 common and grey seals bask at the end of the sand and shingle of Blakeney Point, easily accessible by boat: Bean's boat trips (01263 740505, www.beansboattrips.co.uk) have been running for some 50 years. The reserve itself is run by the National Trust (01263 740241, www.nationaltrust.org.uk).

## Donna Nook, Lincolnshire
The sand bars and dunes of Donna Nook (www.lincsuk.com/donnanookseals.htm) are one of the easiest places to spot seals. Hundreds of grey seals haul themselves on to the beach from October, although mid November to mid December provides the best viewing.

## Farne Islands, Northumberland
Best known as a birders' paradise, these bleak islands are also home to around 4,000 grey seals. Several boats run trips from the harbour at Seahouses village, including *MV Glad Tidings* (01665 720308, www.farne-islands.com), run by the Shiel family. The islands themselves are under the care of the National Trust (01665 720651, www.nationaltrust.org.uk).

## Monach Isles, Outer Hebrides
These uninhabited, treeless islands (www.monachisles.co.uk) have one of the world's largest grey seal populations; the autumn breeding season sees some 10,000 come to shore. *MV Chalice* (01631 720609, www.mvchalice.com) runs boat trips from Oban.

## National Seal Sanctuary, Cornwall
The first and largest of Britain's three Sealife Sanctuaries (the others are at Oban and Hunstanton), the Seal Sanctuary's hospital, nursery pool and resident pools enable you to watch rescued seals that cannot be returned to the wild (Gweek, near Helston, Cornwall TR12 6UG, 01326 221361, www.sealsanctuary.co.uk). Feeding sessions and talks take place throughout the day.

*Shiel's boat trips*

## Ramsey Island, Pembrokeshire
Seals gather on shingle beneath the cliffs of this RSPB-run island (07836 535733, www.rspb.org.uk). Voyages of Discovery (01437 720285, www.ramseyisland.co.uk) and Thousand Islands Expeditions (01437 721721, www.thousandislands.co.uk) run tours.

## Samson and Annet, Isles of Scilly
Most local boat companies will take you out to see the resident seals, basking on dark isolated rocks or bobbing about in the sea (on St Mary's, try the Boatman's Association on 01720 423999, www.scillyboating.co.uk or just turn up at the harbour). Island Sea Safaris (01720 422732, www.scillyonline.co.uk/seasafaris.html) though, offers a magical opportunity to spend three hours snorkelling among them for £40.

## 500

### Sit in the Sitooterie

Like a space-age pin cushion in the unlikely surrounds of Essex, this sitooterie – a Scottish term for a summer house, in which to 'sit oot' and contemplate the world – was designed by the studio of architect Thomas Heatherwick for the National Malus (crab apple) Collection at Barnards Farm in West Horndon (01277 811262, www.barnardsfarm.eu). Hollow spikes extend from a cube-shaped core, lifting the structure off the ground and drawing light from a central source to create its curious orange glow. Certain spikes also extend within, providing a place to sit. Well, what would a sitooterie be without its seats?

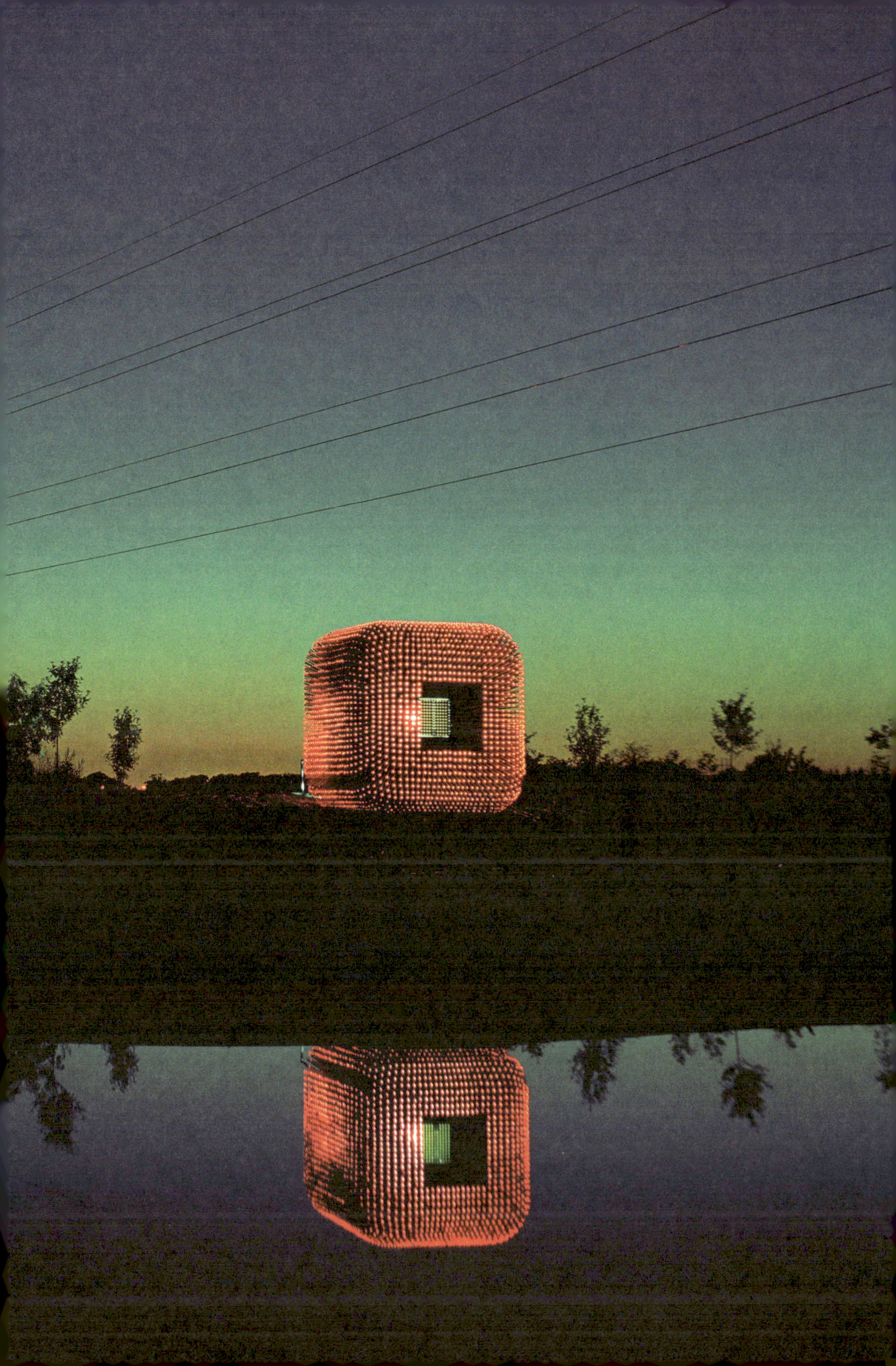

# 501-505
## ...then visit Thomas Heatherwick's other terrific creations

### B of the Bang, Manchester
Made from 180 massive spikes jutting out in all directions (and supported by just five heavy steel legs), *B of the Bang* was commissioned to commemorate the 2002 Commonwealth Games. This star-like structure is the tallest piece of sculpture in England (to put it in perspective, at 184 feet it's about as tall as Nelson's Column or the Leaning Tower of Pisa). Odd as it may sound, the artwork's name comes from a Linford Christie quote: when the pistol is fired to start a race, the athlete once said, he's off at the 'b' of the bang.
**B of the Bang** *Alan Turing Way, Sportcity, Manchester M11 (www.bofthebang.com).*

### Bleigiessen, London
This towering wire and glass sculpture replicates the random shapes formed when molten metal is poured into water; over 400 small samples were produced by this method (known as *bleigiessen*) before a design was selected. Commissioned by medical charity the Wellcome Trust, it rises eight storeys through its headquarters on the Euston Road. The public can view it on the last Friday of the month at 2pm.
**Bleigiessen** *Wellcome Trust, Gibbs Building, 215 Euston Road, London NW1 2BE (020 7611 8888/ www.wellcome.ac.uk).*

### Blue Carpet, Newcastle
Heatherwick's design for this square outside the Laing Art Gallery was completed in 2001. Blue tiles (made from recycled Harvey's Bristol Cream bottles) give the appearance of a carpet across the square; where it meets walls and buildings, the edges curve up like fabric. Protruding bollards appear to have torn through the surface, and benches are formed by similar 'tears', revealing multicoloured lights beneath.
**Blue Carpet** *New Bridge Street, Newcastle NE1 (www.heatherwick.com).*

### East Beach Café, Littlehampton
Located on the beach at Littlehampton in West Sussex, Heatherwick's design for this seafront café resembles an enormous fossil. Long and thin, the structure is made of thick, steel ribbons that are packed together like hollowed-out crusts of bread. The café itself serves the likes of fish pie for lunch and local game at dinner. Thanks to the huge glass frontage, many tables have a terrific view over the Channel.
**East Beach Café** *Littlehampton, West Sussex BN17 5NZ (01903 731903/www.eastbeachcafe.co.uk).*

### Rolling Bridge, London
When fully extended, Heatherwick's innovative Rolling Bridge looks like a simple footbridge, connecting two parts of Paddington Basin over a ten-metre stretch of water. But if a boat needs to pass, the hydraulically powered bridge curls up and over until its two ends are touching – forming a neat circular hoop on one bank. To see it in action, stop by on Friday at noon.
**Rolling Bridge** *Paddington Basin, London W2 (www.heatherwick.com).*

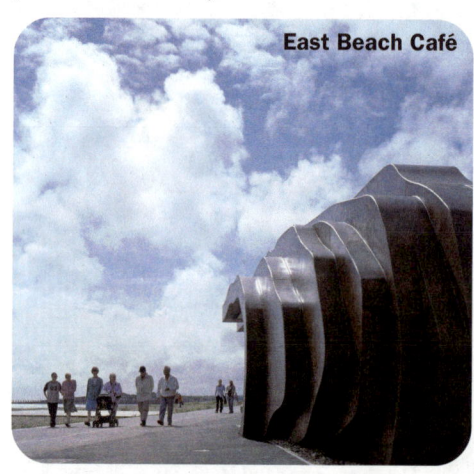

East Beach Café

# 506
## Go bookcrossing

Leaving a copy of your favourite book on the last train home might sound like an unfortunate mishap – but not if you're one of the 600,000 global converts to the joys of bookcrossing. Readers tag books they've read and relished with a unique identity code, before releasing them back into the wild. Next, they post the details at www.bookcrossing.com, to allow other bookcrossers to pick them up, read them and then pass them on again (some books on the site have changed hands hundreds of times). Thus a quick browse on the site might reveal a copy of Asimov's *Foundation* in St Pancras Station, Jane Austen's *Emma* in the White House Hotel in Swansea or Ben Elton's *Stark* in the Dorchester Tesco. The benefits are obvious: homes remain uncluttered with unwanted books, readers can forgo overpriced bookshops in favour of literary adventures of their own, and books themselves get to travel the world with all the globe-trotting ferocity of the gnome from *Amélie*.

# 507
## Catch a film at Britain's oldest working cinema

The Electric Cinema in Birmingham first flickered into life in December 1909. Over the years it took on various incarnations – including an inglorious stint showing soft-core smut and horror movies – before descending into near-dereliction. But in 1993 its original name and dignity were restored, and the Electric was reborn. With comfortable sofa seating and waiter service for drinks, it's now one of the country's most luxurious places to enjoy a film, and a Birmingham institution. But our favourite thing about it is the policy of not showing adverts before films. If only more cinemas did the same…

**Electric Cinema** *47-49 Station Street, Birmingham B5 4DY (0121 643 7879/ www.theelectric.co.uk).*

# 508
## Explore the Bloomsbury set's country retreat

Artist Vanessa Bell set up house in East Sussex in 1916 – accompanied by her lover Duncan Grant, *his* lover, David Garnett, and her two children. Vanessa revelled in the rural freedom, as her sister Virginia Woolf noted: 'Nessa seems to have slipped civilization off her back, and splashes about entirely nude, without shame, and enormous spirit. Indeed, Clive now takes up the line that she has ceased to be a presentable lady – I think it all works admirably.' Bell and Grant daubed every available surface with murals, and filled the farmhouse with textiles, ceramics and art – including works by Picasso and Sickert. The house, now open to visitors, looks as fantastical today as it did 90 years ago: a gloriously uninhibited explosion of colour and creativity. The annual Charleston Festival keeps its intellectual history alive: in 2007, literary heavyweights in attendance included Kiran Desai, Patrick Marber, Claire Tomalin and Colin Thubron.

**Charleston House** *Charleston Firle, Lewes, East Sussex BN8 6LL (01323 811265/ www.charleston.org.uk).*

# 509 Go foraging for your supper

# Walk on the wild side

***Rachel Ragg** boldly samples the great outdoors.*

Given that my own experience of foraging has never gone beyond hunting through the shelves of Harrogate Waitrose, it is with some trepidation that I set off to North Yorkshire on Halloween to meet Chris Bax, forager extraordinaire. Armed with my own emergency supplies (a Marmite sandwich) I'm vaguely anxious about my lack of culinary adventurousness as I head for the huge tepees on Chris's 17.5-acre stretch of woodland near Boroughbridge.

I needn't worry: Chris has spirit enough for us both. And he's not just jumping on a bandwagon. 'Yes, it's fashionable now; chefs are really plugging the whole seasonal produce thing. But there's good reason: things taste so much better at the right time of year.' Late October isn't, he admits, the best time to forage. 'But there isn't a day in the year – unless there's thick snow – when I couldn't go out and pick you a salad.'

Chris was a professional chef before setting up his own catering company. But he wanted to combine his love of food with his love of the outdoors – and thus his company, Taste the Wild, was born. For the last couple of years, he and his sculptor wife Rose have been hosting wild food weekends and introductory bushcraft courses. And his enthusiasm knows no bounds. 'Once you see one or two things you can eat, you see more. The whole foraging thing is a way of seeing. I never used to notice flowers or trees, and now I notice so much.' And there would be something new to notice even a few steps down the road, not to mention in different areas of the UK. 'Our soil here is acid,' he says. 'If we went to Wensleydale, we'd find completely different foods.'

Chris's enthusiasm is infectious as we set off through the forest. 'There's so much edible stuff around, even at this time of year,' he says, stopping to feed me something that looks suspiciously like a weed. It turns out to be sheep's sorrel, with a sharp taste reminiscent

**Time Out** 1000 Things to do in Britain 153

of apple peel. This proves to be the first new experience of many: by the time we're back at the tepees, I'll have eaten hairy bitter cress (mustardy), chickweed (tastes of Outside), elderberries (yum), wood sorrel (sherbert apples) and acorns (pleasantly nutty – they can, apparently, be roasted, ground down and made into anything from biscuits to nut rissoles). We reject the thistles, which are now rather large and bitter, but stop for a spot of nettle: high in protein, and wonderfully versatile, lending itself to nettle tonic, nettle gnocchi and even cheese-making (using rennet made from salt and, yes, nettles).

These wild foods don't just taste good, they do us good too. Pine, for instance, is stuffed full of vitamin C – so for a cold-zapping drink, chop up a few pine needles and add hot water, and you've got a fantastic pine tea. Pine, says Chris, is a great all-rounder: when the cones start to appear, you can eat the shoots; then, later in the season, you can harvest the pollen, which is a great source of energy. The elder tree is another favourite. 'It's looking a bit sad now, but in spring you can make 'gunshot pickle' from the buds, and then you get the berries and flowers in early summer. I love that time of year.'

We amble past the dandelions ('a diuretic'), silverweed and corn mint, searching for burdock root – the most popular food among most attendees on the wild food courses. 'We roast it in the fire – it's a bit like a parsnip,' Chris explains. 'People can't believe how good it tastes. And it provides carbs, which are quite hard to come by in the wild.' Comfrey goes down well too. 'I had one guy who hadn't eaten anything green for 26 years. I made a batter and deep-fried the comfrey in it – and he loved it.' Chris-the-former-chef is warming to his theme. 'If you want to really impress people at a dinner party, give them deep-fried comfrey and elderflowers in a lovely tempura batter with a bit of caster sugar. It's to die for.'

Speaking of things to die for, I can't help noticing that the ground is littered with every kind of fungus imaginable. I tend to think that all wild mushrooms will kill me – but it appears I'm overly cautious. 'Yes, there are mushrooms that are very bad for you,' says Chris, pointing to a scary-looking red and white spotty fungus. 'That one has been used as a psychoactive; lots of shamen use it to get high, especially in Northern Europe.' The Suomi people apparently used to drink the urine of reindeer who had been browsing on such mushrooms.

So why have we demonised mushrooms, when children in Russia or Poland will go out for a happy morning's mushroom-picking? Chris is baffled. 'It makes sense for us to demonise bugs: until the agrarian system, we all ate bugs – but they had to be demonised as they were bad for the crops.' But mushrooms, he says, are a great loss to mankind – and while nobody should go round randomly sampling mushrooms, they shouldn't be scared either. 'We have to learn for the knowledge to come back into our society.'

This is central to Chris's vision: reconnecting modern supermarket-bound humans with the food chain – and getting them to enjoy the great outdoors. 'There are people who can teach you SAS survival techniques, but that's not really what I'm about. Everyone can get something out of the courses.' Recent visitors have included a team of City traders and a coven of Geordie witches. 'Nobody would choose to go out in the wind and rain to pick some fat hen for tea – and yes, of course we go to Sainsbury's like everyone else. Full-time foraging is a subsistence way to live. But if you're out walking for the day and come back with a basket of wild food, how great is that?'

Our foraging over, we return to the 'kitchen' for a restorative brew. The kettle is hung over the fire, and Rose darts off to pick some raspberry leaves for my tea, while an animated Chris waves me over to a little cluster of ceps. After a quick tea-making lesson, we sit around the fire with our raspberry and pine-needle infusions and Chris talks about his big plan for next year: a course in coastline foraging based around Whitby. He's highly excited by the prospect of rock samphire ('great with fish'), marsh samphire ('tastes a bit like Coca Cola'), seaweed and, of course, some freshly caught fish. 'I've always hated shop-bought mackerel, but the first time I caught it and cooked it over an open fire, it was one of the most profound food experiences of my life – it was a revelation. That's what we want to do for people.' And as I leave the North Yorkshire wilds and return to supermarket civilisation with the taste of pine needles still in my mouth, my Marmite sandwich untouched, I'm 100 per cent convinced.

**Taste the Wild** *07914 290083/www.tastethe wild.co.uk). The cost of courses starts from £150 for a weekend's introduction to bushcraft.*

## 510 Re-enact the Battle of Hastings

Squint hard, and you can almost picture the scene in 1066 – despite a few modern anachronisms. The clanking English army are defending the side of Senlac Hill (giving spectators a good view from the top), while King Harold is getting an eyeful of arrow, right by the plaque that marks the historic spot. Once the battle has been fought, the Conqueror's hordes go on to pillage the craft tents and merrye refreshment stalls. This Battle of Hastings may be a remake, but the sight of 1,500 colourful archers, cavalry and footsoldiers, plus a whole ramshackle village of 'living history' extras, leaves an indelible impression. Give in to your inner Norman, and go along – it takes place every year, on the weekend that falls nearest to 14 October.
**1066 Battle of Hastings, Abbey and Battlefield** *East Sussex TN33 0AD (01424 775705/www.english-heritage.org.uk/events).*

## 511 Hear the thwack of leather on willow at the 'cradle of cricket'

There are few things as rewarding in an English weekend as nodding off in a deck chair, cradling a pint of sun-warmed beer, while teams of assorted schoolchildren, estate agents and farm workers cavort on a village cricket field. It's even more hyper-quintessential to do so at the 'cradle of cricket' in Hambledon, Hampshire, where the 1770s village team first 'raised cricket from a sport to an art'. The club's original pitch at Broadhalfpenny Down is still being thwacked and bickered over, and matches rewritten afterwards at the legendary Bat & Ball Inn. There's a fixture list at www.broadhalf pennydown.com, and a full history at www.hambledon-hants.com.

## 512 Visit 'the village that died'

A tiny fishing village on the rugged northern coast of Cornwall, Port Quin was mysteriously abandoned in the 19th century. Some say the villagers left after all the menfolk were drowned at sea one stormy night – though the more prosaic explanation is that it was gradually deserted as pilchard stocks declined. Book into one of the hamlet's National Trust-owned holiday cottages (0870 458 4411, www.nationaltrustcottages.co.uk), or take a stroll out on the lonely promontory and decide for yourself.

## 513 Watch the Isle of Man TT (but resist taking part)

One hundred years old in 2007, this annual time-trial motorcycling race (www.iomtt.com) is considered one of the sternest tests on the motor sports calendar. What makes the week-long summer event so special is that the 40 miles of track used for the race are all ordinary public roads. They are thankfully closed for the event so that the souped-up bikes can zip around them at frighteningly high speeds (there's no speed limit on many of the IOM's roads).
Typical of the event's wildness is 'Mad Sunday', a day during which members of the public can race the mountain section of the course – resulting in more than a few deaths over the years. Nevertheless, the TT itself is taken very seriously, thrilling some 60,000 fans who travel to the island for the two-wheeled drama every year.

## 514 Be awed by the Braunton Burrows

The largest area of sand dunes in Britain is an eerily beautiful natural attraction. Stretching for about four miles along the Braunton Shore in north Devon, the undulating dunes of perfect golden sand – a designated UNESCO reserve – are a truly awesome sight.

## A few of my favourite things

# 515-519
## *Martin Parr, photographer*

Women's Institute markets are great, particularly the one at Bridport (9am-noon Sat, WI Hall, North Street, Bridport, Dorset DT6 3NQ, 01308 485337). They happen all around the country on a weekly basis, and you get a real range of produce – freshly baked cakes, jams, pickles, fruit and bread. The one in Dorset is the best because it's full of nice, middle-class ladies who have lots of time on their hands so they make a lot of food. I inevitably get into conversations with them, and I'm always photographing them. Some have ended up in my books.

**Another Dorset institution is the market at Sturminster Newton on Mondays (8.30am-1pm, Market Place, Sturminster Newton, Dorset DT10 1AR). It's one of those classic markets where you get all sorts of people coming out of the woodwork, bringing all kinds of junk. The atmosphere is slightly quaint, old English. I'm quite nostalgic about the past, although now I collect things like Saddam Hussein memorabilia, which you're not likely to find in Dorset.**

I love going to the Scottish islands. I have a long-term ambition to visit every inhabited Scottish island and I'm two-thirds of the way through. The Island of Barra in the Outer Hebrides has the only airport in the world where the planes take off and land on the beach (01667 462445, www.hial.co.uk/barra-airport.html). You'll be flying along and then you see the sea coming up and wham, there's the beach.

**For the quintessential English seaside resort, I'd elect Broadstairs in Kent. It's got the sandy beach, the cliffs, the beach huts, the fish and chip shop and the games machines. I like the fact the English seaside's a bit tatty. You've also got to have a good Italian ice-cream parlour, and Broadstairs has Morelli's (14 Victoria Parade, Broadstairs, Kent CT10 1QS, 01843 860050), which looks like it hasn't changed since the '50s.**

The British Lawnmower Museum (106-114 Shakespeare Street, Southport, Merseyside PR8 5AJ, 01704 501336, www.lawnmowerworld.com) is one of those eccentric museums that this country does really well. You can see lawnmowers of the rich and famous, including Prince Charles and Nicholas Parsons. They've also got the genuine two-inch lawnmower and the Egg Boiler Lawnmower. Where else in the world would you get a place like that?

# 520 *Become an air guitar legend*

Born to be a rock 'n' roll star but lacking the musical talent? Happily, a complete inability to play guitar is no bar to success at the UK Air Guitar Championship. Regional heats culminate in a hotly contested national final, allowing you to pit your imaginary axe skills against other would-be guitar legends. Judges give points for posture, the realism of your performance and audience reaction as you rock out to your favourite anthem. For the victor, glory awaits: Colin Fulker, winner for the last two years, ended up on telly with his heroes Status Quo. As reigning champion, Colin had his song (Deep Purple's 'Smoke on the Water') imposed upon him, but still blew the other hopefuls off stage. His advice? 'Basically, do what you do when you're at home in your underpants in front of the mirror, but on stage. And try to wear more clothes.' To find your nearest heat, check out www.ukairguitar.com. Then crank it up to 11.

## 521 Spot a Frederick's ice-cream van...

Angelo Frederick arrived in England from Parma and set up shop in Sheffield's Don Valley in the 1890s; four generations and over a century later, the business remains family-owned and staunchly traditional. Sample a scoop of bakewell pudding flavour ice-cream at its gelateria in Bakewell, or play it safe with Frederick's Original 1898 Blend of Vanilla – winner of a coveted gold medal from the National Ice Cream Alliance, beating a staggering 450 samples. You can grab a cone from Frederick's at tourist spots throughout Derbyshire; it could be from a vintage Morris van, painted in swirling colours, or one of the firm's beautifully restored horse-drawn carts, trikes and kiosks.

**Frederick's of Chesterfield** *1 Bridge Street, Bakewell, Derbyshire DE45 1DS (01246 275293/ www.fredericksicecreams.co.uk).*

## 522 ...or hire your own at Lola's On Ice

Rescued from a Land's End parking lot, this ex-Mr Frosty van underwent an extreme makeover and emerged as gaudy gal Lola. Looks aren't everything, of course (although you'll certainly spot this ice maiden from afar); it's the way-out flavours, organic ingredients and infectious enthusiasm of Lola's creator, Morfudd Richards, that's so exciting. Everything is made from scratch, and flavours run the gamut from mint or red summer fruits to hot-and-cold horseradish, star anise and saffron, or caramel and cumin. Jamie Oliver booked Lola's for his birthday; you can too, if you're within a 40-mile radius of central London (07871 797260, http://lolasonice.co.uk). The hire charge is from £200, plus £3 per person for a double scoop, and you can choose up to six freshly prepared flavours. For giving us gin and tonic sorbet, we salute you, Lola.

## 523 Cheer on the London to Brighton rally

Held in November, this annual parade sees around 500 vintage motors (none of which exceeds a stately 32mph) make the long run from London's Hyde Park to Madeira Drive in Brighton. Cars set off at 7.30am, aiming to reach Brighton by 4pm. There's a rest and coffee stop at Crawley at around 1.30pm, during which cars can be admired at closer quarters; alternatively you can wait by the finishing line in Brighton. If you can't make the run itself, check out the handsome, buffed-up vehicles the day before the rally on Regent Street (www.lbvcr.com).

## 524 Spend a penny at the Philharmonic Dining Rooms

The gentlemen's conveniences at this opulently decorated Victorian boozer (better known as 'the Phil') have been voted the best public lavatories in Britain – and rightly so. With their high ceilings, ornate brass fittings, mosaic floors, marble urinals and astonishing ceramic tiles, these loos are a Liverpool landmark. Ladies are welcome to peek – just ask a member of staff, and they'll check that the coast is clear.

**Philharmonic Dining Rooms** *36 Hope Street, Liverpool L1 9BX (0151 707 2837/ www.mbplc.com).*

## 525 Watch the footie from your bedroom window

Built into the Reebok Stadium in Bolton – home of Premiership football team Bolton Wanderers – Whites hotel boasts 19 rooms with windows that look out on the pitch. Prices start at £345 for the night – cheap at the price to any football fan who's dreamed of watching the beautiful game live without having to get out of bed.

**Whites** *De Havilland Way, Bolton, Greater Manchester BL6 6SF (01204 667788/ www.devere.co.uk/venues/Whites).*

# 526-531 *See India in England*

Britain can whisk the curious visitor thousands of miles away in the twinkling of an eye. A glimpse of India, for instance, doesn't require a long-haul flight. Instead, pop down to Brighton to see the Regency splendour of the Indo-Oriental Royal Pavilion (Brighton BN1 1EE, 01273 290900, www.royalpavilion.org.uk). The illicit love nest of the Prince Regent, who set standards of foppish and improvident bad behaviour that some still try to emulate to this day, the pavilion was designed by John 'Marble Arch' Nash from 1815-22. His assemblage of minarets and balconies is far from being an exact copy of any one oriental architectural style, freely mixing Indian, Chinese and Gothic notes in the pursuit of ornate excess.

Deep in the Cotswolds is the inspiration for Nash's pavilion. Sezincote (near Moreton-in-Marsh, Gloucestershire GL56 9AW, 01386 700444, www.sezincote.co.uk), pronounced 'season-cut', was 'indianised' in 1805, transformed into a palatial, Rajasthani Mogul-style abode for Charles Cockerell, who had worked with Warren Hastings in the East India Company. An extraordinary sight with its onion dome, minarets, chajjas and chattris, surrounded by rolling green hills, it also has water gardens designed by Humphrey Repton.

For much of the 19th century, the Indian style was considered far too decadent and actually went out of fashion – though it found its most extravagant expression in the Durbar Wing of Queen Victoria's holiday palace, Osborne House (York Avenue, East Cowes, Isle of Wight PO32 6JX, 01983 200022, www.english-heritage.org.uk). The rooms, designed by Sikh architect Bhai Ram Singh for Princess Beatrice in the 1890s, have now been restored to their original glory.

Less sumptuous, smaller-scale reminders of the subcontinent include the exotic wellhead in the village of Stoke Row in the Chilterns, funded in 1864 by the Maharajah of Benares, and the drinking fountain in the middle of Regent's Park, London, donated in 1869 by Sir Cowasjee Jehangir Readymoney, 'a wealthy Parsee gentleman of Bombay', in gratitude for the British protection afforded to the Parsi community in India. As his sobriquet suggests, he was one of the richest men of his day.

Leonardslee Gardens (Lower Beeding, Horsham, West Sussex RH13 6PP, 01403 891212, www.leonardsleegardens.com) were famously employed as a stand-in for the Himalayas in Michael Powell's superbly camp cult classic *Black Narcissus* (1947). Playing a nun, Deborah Kerr does her magnificent best to run a new convent in the mountains, but is finally undermined by the wind, native eroticism and a sister driven mad with sexual jealousy. The terraces of rhododendrons, magnolias and camellias cultivated by the Loder family provided a glorious technicolour setting for several scenes, including the final frames of the film, in which raindrops slowly begin to fall on to enormous leaves. One thing that obviously couldn't be imported was the weather.

**Brighton Royal Pavilion**

## 532 Sample a proper Cornish pasty

These sturdy, pocket-shaped pastries first came to prominence in the 19th century as a convenient, all-in-one meal for miners, with a savoury filling at one end and jam at the other. In the filthy underground conditions, the miner could hold the crimped edge as he ate, discarding it at the end without soiling the rest of his meal.

So what separates the sumptuous delights of a real Cornish pasty from the bland, mass-produced imitations found all over the UK? Simply being on the Cornish side of the Tamar will greatly improve the quality, while another crucial factor is the mix of ingredients: for a perfect pasty you need a good balance of beef (cut, never minced), potato, onion, turnip (or swede), generous seasoning and golden pastry (either flaky or shortcrust).

One of the best places to pick up a pasty is Ann Muller's award-winning Lizard Pasty Shop in Helston (Beacon Terrace, The Lizard, 01326 290889), which produces huge, tasty pasties of such calibre that they're even delicious cold. In Truro, try WC Rowe (22 Victoria Square, 01872 261281) or Blewetts Bakery (Cathedral Chambers, 13 High Cross, 01872 222856), where eagerly queuing locals are a common sight year-round.

## 533 Flip out on Cardigan Bay

You don't have to head out to sea to see Britain's resident dolphin colonies – they can often be spotted from dry land at Durlston Head or Prawle Point in the West Country, or Scotland's Moray Firth – but when the bottlenoses are flipping in Cardigan Bay in Wales, it's well worth taking a tootle on the briny. On a trip from New Quay's harbour wall (01545 560800, www.newquayboattrips.co.uk), the chugging boat engine and folds of the great sedimentary cliffs are relaxing enough; throw in a pack of inquisitive dolphins, the odd porpoise and a scattering of sunbathing grey seals, and feel your blood pressure plummet 20 points.

## 534 Explore Scotland's prehistoric past

In 1850, a ferocious storm exposed a grassy mound, revealing the ruins of ancient dwellings – and Skara Brae, the best-preserved Neolithic settlement in northern Europe, was discovered. Wonderfully situated on Orkney's curving shoreline, in summer the backdrop of sparkling sea and seagull cries gives exploring the low alleyways and stone buildings a holiday adventure feel; in winter, you'll probably have the place to yourself. (Crunching along the snowy paths is wonderfully peaceful and evocative, but beware skin-flaying winds that can whip out of nowhere.) It's a fascinating site, so archaeology buffs should invest in a guidebook or learn more from the visitor's centre, where a replica house brings alive the remote farming community who lived here between 3200 and 2200 BC. A walk or picnic on the beach at Skaill Bay (accessed via the car park) rounds off the day nicely.

**Skara Brae** *19 miles north-west of Kirkwall on the B9056, Orkney (01856 841815/ www.historic-scotland.gov.uk).*

## 535 Celebrate street theatre in Winchester

Britain's longest-running street theatre festival, the Hat Fair (www.hatfair.co.uk), started in 1974 as a low-key buskers' bash. From these humble beginnings it has grown into a vibrant spectacle, attracting 50,000 people a year. The streets are packed with performers, from fire-breathers and acrobats to off-the-wall costumed characters; you could find yourself exploring the streets alongside flowerpot men on stilts, or picnicking next to Marie Antoinette. There are also markets with quaint old-fashioned stalls, stage shows and displays ranging from gymnastics to clowning. For families, School Day is not to be missed; there's a parade involving over 1,000 children, plus lots of activities and crafts workshops. The festival is named for the street performers' tradition of passing a hat round for donations after shows. And since all this brilliant entertainment is free, do dig deep when the hat comes your way.

# 536-540 *Be a zoo keeper for a day*

'You wouldn't believe how many people want to tap dance with the penguins; they're not all kids, either,' sighs Dave Low, of Bristol Zoo's hugely popular Keeper for A Day scheme (www.bristolzoo.org.uk). 'And we did have to explain to one woman that Asiatic lions are probably not the best animals to be clambering into an enclosure with…' Following the lead of the keeper, this is a day of real work (you have to be over 16 and in good health to take part), rather than a cushy behind-the-scenes tour.

So why would you pay up to £250 to shovel soggy straw, hose down concrete and chop up vast amounts of fruit and veg? As every pet owner knows, there's a lot of satisfaction to be gained from caring for an animal – only here you're dealing with penguin poo instead of Fluffy's litter tray, and might have monkeys climbing over you while dishing out lunch. The schemes are incredibly popular; some animal requests (primates in particular) are booked up a year in advance.

At London Zoo (www.zsl.org) there's a fixed itinerary and you can't choose the animals you want to work with; the same applies to Whipsnade (www.zsl.org/whipsnade), London Zoo's sprawling Bedfordshire outpost and home to larger animals, including Indian rhinos. At both sites, over-16s can experience a day of keeper talks and learn about how zoos are run, along with the usual mucking out, food preparation and feeding. Prices range from £160 for 'introduction days' to £250 for keeper-for-a-day.

The most requested sections at Chester Zoo (www.chesterzoo.org) are the elephants and primates; over-18s can also opt for reptiles and amphibians, parrots and penguins, giraffes (which also includes camels and buffalo), rhinos (plus capybaras, zebras, deer and meerkats), bats and carnivores (tigers, lions, sea lions, bush dogs, kangaroos and, rather bizarrely, the children's zoo); the price is currently £200.

Sessions at Dudley Zoo (www.dudleyzoo.org.uk) run from 10am to 4pm and cost £150; the day is split in two halves and there's the option of working in one or two sections. The minimum age is 14 (for chimps, giraffes and penguins) or 16 (for the big cats). Younger animal-lovers can be 'Little Zoo Keepers' (8-13 years) for £95 and help to feed, clean and care for the animals on the farm. Most zoos offer keeper schemes, so check with your nearest for details.

# 541-550

## Ride Britain's best rollercoasters

According to Andy Hine, founder of the British Rollercoaster Association, it doesn't matter how many drops, corkscrews or loops a 'coaster has – all that counts is whether you want to get straight back on again. 'The best ride will always leave you laughing,' says Hine, 'and desperate to rejoin the queue.' Here's his pick of the best of British rollercoasters.

### Colossus

Opened in 2002, Colossus was Thorpe Park's first major white-knuckle ride, incorporating ten inversions and four corkscrew-like twists in quick succession. Winding within and around itself, this ride is for loop fiends.
**Thorpe Park** *Staines Road, Chertsey, Surrey KT16 8PN (0870 444 4466/www.thorpepark.co.uk).*

### G Force

G Force may not be the fastest of the rides on our list (it reaches speeds of a mere 45mph or so), but it does have a feature unique among UK rollercoasters: you start the ride in a loop, reach the top of it, then swing out and into a further two loops, including the wonderful sounding Bent Cuban Eight. The stomach-churning succession of thrills is responsible for the G-force factor (which measures up to 4.3, we're told). Grasping their 15 minutes of fame by the horns, the band G4 (of *X-Factor* fame) opened the ride in 2005.
**Drayton Manor Theme Park** *Drayton Manor Park, near Tamworth, Staffordshire B78 3TW (08708 725252/www.draytonmanor.co.uk).*

## Grand National
A national treasure, the Grand National is proof that a rollercoaster needn't be high-octane to be thrilling. Opened in 1935 and 'still as exciting as it was then', according to Hine, the ride is based on Britain's most famous horse race. Two cars run in tandem over dips and turns named after famous features of the Aintree course (Becher's Brook, Canal Turn), racing each other to a finishing post at the end. Saddle up!
**Blackpool Pleasure Beach** *525 Ocean Boulevard, Blackpool FY4 1EZ (0870 444 5566/www.blackpool pleasurebeach.com).*

## Jubilee Odyssey
Named to commemorate the Queen's Golden Jubilee (we're not sure whether Ma'am has enjoyed a ride yet), this inverted rollercoaster at Fantasy Island in Skegness reaches 60mph and lasts a whopping three minutes. It's our favourite to look at too: a complex red and white weave of track that – thanks to its loops, rolls, sidewinders and corkscrews – looks as much like a child's scribble as a thrill ride.
**Fantasy Island** *Sea Lane, Ingoldmells, Skegness, Lincolnshire PE25 1RH (01754 872030/ www.fantasyisland.co.uk).*

## Megafobia
Clunky spelling aside, this is Hine's favourite ride in Britain. 'You're constantly out of your seat,' he says of the wooden white-knuckler in Pembrokeshire, Wales. Though travelling at top speeds of just 50mph, 'the airtime is incredible, and you feel like you're floating around the track.'
**Oakwood Theme Park** *Canaston Bridge, Narberth, Pembrokeshire SA67 8DE (01834 861889/www.oakwoodthemepark.co.uk).*

## Pepsi Max Big One
Reaching speeds of over 70mph and heights of over 200 feet, the Big One may have lost its tallest and fastest world records only two years after its launch in 1994 (to Japan's Fujiyama), but it still towers over all in Britain, and has become an iconic feature of the Blackpool skyline. The Lancashire ride's first plunge is particularly harrowing; you might want to save the candy floss until afterwards.
**Blackpool Pleasure Beach** *525 Ocean Boulevard, Blackpool FY4 1EZ (0870 444 5566/www.blackpool pleasurebeach.com).*

## Rita: Queen of Speed
'Faster than a shuttle take-off, speedier than a Ferrari and with more lift than a plane,' boasts Alton Towers of its colourful 60mph ride. The shuttles are designed to look like cars, in keeping with the drag racing theme.
**Alton Towers** *Stoke-on-Trent, Staffordshire ST10 4DB (01538 703344/www.altontowers.com).*

## Roller Coaster
Why bother with an attention-grabbing name when Roller Coaster says it all? This signature attraction at Great Yarmouth's Pleasure Beach was opened in 1933 and is terrifically archaic, requiring a driver on board at all times to pull a lever and stop the thing. 'Unusually, there are no brakes fitted to the track at all,' says the Pleasure Beach. Be brave and climb aboard.
**Pleasure Beach** *South Beach Parade, Great Yarmouth, Norfolk NR30 3EH (01493 844585/ www.pleasure-beach.co.uk).*

## Shockwave
Opened in 1994, this stand-up rollercoaster at Drayton Manor Theme Park is the only upright ride of its kind in Europe. Though not the fastest on our list, Shockwave certainly packs in the thrills, featuring an 80-foot drop, a zero G roll and two corkscrews.
**Drayton Manor Theme Park** *see G Force, left.*

## Stealth
The towering, somewhat phallic, arch of Stealth's track has become an icon of Thorpe Park since the ride opened in 2006. Though it is the shortest ride on our list (just 14 seconds), it's also the fastest, reaching speeds of 80mph in just two seconds, thanks to a 2007 upgrade.
**Thorpe Park** *Staines Road, Chertsey, Surrey KT16 8PN (0870 444 4466/www.thorpepark.co.uk).*

## The Ultimate
At one and a half miles, the Ultimate in Yorkshire's Lightwater Valley park is the longest rollercoaster in Britain (and the third longest in the world). It's also the most scenic, winding over Yorkshire greenery, though that doesn't mean a lack of scares: the 160-foot drop is a real stomach churner.
**Lightwater Valley** *North Stainley, Ripon, North Yorkshire HG4 3HT (0870 458 0040/ www.lightwatervalley.co.uk).*

## 551 Have a Eureka! moment in Halifax

Forget glass cases and notices saying 'please don't touch': everything at Eureka! is there to be poked, prodded, bounced on and banged. Pre-schoolers can use touch-screen technology to design a butterfly, listen to singing lullaby leaves, or make their own inimitable music by bashing the bells and wind-chimes in the Sound Garden; in Desert Discovery, dressing up in hard hats and using the bucket-lift to collect 'rocks' to build desert dwellings is toddler bliss.

Children can also experience the mysteries of grown-up life by withdrawing money from the Eureka! Bank, shopping at the mini-M&S and filling up the car at the garage – the height of mundanity for adults, but oddly enthralling to the infant mind. When that pales, they can drive a lorry to the moon, step inside a giant mouth to find the wobbly tooth, or perform on stage in the Soundspace. Regular afternoon craft sessions for pre-schoolers are led by the superbly child-friendly staff, while the weekend science buskers demonstrate a whole host of tricks (the alka-seltzer and lemon juice rocket is an all-time classic). And let's not forget the marvellous spectacle of Archimedes making a splash in his overhead bath every 30 minutes…

Admission prices are on a sliding scale, from £7.25 for adults to £1 for babies; season tickets pay for themselves a thousand times over, as you can easily spend a whole day just in the bank and M&S. Rather like real life, in fact.
**Eureka! The Museum for Children** *Discovery Road, Halifax, West Yorkshire HX1 2NE (01422 330069/www.eureka.org.uk).*

## 552 Sleep in a fisherman's hut

You can't get much closer to the sea than these converted cockle-fishers' huts in Whitstable: wake up to the sound of seagulls' cries, and go to sleep with the ocean crashing on the shingle. The six huts are booked way ahead in July and August – but autumn's far more atmospheric.
**Hotel Continental** *29 Beach Walk, Whitstable, Kent CT5 2BP (01227 280280/www.hotel continental.co.uk).*

## 553 See volleyball's finest in action

Forget Copacabana Beach; Brighton, Poole, Bridlington, Weymouth and Skegness are among the seaside locations where Britain's top male and female volleyball players get down in the sand and fight for glory (www.volleyballengland.org/Beach). The annual summer tour runs from June to September – and there's usually a spare court for spectators to have a game as well.

## 554 Slather black butter on your toast in Jersey

This Jersey delicacy (*lé nièr buerre*, to give it its official title) is made from apples, lemons, liquorice and spices, and has to be stirred continuously for 30 hours to bring it to its 'proper' consistency – sticky enough to bind a plate to the back of a wooden spoon, according to tradition. Dark and spicy, it's scrumptious on toast or a croissant. La Mare Vineyards (01534 481178, www.lamarewineestate.com) is a popular place to buy a jar.

## 555 Wolf-whistle Miss Transgender

A beauty pageant with a twist, the annual Miss Transgender contest (www.misstg.co.uk) celebrates the glitz and glamour of Britain's transgender community. Held at a different Brighton venue every year, its categories include Miss Transgender, Mr Transgender and Miss Mature, for 'ladies' over 45, with entry open to transvestites, transsexuals, drag kings and queens and cross-dressers. In 2007, a James Bond theme suited dashing guys and diamond-laden girls, who answered coquettish questions on style icons, vital statistics (which are mostly made up), pairs of heels owned ('My name is Imelda!') and proudest and most embarrassing moments in drag, most of which involved public humiliation in extravagant stilettos. With makeovers, a disco, cabaret and burlesque entertainment, it's a great night out for boys and girls – and anyone in between.

## 556 Pull a face at the Egremont Crab Fair

This bizarre competition takes place every September in Cumbria at the decidedly offbeat Egremont Crab Fair (www.egremontcrabfair.org.uk). Competitors have to pull grotesque expressions, with their head stuck through a horse collar or 'braffin'. The fair itself has been taking place since 1267; if the gurning gets too much for you, we strongly recommend the other main event, where intrepid locals attempt to shimmy up a 30-foot pole greased with lard in order to collect a leg of lamb at the top.

## 557 Cross the Tarr Steps

Spanning the River Barle in Exmoor National Park (www.exmoor-nationalpark.gov.uk), this medieval 'clapper' bridge (an ancient type of crossing, made from giant slabs of stone) is an impressive feat of engineering. Legend has it the devil built the bridge to win a bet (some bet – the 180-foot-long bridge comprises 17 spans, with each enormous stone weighing several tons). Visit in spring to see the spectacular bluebells in the surrounding woodland, and look out for otters and red deer.

## 558 Buy wallpaper at Timorous Beasties

Subversive isn't a word you'd generally associate with wallpaper – but the designers at cult interiors company Timorous Beasties have never been afraid to shake things up. Artfully combining contemporary images with ultra-traditional prints, their wallpapers and fabrics are delightfully surreal, if a trifle disturbing. Take the London toile; from a distance, a traditional 18th-century toile de Jouy print that even your grandmother would adore. On closer inspection, all is not as it seems: in place of charmingly rustic scenes, there are delicately-etched depictions of beggars, muggers and underage drinkers. Thanks to the beautiful draughtsmanship and luxurious finishes, it's easy to fall in love with the most unexpected of designs – just don't blame us if your walls end up plastered with giant iguanas, scarily magnified insects or Special Brew-swigging delinquents.

**Timorous Beasties** *384 Great Western Road, Glasgow G4 9HT (0141 337 2622); 46 Amwell Street, London EC1R 1XS (020 7833 5010/ www.timorousbeasties.com).*

## 559

### Cross the causeway to Lindisfarne

Twice a day, the North Sea inundates the causeway linking the island of Lindisfarne to mainland Northumberland. This intermittent isolation only adds to the romance of Holy Island, seat of Celtic Christianity and a pilgrimage destination since Anglo-Saxon times. Viking raids drove away the early monks, who arrived in 635, but the Normans re-established a priory that existed until its suppression in 1537; romantic ruins are all that remain today (01289 389200, www.english-heritage.org.uk). The equally romantic Lindisfarne Castle (01289 389244, www.nationaltrust.org.uk) was built in Tudor times and refurbished in the early 20th century by Lutyens.

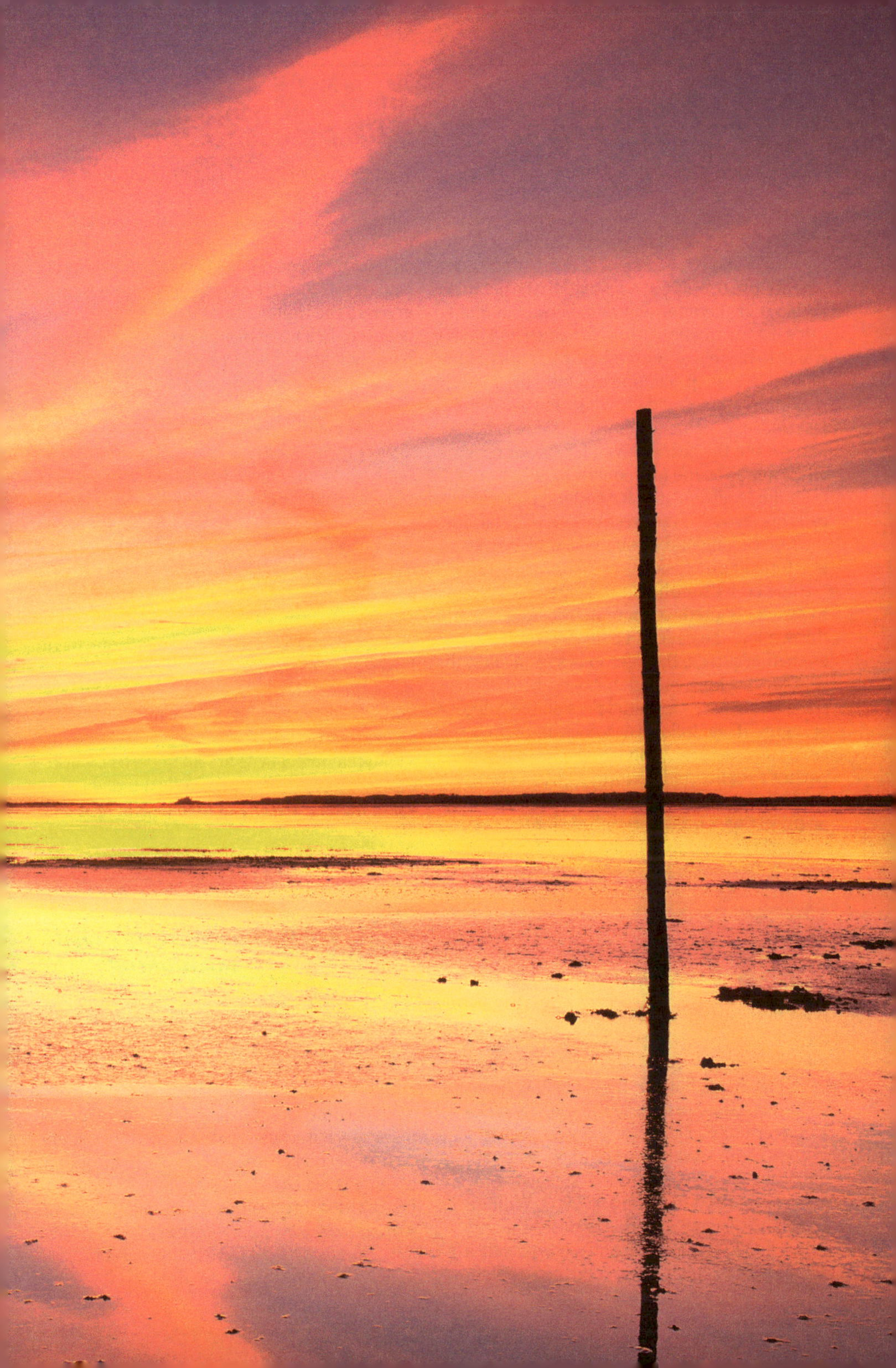

## 560 Burn a boat at Up-Helly-Aa

You've seen in the new year and done the sales; what else could banish the midwinter blues? Head hard north to Lerwick in the Shetland Islands for the last Tuesday of January (Old Yule) and join the islanders in a spot of beer and bonfire revelry, in a festival that celebrates their Viking heritage (www.up-helly-aa.org.uk).

It's not all dressing up as Norsemen and laying waste to barrels of Dark Island ale; painstaking months are spent building a Viking galley ship, making costumes and growing shaggy beards. Daytime events include music sessions and a parade, but the best is saved for the evening, when a brass band and squads of colourfully costumed 'guisers' (not for nothing do locals call this festival Transvestite Tuesday) parade the replica longship through Lerwick's streets in a torchlit procession.

Huge crowds gather at the burning site to watch hundreds of flaming torches being thrown into the galley in a nod to Norse pagan cremation rituals; the inferno is spectacular, the heat far-reaching enough for parents to remove coats and scarves from toddlers on the coldest of nights. Then follows a riotous all-nighter, as the squads do the rounds of local halls and parties to dance and perform satirical sketches. And here's where, as a visitor, it helps to score an invitation, or it'll be a rather more down-to-earth trip to the pub to end your night (although some halls do also sell tickets to the public).

## 561 Remember Graham Greene

Born in Berkhamsted, Graham Greene put the town on the literary map with *The Human Factor*, having already dealt with more exotic locations. In his honour, the town now hosts an annual Graham Greene Festival, held close to his birthday in October (www.grahamgreenefestival.com), with film screenings, a literary quiz, an amiable walk around the town and guest speakers – including, in 2007, William Boyd and Clement Freud. Attendees then gather to hear a selection of Greene parodies and pastiches, followed by a birthday toast.

## 562 Step on American soil in Surrey

There is a corner of an English field that is forever America – an acre at Runnymede in Surrey, scene of the signing of the Magna Carta (01784 432891, www.nationaltrust.org.uk). As an inscription on the Portland stone memorial explains: 'This acre of English ground was given to the United States of America by the people of Britain in memory of John F Kennedy, born 19th May, 1917: President of the United States 1961-63: died by an assassin's hand 22nd November, 1963.' You can reach the memorial by climbing the steep granite steps; one for each year of the president's life. The memorial was unveiled by the Queen in 1965, in the presence of Jackie and the children.

## 563 Wonder at the World of Mechanical Music

As well as repairing and selling antique music boxes and clocks, this place has a one-of-a-kind museum devoted to 'self-playing instruments and automata'. The lovingly maintained musical clocks, boxes, barrel organs, gramophones and violin-playing clowns are all in perfect working order – as you'll discover on the guided tour.
**Keith Harding's World of Mechanical Music** *Oak House, High Street, Northleach, Gloucestershire GL54 3ET (01451 860181/www.mechanicalmusic.co.uk).*

## 564 Sample a star chef in the making

High-flying alumni from University College of Food in Birmingham work in top eateries across the globe: to taste the culinary creations of the next big thing, book a table at the college's student-run fine dining restaurant, Atrium. You're acting as a guinea pig for the students, it's true – but when the menu includes the likes of Bresse chicken and foie gras terrine and honey-glazed Gressingham duck, and costs just £21 for three courses, who's complaining?
**Atrium** *University College Birmingham, Summer Row, Birmingham B3 1JB (0121 604 1000/www.bcftcs.ac.uk).*

# 565
## Buy a miniature masterpiece

The annual RCA Secret Sale gives art-lovers the chance to purchase a big-name original work for a mere £40, as 2,500 postcard-sized artworks by established artists, designers and illustrators, mixed in with the work of RCA graduates, are sold off on a first-come-first-served basis. The 'secret' is that the artists only sign the back of the work, so you don't know who you're buying until you've paid up. Going by previous sales, eagle-eyed collectors could pocket themselves a Damien Hirst or a Tracey Emin. You can only buy four works, though – so choose wisely and well.
**Royal College of Art** *Kensington Gore, London SW7 2EU (020 7590 4186/www.rca.ac.uk/secret).*

*Appropriating Jack Pierson, and Robert Indiana*

# 566
## Take a trip to Monkey World

The monkeys here have been rescued from pet shops and abusive owners around the world – or the ignominy of being dressed up and paraded on Spanish beaches. Set up in 1987, the centre works in conjunction with foreign governments to stop the illegal smuggling of apes from Africa and Asia. There are over 160 inhabitants, including 60 chimps – the largest group outside Africa – plus capuchin monkeys, squirrel monkeys, macaques, marmosets and gibbons. Don't miss the centre's newest arrival, Paulo, a woolly monkey born in November 2007. Your own little monkeys can swing on the ropes and swings in the adventure play area; there's also a pet's corner, café and education centre. The 65-acre woodland site is perfect for ambles and picnics, but not so great on rainy days: when the heavens open, the animals quite sensibly retire indoors, where you won't see much of them.
**Monkey World** *Longthorns, Wareham, Dorset BH20 6HH (01929 462537/www.monkeyworld.org).*

# 567-574 Take a bat walk

With the help of organisations like the Bat Conservation Trust and local bat groups (as well as the brilliant bat detector machines that translate different ultrasound bat calls into audible frequencies), sites all over the UK are offering the public the chance to see these mysterious, flighty creatures up close, and understand a little more about them.

Bat walks usually take place at twilight in the summer months and walk dates tend to be sporadic: ring ahead to check times, make sure you book early, and take torches and warm clothing. For more information on local events, visit the Bat Conservation Trust website: www.bats.org.uk/batgroups. Below are a few good places to start.

## David Marshall Lodge
Perched above Loch Ard Forest, the lodge offers bat walks in the Forestry Commission's Queen Elizabeth Forest Park in summer, following refreshments and a slide show.
**David Marshall Lodge** *Queen Elizabeth Forest Park, Aberfoyle, Stirling FK8 3UX (01877 382258/www.forestry.gov.uk).*

## Dunster Castle
Guided bat walks head out to watch the Daubenton's bats and Pipistrelles that live in and around the wooded garden of this dramatic hilltop fortress. Not that they stay outside: a colony of Lesser Horseshoe bats have also set up camp in the castle's medieval spiral staircase.
**Dunster Castle** *Dunster, near Minehead, Somerset TA24 6SL (01643 821314/ www.nationaltrust.org.uk).*

## Highgate Wood
Ever-popular bat walks are organised among the oaks and hornbeams of this lovely ancient woodland, granted to Londoners as an open space forever by the Lord Mayor in 1886. Book well in advance.
**Highgate Wood** *Muswell Hill Road, London N10 3JN (020 8444 6129/www.cityoflondon.gov.uk/ openspaces).*

## Ilam Park
A splendid combination that involves a walk round Ilam Park in the beautiful White Peak area of the Peak District National Park, then a slap-up dinner of sausages and mash. There is only one walk a year in August: book ahead.
**Ilam Park** *Ilam, Ashbourne, Derbyshire DE6 2AZ (01335 350503/www.nationaltrust.org.uk).*

## London Wetland Centre
After a 30-minute introductory presentation, groups of around ten head out with guides and their bat detectors into the 100-odd acres of this award-winning Site of Special Scientific Interest in Barnes.
**WWT London Wetland Centre** *Queen Elizabeth's Walk, London SW13 9WT (020 8409 4400/ www.wwt.org.uk).*

## Newark Park
The austere setting of this hunting lodge, perched on a 40-foot cliff, is an ideal as well as an atmospheric place to search for bats.
**Newark Park** *Ozleworth, Wotton-under-Edge, Gloucestershire GL12 7PZ (01453 842644/ www.nationaltrust.org.uk).*

## Renishaw Hall
The Italianate gardens of Renishaw Hall provide a delightful setting for 'Going Batty' walks. If there are any injured bats, you'll get a chance to see them close up.
**Renishaw Hall** *Renishaw, Sheffield S21 3WB (01246 432310/www.sitwell.co.uk).*

## Weald & Downland Open Air Museum
The Sussex Bat Group runs the walks around this 50-acre site, which is home to around 50 buildings from all over the country that have been saved from destruction and carefully reconstructed here.
**Weald & Downland Open Air Museum** *Singleton, Chichester, West Sussex PO18 0EU (01243 811464/www.wealddown.co.uk).*

# 575 Hit the slopes in Surrey

If a sedate wander through the 180 acres of parkland, lakes and woods of Priory Farm leaves you cold, try its mountainboarding course instead. Mountainboarding? It's a bit like snowboarding without the snow, and with the addition of four heavy-treaded scooter-sized wheels. That's it: it's off-road skateboarding over ramps and grassy downhill slopes. You can hire all the gear there, or get your own kit and take to the hills on your own.
**Priory Farm** *Nutfield, Redhill, Surrey RH1 4EJ (01737 822458/www.ridethehill.com).*

# 576 Explore a proper wilderness

The 1,470 square miles of ancient granite hills, heather moorland, lochs, rivers, marshes and endless sky that constitute the Cairngorms National Park (01479 873535, www.cairngorms.co.uk) are home to an incredible 25 per cent of all Britain's endangered species. Here are ospreys and lampreys, golden eagles and capercaillies, otters and pine martens, sika deer and reindeer – to name but a paltry few of all that the park has to offer. And if that isn't wild enough for you, it also has the largest area of arctic mountain landscape in the British Isles.

# 577 *Get hands-on at Yorkshire Sculpture Park*

Discover your inner Barbara Hepworth or Eduardo Paolozzi on one of YSP's summer sculpture courses. Covering wood, stone or metalwork, they're suitable for beginners and experienced artists alike. If you're more of a spectator than a sculptor, simply take in the splendid 500-acre sprawl of 18th-century parkland, where sheep amble past Henry Moore sculptures and kids joyfully run riot. Once you've paid the car park charge – £4 for the day – entry to the grounds, visitor's centre and indoor galleries is free. Outdoor highlights include Jonathan Borofsky's 100-foot *Molecule Man*, Elisabeth Frink's bronze water buffaloes, Anthony Caro's tubular sculptures as well as the Moores and Hepworths. Don't expect to find them where you last saw them, though: pieces are moved around the site, and the line-up constantly changes. The Access Sculpture Trail is specially designed for wheelchairs and pushchairs; otherwise, you need sturdy footwear and strong legs – especially in winter, when the rough terrain can get very muddy.
**Yorkshire Sculpture Park** *West Bretton, Wakefield, West Yorkshire WF4 4LG (01924 832631/www.ysp.co.uk).*

## 578 See the Shot at Dawn Memorial

It's thought that 306 British and Commonwealth soldiers were executed for either desertion or cowardice during World War I. Unveiled in 2001 in the National Memorial Arboretum in Staffordshire, the Shot at Dawn Memorial is a long-overdue tribute to the men who faced the firing squad.

The ten-foot statue of a blindfolded young soldier, tied to a stake, was modelled on 17-year-old Private Herbert Burden. Private Burden had lied about his age to join up; at the time of his death, he was still too young to officially be a member of his regiment, the Northumberland Fusiliers. A semicircle of stakes around the statue records the names of all 306 executed men.

**National Memorial Arboretum** *Croxall Road, Alrewas, Staffordshire DE13 7AR (01283 792333/ www.thenma.org.uk).*

## 579 Go letterboxing on Dartmoor

Increasingly popular worldwide, letterboxing is like orienteering with a treasure hunt thrown in. A pot (the 'letterbox') containing a stamp and a visitors' book is hidden, and a map reference (or more cryptic clue) leads seekers to the spot. When they've found the pot, the letterboxer takes a copy of the stamp (rather like getting your passport stamped) and leaves their own personal print in the book.

Letterboxes are stashed away all over the country, but Dartmoor is where it all began. In 1854, James Perrott set up a small cairn with a glass jar inside it at Cranmere Pool; walkers would leave postcards or letters inside, which the next hiker to discover the box would then post. Reaching the early locations was, and still is, a significant achievement; these days boxes are all over the place (some even within ambling distance of car parks), and the allure of stamp collecting appears to have overtaken letterboxing's mental and physical challenges for some people. Nonetheless, it's still a fun excuse for a jolly good wander over the moors (01392 832768, www.dartmoorletterboxing.org).

## 580 Hear a nightingale sing at Rutland Water

When Vera Lynn's song was all the rage in 1940s London, you probably could hear a nightingale sing in Berkeley Square; not so now, given the traffic and dwindling bird population. Nightingales live in dense woodland scrub and usually don't pipe up in exposed areas, hence the scarcity of sightings. To hear one, visit one of their favoured breeding and nesting sites, Rutland Water, between mid April and mid June, when these summer migrants arrive in England. Six pairs are known to nest in Hambleton Wood and Gibbets Gorge at Rutland; a guided walk (in glorious bluebell woods) will maximise your chance of seeing as well as hearing them. Nightingales are nocturnal, so your best chance of catching a tune is at dawn or dusk. The centre's opening times vary throughout the year.

**Rutland Water Nature Reserve** *Egleton, Oakham, Rutland LE15 8BT (01572 770651/ www.rutlandwater.org.uk).*

## 581 Search for samphire

Summer is the season for samphire (*salicornia europea*), which grows wild on the tidal flats and salt marshes of the north Norfolk coast. Head off (cautiously) across the wide, breezy mud plains when the tide has sucked the sea so far back it's almost out of sight and, for an hour or two, you're at one with nature – a hunter-gatherer in green wellies. 'Poor man's asparagus' also appeals directly to the inner tightwad: being able to ignore the bunches that pop up at markets, local shops and at practically every roadside stall in the locality is deeply satisfying. Once home, wash and boil the samphire, simmering for ten minutes or so. Add butter/pepper/vinegar to taste, then suck the fleshy green fronds from the stalks.

# 582
## See pickled bodies at the Surgeons Hall Museum

The grisly collections here trace the history of medicine from 1505 to the present day: sensitive souls may find the preserved human remains unsettling (unaccompanied under-15s are not admitted), and you'll either love or loathe the dentistry section. A pocketbook covered with the tanned skin of William Burke, who, along with his accomplice William Hare, killed at least 16 Edinburgh citizens in 1827-28 and sold their bodies for dissection, is also on display.
**Royal College of Surgeons of Edinburgh**
*18 Nicholson Street, Edinburgh EH9 9DW (0131 527 1649/www.rcsed.ac.uk).*

# 583
## Lay siege to Warwick

Trebuchets were enormous medieval war machines, used to catapult rocks at besieged castles' walls (and sometimes hurl manure and dead animals inside, in an attempt to spread disease). It may sound like something out of a Monty Python sketch, but it's true: see for yourself at Warwick Castle, where there's a historically accurate 22-ton, 59-foot-high wooden trebuchet, which fires twice daily from March through to October.
**Warwick Castle** *Warwick, Warwickshire CV34 4QU (0870 442 2000/www.warwick-castle.co.uk).*

# 584
## Go coasteering in Pembrokeshire

Coasteering involves a scramble along the rocky hinterland between sea and shore; scrambling for footholds on the rocks, traversing narrow ledges and exploring caves and coves, clad in wetsuits, safety helmets and trainers. (It's rather like rockpooling for adrenaline junkies.) The sport sprang up around the Pembrokeshire coast, and this remains its heartland: try an introductory session with TYF Adventure (01437 721611, www.tyf.com), which has been coasteering these cliffs for years.

# 585
## Holiday in a pineapple

There's no need to venture abroad for a taste of the tropics, when you can stay in your very own prickly pear – albeit one made of stone. The 75-foot pineapple folly at Dunmore Park, near Stirling, is one of the oldest examples of the fashion for architectural flights of fancy. Built as a garden retreat for the earl and his wife, the fruit was chosen as it represented the height of gourmet luxury in the 1760s. These days, the peculiar pavilion can be rented out through the Landmark Trust (01628 825925, www.landmarktrust.org.uk), which specialises in rescuing quirky old buildings and turning them into holiday homes with a difference.

If you're after less frivolous accommodation, book in at the austere House of Correction at Folkingham, Lincolnshire; part of a former prison, it sleeps up to four inmates. Other unusual options include the Wardrobe in Salisbury, a cosy attic apartment in a former bishop's storehouse, and the unexpectedly palatial-looking Pigsty in Robin Hood's Bay – probably the world's only folly created for pigs.

# 586 *Learn the art of butchery*

# The first cut

*Will Fulford-Jones gets to grips with slipknots and meat cleavers.*

'First of all,' offers the gentleman behind the counter, 'plasters are five pounds, and medical attention will be 20 quid for 15 minutes.' There's the merest hint of a grin, but the laughter that greets his words arrives just a little too quickly. We are here of our own accord, enthusiastic participants to a man (and we are all male), but we're also a little nervous. After all, many of us have grown quite attached to our fingers. It is a wet Tuesday evening in January, and we are gathered at the Ginger Pig's Marylebone shop to learn the basics of butchery.

Some trades inspire fascination among outsiders. Butchery, though, doesn't generally evoke much more than squeamishness. Most Britons don't want to know how their meat reached their plate – so what are we doing here, forking out a decent chunk of money for the privilege of cutting up a cow?

Our story begins at Borough Market. For one thing, it's where the Ginger Pig started selling its meat in the late 1990s; for another, this corner of the city is arguably where London's food revolution really took hold. The astonishing success of the weekend farmers' market inspired smaller-scale but similar operations all over town, each built on the knowledge that there is an appetite for good-quality raw ingredients and an interest in their origins. And as a result, some foodies have decided to take their curiosity a step further and learn what happens to the meat between the abbatoir and the oven.

Among the participants tonight are Bill, a photographer who's signed up for three of these courses in advance of a move to Suffolk; Jeff, here from Seattle on what amounts to a year-long vacation courtesy of his wife's high-powered banking job; and your correspondent, a reluctant cook and diehard city-dweller who hasn't so much as seen a cow since the last episode of *All Creatures Great and Small.*

Our guides for the evening are a similarly disparate pair. Borut Kozelj spent several years studying to be a butcher in his home country of

Time Out 1000 Things to do in Britain 175

Slovenia, before arriving in London a few years ago. Perry Bartlett, meanwhile, is a dry-witted, Estuary-accented gent from Kent who got into the profession the old-fashioned way: starting at the bottom and clambering up the ladder. A couple of scars act as testament to the fact that one or two of the rungs may have been a little tricky to negotiate.

Together, the pair set the evening in motion by talking us through the basics. We learn the difference between organic and free range meat (which, it turns out, is considerably more complex than mere semantics); between dry- and wet-ageing (in a nutshell, the former results in more flavoursome meat but at a considerably greater cost); between the different cuts of meat found on a cow and how best to cook them; and between the American and British terms for various different steaks. It's a lot to take in, but it's undeniably interesting stuff.

A trip around the cold storage room follows, as Borut and Perry point out the various cuts and explain the age-driven differences in their appearances, textures and tastes. From the rails hangs an array of carcasses, swinging eerily from the ceiling as the eight of us – Borut and Perry, the five amateurs and *Time Out* photographer Charlie, whose girlfriend is a vegan and who seems delighted by such a gallery of corporeal nourishment – duck and weave between them.

Eventually, we get down to business around a butcher's block that's plainly seen plenty of action, but not before sharpening our tools on yellow-handled steels: that old chestnut about blunt knives being more dangerous than sharp ones is apparently perfectly true. It's very much a case of follow the leader, with Perry and Borut taking turns to walk us through the process before we're let loose on the slippery, two-kilo cuts of beef deposited in front of each of us.

Off, first, comes the top layer of fat, gently nicked away with the tip of the knife. Out comes the saw and then, after some more excess baggage has been stripped away, it's time for the beef to be 'frenched', the process of gently scraping the excess meat and fat from the protuding ribs to create a neat and presentable joint. Well, that's the idea, anyway. Sadly, my own bestial creation looks as if it may have spent the last half-hour being used as a football.

A quick glance at the time reveals that this has all taken a surprisingly long time, extended still further by my hopeless inability to tie butcher's string around the joint in a final, and somewhat forlorn, attempt to tidy things up a little. ('It's a slipknot,' offers someone, as the string drops pathetically off the edge of the block for the dozenth time.) But it's also been far less gory than any of us were expecting: blood, both bovine and human, has been conspicuous by its absence.

By the time I finally, mercifully, succeed in tying the final knot, everyone else has wandered into the kitchen to be greeted by the sight of an absolutely mammoth hunk of beef that's been slow-cooking in the shop's Aga for the last two-and-a-half hours. This, it turns out, is the reward for our endeavours, sliced by Borut into gigantic chunks and dished up with salad, a mountain of chips and liberal amounts of red wine. Forty-odd minutes later, full to bursting and with our own cuts of meat tucked under our arms, we shake hands and stagger into the evening.

The real moment of truth arrives two nights later, when the joint comes out of the fridge looking… well, no less amateurish than when I put it in there. After a quick spell of browning in a pan and 45 minutes in a 180-degree oven, out comes the beautifully rare, awesomely tender joint. Job done. Plasters? Who needs 'em.

*For details of the Ginger Pig's regular evening butchery classes, call 020 7935 7788. The £75 fee includes a roast dinner on site, plus the meat you prepared during the evening.*

## 587 Ride high on the Bridgnorth funicular

Bridgnorth, in Shropshire, comprises two towns, High and Low. Both are beautiful old places – but while one's up on the hill, the other's 100 feet below, beside the River Severn. Until 1892, folk in either town were forced to toil up and down 200 steps to reach the other end of town. Enter MP George Newnes, founder of the *Strand* magazine, who promoted the construction of the Bridgnorth Cliff Railway (01746 762052, www.bridgnorthcliffrailway.co.uk). The steepest, shortest and oldest inland funicular railway in the country, it still plays a crucial role in the town's transport infrastructure, affording its passengers effortless views more than 150 times a day, for just 90p return.

## 588 Embrace eccentricity at Snowshill Manor

After inheriting the family sugar fortune, eccentric architect Charles Paget Wade (1883-1956) bought the ruins of Snowshill Manor, restoring its cavernous rooms to their 15th-century grandeur. Not that he ever lived there: instead, he occupied a small cottage in the grounds, using the manor to store his vast collection of arts and crafts, and as a stage for his increasingly odd high-society parties. Guests – who included the likes of Virginia Woolf and John Betjeman – were often forced to dress up in ghoulish costumes from his collection and perform amateur dramatics in the great hall. (The occult intensity of his parlour games wasn't always appreciated; Graham Greene wrote that the host made his 'flesh creep'.) But Wade was a humanist as well as a hoarder, and donated his collection of over 22,000 pieces to the National Trust in 1951, by which time he'd amassed everything from butter stamps and bicycles to clocks and cow bells (not to mention 26 suits of Samurai armour). It makes for a fascinating afternoon's browsing – though the real draw is ruminating on the bizarre goings-on that once took place at this quaint Cotswold manor.
**Snowshill Manor** *Snowshill, near Broadway, Gloucestershire WR12 7JU (01386 852410/ www.nationaltrust.org.uk).*

## 589 Go whale-watching

While backflipping dolphins can be a crowd-pleaser, it's something else entirely to see a whale breach the waves. Nothing matches the thrill of encountering these majestic giants up close: their size can only be fully appreciated this way. That said, whales are elusive and don't perform just because you've paid (around £70-£100 a day) to see them. You could go out day after rainy day and spot nothing more than seagulls, so the first glimpse of a fin or tail – or if you're really lucky, a dive, bellyflop or spot of boat-chasing – is truly memorable; minke and orcas are the most commonly seen. The Whale and Dolphin Conservation Society's website (www.wdcs.org) or the Sea Watch Foundation (www.seawatchfoundation.org.uk) have guidelines on choosing operators; whale-watching hotspots include the Orkney and Shetland islands, the Moray Firth, the Scottish west coast and Cardigan Bay in Wales.

## 590 Welcome spring with Jack-in-the-Green

Dig out the face paint and join this not-so-little green man in Hastings for this weekend of May Day celebrations (www.hastingsjack.co.uk). Its highlight is a procession through the Old Town and along the seafront, where rag-costumed 'bogie' attendants accompany Jack on his way to the castle for a ceremonial 'slaying', to release the spirit of summer. The tradition is thought to have originated in the 17th-century practice of making floral garlands for the beltane festival, with groups competing to outdo each other until the elaborate garlands became man-sized and the foliage-covered Jack-in-the-Green character was born. Along with spectacular costumes, morris dancing and music, places around town host storytelling sessions, theatrical performances and the crowning of the May Queen. You can also take part in this traditional festival in Whitstable, Ilfracombe, Bristol and Knutsford.

## 591 Visit Compton Verney

This cool, elegant 18th-century house, designed by Robert Adam, is a suitably grand setting for a collection of paintings from 16th-century Germany, 17th- and 18th-century Naples, and 19th-century Britain. Check out the signage collection too: in the days when most people were illiterate, it was handy to be able to tell at a glance if you were headed to the butcher's or the baker's. After exploring the exhibitions, stroll through the splendid Capability Brown gardens.
**Compton Verney House Trust** *Compton Verney, Warwickshire CV35 9HZ (01926 645500/www.comptonverney.org.uk).*

## 592 Ramble the South Downs Way

Running over 100 miles of rolling chalk downland between Winchester in Hampshire to Eastbourne in East Sussex, the South Downs Way (www.southdownsway.co.uk) is a National Trail, open to walkers, cyclists and horse riders. Although it never rises higher than 700 feet, the horizons stretch 40 miles over land and sea; closer to your path lie butterflies and orchids, stone circles and dew ponds, windmills, woods and the imperious Seven Sisters cliffs.

## 593 Visit Chatley Heath Semaphore Tower

Each day, thousands of motorists unknowingly pass this relic of naval communications history as they thunder past junction 10 on the M25. It's the last survivor in a line of communication towers used by the Admiralty: flag-signalled messages could pass between London and Portsmouth in a matter of minutes. Stroll through its 700 acres of wood and heathland trails and take in the views of the North Downs from the tower. You can also see demonstrations of the working semaphore mast, and attempt signals yourself on replica models; mastering the flag signals is quite an upper-arm workout.
**Chatley Heath Semaphore Tower** *Pointers Road, Cobham, Surrey KT11 1PQ (01372 458822).*

## 594 Take a seat on Concorde

When Concorde was taken out of service in 2003, one of the sleek supersonic fleet went to the National Museum of Flight, where visitors can enjoy the 'Concorde Experience' – bar actually flying, of course. Concorde G-BOAA now resides in a custom-built hangar, with displays explaining the history and engineering behind this apogee of 20th-century air transport. Climb on board and imagine you're flying to New York at over twice the speed of sound: the big surprise is how pokey the cabin space feels for those of us more used to slow but substantial standard jumbo jets.
**National Museum of Flight** *East Fortune Airfield, near North Berwick, East Lothian EH39 5LF (01620 897240/www.nms.ac.uk).*

## 595 Look for the Lady of the Lake

North Cornwall is steeped in Arthurian legend, with Tintagel Castle – now a weatherbeaten, gloriously atmospheric ruin – famously staking its claim as the king's birthplace. But Arthur aficionados should also squelch across the boggy wastes of Bodmin Moor, in search of Dozmary Pool. It was here, some say, that Sir Bedivere threw Excalibur into the murky depths for safekeeping by the Lady of the Lake. Surveying the pool's eerily still surface, it's not hard to imagine a pale hand rising gracefully from the water to grasp the sword – unless you visit during a summer drought. The lake's not very deep, and spotting a stray beer can on its bed can somewhat dispel the romantic illusion. But although you are more likely to encounter shaggy ponies (and hikers) than a mythical lady in a shimmering gown, there's still a hint of mystery here. It's located past Colliford Lake, on Browngelly Downs (www.visitbodminmoor.co.uk).

## 596 Fill up on a Bedfordshire clanger

For the uninitiated, a clanger may call to mind the squealing space-dwelling mice of children's TV. Here in Bedfordshire, they know better. A clanger is a suet-crust pasty with a meat filling at one end, apple at the other – a sturdy dinner-and-afters-in-one for hardworking labourers, like its better-known Cornish cousin. Gunn's Bakery in Sandy still makes a mean clanger – best sampled straight from the oven (8 Market Square, Sandy, Bedfordshire SG19 GHU, 01767 680434).

## 597 Climb up to a crow's nest

Calling all would-be Jack Sparrows: how about taking to the high seas on a 197-foot square-rigged brig? Tall Ship Adventures run voyages (02392 832055, www.tallships.org) from day sails around the UK to three-week transatlantic crossings. You don't need sailing experience to join the 68-man crew, but be prepared to get hands-on swabbing the decks or setting the sail. The Tall Ships Youth Trust provides a number of bursaries (14-25-year-olds can apply).

## 598 Join the Heritage Seed Library

If you're interested in growing something other than common or garden vegetables, then pay £20 and join the excellent Heritage Seed Library (www.gardenorganic.org.uk/hsl). Members get to choose six seeds from the Library's annual catalogue of traditional vegetable varieties, otherwise in danger of dying out altogether. Bland, mass-grown greens aren't a patch on long-forgotten gems like Mr Bethell's purple podded peas, or Lady Godiva squash.

# 599 Go on a silent retreat

**Nick Rider** *finds perfect peace at the Vipassana Centre.*

Vipassana meditation isn't advertised, so people generally hear about it by word of mouth. At first, the idea of sitting in total silence for ten days sounds odd, if not alarming; but then, depending on who you are and whether you've ever thought of trying any kind of meditation before, the idea grows on you. Some meditation retreats sound like glorified country house weekends – a bit of gentle chanting between chilling in the garden. Hell no, you say, let's go for the real deal.

And then you arrive at the Vipassana Centre, in a farm outside Hereford (www.dhamma.org), wondering why on earth you're there. Having read the imposing-sounding (but very brief) 'Code of Discipline', the rules are clear: you won't be speaking for ten days, will have no contact with the outside world, will have nothing to read or listen to, and will meditate for around 11 hours daily between 4.30am and 9.30pm. No one can say they weren't warned.

Though Vipassana is based on a 2,500-year-old Buddhist practice, there is nothing conventionally 'religious' about it. There is no incense, no chanting, no saffron robes, absolutely no images of any kind. There is a minimum of theory. If you then want to learn about Buddhist doctrine, you can do that in your own time; if not, then that's fine too. The essential Vipassana course is a technique, based on carrying out a series of simple, practical instructions – beginning by focusing all your attention on the nose, and being aware of every breath as it enters and leaves the body.

Which is what you try to do, starting at 4.30am on the first day. And this is when my mind goes twang. I discover that I have the attention span of a deranged gnat, and cannot focus on more than three breaths together. Frustrations, longings and 20-year-old resentments all bubble up to grab my attention, beat me up and then wander off. At times I feel intensely lost, and intensely lonely. I repeat old jokes, and mentally redesign some furniture. By the end of the first day, I feel as if I've been over every memory I could possibly have in my head, and then been round again. This, of course, is all part of it. One interpretation of the word Vipassana is 'to see things as they really are', based on the idea that we normally concern ourselves with the past, the future and the imagination, with memories and vague expectations, never the present. The breath is used as a starting point simply because it is the most universal, most here-and-now human experience. Gradually, over time (and 11 hours a day is a lot of time), you develop more focus, more awareness of the present as a physical experience, and some of the relentless mental chatter dries up. This is a physical, mental and emotional process, for Vipassana assumes that all three are interlinked. Physical pains and tensions rooted deep down in the mind stand out like lamps in the dark, but you only observe them, as they ebb and flow in the body.

At the end of each day you are given your instructions for the next day in a video talk by the founder of international Vipassana, Mr SN Goenka of Mumbai. Being averse to anything with the remotest whiff of a cult, I was initially suspicious of the idea of having a video chat from a guru. No need. Goenka immediately lets you know he isn't anyone's guru, just a wise old owl who's been where you are. And he's very funny, understanding full well that after a day in your own head, some light relief is necessary. Vipassana is also one of the most generous, genuinely collective organisations around. There is no charge for a course; you just give a donation of whatever you can afford once it's over, and there's no pressure to leave anything.

In silence, time goes in strange directions: when the sign went up in the dining hall for day three, I was convinced they'd got it wrong, and that I'd been there at least a week. You feel as if you've been on a very long journey when, on the morning of day ten, silence is lifted, the faces around you suddenly acquire voices, and many of them begin chattering away vaguely euphorically. One of the features of Vipassana, of getting to appreciate 'reality as it is', is that people should never assume that their experience of meditation will be the same as anyone else's (or even that their own experience will be repeated). But I can say I've noticed that as they leave, most people seem to go out into the world with a new, bright clarity.

# 600-603
## Go to Gordon's gastropubs

If you've had enough of the shouty, sweary and generally ubiquitous Gordon Ramsay on telly, it might be time to sample first-hand the food that made his name. If his fine dining restaurants are out of reach, then his London gastropubs (www.gordonramsay.com) are an excellent compromise. The Narrow opened in 2007 to some fanfare, thanks in part to its Thames-side Wapping location, but also due to the defiantly British menu, which includes devilled lambs' kidneys, pork pie and London Particular (pea and ham soup). Ramsay's second venture, the Devonshire in Chiswick, offered more of the same: retro British recipes with the cobwebs brushed off them for the 21st century. Meaty Brown Windsor soup, a favourite with Queen Victoria, is a winner; for afters, the comforting lemon possett served with sponge fingers is perennially popular. The last in the Ramsay triumvirate, the Warrington in Maida Vale, opened in early 2008 – another polished-up Victorian boozer with traditional British grub. Thanks to the might of the Ramsay brand, you'll need to book well in advance. Though it's a bistro rather than a gastropub, Foxtrot Oscar in Chelsea is another affordable option, serving up classic dishes at surprisingly modest prices.

**The Narrow**

# 604
## Take the Inklings tour of Oxford

JRR Tolkien and CS Lewis – not a bad couple of members to start with, if you're setting up a literary discussion group. There were other important Inklings besides these two, though, as you'll discover on this walking tour – which also provides the chance to have a good poke around Oxford and some of its colleges. The tour takes place on Wednesdays at 11.45am, starting at Blackwell's bookshop. Set aside some time to explore the shop as well, especially the Norrington Room. With over three miles of shelving, it was once the largest single room dedicated to bookselling in the world.
**Blackwell Bookshop** *48-51 Broad Street, Oxford OX1 3BQ (01865 333606/www.blackwell.co.uk).*

## 605 Discover David Hockney at Salts Mill

When Jonathan Silver took over the semi-derelict 19th-century Salts Mill in 1987, he thought it would make the ideal showcase for David Hockney's talents. Hockney agreed – and was so keen that he even designed the napkins, menus and crockery for the café (which serves the biggest, tastiest scones in the world). Three galleries of Hockney's work cover everything from early sketches to photography, stage-sets and recent oils; once you've had your fill of artwork and scones, take a walk around the quaint streets of Saltaire. A purpose-built Victorian 'model' village, constructed by the mill's enlightened owner, Sir Titus Salt, it's now a World Heritage Site. Alternatively, venture further afield by taking the Victorian tramway to Shipley Glen. A fabulous day out – and (refreshments aside) all for free.
**Salts Mill** *Shipley, Saltaire, West Yorkshire BD18 3LA (01274 531163/www.saltsmill.org.uk).*

## 606
## *Puzzle over the Mathematical Bridge*

Legend has it that the curious-looking bridge spanning the River Cam at Queens' College (www.queens.cam.ac.uk) was the handiwork of none other than Isaac Newton, ingeniously constructed from interlocking wooden pieces that didn't need bolts to hold them together. Amazed, the college dons took it apart to investigate – and couldn't work out how to put it together again (hence the nuts and bolts that are now in place). In truth, the bridge was built in 1749 by James Essex the Younger and designed by William Etheridge; Newton died in 1727, so it's unlikely he was involved. Some insist the bridge was originally made without bolts, and would hold firm if they were removed – a theory generations of undergraduates have drunkenly contemplated putting to the test. Meander across and make up your own mind.

## 607 Hide away on romantic Burgh Island

Although easily reached from shore, ten-acre Burgh Island feels wonderfully remote. Pilchard fishermen and pirates once made a lonely living here – one Tom Crocker was shot by customs men right outside the 14th-century Pilchard Inn – but for most of the 20th century the island was the preserve of socialites, who holed up in the Burgh Island Hotel (01548 810514, www.burghisland.com). Noël Coward came for three days and stayed three weeks, and Edward brought Wallis Simpson here.

'Uncle' Archibald Nettlefold built the 'country house by the sea', with its copper-green turret, ballroom and sea-fed Mermaid Pool in 1929. After a period of post-war decline, painstaking restoration has returned the hotel to its art deco glory. Nowadays, Burgh offers a distinctly old-fashioned luxury. Televisions are out; ballgowns and billiards are definitely in. (As are weekly arrivals by helicopter, greeted with champagne.) The evening brings dances to the strains of a white grand piano, cocktails and excellent meals made from local produce.

Can't afford the hotel? There's still fun to be had. For £1.50 you can ride the hotel's 1969 hydraulic sea tractor (designed by nuclear engineer Robert Jackson in return for a case of bubbly), which raises passengers above the waves even as the wheels trundle along the sea-bottom. And less expensive sustenance can be found – along with Tom Crocker's ghost – at the Pilchard Inn (01548 810514).

## 608 Ride the Crab & Winkle Way

This evocatively named seven-mile cycling and walking trail runs from Canterbury to Whitstable (www.sustrans.org.uk), following the disused railway track of the Crab & Winkle Line. Mainly traffic-free, the route meanders through the Kentish countryside and ancient woodland at Blean Woods, before emerging close to the harbour at Whitstable. You can hire bikes at Downland Cycles (Malthouse, St Stephens Road, Canterbury CT2 7JA 01227 479693), a five-minute walk from Canterbury West Station.

# 609
## *Do as the Romans did in Bath*

The Thermae Bath Spa is Britain's only natural thermal spa, fed by the same springs that tickled Roman toes almost 2,000 years ago. A two-hour session at the spa costs a very reasonable £22, and includes access to either the New Royal Bath or Cross Bath plus the aroma steam rooms, waterfall shower and stunning open-air rooftop pool with views across the city. Over 50 spa treatments are available, including Watsu, a form of massage that takes place in the mineral-rich waters.
**Thermae Bath Spa** *Hetling Pump Room, Hot Bath Street, Bath BA1 1SJ (0844 888 0844/ www.thermaebathspa.com).*

## 610 Visit Lawrence of Arabia's cottage

Fêted for his manly adventures fighting the Ottomans in the Arabian desert during World War I, TE Lawrence sought to escape his post-war celebrity status at Clouds Hill, a secluded cottage near Wareham in Dorset; it was here that he completed his dramatic account of his experiences in the desert, the *Seven Pillars of Wisdom*. Thirteen years later, following a motorcycle accident, he fell into a coma and died. His home – now owned by the National Trust – reflects his complex personality, and has an exhibition devoted to his extraordinary life. Lawrence is buried at nearby Moreton Church, and a stone memorial marks the site of the accident.

**Clouds Hill** *Wareham, Dorset BH20 7NQ (01929 405616/www.nationaltrust.org.uk).*

## 611
## Sip Britain's strongest ale

First brewed in 1968, Thomas Hardy's is Britain's strongest, rarest and strangest ale. Matured in oak sherry casks for nine months, the nigh-on 12 per cent tipple is often drunk as a digestif and, unlike most other beers, can be 'laid down' for several years before drinking. Served only in selected outlets, this celebratory booze was conceived in honour of the 40th anniversary of the writer's death. O'Hanlon's Brewery (Great Barton Farm, Whimple, Devon EX5 2NY, 01404 822412, www.ohanlons.co.uk), now produces this annual 'vintage', some bottles of which are bound for as far afield as Japan. Dart's Farm (Topsham, Exeter, Devon EX3 0QH, 01392 878200, www.dartsfarm.co.uk) at nearby Topsham is the handiest local outlet if you believe that beer shouldn't travel; heathens, however, can also buy the tipple in Waitrose for around £3.70 per 25cl. A special vintage is being produced for the summer of 2008, 40 years after the first.

## 612 Pick your own lavender at Carshalton

When Queen Victoria was on the throne, the fields of Carshalton (now in the London Borough of Sutton) were given over to lavender farming. The oil was used in the popular ladies' scents, as well as in disinfectants and herbal remedies. In midsummer, just before the August harvest, the whole area was magically transformed by swathes of the fragrant mauve-blue plant. Those days are long gone, but a small vestige of what was once a great industry remains on three acres of disused allotment ground managed by a dedicated lavender-growing community group. The harvest has become a memorable annual event locally, and is usually held in mid July (the harvest is earlier these days, possibly due to climate change); any volunteer pickers are welcome.

**Carshalton Lavender** *Stanley Road Allotments, Oaks Way, Carshalton, Surrey SM5 4NQ (07948 174907/www.carshaltonlavender.org).*

## 613
## Visit Whipsnade Tree Cathedral

The Tree Cathedral near Dunstable is exactly that – trees, hedges and shrubs set out in the form of a medieval cathedral. It was planted between 1931 and 1939 by a Mr EK Blyth, who created it in the spirit of 'faith, hope and reconciliation' following the deaths of two World War I comrades. Visitors walk along grass avenues that form the nave, chancel, transepts and chapels; a pond is set at the centre of a cloister-garden. During World War II, the young garden was left untended while Blyth went back to war but on his return, the undergrowth was cleared to allow services to be held. Today, around five services are held here each year; although the cathedral hasn't been consecrated (worship has been led by many Christian denominations), the spirit of this serenely beautiful spot is quietly affecting, whatever your faith.

**Whipsnade Tree Cathedral** *Chapel Farm, Whipsnade, Dunstable, Bedfordshire LU6 2LL (01582 872406/www.nationaltrust.org.uk).*

# 614
## Ride the Tarka Line to follow the Tarka Trail

Henry Williamson first came to north Devon by motorbike, escaping suburban London and his experiences in World War I. His forays into the local countryside and experiences of caring for an abandoned otter cub inspired his classic novel, *Tarka the Otter*, first published in 1927. The name 'Tarka' has since been adopted for a railway line (running between Exeter and Barnstaple and following the Taw river) and a walking and cycling route – not to mention dozens of tea shops throughout the region.

The unspoiled countryside that provides the backdrop for the trials and tribulations of the eponymous mustelid is best seen via the impressive Tarka Trail (www.tarka.org.uk), a 180-mile path. Alight from the train at Eggesford to join the route, which loops in a figure of eight from Barnstaple south to the rural heartland of the county, north to the cliffs and beaches of the north Devon coast and east into Exmoor. For 32 miles between Braunton and Meeth, it follows a disused railway line – a flat, traffic-free route that's perfect for cycling.

# 615
## See the Northern Lights

That roiling mass of nuclear fusion that we call the sun occasionally spews out material into the solar system, which travels enormous distances then bumps into the earth. The planet's magnetic field deflects most of it, but at the poles it interacts with the atmosphere to create the Aurora Borealis, or Northern Lights. It's a startling show of fast-flickering greens, reds and purple-blues – sometimes with pulses of extraordinary intensity. A bona fide natural wonder, it is best seen on the clear, cold evenings of midwinter, as far north in the UK as you can manage. Orkney (www.visit orkney.com) is a decent bet; not only are the Lights far from uncommon there, it also offers alternative attractions (neolithic sites, clifftop scenery) should the gods fail to deliver.

# 616
## Drop by the Baltic

Part of Gateshead's bells-and-whistles Baltic Quays development, this disused 1950s grain warehouse underwent a spectacular £46 million transformation and opened in July 2002 as a contemporary arts venue. Its galleries house a changing calendar of exhibitions, ranging from international urban art exhibitions (the first 'official' commission Banksy ever agreed to was for the 'Spank the Monkey' exhibition) to projects involving locals and Yemeni refugees. There are also artists' studios, a library and archive and a cinema/lecture space. The rooftop restaurant enjoys views over the Tyne and Millennium Bridge, but note that the best aspects are from the swanky Viewing Box private dining room and lounge – unfortunately, you can't just wander in for a quick peek, unless you're also booked in for dinner.

**Baltic Centre for Contemporary Art** *South Shore Road, Gateshead, Tyne & Wear NE8 3BA (0191 478 1810/www.balticmill.com).*

# 617

### Take flight at the Bristol International Balloon Fiesta

Fingers crossed for fair winds and blue skies at this annual ballooning spectacle (0117 953 5884, www.bristolfiesta.co.uk). Over a hundred colourful crafts are launched into the heavens at 6am and 6pm, weather permitting; when the skies darken, the 'night glow' takes over, with around 30 lit balloons taking off, accompanied by music and fireworks. The novelty balloons are always the stars, as the sky fills with enormous, improbable floating objects – a Scottish piper, perhaps, or a vast fire extinguisher. Entry is free, but even if you're not on site and up close to the tethered balloons, they can be seen in the skies for miles around. Contact the organisers for a list of operators offering rides.

COWLIN
www.cowlin.co.uk
IKEA
HOME FURNISHINGS
NOKIA
HB-QET
sloggi

# 618
## Discover chocolate heaven at Paul A Young's

Yorkshire-born Young, former head pastry chef at Quo Vadis, is the creative force behind this award-winning north London chocolate shop. Offering a sophisticated alternative to mass-produced confections, his treats are miniature works of art, made in small batches every day. Unconventional flavour combinations are Young's hallmark, with a range that runs from orange and geranium-infused artisan bars to cedar-oil flavoured dark chocolate; still more adventurous gourmets can sample the best-selling sea-salted caramel, or brave the Marmite Guinness ganache. The shop runs regular after-hours tasting workshops for chocoholics who want to educate their palates, with a small goodie bag included in the £45 cost.

**Paul A Young Fine Chocolates** *33 Camden Passage, London N1 8EA (020 7424 5750/ www.paulayoung.co.uk).*

# 619
## Stargaze at Kielder

Covering 230 square miles, Kielder Forest (www.forestry.gov.uk) is the UK's largest forest. At its heart lies Kielder Water, an immense man-made lake with 27 miles of shoreline. Home to England's biggest colony of red squirrels, the unspoilt woodland is a beautiful place for a hike.

What's more, it's one of the least light-polluted areas in England: perfect for stargazing. You're also just far enough north to (very occasionally) be treated to a Northern Lights show. Kielder Forest Star Camp (www.richarddarn.demon.co.uk/starcamp) runs two events a year, when you can camp out with up to 200 stargazers to train telescopes and binoculars on the heavens and look for meteors. Spring is a good time for viewing the Leo and Virgo constellations, while the best view of the Milky Way is in autumn.

# 620
## Follow the Stations of the Cross at Carfin's Lourdes

Built largely by local Catholic miners in the early 1920s, and inspired by a priest's visit to the celebrated site at Lourdes in France, the Carfin Lourdes Grotto is one of the most extraordinary religious centres in Scotland. Much of its surprise value comes from the location – in the industrial hinterland east of Glasgow, just outside Motherwell. To the average lay person used to British Protestant culture, the area looks like a small park dotted with a chapel, outdoor altar and several alien-seeming reliquaries, shrines and statues. To a practising Catholic, it's far more familiar. Over the years, the grotto has become a place of pilgrimage for Scotland's Catholic population, Lithuanian and Polish communities as well as thousands from further afield – but anyone can pop in to follow the Stations of the Cross, or simply take a look around.

**Carfin Lourdes Grotto** *Taylor Avenue, Carfin, Motherwell, North Lanarkshire ML1 5AJ (01698 263308/www.carfin.org.uk).*

# 621
## Swan about at Abbotsbury

There was a time when swans were considered quite a delicacy – and the Benedictine monks who built St Peter's monastery during the 1040s once farmed the birds for their lavish banquets. Although the monastery was destroyed in 1539 during Henry VIII's Dissolution (you can see its remains around St Nicholas's Church in the village), the swans remain. Uniquely, you can walk through a colony of nesting mute swans here; don't miss the twice-daily mass feeding sessions. From mid May to late June, hundreds of tiny, fluffy cygnets hatch, and it's possible to see them up close – some of the nests are even on the pathways. It's a fairytale sight that'll melt even the most cynical of hearts.

**Abbotsbury Swannery** *New Barn Road, Abbotsbury, near Weymouth, Dorset DT3 4JG (01305 871858/www.abbotsbury-tourism.co.uk/swannery).*

# 622
## Discover Watts in Surrey...

This idiosyncratic and utterly charming gallery displays the work of George Frederick Watts (1817-1904), a man famous enough in his day to be nicknamed 'England's Michelangelo'. The Arts and Crafts gallery houses landscapes, social comment pieces, allegories, portraits, drawings and sculptures. Watts's ideal was to do good through art, and much of his work features either a moral dimension or a social comment – for many years, his painting *Hope* was one of the most reproduced pictures in the world. His wife Mary designed the nearby Watts Chapel (off Down Lane, open 9am to dusk daily), a riot of symbolism and blend of styles that is something of a surprise in the Surrey countryside, but still demands to be seen. A visit to the hut-like tearoom just along the road rounds off a trip nicely.
**Watts Gallery** *Down Lane, Compton, Surrey GU3 1DQ (01483 810235/ www.wattsgallery.org.uk).*

# 623 ...and in London

Although you are more likely to bump into Watts's work in Tate Britain (Millbank, London SW1P 4RG, 020 7887 8888, www.tate.org.uk) or the National Portrait Gallery (St Martin's Place, London WC2H 0HE, 020 7312 2463, www.npg.org.uk) if you're in London, it's worth seeking out his splendid *Physical Energy*, silhouetted against the sky in Kensington Gardens (020 7298 2117, www.royalparks.org.uk). The large-scale bronze overlooks the Serpentine and depicts a naked man on horseback, shielding his eyes from the sun. The secret oasis of Postman's Park, off Aldersgate Street in EC1, also has Watts' *Heroes Wall*, a display of 34 plaques commemorating various valiant, but fatal, acts of bravery on the part of Londoners.

# 624-641 See Britain in bloom

# Flower power

*Gardener's World's* **Carol Klein** *tours Britain's loveliest gardens.*

At Hodsock Priory in Nottinghamshire (Blyth, near Worksop, Nottinghamshire S81 0TY, 01909 591204, www.hodsockpriory.com), snowdrops reign supreme in mid to late January and you can wander through woods carpeted with their white bells. There are magical vistas across the lake, surrounded by scented winter-flowering shrubs, and the whole garden is permeated by a mysterious, slightly eerie ambience.

Another garden best explored in spring is Colesbourne Park (Colesbourne, near Cheltenham, Gloucestershire GL53 9NP, 01242 870264, www.snowdrop.org.uk), described by *Country Life* as the best place in the country to see snowdrops. Groups of galanthophiles (snowdrop fanciers) flock here for the winter open days.

In other gardens, snowdrops are just the hors d'oeuvre, and the courses that follow provide delicious excitement right through the year. At Marwood Hill Gardens (Marwood, Barnstaple, Devon EX31 4EB, 01271 342528, www.marwoodhillgarden.co.uk) you're in for a treat whenever you visit. It's a horticultural nirvana, with acres of plants. Despite its size, the garden feels manageable and on a human scale – perhaps because you are always aware of its enclosed nature, nestled in a wooded valley.

If Marwood exploits its lovely setting in the wild Devonshire countryside, so too does the deeply romantic Garden House (Buckland Monachorum, Yelverton, Devon PL20 7LQ, 01822 854769, www.thegardenhouse.org.uk). Climb the 16th-century tower and look out over the old sunken garden and bulb meadow, full of spring jewels in April and May. Beyond, panoramic views stretch across Dartmoor.

Gardens run by big organisations can sometimes have an offputting institutional feel, but Logan Botanical Gardens (Port Logan, Stranraer, Dumfries & Galloway DG9 9ND, 01776 860231, www.rbge.org.uk/the-gardens/logan), an outpost of the world-renowned Edinburgh Botanic Garden, is an enclave of creative landscaping and unexpectedly exotic planting: big blue poppies from the Himalayas and enormous, spiky phormiums (the size of a

Coton Manor

Great Dixter

Garden House

Beth Chatto Gardens

**Time Out** 1000 Things to do in Britain **191**

small house) enjoy the benefits of a climate tempered by the Gulf Stream. While you're in the area, take in Cally Gardens (Gatehouse of Fleet, Castle Douglas, Kirkcudbrightshire DG7 2DJ, 01557 815029, www.callygardens.co.uk), a horticulturalist's paradise. The walled gardens offer a botanical world tour, the plants within a living catalogue of those offered for sale by owner Michael Wickenden, who goes on plant-hunting expeditions across the globe to find new stock, from Ecuador to Ethiopia.

The RHS Rosemoor Garden at Torrington (Great Torrington, Devon EX38 8PH, 01805 624067, www.rhs.org.uk) is another garden that's packed with unexpected treasures – including an underpass opening on to stacks of monumental rocks, and mind-boggling bamboos.

If you're Lakeland bound, put Holehird (Patterdale Road, Windermere, Cumbria LA23 1NP, 01539 446008, www.holehirdgardens.org.uk), at the top of your list. Not only does the ten-acre hillside site offer some spectacular views of mountain, lake and sea, but it's filled with interesting features, including a delightful walled garden with colour-themed beds and borders over the spring and summer months. It's run by a team of around 250 volunteers, who take huge pride in the garden and are only too pleased to talk to visitors.

Some gardens, though, are so intimately connected with the individuals who created them that their spirit always predominates – and, in the best scenarios, continues to inspire those charged with their upkeep.

Whether or not you're an admirer of the late, great gardening guru Christopher Lloyd, his garden at Northiam, Great Dixter (Northiam, Rye, East Sussex TN31 6PH, 01797 252878, www.greatdixter.co.uk), is a must-see. The unique topiary includes the famed peacocks, the long border is the most imaginative around, and the wild flower meadows are second to none. Christopher's spirit permeates the whole place, and the garden continues to move forward as a place of experimentation and creativity.

One of Christopher's gardening friends was Beth Chatto, whose wonderfully diverse garden in Essex (Elmstead Market, Colchester, Essex CO7 7DB, 01206 822007, www.bethchatto.co.uk) opens its gates to visitors almost year round. Enthusiasts flock from all over the world to see the woodland, damp and dry gardens, all created from scratch over the last 40 years. The drought-resistant gravel garden, built on an old

Coton Manor

car park, is a masterpiece of the 'Right Plant, Right Place' genre: it hasn't had to be watered since its creation in 1992.

Another impressive Essex garden, albeit on a more modest scale, is Glen Chantry (Ischams Chase, Wickham Bishops, Essex CM8 3LG, 01621 891342, www.glenchantry.demon.co.uk). It's a privilege just being able to share in the poetry of the place, created and tended lovingly and expertly by Sue and Wol Staines. Glen Chantry also boasts one of the best nurseries in the country, oozing with the very special plants with which the garden abounds.

In the same area, Derek Jarman fans should stroll by Prospect Cottage, his iconic sanctuary on the beach at Dungeness. Jarman took his planting plan from the indigenous local plants: sea-kale with thick, glaucous, undulating leaves and clouds of honeyed flowers, horned poppies and gorse. The garden, seemingly without boundaries, merges into the seashore.

Heading further up the east coast is a treasure trove of a garden, whose reputation precedes it in gardening circles. Cactus and eucalyptus in Norfolk? On an exposed and inhospitable site, Alan Gray and Graham Robeson have constructed one of the wonders of the modern horticultural world. The 20-acre site at East Ruston Old Vicarage (East Ruston, Norwich, Norfolk NR12 9HN, 01692 650432, www.e-ruston-oldvicaragegardens.co.uk) has the lot, and is open on selected days from late March to October.

If you want to see how to grow your own vegetables, or simply revel in some gloriously productive gardens, West Dean Gardens (West Dean, Chichester, West Sussex PO18 0QZ, 01243 811301, www.westdean.org.uk) is the pinnacle of veg perfection. Its pristine glasshouses, perfect cold frames and immaculate raised beds display the finest edibles. Edward James, patron of the Surrealist movement, once owned West Dean: two of his tree sculptures stand in the spring garden, and his simple, slate-topped grave is in the arboretum.

Garden Organic at Ryton (Ryton, Coventry, Warwickshire, CV8 3LG, 02476 303517, www.gardenorganic.org.uk) is a mecca for organic veg addicts. The prize-winning café uses own-grown produce, and there's friendly, hands-on advice on everything from compost-making to bee gardens. Garden Organic at Yalding in Kent (Benover Road, Yalding, near Maidstone, Kent ME18 6EX 01622 814650, www.gardenorganic.org.uk) is an up-and-coming offshoot with different soil and much less water.

The new National Botanic Garden of Wales (Llanarthne, Carmarthenshire SA32 8HG, 01558 668768, www.gardenofwales.org.uk) is also dedicated to education and conservation. There's masses to see here, including Norman Foster's inspiring Great Glasshouse. Built to house a lush profusion of Mediterranean plants, it's in total contrast to the green Carmarthenshire hills that surround it.

Wherever you go in Britain, you're never far away from esoteric and exciting gardens. I am already conscious of all the glaring omissions from this list, like Coton Manor Garden (Coton, near Gillsborough, Northamptonshire NN6 8RQ, 01604 740219, www.cotonmanor.co.uk), with its poetic colour schemes and evocative scents – not to mention its flamingos and black swans. Then there are the lovely gardens of Cheshire, Lancashire and Yorkshire. How could I leave them out? But you'll discover them for yourself wherever you wander.

*Carol Klein's latest book is* Grow Your Own Veg *(Mitchell Beazley, £16.99).*

**Great Dixter**

## 642 Stroll Tintern's romantic ruins

The first abbey at Tintern was founded in 1131 – although most of what survives dates from the 13th and 14th centuries. The building fell into ruin after 1536, and only began to be appreciated again with the vogue for the 'picturesque' at the end of the 18th century. Early tourists might not have been encouraged by the opinion of the 18th-century traveller and author William Gilpin, who pronounced that 'Though the parts are beautiful the whole is ill-shaped.' Happily, after inspiring Wordsworth's 'Lines Composed a Few Miles above Tintern Abbey, on Revisiting the Banks of the Wye during a Tour, July 13, 1798', in which the poet hears the 'still, sad music of humanity', the abbey's future celebrity was secure. It was also immortalised in one of Turner's early watercolour drawings, which captures the exquisite, pale ochre stonework to perfection.

**Tintern Abbey** *is off the A466 4 miles north of Chepstow, Monmouthshire (01443 336000/ www.cadw.wales.gov.uk).*

## 643 Go in search of William Morris

Kelmscott Manor, that great Tudor farmhouse by the Thames in Gloucestershire, inspired William Morris with its sense of organic harmony amid barns, meadows and gardens. Today, the Arts and Crafts pioneer's presence (as well as that of Rossetti, Burne-Jones and May Morris) is everywhere: in the furniture, original textiles, ceramics and carpets. Morris and his family are buried nearby in the 'heavenly' village churchyard, where a ridged tomb is hidden away behind a bay bush. Note that the manor is only open on Wednesdays and some Saturdays, from April to September.

**Kelmscott Manor** *Kelmscott, Lechlade, Gloucestershire GL7 3HJ (01367 252486/ www.kelmscottmanor.co.uk).*

## 644 Follow the 'Obby 'Oss in Padstow

This is one of Britain's longest surviving Beltane celebrations, possibly originating from the pre-Christian people who settled at Padstow's harbour mouth 4,000 years ago. After midnight singing around the town, in the early hours of May Day, the two 'Obby 'Osses are 'released' from their respective stables; the Old 'Oss resides at the Golden Lion Inn, while the Blue Ribbon 'Oss emerges from the Harbour Inn (http://blueribbonoss.org.uk).

Crowds flock to watch the dancers and musicians wind through Padstow's streets, which are decorated with greenery and flags; celebrations carry on throughout the day. Find a good spot by the maypole; otherwise, unless you're tall, you might miss the 'osses in the crowded lanes – the costumes are (very) stylised horses and only a little higher than the person dressed in them. Black-cloaked and gruesomely masked, accompanied by 'teasers', they pass through the streets trying to catch young maidens, then meet at the maypole at noon for a mock battle. There are plenty of activities around town, from boat trips to the simple pleasures of a pint and a pasty. This being 'Padstein', you could also pick one of the five Rick Stein eateries for a gourmet feed – but make sure you book ahead.

## 645 Bike across Britain on the C2C

The C2C (it stands for Sea to Sea) is all about dipping your bicycle wheels in the Irish Sea (at Whitehaven), then cycling the scenic 140 miles up hill and down dale through the Lake District, over the Pennines and down through the Durham Dales to the North Sea in Sunderland (www.c2c-guide.co.uk). Opened in 1994, just four per cent of the route is on main roads; the rest comprises small country lanes, disused railway tracks and off-road paths. The route has been hugely popular, with several new branches opening up in the last few years, and commissioned artworks by the likes of sculptors Andy Goldsworthy and Tony Cragg beautifying certain sections.

# 646 *Ski Scotland*

Skiing and snowboarding in Scotland is a big risk – and we're not referring to the possibility of avalanches. If only. For the last ten years, Scottish resorts have been suffering shorter seasons, a rise in the rideable snowline and a reduction in overall snowfall, making for slopes that are all too often short on the soft stuff.

'Pre-emptively planning a holiday in Scotland is no longer an option,' says snowboarder Orlando Einsiedel, a devotee of the Scottish mountain experience. 'The only way to do it is to keep an eye on the weather reports and jump in the car the moment it starts dumping in the mountains – although even when it is snowing in Scotland, it's often blowing such a ferocious gale that the lifts may be shut for days on end.'

All the more reason, you might think, for cutting your losses and blazing a trail to the Alps. Yet there remains some credence to the claim that no Brit can call himself a serious skier until he's tackled a Scottish slope. For starters, Scotland does still get the odd amazing day, and nothing beats the chairlift camaraderie between skiers who know they've beaten the odds to ski on home turf – especially if they've just woken up refreshed after a night on the 12-hour Caledonian Sleeper train from Euston (www.firstgroup.com/scotrail). On top of that, a Scottish sense of the epic extends from the bone-rattling chairlifts and rugged landscape – criss-crossed by spiked fences with potential for eviscerating the unwary – to the unrivalled intensity of the après-ski piss-ups.

The big destinations are Cairngorm Mountain (01479 861261, www.cairngormmountain.co.uk) and the Nevis Range (01397 705825, www.nevisrange.co.uk) – the former a good beginner's hill, the latter claiming the lion's share of steeper red and black runs for the brave. Nearby Lecht (01975 651440, www.lecht.co.uk), meanwhile, is a hit with the freestyle contingent thanks to the ramps and rails of its dedicated terrain park. Bear in mind that none has enough pistes to engage serious skiers for more than a weekend – but then one good weekend in Scotland is a full season by most standards.

## A few of my favourite things

# 647-652

*Julie Myerson, author*

The car journey from London to Suffolk has three exquisite pleasures, listed here in strict order of appearance. Driving over the Orwell Bridge is breathtaking. Soaringly beautiful in summer, slightly scary in the autumn wind. There's an incredible moment when you're at its peak: for about three seconds, the land drops away and all you see is the vast East Anglian sky. About 20 minutes after that, you pull in at the **Farm Café at Marlesford (A12, Marlesford, Woodbridge, Suffolk IP13 0AG, 01728 747717, www.farmcafe.co.uk)**, a kind of famous secret and the loveliest place to stop off for breakfast or lunch. With a fire burning in the grate, really high quality, locally sourced food, wine, good coffee, and all the newspapers, it feels like home. In summer you can sit in the back bit, which is open to the fields, and there's water for dogs, who are welcome too. Ten minutes after that, the **Antiques Market at Yoxford (Askers Hill, Yoxford, Suffolk IP17 3JW, 01728 668844, www.yoxfordantiques.com)** is such an obsessive favourite of mine that the dog – having just been refreshed at the Farm Café and now doubly anxious to get to the sea – sometimes yelps in horror when I turn off the A12 towards it. Housed in a huge old barn-like building, this is one of those places where not only old things but entire past lives seem to be offered up for sale. I've bought old photos, old chairs, old books and maps, and fallen in love with a gargantuan Victorian weathervane I can't afford. Mooching around on a wet afternoon with the rain beating loudly on the roof just seems to make me feel happy.

In London, wandering alone around **Columbia Road Flower Market** on a Sunday morning gives me the same sort of pleasure. I get there as early as I can bear and am very methodical – I check out the junk and antiques first, then buy as many plants as I can carry. It's glorious on a hot summer's morning, but I almost prefer it in darkest winter, when the bulbs and shoots look like small miracles.

We moved out of Clapham two years ago and **Gastro**, a French café on Venn Street **(63-67 Venn Street, London SW4 0BD, 020 7627 0222)**, is the one thing I really miss. It's only about ten years old, but feels as if it's been there 60 years – the kind of place where you can sit for hours with one coffee and no one will bother you. In the evening, it transforms itself into a glamorous fish-and-seafood-serving dive. Half the dramas of my life seem to have unravelled within its walls and, even though we have to make a special journey to get there now, I can't imagine life without it.

In spite of (or maybe because of) the loss of Gastro, **Wright Brothers in Borough Market (11 Stoney Street, London SE1 9AD, 020 7403 9554, www.wrightbros.eu.com)** has become a slightly guilty obsession for my husband and me. We perch on not especially comfortable, hard, high chairs and drink fizzy wine and eat a deliciously simple menu of fresh fish and seafood. It has a slightly celebratory atmosphere, and something about being in there feels like being on holiday. We sneak off at every opportunity – even Friday lunchtime, if we think we've done enough work to justify it.

*Julie Myerson is the author of nine novels. Her latest novel is* Out of Breath *(Jonathan Cape, £12.99).*

# 653 *See Overbeck's Rejuvenator*

Overlooking Salcombe and the sea, the seven-acre gardens at this stately Edwardian villa are a subtropical delight, where palm trees, lofty cypresses and pink magnolia flourish. The former owner was scientist Otto Overbeck; inside the house, don't miss seeing his oddest invention, the 'Rejuvenator' – a scary-sounding device used to self-administer electric impulses.
**Overbecks Museum & Garden** *Sharpitor, Salcombe, Devon TQ8 8LW (01548 842893/ www.nationaltrust.org.uk).*

# 654-656
## Eat curry in Southall
Forget the Indian restaurants that line Brick Lane in east London: for an altogether more authentic experience, head west to Southall. Here, the Broadway and its surrounding streets are a corner of Middlesex that will be forever Punjabi. The cuisine here is as you'd find it in the Punjab itself – lots of hearty meat curries, dahls and smoky kebabs.

The best of the bunch are the New Asian Tandoori Centre (114-118 The Green, Southall UB2 4BQ, 020 8574 2597), which is good for meat skewers, and Madhu's (39 South Road, Southall UB1 1SW, 020 8574 1897, www.madhusonline.com), whose signature dish is lamb ribs; the owners hail from Nairobi, so the dishes have a unique Kenyan twist. Before you eat, call in for a quick pint at the Glassy Junction (97 South Road, Southall UB1 1SQ, 020 8574 1626), the only pub in Britain to accept rupees.

# 657
## Follow the herd to the Big Sheep
The undoubted highlight of a day out at this working sheep farm has to be the entertaining sheep races. Place your bet on one of the woolly racers (ridden by knitted jockeys with names like Red Ram, Sheargar and Alderknitt), then cheer on your favourite as they race for the finish line. Children who enjoyed Dick King-Smith's *The Sheep-Pig* will also love the dog and duck trials; pony rides and tractor rides, sheep shows and feeding sessions with baby lambs round off the entertainment. Outdoor activities for older children include mountain boarding and laser gun games, while cream teas are on offer for those in need of refuelling. In damp weather, younger visitors can hare around the huge indoor soft play tumble towers and create wonky pottery to take home. Check the website for details of special seasonal events, such as autumn's Halloween festival and conker championships.
**Big Sheep** *Abbotsham, Bideford, Devon EX39 5AP (01237 472366/www.thebigsheep.co.uk).*

# 658
## Join the beach hut brigade
Beach huts began life as mobile contraptions, wheeled to the water's edge to preserve the modesty of Victorian ladies with a horror of showing so much as an ankle in public. Sadly, they became somewhat redundant once we all stripped off into swimsuits and cavorted merrily on the sands – until someone had the bright idea of turning them into static huts; a little piece of privacy on increasingly busy beaches.

These days, you'll be lucky to get your hands on one: price tags of £50,000 and upwards aren't unheard of, even though you're generally not allowed to stay in them overnight. A rare exception is Mudeford Spit in Dorset, where you can sleep in the huts overnight between March and November. Prices to buy are eye-watering – but renting is more manageable, at around £400 a week in high season (www.mudeford-beach-huts.co.uk). Traditionalists, though, favour the jaunty row of beach huts at Southwold, a charmingly old-fashioned resort on the Suffolk coast. Waveney District Council recommends calling Durrants Estate Agents to find a hut for rent (01502 723292), or you can call the tourist information office in Southwold (01502 724729). Expect to pay around £200 a week in the school summer holidays.

# 659-673
## *Pitch up at a festival*

### All Tomorrow's Parties, Somerset & East Sussex
Even when you've exhausted the Redcoats gags, there's much to love about this intimate, artist-curated holiday camp (Butlins Minehead and Camber Sands) weekender (www.atpfestival.com). The likes of the Shins, Dinosaur Jr and Mogwai have taken the reins in past years, resulting in a post-rock musical mix that makes Glastonbury's main stage look like a cheesy school disco. Best of all, it's a tent-free zone.

### Bestival, Isle of Wight
Celebrating its fifth year in 2008, Bestival (www.bestival.net) has come a long way since the chaotic early days. Its friendly, boutique feel remains intact, with quirky surprises at every turn – a baby temple for breastfeeding mothers (Breastival), freaky cabaret and spontaneous morris dancing – and no room for muso posing when you get sandwiched between a camp cowboy and a semi-naked trapeze artist at the bar. Also check out new sister fest Camp Bestival (www.campbestival.net) from 2008.

### Big Chill, Herefordshire
'Big Chill is a medium-sized festival, with a small-festival's heart,' says co-founder Katrina Larkin. There's no escaping the fact that sharing a field with 35,000 people is far from boutique, but Big Chill's (www.bigchill.net) layout means there's always a tranquil spot to be found. No one gets left out, either – there's a kids' area, a Teen Tent, a Body & Soul Village, bleeding-edge dance music and live acts, circus freaks, storytelling and racing human snails. New partnerships with the ICA, Roundhouse and Underbelly will pack in even more from 2008.

### Blissfields, Hampshire
Blissfields' new Matterley Bowl site (www.blissfields.co.uk) belies its humble farm origins – it started as a party for just 70 in 2001. Its recent success (Best Small Festival at the 2007 UK Festival Awards) means no more tractor rides, but the home-grown ethos remains. 'It's taken on a life of its own,' says organiser Paul Bliss, 'but it still feels like everyone's a friend of a friend.' Expect soapbox ranting, local bands, loads of kids' stuff and an indie vibe.

### Creamfields, Cheshire
Club kids and old ravers unite at this spin-off of the legendary Liverpool club. Creamfields (www.creamfields.com), ten years old in 2008, pulls in a shiny, happy crowd with its top-notch line-ups (Chemical Brothers, Mark Ronson and Groove Armada have all graced its stages), quality sound systems and hedonistic spirit. Not for the fainthearted, this may be a one-day event but you'll need energy levels that will see you through five.

### Glade, Berkshire
Breakaway Glastonbury stage the Glade (www.gladefestival.com) attracts over 10,000 revellers to its annual dance festival. Since its inception in 2004, Glade has been known for its hedonistic vibe and impressive luck with the weather – until the washout that was 2007, that is. Still, the Glade crowd is way too hardcore to let damp trainers and frizzy hair ruin its buzz. There's the likes of 808 State, Dreadzone, the Orb and A Guy Called Gerald to check out for starters.

### Glastonbury, Somerset
Bagging a ticket requires a five-month organisational campaign, the toilets are grim and a stagnant quagmire is guaranteed, but Glasto still pulls a crowd like no other (www.glastonburyfestivals.co.uk). 'It's shit when it's muddy,' says Deborah Armstrong, one of the original producers of Lost Vagueness, 'But – and sorry for sounding like an old hippie – magical things happen at Glastonbury. Things that just don't happen anywhere else.' Need to know: debauchery centralis Trash City (2007's in-the-know tip) will join Armstrong's as yet unnamed new area in the old Lost Vagueness fields for subversive madness from 2008.

## Green Man, Powys
Despite its phenomenal growth (300 people in 2003; 10,000 in 2007), Green Man (www.thegreenmanfestival.co.uk) remains a blissfully sponsorship- and corporate-free zone. 'It's a real escape from everyday life,' says organiser and musician Jo Bartlett, who set up the festival with husband Danny Hagan to provide an outlet for the new folk music they themselves play and love. Sugar Loaf Mountain, looming over the main stage, is a magical backdrop, while the spontaneous, free-and-easy vibe makes this one of the best festival experiences around. Head for the campfire, which will have a new piano bar area for impromptu sets from 2008.

## Isle of Wight
So you missed Jefferson Airplane in '68, Dylan in '69 and 'Britain's Woodstock' in 1970? The days of £1.25 tickets and free love may be long gone, but the Isle of Wight Festival (www.isleofwightfestival.co.uk) has still got the goods. Spot rock stars on the ferry, swig cider in the Strawberry Fields and watch local bands on the Bandstand. Oh, and ditch the wellies: this is one UK festival where – usually – mud doesn't reign.

## Latitude, Suffolk
Latitude (www.latitudefestival.co.uk) mixes musical clout with idyllic scenery (Southwold's tranquil Henham Park) to harmonious effect. Its

intellectual blend of music, art, literature, comedy, cabaret and theatre packs a serious punch too. Even the festival's pastel-coloured sheep are clever: 'They organise themselves into flocks in accordance with their wool colour,' says organiser Melvin Benn.

## Secret Garden Party, Cambridgeshire

Secret Garden Party (www.secretgardenparty.com) is a real one-off. We're talking naked saunas, offbeat art installations, campfires, hula Olympics and late-night insanity you won't remember in the morning. 'We feel there's far more fun to be had in a field than just watching bands,' says founder Fred Fellowes (aka the Head Gardener). Quite. Though they do have them too.

## Shambala, Northamptonshire

Word-of-mouth success Shambala (www.shambalafestival.org) makes a great escape from the festival norm. 'There's a beautiful sense of anarchy,' says co-organiser Dan. 'Festivals now are just so tame. Shambala is really participatory and it brings out the best in people.' The organisers certainly take green issues seriously (subsidised coach journeys to the site and the like). Add on a huge kids' area, open-air hot tubs and music that spans folk, hip hop and world music, and what's not to love?

## Standon Calling, Herefordshire

One of a new breed of small, independent festivals, Standon Calling (www.standoncalling.com) still has a 'we're all mates here' anti-commercial vibe. The organisers have an eye for talent – bands tend towards the high-quality but on-the-up variety (New Young Pony Club, the Noisettes) – and a knack with quirky themes. Head for the bar, built into a semi-circle of horse chestnut trees, and gawp at the Hertfordshire countryside. The festival-jaded should reserve tickets immediately.

## Tapestry Goes West, Glamorgan

A festival for those who've realised that 20,000 people standing in a field really isn't the way the future's meant to feel. Having moved from a wild west theme park in Cornwall to a Welsh deer park (complete with abbey ruins) in 2006, Tapestry Goes West (www.tapestrygoeswest.com) is about as intimate as festival-going gets. The crowd is small (around 1,000), the bands are far from mainstream and the medieval theme – mead, jousting, freaks in robes – adds a delicious touch of insanity to proceedings.

## T in the Park, Kinross-shire

Doing its bit for north-of-the-border music obsessives, T in the Park (www.tinthepark.com) is big: big bands, big crowds, big site, big business. Expanded into a three-day event in 2007, its size means it suffers from the usual festival irritations – traffic/parking chaos, toilets of doom, chanting drunkards – but for serious line-ups (Arctic Monkeys, Scissor Sisters and Arcade Fire) and spirited main-stage sing-a-longs, T rocks.

# 674 Return to Eden

The Eden Project has transformed an unlovely former clay pit into one of Cornwall's biggest tourist draws – two giant, domed greenhouses that recreate the earth's different climatic zones. The most dramatic is the humid tropics biome – a steamy haven where banana plants, bamboo, mahogany and mango trees stretch towards the sky. Allow at least half a day to do the whole site justice, and avoid the middle of the day and bank holidays, when traffic queues can last for hours. If you opt for the gift aid entrance option (which costs the same as the normal entry fee), you'll be given a membership card that entitles you to free entry for a year.
**Eden Project** *Bodelva, near St Austell, Cornwall PL24 2SG (01726 811911/www.edenproject.com).*

# 675 Visit the World Pipe Band Championship

There's no two ways with pipe bands – either they make the hair on the back of your neck stand up, or they sound like a phalanx of ailing cats with gout. To settle the question once and for all, why not visit the pinnacle of pipe band achievement, the annual world championship? Organised by the Royal Scottish Pipe Band Association (www.rspba.org) and held in Glasgow every August, it attracts hundreds of bands and thousands of bagpipers from across the globe. The big name on the scene in recent years has been the Field Marshall Montgomery Pipe Band from Northern Ireland – although Canada's Simon Fraser University Pipe Band and Scotland's own Shotts and Dykehead Pipe Band are also pretty talented ensembles.

# 676 Enjoy Chatsworth – for free

We're not saying that the magnificent stately home of the Duke and Duchess of Devonshire isn't worth paying to see, but even more of a treat are the beautiful grounds. The whole place is in the Peak District National Park, so the approach is also a joy, but there are miles of walks (of varying degrees of difficulty) once you're inside the estate, which includes the River Derwent and Stand Wood. Sculptures dot the parkland – including the water-powered *Revelation*. It's free to enter, and while there are tearooms, picnicking is also welcomed.
**Chatsworth** *Bakewell, Derbyshire DE45 1PP (01246 565300/www.chatsworth.org).*

## 677 Spot a celebrity on a tour of the BBC

Sadly, having paid your licence fee doesn't qualify you for a free peek at the Beeb's west London nerve centre, but fork out £9.50 and you'll be amply rewarded by the award-winning tour. It takes in the news desk, weather centre, TV studios and dressing rooms (depending on daily circumstances); because you're wandering around a busy workplace, you get a real sense of the frenetic nature of broadcasting – and if you're really lucky, you may even get a glimpse of Terry Wogan popping in for an early shift. Tours run Monday to Saturday; book well ahead.
**BBC Television Centre** *Wood Lane, London W12 7RJ (0870 603 0304/www.bbc.co.uk/tours).*

## 678 Sample a slab of Grasmere gingerbread

Grasmere, deep in the Lake District, was described by Wordsworth (who lived there) as 'the loveliest spot that man hath ever found'. It's also famed for its gingerbread – a delightfully dense, spicy affair. The recipe was concocted by Sarah Nelson in the mid 19th century, and remains a closely guarded secret. It is now generally considered the acme of the confection: call in at the shop (tucked away at the corner of the lovely St Oswald's churchyard) and see if you agree. Such is the demand, the company also offers a mail order service.
**Grasmere Gingerbread Shop** *Church Cottage, Grasmere, Ambleside, Cumbria LA22 9SW (01539 435428/www.grasmeregingerbread.co.uk).*

## 679 Stay in a station

Set on the gloriously scenic Settle to Carlyle line, high above the Yorkshire Dales, Grade II-listed Dent Station is now an unusual holiday let (07824 665266, www.dentstation.co.uk). This is a true rural retreat, and no mistake: the nearest village is four miles away. You can roam the countryside in splendid isolation – although with regular train services passing through, you're not completely alone.

## 680 See a red squirrel at Formby Reserve

There are just 160,000 native red squirrels left in Britain; their decline was brought about by the introduction of the American grey squirrel in the 1870s, which spread rapidly throughout the UK (population now around two-and-a-half million), invading and destroying the habitat of the reds. Red squirrels, extinct in most southern counties, can still be found in Scotland and the Lake District, with smaller populations existing in Wales, Norfolk and parts of the North.

The National Trust's Formby estate in the Sefton Coast Woodlands is one of only three red squirrel refuges in the UK, and is home to around 1,000 of the little critters – with a three-mile buffer zone to prevent a grey invasion. The 'red squirrel walk' through the pinewoods offers opportunities to spot them (and woodland birds), with ample rest and picnic spots. This is also a good starting point for walks along the Sefton Coastal Path, which has stunning views.
**Formby Point Red Squirrel Reserve** *Victoria Road, Freshfields, Formby, Liverpool L37 1LJ (01704 878591/www.nationaltrust.org.uk).*

## 681 Bathe in safety at Ilfracombe

In 1823, a team of Welsh miners was hired to carve out a network of tunnels under the cliffs at Ilfracombe, north Devon, giving easy access to two secluded sandy coves (www.tunnels beaches.co.uk). While they were there, the miners also built two tidal pools, one of which has now been restored. Cut off from the open water at low tide, it's a great bathing spot for families, with no danger of dingies floating out to sea (though it is very deep in places). Once you've paid the modest entry fee and had a swim, hire a deckchair and sprawl in the sunshine or play a sedate game of boules: there's also a play area and table tennis to keep the kids occupied.

## 682 Eat organic at Riverford's Field Kitchen

Riverford Farm in south Devon is determined that you get your five portions of vegetables a day – it grows 85 different kinds, all of them organic. Sign up for the home delivery service or get your wellies on and pay a visit; after a tour of the fields, you finish off in the farm kitchen, naturally starring some of that lovely veg. Head chef Jane Baxter trained at the Carved Angel in Dartmouth and used to work at London's legendary River Café, so the grub's top notch. Farm regulations mean you must call and make a reservation in advance.
**Riverford Farm** *Wash Barn, Buckfastleigh, Devon TQ11 0LD (0845 600 2311/www.riverford.co.uk).*

# 683 Escape to the Isle of Man

**Long considered a backwater, the Isle of Man is now a hot filming location and celebrity getaway. Rob Crossan meets the locals.**

It's way past midnight in the Mitre, the tiny village of Kirk Michael's sole boozer, and I'm being taught a stern lesson in Isle of Man etiquette by the clientele. Many of them have had a little more of the local whisky, ManX, than is advisable and are telling me what to do if anybody should be foolish enough to say the word 'rat' while on the island. 'You absolutely have to whistle, then place your hand on the nearest piece of wood, and then turn around if you ever mention that animal's name,' says one particularly garrulous local. Not for the first time in my stay, I'm reasonably convinced that the citizens of the Isle of Man are embroiled in a number of elaborate jokes at the expense of outsiders (or 'come-overs', as we're known).

Poor old Isle of Man. Marooned in the Irish Sea, long derided as a windswept backwater populated by greying *Daily Mail* readers, the place has the feel of a bullied child at school, never invited to the mainland's parties. Sympathy, however, is not what the island is looking for. Without anyone realising, the Isle of Man has become a desirable destination for celebrities seeking an escape; regular visitors include Jeremy Clarkson, Robin Gibb and *Morvern Callar* author Alan Warner, who owns a lighthouse on the far north of the island.

The appeal of the Isle of Man is obvious within seconds of arriving, even in winter; it's impossible to drive for more than a few minutes without having an ocean view by your side. Untamed and independent (it is neither part of the UK nor the EU, but is part of the British Isles), it's a brooding landscape of verdant green and black fields that fall away to a constantly turbulent sea. It's hard to believe you're only an hour's flight from London.

The tiny towns and villages remain almost completely bypassed by modernity. Peel, on the west coast and technically the only city on the island (owing to its bijou cathedral), is an exquisitely preserved 1950s working fishing harbour. To stroll along the seafront is to experience an assault of the senses as you pass the living museum of Moores; the last of the island's curing yards, it still produces oak-fired, chimney-smoked Manx kippers straight out of the adjacent River Neb. Walk on and you encounter the Harbour Lights tearoom, cosy Creek Inn and a warren of snug-looking fishermen's cottages. The annual TT motorbike race fortnight in late May-early June is about the only thing that disturbs the island's perfect peace.

For the past decade, the island has also been promoting itself as an ideal film location, masquerading as Ireland in *Waking Ned*, bygone Bristol in *Treasure Island* and even as Oregon in Simon Pegg and David Schwimmer's flick *Big Nothing*. Guy Ritchie's been here filming chase scenes with OutKast's Andre 3000, and Bill Nighy has visited so often he now has his favourite hotel room on standby at the Regency in Douglas. And the story of how every single eligible woman on the island crammed into Colours nightclub when Johnny Depp popped in while filming *The Libertine* has already passed into legend.

Back in the Mitre, the eccentric tales just keep on coming. Did you know you can still shoot a Scotsman on sight if he runs towards you on a beach? 'We always welcome the come-overs,' a local whispers to me. 'Though you have to get used to the fact that things are different around here. Not at all like where you come from.'

# 684 *Experience monastic life at Pluscarden*

This 13th-century priory, set in the beautiful Morayshire countryside, fell into disprepair for centuries, before being restored in the 1940s. It's now a thriving Benedictine community, where visitors are welcome to come on retreats (free of charge), on application to the warden. There are 12 guest rooms for women, in a self-contained annexe called St Scholastica's Retreat, and 14 rooms for men in a new wing.
**Pluscarden Abbey** *Elgin, Morayshire IV30 8UA (www.pluscardenabbey.org).*

# 685 *Hop on a toboggan in Derbyshire*

You might think dry ski slopes are strictly for brushing up on your technique before your winter holidays, but Swadlincote Ski & Snowboard Centre in Derbyshire has broken the mould with its wildly exhilarating artificial toboggan run. Because pack ice is a bit thin on the ground in the Midlands, it's a slick steel slipway that winds down around the slopes – 1,135 feet of high-speed helter-skelter that'll have you clinging to your brake on the bends.
**Swadlincote Ski & Snowboard Centre** *John Nike Leisuresport Complex, Sir Herbert Ragg Way, Swadlincote, Derbyshire DE11 8LP (01283 217200/www.swadlincoteskislope.co.uk).*

# 686
## Snoop behind closed doors

Every September, a series of linked events held around the UK gives us all the chance to explore behind doors that usually remain resolutely closed for the rest of the year. European Heritage Days – aka Heritage Open Days in England, Doors Open Days in Scotland and the Open House Weekend in London (www.heritagedays.net) – are all about having a nose around out-of-bounds architectural treasures, from eco-friendly private abodes to elaborate Buddhist temples and state-of-the-art skyscrapers.

# 687
## *Enrol the kids at Knight School*

The perfect pairing of castles and knights has been cannily recognised by English Heritage, which, being in charge of many fine examples of the former, but with no ready access to the latter, has set up a series of training sessions to create its own champions of courage, valour and honour (www.english-heritage.org.uk). Here, children can try on armour, learn the art of chivalry and indulge in swashbuckling swordplay and play jousts.

Fitting in around would-be heroes' more mundane curricular activities, Knight Schools take place in the summer holidays: among the castles taking part in 2008 are Helmsley, Dover, Pendennis, Beeston, Scarborough, Kenilworth, Framlingham and Bolsover. Dragons, alas, are not included.

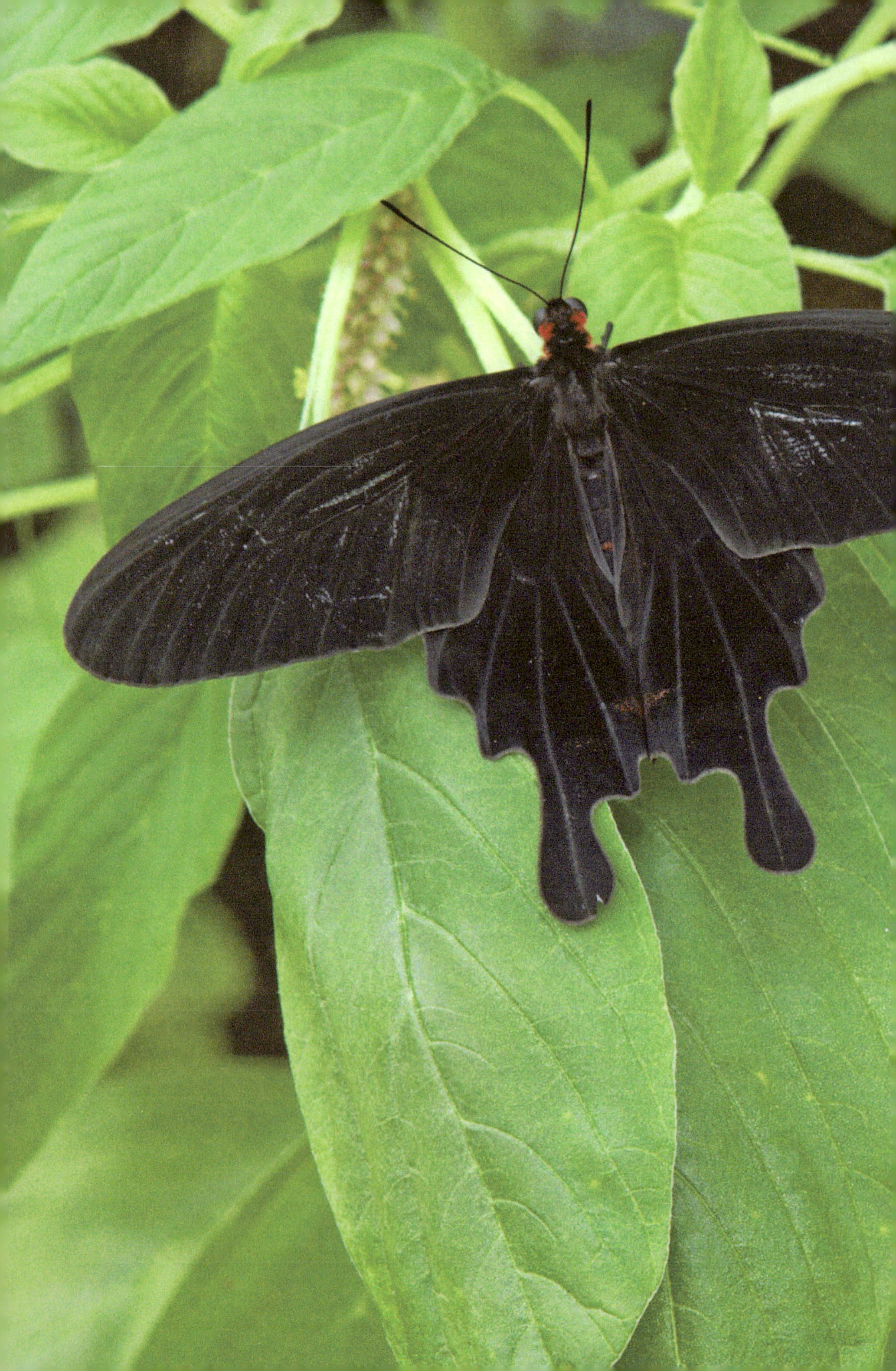

## 688

**See butterflies in Bedford**
While the famed butterfly house at London's Syon House has, sadly, been mothballed, Bedford Butterfly Park (01234 772770, www.bedfordbutterflypark.co.uk) has morphed into Wild Britain, adding new nature trails, keepers' talks and puppet shows. The ten-acre wildflower meadows are a delight, but the star attraction remains the hot and steamy Tropical House, where the beautiful insects flutter around visitors against a backdrop of exotic plants and cascading waterfalls – a particularly surreal experience in the depths of winter.

## 689 Visit Sidmouth's Donkey Sanctuary

Fan of Eeyore? Then this haven for neglected and retired donkeys is a must-visit. Home to around 500 donkeys at any time (over 12,000 have stayed here since the sanctuary opened in 1969), the centre welcomes visitors, who are encouraged to amble around the grassy expanses and meet the animals; apparently, the donkeys 'adore the fuss and attention'. The sanctuary is open until dusk every day, year round, and admission is free. Remember to make a contribution, though – without these chaps, there'd be many more miserable donkeys than just AA Milne's famous creation.
**Donkey Sanctuary** *Sidmouth, Devon EX10 0NU (01395 578222/www.thedonkeysanctuary.org.uk).*

## 690 Ride Scotland's most scenic rail line

The journey by rail from Inverness to the Kyle of Lochalsh is a visual stunner. The journey takes around two and a half hours, so it's possible to do a round trip in a day – or carry on (sadly, not by train) to Skye, just over the water from the Kyle of Lochalsh. Contact Scotrail for times of trains (0845 601 5929, www.firstgroup.com/scotrail).

## 691 Hide out in Forbidden Corner

Anyone who was delighted – or disturbed – by the film *Labyrinth*, starring David Bowie in a fetching codpiece, will particularly appreciate the experience of wandering through the tunnels, chambers and turrets of this bizarre walled garden. Set across four acres in the heart of the Yorkshire Dales, the Forbidden Corner is a Gothic maze of living gargoyles, spitting stones, walls with eyes and mysterious caverns – where you might just meet the King of the Underworld himself (no, not Bowie). Admission is by pre-booked ticket only, so call ahead.
**Forbidden Corner** *Tupgill Park Estate, Coverham, Middleham, North Yorkshire DL8 4TJ (01969 640638/www.theforbiddencorner.co.uk).*

## 692 Make a masterpiece at the National Glass Centre

To go with the traditional Mother's Day flowers, why not make your mum an original vase – you know she'll love it, even if it is wonky – or try your hand at glass jewellery-making. The NGC offers a range of courses for adults and families where you can learn how. Most courses run for around six weeks, and there are also sessions during school holidays for children who've watched the glassmakers at work in the studio and fancy a go themselves. If you're only visiting for a day, admire the stunning glass collections and installations, then scare yourself silly by looking down while walking across the super-cool glass roof. Just watch what you wear – there are people gawping up from below.
**National Glass Centre** *Liberty Way, Sunderland SR6 0GL (0191 515 5555/ www.nationalglasscentre.com).*

# 693
## Admire the carvings at Kilpeck

The fantastical, the animal, the mythical and the magical join human faces angelic, humorous and grotesque in the carvings of Kilpeck's 12th-century church. Concentrated on the south door, the west window and the chancel arch, these ebullient outpourings are very different from the geometric motifs that characterise much Norman stonework – they're organic, and in places almost pagan (there are representations of the Green Man as well as the Sheelah-na-gig, a famously shameless Celtic fertility symbol). A puppy sits alongside a rabbit; a pair of fish interlink; a circle of four dragons hungrily devour each other; jesters and wrestlers cavort; and foliage and grape clusters form the Tree of Life – all revealing the role of symbolism and imagery in medieval thinking.

**Parish Church of St Mary & St David** *Kilpeck, Herefordshire HR2 9DN (01981 570315).*

# 694
## Get intimately involved in opera at Iford

Tucked away in a pretty valley on the Wiltshire-Somerset border, not far from Bath, is the Italianate, wisteria-clad Iford Manor – an idyllic setting for a little opera of a summer's evening. The performance area is a gloriously intimate cloister that holds just 90 people, designed by architect Harold Peto, which he described as his 'Haunt of Ancient Peace'.

For the past 12 years, Iford Arts has run a summer season of music here (mainly opera, but also some jazz, world and chamber music), performed by a host of budding young UK ensembles as well as their own Iford Opera company. Performances are standing room only, as there are no seats in the cloister – but in such delightful and high-brow surrounds, who's complaining? You can picnic in the lovely garden first.

**Iford Manor** *Bradford on Avon, Wiltshire BA15 2BA (01225 868124/www.ifordarts.co.uk).*

# 695
## Skip straight to dessert at Lucy's

Held on the first Wednesday of the month, the 'Up the Duff' pudding night at Lucy's On a Plate (next door to the owner's superlative deli) is a dessert-lover's dream. Instead of feeling duty-bound to fill up on pesky starters and mains before being let loose on the sweet stuff, diners can feast on puddings alone. Pick six from a list a dozen strong, along with a glass of dessert wine and a cup of coffee to round things off nicely. The menu changes every month, but might include the likes of spiced apple, pear and cranberry crumble, damson syllabub, deliciously rich chocolate almond torte or delightfully old-fashioned steamed ginger pudding. Not to mention the signature Borrowdale sticky banana pudding – a cross between sticky toffee pudding, banoffi pie and bread and butter pudding. Of course, you can pop into the restaurant for a pudding at any time – but the chance to guzzle down six in a row without being considered a pig is an opportunity not to be missed.

**Lucy's On a Plate** *Church Street, Ambleside, Cumbria LA22 0BU (01539 432288/ www.lucysofambleside.co.uk).*

# 696 *Learn to surf*

# Surfin' UK

*Donning his wetsuit,* **Sam Le Quesne** *hits Britain's shores in search of the big one.*

Little more than a decade ago, surfing was still considered a minority sport in Britain. Struggling into your wetsuit in an icy car park and paddling out into the gun-metal smudge of another British dawn was the preserve of the lunatic few. A combination of unpredictable swells yet predictably poor weather prevented the UK from getting caught up in the surfing fever that took hold of its warm-water siblings, America and Australia. Somehow, five inches of neoprene and a thermos of Cup-a-Soup didn't quite measure up to the aloha shirts and bikinied babes of California. But these days, none of that seems to matter.

Put it down to fashion and clever marketing; blame it on that Guinness ad – but the fact remains that unprecedented numbers of first-time surfers are now flocking to the British shoreline in search of the ultimate ride. And springing up in their wake are myriad surf schools and hire outlets, all with one purpose in mind: getting you on to a board, into the white water and out of the spirit-killing shackles of modern life. All you need to do is point the surfmobile towards the coast, slide *Pet Sounds* into the CD player and not take your foot off the gas until you see the ocean.

As is the case elsewhere in Europe, Britain's surf scene can be summed up with one simple maxim: West is best. It's not that there is no surf to be found in the south or the east, it's just that the long stretch of beaches, points and reefs that face the storm-battered expanse of the Atlantic are treated to the best of the swells. Generally, the good-quality waves tend to arrive either side of summer in the early autumn and spring, when low pressures out to sea usher in clean lines of larger, rideable surf. These are the times when serious surfers will be out in force, causing the line-ups at some of the more popular spots to get a bit competitive – with enough hot tempers and argy-bargy to make beginners feel out of their depth. Best, then, to try your luck in summer if you're new to the sport, when smaller waves, carefree crowds and (marginally) warmer water make the sea feel like an altogether friendlier place. You may be jostling for space, but the general vibe is usually far more laid-back, with rookie errors such as 'dropping in' (taking off on someone else's wave) being treated with a degree of good-humoured tolerance.

So where to start? Well, the obvious jumping-off point would be Britain's biggest and busiest surfing strip, otherwise known as England's south-west coast. The meandering line of coves, cliffs and coastal resorts that connects the dots between Land's End and the north Devonian beaches of Croyde and Woolacombe is where the vast majority of wave-riding is done. It is also where you'll find the headquarters of the British Surfing Association (in Newquay) and its National Surfing Centre, along with the highest concentration of surf schools in Britain.

Starting at the southernmost point, try your luck at Sennen Cove, a short drive west of Penzance and just a couple of miles up the coast from Land's End. This gorgeous stretch of sand is served by the Sennen Surfing Centre (01736 871227, www.sennensurfingcentre.com), which offers everything from two-hour starter lessons to lengthy courses under the auspices of qualified, experienced instructors. Alternatively, get your own board and suit from the hire shop next door and brave the elements alone (full-time lifeguards work the beach from March to

September). Or you could just buy what you need from the slickly appointed Chapel Idne surf shop (01736 871192, www.chapelidne.com), also located right on the cove.

Heading further north, beyond St Ives and St Agnes (also home to vibrant surf scenes), Newquay is the seat of the National Surfing Centre (01637 850737, www.nationalsurfing centre.com) and a good base from which to explore the region's best surfing beaches, such as Fistral, Lusty Glaze and Watergate. The NSC is one of Britain's top surf schools, with courses tailored to all levels and requirements. The beach breaks along this coast are friendly and (especially in summer) accessible even to complete novices, making it the perfect place to launch a mini surf safari. To that end, a very well-stocked hire outlet is Surfer's Paradise (64 Tower Road, Newquay TR7 1LY, 01637 877373, www.surfersparadise.co.uk), which offers deals on all manner of boards (customs for improving beginners and foam pop-outs for full-blown groms), bodyboards and wetsuits.

Last stop on the Cornish express is Bude, at the very tip of the county, where excellent beach breaks and a well-established surf culture allow plenty of opportunities to get involved in the sport at any level. The best surf school is Big Blue (01288 331764, www.bigbluesurfschool. co.uk), which runs lots of courses and visits all the best local beaches, including Summerleaze and Crooklets. Bude also has an interesting take on surf hire, with NCS Surfboards (0845 500 8550, www.ncssurfboards.co.uk) delivering equipment to your hotel and picking it up at the end of the hire period (minimum two days).

Next up is north Devon, a mythical land where verdant countryside trails off into surf-fringed beaches, and to whose shores surf-starved Londoners make frequent pilgrimages, caning it down the M5 on a Friday night, stopping only for pasties and petrol until the sound of the sea is roaring in their ears. The two surfside meccas here are Croyde and Woolacombe. The former, a charmingly old-fashioned English village, is the indicator for the area thanks to its solid, reliable beach break and consistent swells. If you find yourself in luck (and do bear in mind that the dreaded flat spells are something of a summertime affliction), the one-stop Surfing Croyde Bay (01271 891200, www.surfingcroyde bay.co.uk) is an excellent resource. Offering lessons, equipment hire and accommodation, SCB is the focus of the local scene. Hire here and check out the break at Croyde, or strap your board on to the roof and bimble over to the less crowded Woolacombe, where an easy wave and the absence of any rips provide ideal conditions for the newbie wave-rider.

Crossing the border, probably the best-loved surf spot in Wales is the jewel of the Gower coast, Llangennith. Simply put, this is one of the most beautiful bays in Britain. Beyond a rugged spine of dunes, a wide sandy beach stretches for miles with no adornment other than the canopy of the sky and the pounding sea. A campsite and thriving local surf culture ensure that there are always lots of boards in the water (kayaks and kite surfers also join the fray), and yet there is rarely the suggestion of congestion, thanks to the bay's shifting peaks and sand bars that guarantee waves enough for everyone. The traditional stop-off for board hire is PJ's Surf Shop (01792 386669, www.pjsurfshop. co.uk), which is run by the eponymous PJ (an outstanding surfer himself, and a tireless ambassador for the sport). Instructions in the art of how to stay on your feet and not wipe out are available from the tutors at the nearby Welsh Surfing Federation Surf School (01792 386426, www.wsfsurfschool.co.uk).

Meanwhile, continuing in a westerly direction, you will reach the ultimate outpost of Welsh surfing, Pembrokeshire. Quality breaks are plentiful in these parts, but many will require supervision and a certain amount of insider knowledge, both of which are available from Pembroke's excellent Outer Reef Surf School (01646 680070, www.outerreefsurfschool.com).

And so to the best of the rest. On the east side, Scarborough is a big crowd-puller, thanks to consistently rideable waves (try Scarborough Surf School; 01723 500467, www.scarborough surfschool.co.uk). Alternatively, leave the car on the mainland and head out to the island of Jersey, whose St Ouen's Bay has some of the finest shore-break surfing in the UK – hire gear and find out about lessons at the Watersplash (01534 484005, www.jerseysurfschool.co.uk).

The list could go on, and on, and on. But, when it comes down to it, there's only one thing you really need to remember about surfing in Britain: keep your sense of humour, don't care about how you look in your wetsuit, and surf like no one's watching.

# 697
## Take tea at a Buddhist monastery

Kagyu Samye Ling was not only the first Tibetan Buddhist monastery in Britain, but the first in the western world. Established in 1967 just outside the small Dumfriesshire village of Eskdalemuir, it functions as a religious and training centre, offering various courses and spiritual retreats. Day visitors are always welcome too, to look at the temple, peace garden and grounds, or pop into the brightly painted Tibetan Tea Rooms for a cuppa and a vegetarian snack.

**Kagyu Samye Ling Monastery & Tibetan Centre**
*Eskdalemuir, Langholm, Dumfriesshire DG13 0QL (01387 373232/www.samyeling.org).*

# 698
## Go underground at Geevor

Set on Cornwall's far western coast, the mining works at Geevor reach beyond the cliffs and out under the waves. A working tin mine until 1990, this is the UK's largest mining heritage centre. The dramatic setting alone warrants a visit, but the 67-acre site also allows you to explore a forgotten way of life. There are displays of mineral samples and big machinery galore, but it's the human element that's most interesting. The miners' changing rooms are wonderfully atmospheric and, unless you're claustrophobic, the 25-minute tunnel tour is not to be missed. Although the way is well lit, walking in single file along the uneven surface of this abandoned late 18th-century tunnel is a goosepimple-inducing experience. Guides talk about the various shafts and mineral veins, but all you'll be thinking is how cramped, cold, dark and damp it was for the workers, 50 feet down. Back out in the open air, safety helmet off, you'll never complain about crowded picnic areas again.

**Geevor Tin Mine** *Pendeen, Penzance, Cornwall TR19 7EW (01736 788662/www.geevor.com).*

# 699-705 Buy bread at Britain's best bakeries

Forget serving squishy supermarket loaves and Mr Kipling's finest at teatime; according to baking legend Dan Lepard – a man who's made bread for the likes of Giorgio Locatelli and Fergus Henderson – British baking is undergoing a renaissance. Inspiration is starting to come from closer to home, and unassuming classics like the eccles cake are coming into their own. 'The big change is a shift back to British baking, with a new generation of artisan bakers working to rediscover traditional recipes and methods,' says Lepard.

A wealth of independent bakeries has sprung up across the country: here are seven of Lepard's favourite spots to pick up a freshly baked loaf or sample some superlative cakes.

## Cinnamon Twist

There's an ever-changing cornucopia of goodies at this tiny artisan bakery and pâtisserie – from baked chocolate tart or macadamia and sultana brownies to mature cheddar scones with caramelised onion and flatleaf parsley. It's a glorious find in a small market town, with real talent in the kitchen – owner Mark Lazenby, whose CV includes stints at Baker & Spice and Villandry.

**Cinnamon Twist** *17 Church Street, Helmsley, York, North Yorkshire YO62 5AD (0790 170 1120).*

## Common Loaf

Baking with spelt flour, the Common Loaf produces everything from olive-studded focaccia to maple syrup-glazed blueberry muffins. Lepard also praises the 'beautifully dense, moist fruit bread' – 70 per cent fruit, it's packed with sherry-soaked raisins, figs, prunes and dates. The bakery is run by a community who live and work on the farm near where the main shop is based; on Fridays, look out for the stall at Totnes farmers' market.

**Common Loaf** *Stentwood Farm, Dunkeswell, Devon EX14 4RW (01823 681155/www.commonloaf.com).*

## Daylesford Organic

Better-known than some of the other bakeries on our list, Daylesford is a particular favourite with Lepard. 'Daylesford does exceptionally good sourdoughs and, more unusually, baguettes – in this country, we've never really perfected the baguette. Its breads have the most beautiful blistered, deep golden crust, thanks to a long fermentation of the dough in its final shape.'

**Daylesford Organic** *Daylesford, near Kingham, Gloucestershire GL56 0YG (01608 731700/ www.daylesfordorganic.com).*

## Flour Station

'This place really is very good,' says Lepard, who singles out the 'wonderful' sourdoughs and focaccia for particular praise. 'It's down to a very, very slow fermentation,' says manager Raphael Lennon. 'We leave the dough to rest for up to 36 hours, and a lovely flavour develops.' Lennon's own favourites

are the walnut levain (best eaten with blue cheese) and sugar-encrusted eccles cakes (made with boozy fruit and 'an awful lot of butter'). Sample one at Flour Station's market stall, in Borough Market, Wimbledon or Queen's Park.
**Flour Station** *22-24 Gwynne Road, London SW11 3UW (020 7223 5656/www.theflourstation.com).*

## Phoenix Bakery
Getting out of bed to arrive as the Phoenix opens is well worthwhile, if you can bag one of baker Iain Smith's amazing spelt loaves or Highland rye breads, fresh from the oven; the sourdough, says Lepard, is sublime. While the bakery shuts up shop at lunchtime, its bread is also sold at the nearby Phoenix Store – see the website for details.
**Phoenix Bakery** *Street, Findhorn, Morayshire IV36 3TZ (01309 691600/www.bakery-findhorn.co.uk).*

## Potting Shed Tea Room
Presided over by Norwegian Gunn Borrowman, this diminutive tearoom is set in a humble potting shed in a Cairngorms garden centre. 'People often recommend places to me – and they're normally dreadful,' says Lepard. 'This place, though, is exceptional – Gunn makes a beautiful almond cake with apricots.'
**Potting Shed Tea Room** *Inshriach Alpine Nurseries, Aviemore, Inverness-shire PH22 1QS (01540 651287/www.drakesalpines.com).*

## Town Mill Bakery
A slice of sourdough from the Town Mill is a sensory revelation, thanks to an unhurried fermentation process and top-quality organic flour; the cakes are splendid too. Until midday, passers-by can stop by the open kitchen and chat to baker Aidan Chapman as he works – and inhale the heady smell of baking bread. The in-house café serves up everything from hunks of Dorset rarebit to scrumptious sourdough pizzas; try the florentine, made with local eggs and organic spinach from the farm up the road.
**Town Mill Bakery** *Coombe Street, Lyme Regis, Dorset DT7 3PY (01297 444035/www.thetown millbakery.com).*

*Dan Lepard is the author of* The Handmade Loaf *(Mitchell Beazley) and* British Baking *(Harper Collins/Fourth Estate), published in September 2008. For a UK-wide list of independent bakeries, see www.danlepard.com.*

# 706

## Step back in time at the English Heritage Festival of History

*Derek Hammond joins the fray with the Britons of yesteryear.*

IT'S HISTORY IN THE FAKING! proclaimed a *Daily Mail* story of August 2007, when the English Heritage Festival of History was staged at Kelmarsh Hall in Northamptonshire. But in the ensuing trawl through the absurdities of 'more than 1,000 glorious British eccentrics' from 80 re-enactment societies simultaneously playing out historical scenes involving the Roman Army, medieval knights and Queen Victoria – to name but a few – the newspaper managed to miss out on the fun, as well as the point of this wildly popular event.

It's a transforming experience, dressing up in Robin Hood tights, armour and chainmail, or donning a wimpole. Serious re-enactors aren't merely playing out their historical fantasies, they're living them – and the sense of escape can be infectious. After a mere 30 minutes wandering through the tented landscape, it's impossible not to be caught up in the passion, the obsessive attention to detail, and the sheer belief of everyone involved.

In one corner, vaguely recognisable Tudor royalty and sundry servants are flying their falcons on the lawn. A Roman soldier has unfortunately – in real life – had the end of his finger cut off in a skirmish with an oiled-up gladiator, and the carefully researched skills of a Georgian apothecary are being stretched to the limit. 'Hold still,' he says. 'It's a shame you don't have syphilis.' Bi-planes dogfighting over a worryingly authentic World War I trench add to the sheer confusion experienced by unwitting drop-by time-travellers on this ultimate lost weekend. Meanwhile, Civil War veterans run through their battle drill to the echoing beat of a snare: curse the king's name around these parts, and you could risk being hung, drawn and quartered.

Members of the Sealed Knot Society effectively live double lives, split between the present and the past. Every weekend they make like the English Civil War is still being waged, rallying under Cavalier and Roundhead banners, dressing up and fighting for their historical beliefs. But what do these rotund real-alers do for a living? What do their comely damsels do when they have to cease their quaffing and banqueting and pour their overflowing bosoms back into more practical attire? What, in short, is the attraction of becoming a character from another era?

'It's something to do with the certainty and simplicity of the past,' muses Tony, a civil servant hailing from Birmingham. 'And personally, I really like the fact that everything was handmade – made to last.'

'If you look around the Festival, you'll see how there are whole industries springing up again,' agrees fellow-Brummie Christian, who's an armourer. 'There are musket-makers, embroiderers, woodworkers. A whole suit of armour can cost over £1,000, but there's a pride in it.'

But even if you're not prepared to squander your savings in pursuit of historical perfection, Kelmarsh is a wonderfully surreal and spectacular day out; escapism in its purest form. As Christian sagely observes, 'It's one thing to read about history, another to experience what it looked and felt like.' The Festival of History returns to Kelmarsh Hall on the weekend of 19 and 20 July 2008. See www.english-heritage.org.uk for more details.

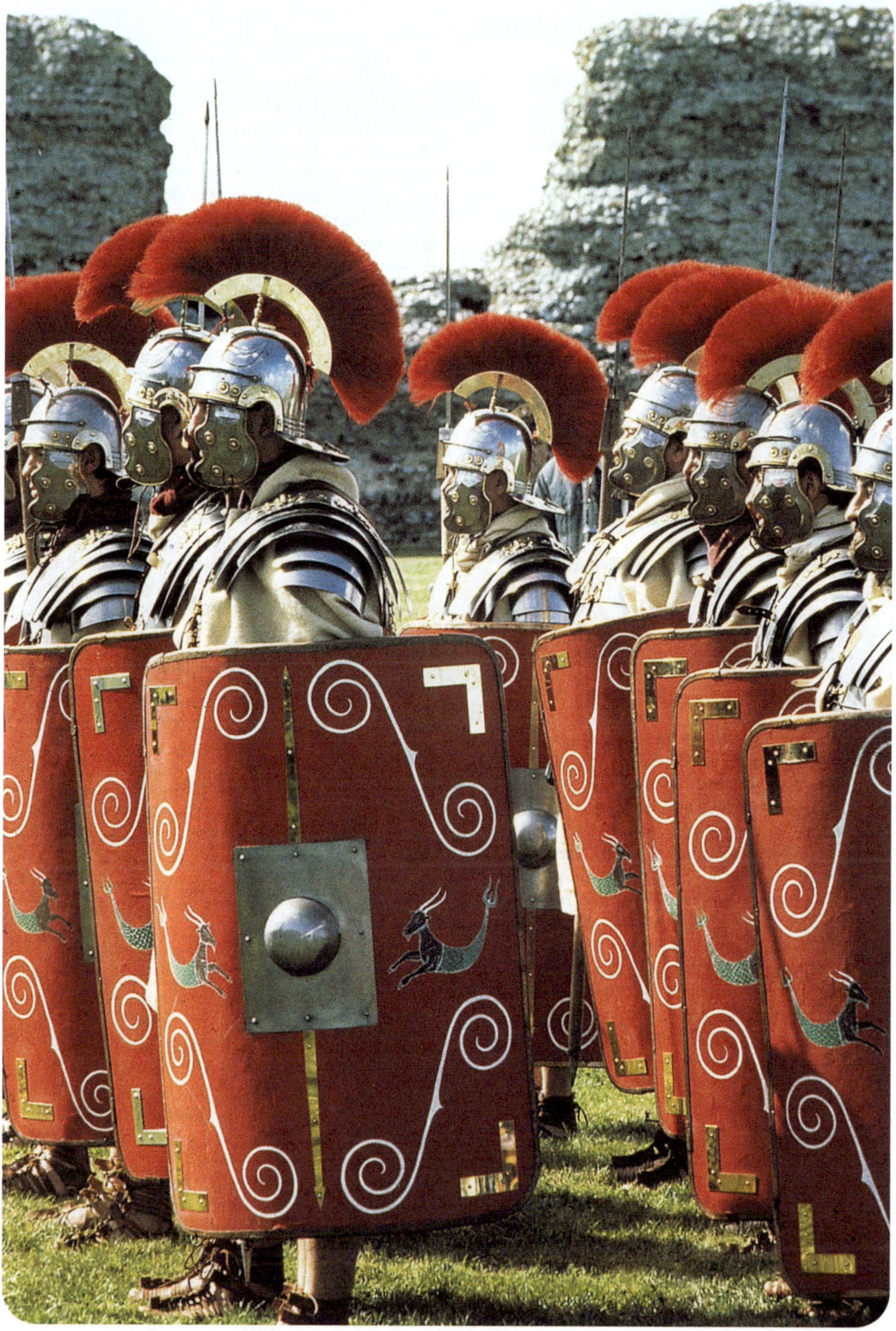

# A few of my favourite things

# 707-714

## David Starkey, historian

One of my favourite National Trust properties is Ightham Mote (Mote Road, Ivy Hatch, Sevenoaks, Kent TN15 0NT, 01732 810378, www.nationaltrust.org.uk). Like many early Tudor manors, it's built in a hollow and is surrounded by water. It's a really wonderful, half-timbered house, which presents a completely romantic vision of a country house. It also has unrecognised regal connections – the long gallery is decorated with the badges of Henry VIII and Catherine of Aragon, which means the house was built by a very important member of the royal court – and it's quite probable that the king visited at some point.

I'm particularly fond of the gardens at **Levens Hall (Kendal, Cumbria LA8 0PD, 01539 560321, www.levenshall.co.uk).** I was born in Kendal and first saw them as a boy. It's the best-preserved topiary garden in England, and dates back to the late 17th century; one of the few cases where you can trace the direct history of a garden. In some places, the topiary is actually original.

The most important recent acquisition on behalf of the nation is Dumfries House, near Cumnock in Ayrshire (www.ayrshirescotland.com/mansions/dumfries.html), which was rescued thanks to the Prince of Wales's intervention and should be open to the public soon. It probably has the best-preserved 18th-century interior in Britain. Like so many of these houses, it was never really lived in by the family that owned it. As a result, all the original furniture is in place, including pieces by Thomas Chippendale, along with the bills for each item. You have the sense of the house being just as it was when the decorators left.

You can find a very political garden at Stowe House (Stowe School, Stowe, Buckingham, Buckinghamshire MK18 5EH, 01280 818229, www.stowe.co.uk). The Viscount Cobham used sculptures, busts, temples and images in the garden to make a comment on his political enemies, so an attack on Prime Minister Robert Walpole takes the form of a so-called Temple of Modern Virtue – built as a ruin with a hideous caricature of Walpole at the centre.

I love staying at country hotel Llangoed Hall (Llyswen, Brecon, Powys LD3 0YP, 01874 754525, www.llangoedhall.com). The building is stunning: the main design is by the great Welsh architect Sir Clough Williams-Ellis. It's where I go whenever I speak at the Hay-on-Wye Festival, and it's the kind of place where Clive Anderson is to be seen kissing Germaine Greer, with both of them looking equally awkward.

**The restaurant in London with the most interesting interior around has to be the Wolseley (160 Piccadilly, London W1J 9EB, 020 7499 6996, www.thewolseley.com).** It's a converted car showroom from the 1920s, and has a combination of grand columns and very noble architecture and, on the other hand, frilly, chinoiserie decoration. On the whole, I think town architecture is very much a function of good manners, and most modern building is deliberately bad-mannered. Of all the major recent buildings, the most successful is the British Library (96 Euston Road, London NW1 2DB, 0870 444 1500, www.bl.uk). The exterior is uncomfortably like a suburban Tesco, but the interiors are superb. The sense you get when you first enter and confront the great columns of the King's Library rearing up as a gigantic glass book stack in the centre of the building is monumental.

**A landmark far too little registered is the Monument to the Great Fire of London (Monument Street, London EC3R 8AH, 020 7626 2717, www.themonument.info).** It's extraordinarily striking. It's the first and most impressive of the great columns that were built in the capital and is profoundly political in message – it drops heavy hints that the fire was a Catholic conspiracy. But it's also a symbol of the wealth of London and its ability to reinvent itself.

# 715
## Hunt the Earl of Rone

This utterly bizarre festival takes place every year over the spring bank holiday in Combe Martin, north Devon, as locals dress up to re-enact the ancient tale of the Earl of Rone (www.earl-of-rone.org.uk). The precise provenance of the story is disputed – was the earl a shipwrecked Irishman called Hugh O'Neill, or a famous outlaw from Chichester? – but that doesn't seem to dampen participants' enthusiasm. They spend the four-day weekend hunting the unfortunate 'Earl', before finding him on Monday evening, at which point he is paraded to the beach on a donkey – backwards, naturally – and dumped into the sea. His demise is then celebrated with a hobby horse procession. Fancy yourself in the role of the earl? Sadly, only residents of Combe Martin – or inhabitants of the surrounding parishes of Berrynarbor, Trentishoe and Kentisbury – are allowed to dress up and take part, but visitors can come and watch (in return for a small donation).

# 716
## Visit a surreal Russian puppet theatre in Glasgow

The Sharmanka Kinetic Gallery in Glasgow is an absolute gem, using hundreds of carved wooden figures, bits of scrap, clever lighting and music to create magical mechanised shows. Sculptor Eduard Bersudsky and theatre director Tatyana Jakovskaya founded the Sharmanka (which means 'hurdy gurdy' in Russian) in St Petersburg in 1989, before upping sticks and moving to Scotland in 1996. There are usually three scheduled Sharmanka shows a week at their Glasgow base, or you can call in advance to arrange a special performance. It's strangely creepy when the figures spring to life in the shadowy sets – so probably best avoided by nightmare-prone small fry.

**Sharmanka Kinetic Gallery/Theatre** *64 Osborne Street, Glasgow G1 5QH (0141 552 7080/ www.sharmanka.com).*

# 717
## Step aboard the SS Great Britain

The world's first propeller-driven, iron-hulled passenger liner, *SS Great Britain* today lies in the dry dock from which she floated in 1843 as the largest ship in the world. Designed by Isambard Kingdom Brunel, she completed her maiden voyage to New York in a stunning 14 days. In later years she carried emigrants to Australia, but ended up rusting off the Falkland Islands, until a rescue plan returned her to her place of origin in 1970. Beneath the glass sea on which the great ship appears to float, visitors can walk alongside the hull, with its immense propeller and rudder. Inside is Brunel's huge steam engine, three storeys high, and the passenger accommodation: tiny steerage cabins crammed with narrow bunks, human figures and the odd model rat, along with the more salubrious first-class cabins and sitting areas. Next to the ship is a dockyard museum and (when in port) *The Matthew*, a replica of the ship John Cabot sailed to Newfoundland in 1497.

**SS Great Britain** *Western Dockyard, Gas Ferry Road, Bristol BS1 6TY (0117 926 0680/www.ss greatbritain.org).*

## 718
### Ramble over Kinder Scout – without getting arrested

Kinder Scout, midway between Manchester and Sheffield, played a crucial part in the great 'right to roam' debate. Its open moorlands had always been the private domain of the grouse-shooters – but in 1932, several hundred ramblers lobbying for open access to the moors set off on a mass trespass. As they tried to ascend the plateau, they clashed with gamekeepers in the 'Battle for Kinder Scout', and six arrests ensued. Kinder was officially opened to the public in 1953, though it wasn't until the Countryside and Rights of Way Act of 2000 that wider rights of access to the moors really opened up.

You may not get arrested on Kinder Scout these days, but the right to roam has caused problems: the peat layer is being seriously eroded, partly due to the number of walkers. You can see why they come, though; at around 1,970 feet above sea level, the windswept plateau affords stunning views. The National Trust is taking steps to tackle the damage: in 2007, to mark the 75th anniversary of the mass trespass, members of the public helped to plant over 150,000 cotton grass plants and re-seed the bare peat with heather. If you want to follow in the footsteps of the trespassers, the National Trust's website (01433 670368, www.nationaltrust.org.uk) has a downloadable walk sheet and map, designed to allow access to the area while preserving the environment. And a map is what you'll need: if you get lost, there's no mobile reception.

## 719
### Drink cider from the barrel at Tucker's Grave Inn

Step inside this tiny pub and enter a timewarp, where Bass and Butcombe are served straight from the barrel (it's too small to have a bar), along with Cheddar Valley cider. Skittles and shove ha'penny add to the old-time ambience.
**Tucker's Grave Inn** *Faulkland, Radstock, Bath BA3 5XF (01373 834230).*

## 720
### Petition the PM

Got a grievance you think the government ought to sort out? Log on to http://petitions.pm.gov.uk, and state your claim. Issues getting other petitioners hot under the collar include everything from scrapping the ID card plan to campaigns to make Jeremy Clarkson prime minister and (coincidentally) declare banger racing an Olympic sport.

## 721
### Get Back to where John Lennon once belonged

Unlike the National Trust's other stately piles, the childhood homes of Lennon and McCartney are defiantly ordinary – a 1930s semi set on a suburban dual carriageway, and a modest terrace house. Uniquely for the NT, these are painstaking re-creations of just 50 years ago: inside, every beige and Bakelite detail of 1950s Scouse normality is checked. But for any trace of teenage John lingering in his bedroom, it's up to you to Imagine… Visits are restricted to pre-booked minibus tours of the two sites (0151 427 7231, www.nationaltrust.org.uk/beatles).

## 722
### ID your fruit trees

With a whopping 1,881 varieties growing on site, the apple collection at Brogdale Farm is probably the best in the world. Take a guided tour of the lovely orchards before quaffing an apple juice in the tearoom – or take advantage of the unique fruit identification service. If you've always wondered which variety that apple or pear tree in your garden is, post three samples of its fruit to Brogdale along with some leaves, details of the tree it came from and a fee. Within 28 days, the mystery will be solved.
**National Fruit Collection** *Brogdale Road, Faversham, Kent ME13 8RZ (01795 535286/ www.brogdale.org).*

# 723 See world art at the Sainsbury Centre

At the Sainsbury Centre, modernist aficionados can not only admire works by Epstein and Moore (among many others), but in an early Norman Foster building to boot – a striking, 1978 steel-clad and semi-glazed cube on the UEA campus. You'll also find everything from shell-set Polynesian carvings to Japanese scrolls. If your visit is fleeting, must-sees include Henry Moore's *Mother and Child*, Degas' *Little Dancer Aged Fourteen*, Picasso's *Female Nude with Arms Raised*, a 500-year-old silver Inca llama effigy and the 16th-century bronze *Head of an Oba* from Benin.
**Sainsbury Centre for Visual Arts** *University of East Anglia, Norwich NR4 7TJ (01603 593199/ www.scva.org.uk).*

# 724 See the sea from Spinnaker Tower

Spinnaker Tower's distinctive sail-shaped silhouette was designed to reflect Portsmouth's rich maritime history; its three observation decks mean that landlubbers can avoid going afloat, yet still feast on the sort of views usually only visible from a ship's crow's nest. Standing at 558 feet high, the slender structure is two-and-a-half times taller than Nelson's Column; on a clear day you can see for over 20 miles. Ride the panoramic lift to the top, then make your heart race by walking across the glass floor and getting whipped by the wind on the open-air top deck.
**Spinnaker Tower** *Gunwharf Quays, Portsmouth, Hampshire PO1 3TT (023 9285 7520/www. spinnakertower.co.uk).*

# 725 Take a handbrake turn in time at the Goodwood Revival

The Revival is an annual institution at this famous old motor circuit, allowing the world's retro petrolheads to converge on the Earl of March's West Sussex estate to top up on fumes, vrooms and champers-tinted memories of British motorsport's halcyon days. Dressing up like Dick Dastardly is only nominally optional.
**Goodwood Revival Meeting** *Goodwood, Chichester, West Sussex PO18 0PX (01243 755000/www.goodwood.co.uk/revival).*

# 726
## Watch the skies fill with starlings at Slimbridge

The starlings' white-spotted, green and purple iridescent plumage mark it out from the other crumb-snatchers hopping around your lunchtime park bench, but these little birds really come into their own when they fly en masse at dusk. No one really knows why they do it; one theory is that it's to confuse predatory birds while the flocks head for a roosting site for the night. The sight of hundreds – if not thousands – of starlings wheeling and turning in synchrony in the darkening sky is something to turn the heads of even the busiest of commuters – but it's best seen in the countryside. At Slimbridge nature reserve, the wide expanse of sky offers an awe-inspiring backdrop: autumn is a good time to visit, as large starling numbers arrive to winter here. As the temperature drops and the light slowly fades, watching the swooping and swirling patterns of the starlings is a surreally beautiful experience. The best viewing spot is at the southern end of the grounds, around the tropical house or in the South Finger – then just wait and listen for the sound of beating wings (a flock of starlings is aptly called a murmuration). You won't need binoculars for the show; there's a cast of thousands, after all.
**Wildfowl & Wetlands Trust** *Slimbridge, Gloucestershire GL2 7BT (01453 891900/www.wwt.org.uk).*

# 727
## Whoop at the BritBowl

American football in the UK received a huge boost when the Miami Dolphins and New York Giants played the first regular-season NFL game to be staged outside North America at Wembley Stadium in October 2007. British gridiron's showpiece, though, is the BritBowl, contested by the two top teams in the British American Football League (www.bafl.org.uk) at the Don Valley Stadium each September.
**Don Valley Stadium** *Worksop Road, Sheffield S9 3TL (0114 223 3600/www.donvalleystadium.co.uk).*

# 728
## Go the whole hog at St John

'Nose to tail eating' is chef Fergus Henderson's description of the Modern British cooking he pioneered at St John – situated, appropriately enough, around the corner from London's Smithfield Market. Henderson's genius was to put back on the menu parts of animals most diners had long forgotten about – his roast bone marrow and parsley salad, for instance, is a bona fide culinary classic. Another show-stopper is the whole roast suckling pig, which feeds 14 to 16 people (note that a week's notice is required). Henderson also transformed forever the visual grammar of British restaurants: St John's white walls and pared-down, vaguely post-industrial aesthetic set an example that has been copied a thousand times.
**St John** *26 St John Street, London EC1M 4AY (020 7251 0848/www.stjohnrestaurant.com).*

# 729
## Walk Britain's last battlefield

More than lives were lost at Culloden. On a bitterly cold, wet day in April 1746, a few miles east of Inverness, the last Jacobite uprising reached its endgame. The House of Hanover was reaffirmed as Britain's royal family, while the Stuarts – who had ruled Scotland from the 14th century, and Britain for much of the 17th – were written out of history. The British Army carried the day, the Jacobite threat was extinguished, and Bonnie Prince Charlie fled to France – leaving the clans who had supported him face to face with a modernity that would extinguish their way of life. A new visitors' centre opened in late 2007, but simply walking amid the wind-scoured heather, past the simple gravestones, is enough to evoke a tremendous sense of loss.
**Culloden Moor** *Inverness, IV1 2ED (0844 493 2159/www.nts.org.uk/culloden).*

# 730 Head for a lighthouse

Holidaying in a lighthouse keeper's cottage is about as remote and romantic as you'll get. Views of the open sea, the sound of waves as a bedtime lullaby – there's no better place to unwind and relax those stiff city shoulders. Trinity House, the UK's Lighthouse Authority, has converted over 30 former keepers' cottages into holiday lets, dotted all around the coast (01386 701177, www.ruralretreats.co.uk). They're great spots for wildlife watching, and there's something thrillingly Enid Blytonesque about seeing the sweep of a lighthouse beam in the darkness. Just be aware that some of the lighthouses are still operational, which means a powerful foghorn is liable to sound on misty nights; earplugs are thoughtfully provided.

# 731-736 Cross Britain's greatest bridges

## Clifton Suspension Bridge
The great Victorian engineer Isambard Kingdom Brunel won his first major commission in 1830, aged 24, with his design for the west of England's most famous bridge. It spans the Avon Gorge in Bristol at a height of 245 feet, but Brunel himself never got to cross it. Funding problems delayed its completion until 1864 – five years after his death from overwork on the massive steamship the *Great Eastern*, the ship that first bridged the Atlantic with a telegraph line.

## Humber Bridge
The quickest way south from Hull is over the Humber Bridge, which crosses the Humber estuary. On its opening in 1981, it was the longest single-span suspension bridge in the world (at almost one mile from tower to tower), a boast it could make until the construction of longer spans in Denmark and then Japan in the late 1990s. In 2005, it was knocked into fourth place by the completion of the Runyang Bridge over the Yangtze in China.

## Forth Road Bridge
Opened in 1964, the Forth Road Bridge is the 19th longest suspension bridge in the world. It is best appreciated for its superb setting, its convenience (it connects Edinburgh with Fife over the Firth of Forth), and for the fact that in February 2008 it finally became toll-free. The one-and-a-half mile roadway is flanked by cycle paths and footpaths – although only the foolhardy would think about trying to walk or ride across on a windy day.

**Humber Bridge**

## Tower Bridge
One of the most foolish questions that tourists apparently ask the chief Beefeater of the Tower of London is which side of the Thames this bridge is on. In fairness to the questioner, though, it might be useful to know that the entrance to the Tower Bridge Exhibition (and the spectacular viewing galleries along the top of the bridge) is in the north tower. A much-loved London icon, up there with St Paul's and Big Ben, Tower Bridge was opened in 1894 and still raises its bascules now and again for passing river traffic.

## Tay Road Bridge
One of the longest bridges in Europe, some one-and-a-half miles long, the Tay Road Bridge links the county of Fife to Dundee. As well as giving splendid views of the 'silvery Tay', the trip north is the most impressive approach to Scotland's fair city of 'jam, jute and journalism'. Constructed in the early '60s, the bridge slopes into town at a gradient of one in 81.

## Isle of Skye Bridge
Dogged by controversy from its inception, largely because it was going to render the ferries (and hence the *Skye Boat Song*), redundant, the Isle of Skye Bridge was completed in 1995 and immediately caused further outrage with the level of its tolls. These were abolished in 2004, and the bridge can now quietly get on with doing what it does best: providing easy, 24-hour access to one of the most beautiful corners of the country.

# 737 Globe-trot in London's Horniman Museum

Victorian tea trader Frederick J Horniman had a mission: he wanted to bring the world to Forest Hill, SE23. To that end, he collected artefacts and specimens from around the globe, stuck them in his house and opened his doors to the public. Over a century later (having hastily relocated in 1901, when the house became too cramped), the Horniman Museum is still edifying and entertaining visitors with its pickled animals, stuffed birds, Egyptian mummies, masks, models and weird musical instruments – not to mention the stunning new aquarium, opened in 2006. Horniman gave the museum to the people of London when it relocated in 1901, so you can visit this splendid establishment – and tickle a stingray – for free. **Horniman Museum** *100 London Road, London SE23 3PQ (020 8699 1872/www.horniman.ac.uk).*

# 738-741
## Get lost in a maize maze

The maize maze season lasts for just a couple of summer months before the fields are harvested for cattle feed, so why bother painstakingly laying out designs and pulling out paths for people to get lost in? Well, why not – there's something wonderfully appealing about sunny cornfields, so you might as well make an afternoon out of it, wandering in circles and solving puzzles. The work that goes into creating the large-scale labyrinths can only be properly appreciated from aerial pictures. At York Maze (01904 415234, www.yorkmaze.com) a different design is created each year in an area the size of 15 football pitches, carved out of 1.5 million growing maize plants. Themes vary: at Hampshire's seven-acre Mega Maze (www.forty-acres.co.uk) last year, visitors could spot Portsmouth destinations on a recreated road network, while dinosaurs ruled at Smeaton Farm, Saltash (01579 351833, www.amazingcornishmaizemaze.co.uk). At Cumbria's Lakeland Maze (01539 561760, www.lakelandmaze.co.uk) there's a mini-maze for little ones. See also www.maizemaze.com.

# 742
## Join FRED's art invasion

Why pay to look at art in a plain old gallery when you can see it for free in an area of outstanding natural beauty? FRED, Europe's largest festival of site-specific art, provides some beautiful, quirky and frequently bizarre additions to the Cumbrian landscape for 16 days every September and October, when more than 60 artists turn the area into their canvas (01768 371561, www.fredsblog.co.uk).

Previous years have seen members of the public invited to partake in a transparent floating steam sauna and ponder climate change, courtesy of Gareth Kennedy's *Weathercube* at St Patrick's Boat Yard in Glenridding, and revisit childhood fantasies of flying by walking through Jo Lathwood's enormous disc-shaped sculpture, *Flying Inside*, at Whitehaven Harbour.

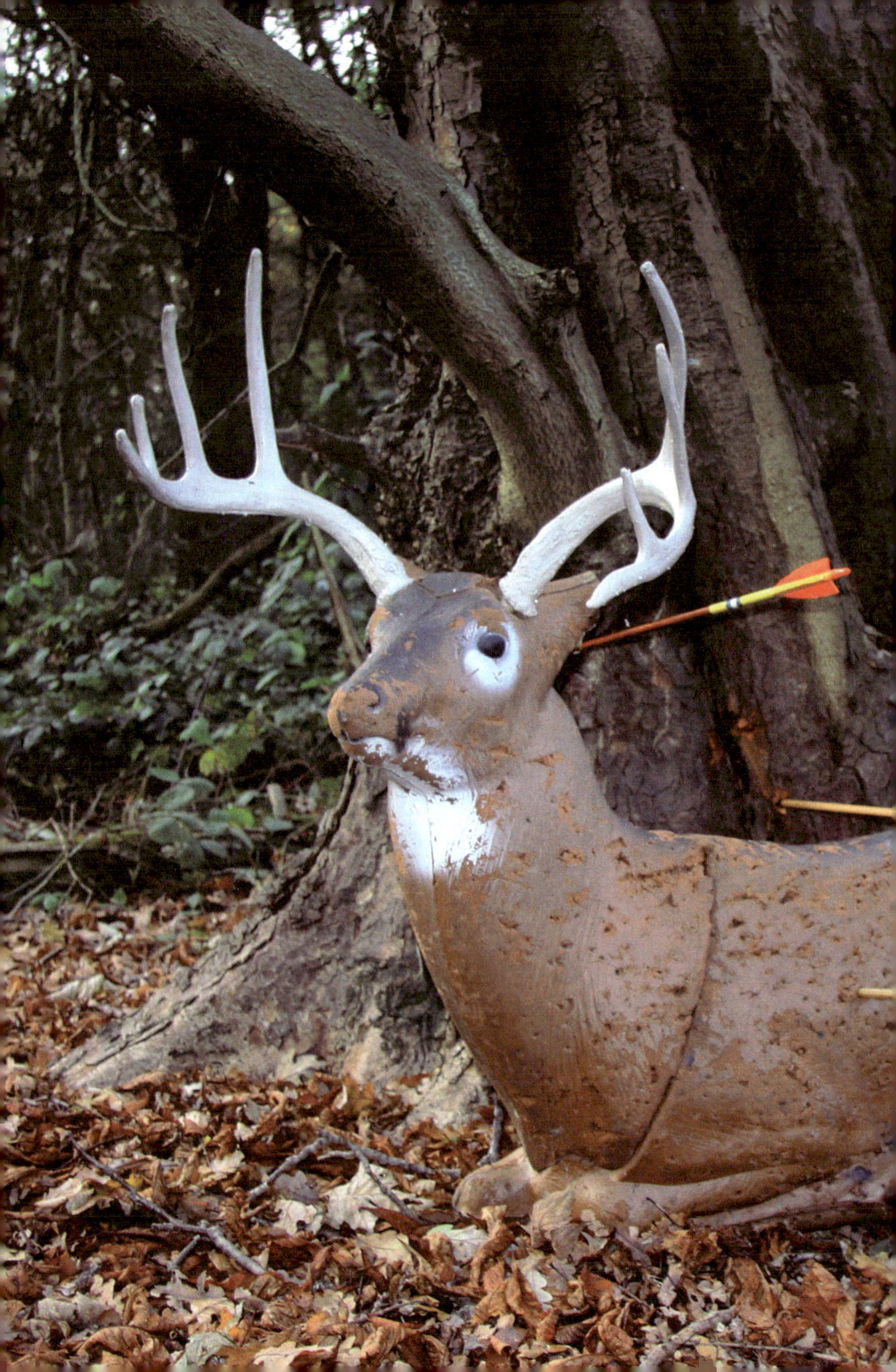

## 743

### Try field archery
These days, archery generally involves shooting at static boards marked with concentric circles – a far cry from the days of Robin Hood. Field archery, on the other hand, is a much more exciting proposition, restoring the sport to its hunting and warfare roots. The first challenge is to find your virtual prey (images or 3D models of anything from deer to dinosaurs) amid the undergrowth. Then comes the thrilling shot at the target: across water, perhaps, or downhill between overhanging branches. For dozens of clubs across the UK that organise 'shoots' for adults and children, check out the National Field Archery Society's website (www.nfas.net).

## 744 Bake bread on St Martin's

Set on the tiny Scilly island of St Martin's (it's two-and-a-half miles long and a mile wide), St Martin's Bakery is a tiny delight. Thanks to the remote location, its focus is firmly on local produce: sterling Cornish pasties are rustled up from island-reared beef, while the eggs in the cakes and quiches come from the owner's flock of chickens. What better place to learn to bake? Week-long courses take place in November and between January and March; at £745 they're not cheap, but everything (including helicopter flights from Penzance) is included.
**St Martin's Bakery** *Moo Green, St Martin's, Isles of Scilly TR25 0QL (01720 423444/ www.stmartinsbakery.co.uk).*

## 745 Take the train to the National Railway Museum

Take in over 300 years of world railway history at this vast museum, as you clamber aboard a steam train, pretend to be a Japanese commuter on a bullet train, see the mechanics at work or watch one of the daily steam demonstrations. Entry is free, while long-stay car parking costs £7 – though for true train aficionados, the railway station is just a short walk away.
**National Railway Museum** *Leeman Road, York YO26 4XJ (08448 153139/www.nrm.org.uk).*

## 746 Explore the garden rooms at Hidcote

When Gertrude Winthrop bought Hidcote Manor estate in 1910, the house was surrounded by fields. Her son, Arts and Crafts enthusiast Lawrence Johnston, embarked on an ambitious plan to transform the farmland into a garden, aided by a 12-strong team of gardeners. These days, it is often likened to a series of outdoor rooms, divided by topiary, walls and hedges. Each 'room' has a different feel; finding your favourite is a lovely way to spend an afternoon.
**Hidcote Manor Garden** *Hidcote Bartrim, near Chipping Campden, Gloucestershire GL55 6LR (01386 438333/www.nationaltrust.org.uk).*

## 747-748 See a kilted man toss a caber

Various sporting, musical and dance events have gone on in the Scottish Highlands for untold centuries, but it wasn't until the 1820s that they were aggregated into the modern Highland games format. This involves a summer get-together with something of the atmosphere of a village fête, taking in specific sports (caber tossing, hammer throwing and stone putting, among others), fiddlers, pipe bands, Highland dancing competitions and more. Scotland's largest event is the Cowal Highland Gathering, held at Dunoon every August (www.cowalgathering.com) – although the Queen usually attends September's Braemar Gathering (www.braemargathering.org) when she's in residence at nearby Balmoral Castle.

## 749 Peep at the Lincoln Imp

Victorian arbiter of good taste John Ruskin declared Lincoln Cathedral to be 'out and out the most precious piece of architecture in the British Isles and roughly speaking worth any two other cathedrals we have'. Its soaring towers are visible from 25 miles away; close up, it is equally impressive, with its Christopher Wren-designed library and medieval rose window. Don't miss the famed Lincoln imp, a grinning gargoyle perched on a pillar in the Angel Choir. Legend has it he's one of a pair of mischievous creatures sent by Satan to cause trouble on earth, who were caught by an angel as they wreaked havoc in the cathedral. One fled, while the other scampered up a column to throw rocks at the angel and was turned to stone – a less than repentant sinner, judging by his expression.
**Lincoln Cathedral** *Minster Yard, Lincoln, Lincolnshire LN2 1PX (01522 561600/ www.lincolncathedral.com).*

# 750
## Help Britain's oldest orchestra celebrate its birthday

As luck would have it, the Hallé has chosen its 150th anniversary to come into spectacular form. The Manchester-based orchestra, founded by Sir Charles Hallé in 1858, has enjoyed something of a renaissance under current music director Mark Elder: in the last five years he has lifted it from the brink of ruin to being named the country's best orchestra in *The Times* in 2007. The Hallé has a fearsome reputation in all kinds of repertoire, but perhaps most notably in the music of Edward Elgar. Listening to the orchestra's iconic British conductor playing so quintessentially British a repertoire can't fail to stir feelings of pride in even the most cynical internationalist. During the extended birthday celebrations, which began in 2007 and will continue into 2009, the focus will be on works that received their world and British premières with the Hallé, many of them now favourites of the repertoire.

**Hallé Orchestra** *Bridgewater Hall, Lower Mosley Street, Manchester M2 3WS (0161 907 9000/ www.halle.co.uk).*

# 751
## Raise a toast to Crick and Watson in the Eagle

Cambridge University lays claim to several monumental discoveries – not least of which is James Watson and Frances Crick's 1953 unravelling of the double helix structure of DNA. The pair supped at the Eagle pub between stints in the lab and it was here that they announced their results, making this charming boozer a place of pilgrimage for science fanatics the world over.

The pub was also popular with American pilots stationed in Cambridge during World War II, and its memorabilia-packed rear room remains a temple to the airborne forces. Most powerful is the ghostly graffiti that covers the ceiling – a largely illegible mass of overlapping names, dates and divisions, which were burned on with cigarette lighters by pilots between missions. A naked lady is supposedly scrawled somewhere among them; framed on the far wall, the signature of the pilot of the Memphis Belle is far easier to locate. Those with an interest in Cambridge's wartime connection with the American military can also visit Madingley American Cemetery in outlying Coton, with its sprawling graveyards, serene mausoleum and Portland stone memorial.

**The Eagle** *8 Benet Street, Cambridge CB2 3QN (01223 505020).*

# 752
## Discover the Orient in Durham

Exhibits at the impressive Oriental Museum at Durham University, opened in 1960, include prized possessions of China's Ming and Qing dynasties, woodblock prints by Japanese artist Hokusai (best known for his iconic *Great Wave off Kanagawa* print) and ancient Egyptian antiquities – including a splendid bronze coffin designed for a mummified cat. Special events range from Chinese New Year celebrations to demonstrations of how to tie a kimono.

**Oriental Museum** *Elvet Hill, Durham DH1 3TH (0191 334 5694/www.dur.ac.uk/oriental.museum).*

# 753-761 Inspect a sports stadium

Andrew Shields *tours hallowed sporting halls and shiny new stadiums.*

**Arsenal Museum & Tour**
*Emirates Stadium, Drayton Park, London N5 1BU (020 7704 4504/www.arsenal.com).*
For a club as acutely aware of their past as Arsenal, the move to the Emirates Stadium represented a glorious opportunity to celebrate the new while paying tribute to more than 120 years of history, right back to 1886 and the original Dial Square FC. There are artefacts aplenty in the new museum – including Michael Thomas's boots from the title-winning game at Anfield in 1989 and Charlie George's 1971 FA Cup Final shirt – but plasmas and projectors are to the fore. Themes include 'The Arsenal Spirit' and 'The Invincibles' and the tour visits the dressing rooms, players' tunnel and dugouts, directors' box and media centre.

**Manchester United Museum & Tour**
*Sir Matt Busby Way, Old Trafford, Manchester M16 0RA (0870 442 1994/ www.manutd.com).*
United fans can stand in Fergie's spot in the dugout, sit in the home changing room and admire the vast array of honours won since 1908 in the Trophy Room. The museum honours the club's greats – Charlton, Law, Best, Cantona – in its hall of fame, while the 1958 Munich Air Disaster is poignantly covered.

**MCC Museum & Lord's Tour**
*Lord's, St John's Wood Road, London NW8 8QN (020 7616 8595/www.lords.org).*
The museum at the home of cricket is full of evocative paintings, photos, bats, balls and kit going back more than 400 years – plus the tiny, fragile Ashes urn (which most Australians believe should reside down under rather than in north-west London, since they're the near-permanent holders). The tour takes in the pavilion, Long Room, indoor cricket school and dressing rooms, which include the honours boards on which are inscribed the names of every Lord's Test match century-maker or bowler taking five wickets in an innings.

**Museum of Rugby & Twickenham Stadium Tour**
*Twickenham Stadium, Rugby Road, Twickenham, Middlesex TW1 1DZ (0870 405 2001/ www.rfu.com/museum).*
You can almost smell the embrocation as you wander round this splendid collection of memorabilia, showing how the oval-ball game has spread around the world. The beautiful Calcutta Cup, made out of 270 melted silver rupee coins, is a highlight, as is an England shirt from the very first international match, held in 1871. Film footage dating back to 1901 is fascinating, while visits end with a 15-minute presentation in the AV theatre. The stadium tour includes a peek into the England changing room.

**MCC Museum**

**National Football Museum**
*Sir Tom Finney Way, Preston, Lancashire PR1 6PA (01772 908442/www.national footballmuseum.com).*
Preston North End may no longer be one of the big names in English football (despite being one of the Football League's 12 founder members) but their Deepdale home is worth a trip for this museum. The 'First Half' gallery concentrates on the past, including the Jules Rimet Trophy from the 1966 World Cup Final and Maradona's shirt from the infamous 'Hand of God' game in 1986. The 'Second Half' is more interactive, exploring themes such as grounds, players, rules and fans, along with a chance to be guest pundit on a special edition of *Match of the Day*.

Wembley Stadium

### River & Rowing Museum
*Mill Meadows, Henley on Thames, Oxfordshire RG9 1BF (01491 415600/www.rrm.co.uk).*
This award-winning museum has enjoyable displays about the River Thames, its regattas and the town of Henley. Oarspersons should head for the Schwarzenbach International Rowing Gallery, which tells the story of one of Britain's most successful Olympic sports through memorabilia and interactive exhibits. One such is 'In the Cox's Seat', affording a 360 degree panoramic experience of what it's like to take part in a race at the Henley Regatta.

### Scottish Football Museum & Hampden Park Tour
*Hampden Park, Glasgow G42 9AY (0141 616 6139/www.scottishfootballmuseum.org.uk).*
The world's first international football match was a 0-0 draw between Scotland and England in 1872. Remarkably, a cap awarded to one of the Scottish players and a match ticket have survived – and they're both on display here. Six years later, Scottish Cup holders Renton FC played their English equivalents, West Bromwich Albion, in a game dubbed 'The Championship of the United Kingdom and the World'. Since it never took place again, the winners – a now-defunct club from a village in Dunbartonshire – are still officially world champions; you can see the trophy they won. The stadium tour takes in the changing rooms, players' tunnel and royal box.

### Wembley Stadium Tour
*Olympic Way, Wembley, Middlesex HA9 0WS (0844 800 2755/www.thestadiumtour.com).*
Now that its giant arch is a fully integrated part of the London landscape, Wembley has opened up for a look behind the scenes. The 90-minute tour includes the changing rooms, executive suites, players' tunnel, press room and dugouts. You even get to hoist aloft the FA Cup (replica, of course). There's also a chance to try the best seats in the house: the Corinthian Club. Ten-year membership requires a £16,100 joining fee, plus an annual payment of £5,450. Start saving.

### Wimbledon Lawn Tennis Museum & Tour
*Church Road, London SW19 5AE (020 8946 6131/ www.wimbledon.org/museum).*
This is not the place to kill a few minutes when rain stops play. It repays far longer inspection, justifying its many awards. A unique film shot using five simultaneous cameras immerses you in the science and technology of the sport, while a combination of an old illusionist trick known as 'Pepper's ghost' and contemporary projection techniques enable a spectral John McEnroe to appear in a re-creation of the 1980 men's locker room and reminisce about his epic battles with Connors and Borg. The tour takes in No.1 Court (and Centre Court when building work permits), the water gardens and the picnic terrace forever to be known as Henman Hill.

# 762
## Ride the spectacular Dawlish Sea Wall

To enjoy one of Britain's most scenic train journeys, and to experience plucky Victorian engineering at its best, take a ride on the Exeter to Plymouth line, one of the UK's last remaining coastal railways (0845 700 0125, www.firstgreatwestern.co.uk). The key stretch starts a few miles outside Exeter, at Powderham Castle, where the train tracks head by the River Exe estuary, through the village of Starcross, past the sand dunes at Dawlish Warren and then turn to run next to the open sea. For the four miles between Dawlish Warren and Dawlish, the train runs on top of the purpose-built Dawlish Sea Wall, right over the beach – any closer to the water and you'd be swimming.

In good weather, it feels as if you're skimming across the top of the waves; when the sea is rough, it turns into a nerve-wracking thrill ride – better than any theme park – as waves batter the sea wall, crash over the top of the train and threaten to swallow it whole. In winter, services are often suspended during particularly fierce storms. After Dawlish station the train rattles through a series of five tunnels cut into the cliffs – the longest 521 yards, the shortest 49 yards – before arriving at Teignmouth. Phew.

The man responsible for the spectacular route (rather than tunnelling through the hills inland) was the pioneering Victorian Isambard Kingdom Brunel, who once famously claimed that 'Nothing is impossible for an engineer'. Opened in 1846, the line was originally operated by 'atmospheric power' – one of Brunel's inventive but ultimately unsuccessful schemes. An intricate network of vacuum pipes laid between the tracks 'sucked' the train along, but the system proved costly and difficult to maintain, and was abandoned after a year in favour of conventional steam engines. A few reminders still exist: Starcross's pub is called the Atmospheric Railway Inn, and one of the original atmospheric pumping houses stands next to Starcross station.

# 763
## Stay in a stately home (without spending a fortune)

Forget your preconceptions about dank dorms and basic huts: there are some seriously stylish joints on the Youth Hostel Association's books (www.yha.org.uk). Planning a trip to London? You can stay in the middle of Holland Park (one of the capital's costliest neighbourhoods) in a Jacobean mansion for around £20 (0870 770 5866). Equally impressive surrounds can be found at Bath's Youth Hostel – an Italianate mansion, refurbished in early 2008 (0870 770 5688). Grander still is Hartington Hall in Derbyshire, a sprawling Tudor mansion set in lovely grounds (0870 770 5848). Many of the rooms have en suite bathrooms, and there's even a little romantic luxury to be had in the two-bed apartment known as the Roost. Bonnie Prince Charlie once slept here, so it's got the almost-royal stamp of approval.

# 764
## Admire the artistry of Rosslyn Chapel's unlucky apprentice

Few buildings are more swathed in myth, mystery and legend than Rosslyn Chapel – and a bit part in *The Da Vinci Code* only served to intensify interest. A fantastic blend of pagan, Celtic, Christian and Masonic symbolism, stone carvings are everywhere; hardly a suface has been left bare. One intricately carved pillar has eight dragons at its base; from their mouths emerges a vine that twists itself around the pillar. It's most likely a representation of the Norse tree of knowledge, although its medieval creator probably justified it in Christian terms as representing the Tree of Life. Legend has it that the mason's apprentice who carved this masterpiece was struck on the head and killed by the mason in a jealous rage. Elsewhere in the chapel is a stone carving of the unfortunate apprentice's head, complete with a scar on his right temple. Next to him is his grieving mother, while another carving is said to represent the jealous master mason himself.

**Rosslyn Chapel** *Roslin, Midlothian EH25 9PU (0131 440 2159/www.rosslynchapel.org.uk).*

## 765 Play peeping tom with an osprey

Ospreys are large and impressive birds of prey – watching one career out of the sky to pluck an unsuspecting fish from the water is pretty spectacular. They were persecuted out of existence in Scotland around the time of World War I, departing for more hospitable climes – but gave us another chance in the 1950s, when a breeding pair settled at Loch Garten on Speyside. Round-the-clock protection of the nest and its eggs was mounted by the Royal Society for the Protection of Birds, which now runs an Osprey Centre at the loch (01479 831476, 01767 693690, www.rspb.org.uk). A CCTV camera is trained on the nest from roughly spring to late summer, allowing visitors to see the adults and chicks at remarkably close quarters.

## 766 Get animated in Bradford

An annual celebration of all things animated, Bradford Animation Festival will celebrate its 15th year in 2008. Expect films, seminars, children's workshops and some big-name talents: highlights in 2007 included a visit from Nick Park and a screening of *Persepolis* – adapted from Marjane Satrapi's cult graphic novel.
**National Media Museum** *Bradford, West Yorkshire BD1 1NQ (0870 701 0200/www.nationalmediamuseum.org.uk/baf).*

## 767 Visit Little Sparta

The poet Ian Hamilton Finlay was associated with so-called 'concrete poetry', and it's hard not to see Little Sparta, the extraordinary garden he designed in the 1960s on an abandoned farm in the Pentland Hills near Edinburgh, as itself a kind of concrete poetry. There are words everywhere amid the greenery, inscribed on headstones, benches, bridges and tree trunks. Little Sparta is only open on summer weekends.
**Little Sparta** *Dunsryre, Lanarkshire ML11 8NG (www.littlesparta.co.uk).*

## 768 Find peace at Faith House

The UK's only purpose-built exhibition space for disability arts, Faith House is set in 350 acres of unspoilt woodland, heath and reedbeds. Wheelchair accessible pathways connect all the varying habitats, and £15 buys you a year-round parking permit to visit the estate. The building has won several awards for its sleek, inspiring architecture: built in 2002, it comprises a flat-roofed, timber-framed structure, rather like a miniature Greek temple, with floor-to-ceiling windows that allow the light to flood in. The building hosts year-round exhibitions ranging from film to print-making, and has a quiet room for spiritual contemplation, with a circle of cut silver birch trunks forming elegant pillars. Call ahead before visiting.
**Holton Lee** *East Holton, Holton Heath, Poole, Dorset BH16 6JN (01202 625562/www.holtonlee.co.uk/arts).*

# 769 Go wild swimming

# Take the plunge

*You're never far from a great wild swim in Britain.* **Kate Rew,** *founder of the Outdoor Swimming Society, tests the waters.*

I'm standing on the banks of Loch Ness with my fellow swimmers Dom and Kari, putting on triathlon wetsuits, booties and gloves. The autumn sky is blue and sunny, the dark water in sharp contrast to the trees ablaze on the far shore: yellow and green by the water, rising to oranges and reds on the hills.

Looking out from the edge of the forest, we scan the waters, hoping to catch a glimpse of Nessie. We're keen to identify the wave pattern against the sharp grey shore stones as 'unusual', but that seems unlikely, so Kari, a sculptor, fashions a model Nessie for us out of some wood and moss instead and carries it down to the water's edge.

Today, we're planning to swim in each of the three lochs of the Great Glen, a 60 mile-long rift valley that divides Scotland, running east to west across the country and containing the long, narrow forms of Loch Ness, Loch Oich and Loch Lochy. We run a sweepstake to guess the water temperature as we enter. In summer, rivers and lakes across Britain reach balmy temperatures – up to 18 or 22 degrees centigrade where the water is shallow and the sun hot. The Great Glen can be cycled in a day, with refreshing dips along the way if the weather's warm. But this is the season when grouse are fattening and clouds of mist hover over the grass before the sun sets; when stags roar at night as dead silvery thistles grow rimy with frost. For inland swimmers, temperatures are rapidly dropping, and a cruel trickle of cold water makes its way down my breastbone as we guess at between nine and 13 degrees.

The water is black as outer space, and it tastes of salt. In our wetsuits and gloves we are weightless, and bob about doing somersaults like aquatic astronauts. Nosing along at water level, the scenery has become all the more epic: sunk below the level of cars, roads or people, it's just nature and us. Outdoor swimming has

Time Out 1000 Things to do in Britain 235

*'Autumn is my favourite time of year for a swim: the sea is warmer and the beaches wilder.'*

a way of restoring the magic to even familiar environments, giving you a unique experience of landscapes that may have come to seem packaged. We abandon our Nessie to the depths and head out like great explorers, breaststroking towards the horizon.

Pre-holiday worries about unfinished work have left us now, and we're immersed in this place. Whatever mood you are in when you enter natural water, you exit feeling buoyant – and the invigorating, bright chill intensifies the experience. We get out an hour later with broad smiles on our faces, deep-down happy.

After lunch by a fire at Fort Augustus we move on to Loch Oich, a small loch – currently deserted by boats – that looks both wild and approachable. We know daylight is limited, so decide on a quick crossing.

Autumn is my favourite time of the year to swim: the sea is at its warmest and beaches are becoming wilder, cleaner and more deserted, while on crisp, sunny days, rivers and lakes are at their most colourful and vivid. At the height of summer, it's wonderful to spend afternoons swimming and snoozing by the banks of the Cotswold Thames or the Cam; to join merry throngs swimming and jumping off rocks in traditional bathing spots like Stainforth Force in Yorkshire, or Deeper Marsh in Devon. It's a treat to climb to remote tarns and waterfalls like Lyn Arenig Fach in Wales, or the Isle of Skye's Fairy Pools, then strip off and skinny dip in the gloriously cool water. But for me, there's a special intensity to swimming when it's least expected – to taking a moonlit dip at a familiar place, to plunging in before other visitors are up at Crummock or Windermere in the Lake District, and carving your own route through well-trodden places.

Kari and I identify an orange-hued tree on the opposite bank and head for it, the autumnal colours making it easy to keep on course. It's a wonderful crossing: yellow leaves hang in the black water, suspended at different heights. We set out with a smooth, rhythmic stroke: seven minutes to the bank opposite, seven minutes back. Feeling invigorated, we set off for our final swim of the day: Loch Lochy, which empties water into the Atlantic that started at the North Sea, gathering highland rivers and rain on its journey.

After parking by a pine wood, we walk down to the shore. Up close, nothing seems quite as it should be. The moss is a vivid yellow, while the bay looks curiously like a mangrove swamp: on the bank a few hundred metres opposite is a line of truncated tree trunks, black and stubby. We leave our clothes spread out on the rocks, towels thrown up on to branches above our heads to sway and dry in the breeze, and swim across. There is grass under the water, and the perfect prints of wading ducks. Loch Ness was a playful swim, astronauts in freefall; Loch Oich was a short, wild crossing. Making our way across Loch Lochy in long, gliding strokes, by contrast, is transfixing and stilling. The loch has corrugated sides, and the landscape is rich and soft: felted hills and pillowy forests. It's a tranquil, magical swim. Every now and then we hear the slap of a jumping fish, or see its belly flash silver. We snorkel around looking at the untouched footprints and blackened trees, unable to work out how everything got here.

The sky turns pink, and clouds snag on the mountains. We get out and pull our clothes on, driving away as the light is fading. Elegant birches with silver trunks and yellow leaves pick up the last of the light as it fades; in the dark, the lochs shine like tin foil. We head back up towards the Isle of Skye; our next swim spot, the Fairy Pools of Glen Brittle, beckoning.

*Kate Rew is the author of* Wild Swim *(Guardian Books), which contains over 100 great swims in rivers, lakes, lidos, tidal pools and the sea around Britain.*

- Do not undertake wild swimming recklessly.
- Always swim within your ability, being aware of currents, cold and boats.
- Never swim alone, swim close to the shore unless experienced and with boat cover, and wear brightly coloured hats.
- For advice see the website www.outdoor swimmingsociety.com.

# 770
## Take in the North-east's public art

Commissions North – a branch of Arts Council England – is the reason that the North-east has become so impressively littered with artistic showpieces in the last decade. We've all marvelled at Antony Gormley's *Angel of the North*, but Commissions North has also been involved in hundreds of more low-profile, but no less worthy, projects. Various commissions now beautify hospitals and community centres throughout the North-east – art that makes a difference on a humble, everyday level. Larger-scale projects – heirs to the *Angel*, if you like – include *Conversation Piece*, a 22-piece bronze sculpture at the mouth of the Tyne in South Shields, and *Couple* – a lonely, haunting duo (also bronze) that stand atop the recently completed Newbiggin Breakwater sea defence. To see a full list of the permanent works and temporary installations Commissions North has been involved with, visit its website at www.commissionsnorth.com.

# 771
## Quaff an oyster in Whitstable

Whitstable has been praised for its oysters since Juvenal first shucked a few here a couple of thousand years ago. These days, the oyster beds granted royal protection by Elizabeth I are no secret, and day-trippers head down from the capital in droves at the weekends. And, in what seems like a brilliant piece of marketing by the Whitstable tourist office, during the spawning season when it's advisable to steer clear of them (May-August – when there's no 'R' in the month), there's still good reason to visit: celebrating the feast day of St James of Compostella (25 July) seems like the most natural thing in the world once you realise that he's the patron saint of oysters. The Whitstable Oyster Festival (www.whitstableoysterfestival.co.uk) spans nine days around the feast day: as well as oyster processions and fish dances of the Monty Python variety, there is also the Whitstable Regatta, which takes place on the festival's second weekend.

# 772
## Catch some top-class eventing at Burghley

Zara Phillips is probably Britain's best-known exponent of three-day eventing – the supreme sporting test for horse and rider. After the discipline of dressage comes the challenge of riding cross-country at speed, navigating ditches, fallen trees and gates. The final stage is show jumping, with competitors jumping in reverse order to create maximum tension: very few penalty points usually separate the top riders, and knocking just a single pole can drop them out of contention.

Burghley Horse Trials are held in September – as they have been every year since 1961. The annual gathering of equestrianism's great and good forms the centrepiece of a country fair that is held in the parkland surrounding the Elizabethan mansion. With shopping arcades, rural craft pavilions and specialist food stalls, it's a green-wellied extravaganza.

**Burghley Horse Trials** *Barnack Road, Stamford, Lincolnshire PE9 2LH (01933 304744/www.burghley-horse.co.uk).*

Time Out 1000 Things to do in Britain **237**

# 773-778 Submit a script

*Nuala Calvi finds out how to get your name in lights.*

Fancy yourself as the next angry young man or woman of British playwriting? Then take advantage of the profusion of masterclasses, workshops, awards and fellowships on offer from leading theatres around the UK.

At the Royal Court Theatre (Sloane Square, London SW1W 8AS, 020 7565 5050, www.royalcourttheatre.com), famed for its boundary-pushing plays and fierce commitment to new writing, the Young Writers Programme has been up and running since 1966. Open to anyone aged between 13 and 25, in recent years the programme has seen the launch of the careers of Joe Penhall, Leo Butler and Jonathan Harvey, among others. There are various playwriting courses, competitions and projects on the boil, and projects for writers from ethnic minorities and the over-26s.

Also in London, the Writers' Centre at the Soho Theatre (21 Dean Street, London W1D 3NE, 0870 429 6883, www.sohotheatre.com) offers one of the most comprehensive programmes of support for aspiring playwrights in the country, with its own script library and writers' rooms to help scribblers avoid distraction. The literary team gives feedback on over 1,500 scripts a year, as well as running weekend masterclasses, monthly Launch Pad readings of new works, and attachments of varying lengths. The theatre also runs the prestigious Verity Bargate Award – with £5,000 in prize money to be won.

Outside the capital, the excellent West Yorkshire Playhouse (Playhouse Square, Quarry Hill, Leeds LS2 7UP, 0113 213 7800, www.wyplayhouse.com) has a rather cut-throat script-reading policy, which involves deciding whether or not your creation is worth reading based on the first ten pages. It does, however, offer the lucky few up to £1,500 to develop their idea further.

Theatre Writing Partnership (0115 947 4361, www.theatrewritingpartnership.org.uk) is a unique new venture that has sprung up in recent years between theatres in the East Midlands. Its activities include a script-reading service for writers in the region, a Playwrights' Studio group mentored by established local writers such as Stephen Lowe and Amanda Whittington, and the five-day Momentum Festival of new writing, held at Lakeside Arts Centre in Nottingham.

Birmingham Rep's Transmissions scheme (www.transmissions.org.uk) also focuses on cultivating local talent, offering 12- to 25-year-olds from the region the chance to develop an idea for presentation at a festival each July, with the help of professional playwrights. Writers are selected from workshops held at the Rep (Centenary Square, Broad Street, Birmingham B1 2EP, 0121 245 2000, www.birmingham-rep.co.uk) every Saturday afternoon between November and April.

North of the border, the award-winning Traverse Theatre (10 Cambridge Street, Edinburgh EH1 2ED, 0131 228 3223, www.traverse.co.uk), founded in 1963, remains dedicated to seaching out new talent. To that end, it offers a script-reading service, Young Writers Group, writing workshops and post-show discussions, with the aim of commissioning at least six new plays a year by writers from (or based in) Scotland.

# 779 *Walk among the undead at Whitby Gothic Weekend*

Don't be alarmed if you've popped into the Elsinore for a quiet pint, and you're the only punter who doesn't look like an extra from *Interview with the Vampire*; you've probably visited Whitby during one of its twice-yearly Gothic Weekends (http://wgw.topmum.co.uk). Started ten years ago by a goth who invited a clutch of her penfriends, it has escalated into a goth-rock music festival and general shindig attended by devotees of the dark side from the world over. Whitby was chosen because of its connections with *Dracula* (take in the view from the Bram Stoker Memorial Seat, perched high on West Cliff) – and with its cobbled streets and ruined abbey, this Yorkshire harbour town is weirdly, wonderfully atmospheric.

## 780 Board the RRS Discovery

Captain Robert Falcon Scott is best known for his ill-fated Antarctic expedition of 1912, which ended in the deaths of all five men in the party. His earlier scientific research trip of 1901-04, however, was a resounding success, and was dubbed the 'Discovery Expedition' after the vessel that carried his team to the Antarctic. The magnificent three-masted ship was built in Dundee specifically for polar research; after a long and eventful career – which also involved running munitions to Russia during World War I – she was restored and returned to her home port in 1986. Since then, the *Royal Research Ship Discovery*, with displays telling the story of her assorted adventures, has been one of the city's major attractions.
**RRS Discovery** *Discovery Quay, Dundee DD1 4XA (01382 309060/www.rrsdiscovery.com).*

## 781 Go crabbing at Walberswick

This pretty coastal village in Suffolk is home to the British Open Crabbing Championship, held every August on the banks of the river (www.walberswick.ws/crabbing). Armed with a single crabbing line and their bait of choice, competitors try to entice the resident crabs. After 90 minutes, the person who's captured the weightiest crustacean wins.

Entry costs a mere £1, and all equipment (buckets, bait and line) is available on site for a small charge. Last year, Oscar Kane walked away with the first prize (a medal and £50), beating off more than 700 competitors with a crab weighing 5.75oz. If none of the little nippers bite, take solace at the Sole Bay Fish Company on Blackshore Road (01502 724241), which dispenses divine dressed crab from its converted fishing hut premises. With just ten yards between river and plate, it doesn't get much fresher than this.

## 782 Admire the Ashmolean

Oxford's Ashmolean Museum of Art and Archaeology is one of the first examples of museums as we know them today; its opening in 1683 marked the beginning of the era when private collections were first revealed to the public at large. This wasn't initially to everyone's taste, with one visitor in 1710 complaining that, 'Even women are allowed up here for sixpence, they run here and there, grabbing at everything'. The museum is currently undergoing a massive £61 million redevelopment, due for completion in 2009 – though it remains open while works are carried out. Among the highlights of the collection are the Alfred Jewel, an exquisite Anglo-Saxon ornament, Guy Fawkes's lantern and the mint-condition Messiah Stradivarius – never played in a performance, and one of the most valuable violins in the world.
**Ashmolean Museum** *Beaumont Street, Oxford OX1 2PH (01865 278000/www.ashmolean.org).*

## 783 Follow Byron to Newstead Abbey

Newstead Abbey started life in the late 12th century as an Augustinian priory. Following the Reformation and the Dissolution of the Monasteries in the 16th century, however, Henry VIII gave the priory to Sir John Byron, to convert into an imposing country house. Sir John's grandson was, of course, the infamous poet – who inherited the by-then dilapidated Abbey at the tender age of ten. With his tame bear and pet tortoises in tow, he lived at Newstead from 1808 to 1814, occupying a few rooms as the rest of the house sank further into dereliction: in the once-opulent great hall and dining room, he and his friends perfected their fencing and pistol-shooting. Finally, in 1818, he was forced to sell up. His private apartments are now the mansion's key attraction, along with the lovely gardens and parkland: don't miss the deliciously over-the-top memorial to his beloved dog, Boatswain.
**Newstead Abbey** *Newstead Abbey Park, Nottingham NG15 8NA (01623 455900/www.newsteadabbey.org.uk).*

**Sark**

# 785
## ...then walk the length of Herm

Take the Trident ferry from St Peter Port on a sunny day, and within 20 minutes you're on what could almost be a private Caribbean island. Herm's just half a mile wide and one-and-a-half miles long; don't miss gorgeous Shell Beach, which stretches for nearly half the island's length and is covered with thousands of tiny shells, washed up by the Gulf Stream (01481 722377, www.herm-island.com). The car-free islanders get about by tractor, bike or on foot, and there are paths around the whole island, from easy ambles (even if you've turned up in flip-flops) to more strenuous cliff hikes.

# 784
## Cycle car-free Sark...

OK, so there are vehicles on Sark. But don't try hitching a lift on the couple of tractors that slowly trundle around this minuscule outpost of the Channel Islands (www.sark.info). Local law dictates that they are strictly for agricultural purposes only. Driving one down to the UK's most southerly hotel, La Sablonnerie, is likely to land you in trouble with Seigneur Michael Beaumont, who presides over Sark. Biking, then, is the best way to get around the island's three square miles. Narrow, unpaved lanes wind around scenery that looks like it's straight out of *Cider with Rosie*. Cows and sheep graze in open fields, small tables with eggs for sale outside farmhouses rely on honesty jars, and the inky darkness at night will be truly startling if you're a city dweller.

Eccentricities abound in this ancient land, where the clocks seem to have stopped shortly before World War I. The Seigneur is the only man on the island allowed to own an unspayed bitch, the death penalty was only abolished in 2004 and anyone who thinks that their rights have been infringed can secure legal protection by reciting the Lord's prayer (in French) and crying out 'Haro, Haro, Haro!', under the ancient Viking 'Clameur de Haro' ruling. Sark may only be an hour's ferry ride from Guernsey, but it's a world away from everyday life.

# 786
## Be a pilgrim at Norfolk's Nazareth

If pilgrimage was the Middle Ages equivalent of modern tourism, then Walsingham was a holy Costa del Sol of its day – an immensely popular destination, on a par with Jerusalem or Rome. It all began in 1061, when a Saxon noblewoman had a vision in which she was taken by the Virgin Mary to the house in Nazareth where Gabriel had announced the birth of Jesus. Mary asked Richeldis de Faverches to build an exact replica of the house in Walsingham. The story of 'England's Nazareth' spread, and soon the house and the priory built around it were welcoming pilgrims in their thousands. During the Reformation, Henry VIII ordered its destruction, but the 19th century saw renewed interest in the shrine, and its restoration. Today, Catholics head for the restored 14th-century Slipper Chapel, originally the spot where pilgrims would remove their shoes to make the last mile of pilgrimage barefoot, and the modern Chapel of Reconciliation. For Anglicans there's the 20th-century Shrine Church, which contains a modern version of the Holy House and a new statue of Our Lady of Walsingham.

**RC National Shrine** *Friday Market Place, Little Walsingham, Norfolk NR22 6DB (01328 820495/ www.walsingham.org.uk).*

# 787-799
## Eat your way around Britain in London

Some of the best British food can be sampled in London – and we don't mean pie and mash. Try posh jellied eels while perched on wooden benches at the Quality Chop House (92-94 Farringdon Road, EC1R 3EA, 020 7837 5093, www.qualitychophouse.co.uk), West Mersea oysters at venerable City haunt Sweetings (39 Queen Victoria Street, EC4N 4SA, 020 7248 3062), or hot buttered Arbroath smokies in casual, modern surroundings at Canteen (2 Crispin Place, off Brushfield Street, E1 6DW, 0845 686 1122, www.canteen.co.uk).

For first-rate meat from Britain, try the steaks from Top Floor at Smiths (67-77 Charterhouse Street, EC1M 6HJ, 020 7251 7950, www.smithsofsmithfield.co.uk) or the roasts at Roast (The Floral Hall, Borough Market, Stoney Street, SE1 1TL, 020 7940 1300, www.roast-restaurant.com); or call Franklins (157 Lordship Lane, SE22 8HX, 020 8299 9598, www.franklinsrestaurant.com) to see if its organically farmed mutton from Berkshire is currently on the menu.

For game, eat at Lindsay House (21 Romilly Street, W1D 5AF, 020 7439 0350, www.lindsayhouse.co.uk) or Rules (35 Maiden Lane, WC2E 7LB, 020 7836 5314, www.rules.co.uk); for haggis, at Boisdale (13 Eccleston Street, SW1W 9LX, 020 7730 6922, www.boisdale.co.uk). For a proper pudding, have trifle while enjoying the sedate, gentlemen's club atmosphere at either Wilton's (55 Jermyn Street, SW1Y 6LX, 020 7629 9955, www.wiltons.co.uk) or Bentley's (11-15 Swallow Street, W1B 4DG, 020 7734 4756, www.bentleysoysterbarandgrill.co.uk); alternatively, devour your spotted dick and custard in more 21st-century surroundings at the Rivington in Shoreditch (28-30 Rivington Street, EC2A 3DZ, 020 7729 7053, www.rivingtongrill.co.uk).

Too much choice? Then plump for the National Dining Rooms (Sainsbury Wing, National Gallery, Trafalgar Square, WC2N 5DN, 020 7747 2525, www.thenationaldiningrooms.co.uk), where the menu reads like a sampler menu of British classics, and there's a splendid afternoon tea.

# 800
## Celebrate Burns Night

When advocates of a romanticised Caledonia were searching around for a national bard in the early 19th century – a Scottish Shakespeare – Robert Burns was the obvious choice. A farmer's boy from Ayrshire, the poet died in 1796 aged just 37, yet poems like *To a Mouse* and *Ae Fond Kiss* have ensured his literary immortality. His life and work have subsequently been celebrated every year on his birthday, 25 January. There is no single official event and Burns Night (http://burns.visitscotland.com/festival) is celebrated both in Scotland and worldwide. Formal gatherings can be highly structured, and involve a bagpiper, speeches, an address to the all-important haggis – served with mashed neeps (turnips) and tatties (potatoes) – readings of other Burns's poetry and a ceilidh. Domestic versions can simply be an excuse for a get-together with friends (and a bottle of whisky) round the dining table.

# 801
## Check out the Twentieth Century Society

Until the late 1980s, English Heritage refused to list post-war buildings. That it relented in 1987 and listed Sir Albert Richardson's neo-classical *Financial Times* HQ in the City of London was due largely to the efforts of the Twentieth Century Society. Founded in 1979 as the 'Thirties Society', the group soon turned its attention to saving architecture from other decades. Many notable modern buildings, such as Ernö Goldfinger's house in north London, owe their survival to campaigns led by the society. So if a 20th-century masterpiece in your area – no matter how recently built – is threatened with demolition, contact the society and encourage it to add it to its caseload. Better still, join the society: you'll be sent the thrice-yearly magazine, and be able to attend the members-only talks, guided walks and events.

**Twentieth Century Society** *70 Cowcross Street, London EC1M 6EJ (020 7250 3857/www.c20society.org.uk).*

## 802 See Papplewick Pumping Station

The water-pumping station at Papplewick represents Victorian industrial engineering at its finest. The magnificent red-brick building, with its stained-glass windows and unexpectedly opulent decor, is open to visitors every Sunday afternoon, while its two immense steam engines are still stoked up on bank holiday weekends.
**Papplewick Pumping Station** *Off Longdale Lane, Ravenshead, Nottinghamshire NG15 9AJ (0115 963 2938/www.papplewickpumping station.org.uk).*

## 803 Find your mojo in the Brecon Beacons

Generally held over the second weekend in August, and celebrating its 25th anniversary in 2008, the Brecon Jazz Festival (01874 611622, www.breconjazz.co.uk) has quietly made a name for itself over the years, and now attracts artists from all over the globe who perform at a huge selection of free and individually ticketed gigs. The setting is the lovely Brecon Beacons National Park, the jazz world-class.

## 804 Have a brief encounter at Carnforth

It would be a frightfully bad show to give the ending away; worse still to cast aspersions. Suffice to say, when thoroughly decent family doctor Trevor Howard bumps into awfully nice housewife Celia Johnson in David Lean's post-war classic *Brief Encounter*, it isn't in the unseemly sense. Nothing untoward occurs. It's this splendidly British repression and sense of fair play that still draws lovestruck couples to the station tearooms at Carnforth in the Lake District, where the film was set. Nowadays, the film might play non-stop amid gift-shop memorabilia, but you can still enjoy an authentic stewed cuppa, freshly baked scone and a whispered sweet nothing.
**Carnforth Station** *Warton Road, Carnforth, Lancashire LA5 9TR (01524 735165/ www.carnforthstation.co.uk).*

#  805-810 *Get hands-on at a science museum*

Science doesn't get much more hands-on than at Magna Science Adventure Centre (Sheffield Road, Templeborough, Rotherham S60 1DX, 01709 720002, www.visitmagna.co.uk). Housed in a huge former steelworks, Magna is divided into four pavilions: air, earth, fire and water. Everything is for exploring and experimentation, including JCBs, sandpits, a fire tornado, wind machines, and the Big Melt, a dramatic reconstruction of steel-making. Adrenalin junkies can even take a 130-foot plunge with the world's only indoor bungee jump into the abyss of the steelworks.

Come prepared, as Magna is dark and noisy; it's also cold in winter, so pack your anoraks and woollies. You may also need a change of clothes for all the family: even if you're just watching, it's near-impossible to stay dry in the water pavilion. In summer, you can get even more wet scooting around the outdoor Aqua-tek play zone.

Interaction is also at the heart of Thinktank, at the Birmingham Museum of Science and Discovery (Curzon Street, Birmingham B4 7XG, 0121 202 2222, www.thinktank.ac). Each of its ten galleries is relevant to specific areas of the National Curriculum – but this is learning the fun way. Children can work in a café or become market traders, doctors and dentists in Kids' City; when that pales, they can find out how their bodies work, see steam engines, explore forensic science or marvel at cutting-edge technology – including robotics and space exploration.

Could you lift a Mini, compose a symphony, function in a back-to-front world or launch a rocket? Find out in Manchester's Xperiment (Liverpool Road, Castlefield, Manchester M3 4FP, 0161 832 2244, www.msim.org.uk) – an interactive gallery within the Museum of Science and Industry. Entry is free, and with over 30 interactive displays the gallery offers lots of hands-on fun, ranging from the simple – testing your senses, experimenting with energy – to the fiendishly difficult; solving the Tower of Hanoi puzzle, which makes Rubik's Cube look like child's play.

Alternatively, try out Launchpad, the London Science Museum's most popular gallery, with over 50 interactive exhibits (particularly suitable for eight to 14s), electrifying shows and lively demos (Exhibition Road, London SW7 2DD, 0870 870 4868, www.sciencemuseum.org.uk).

If you're around the South-west, try getting into a spin on a human gyroscope or plucking a magical harp at Explore-At-Bristol (Anchor Road, Harbourside, Bristol BS1 5DB, 0845 345 1235, www.at-bristol.org.uk). This place combines hands-on activities with the latest multimedia techniques. Walk through a tornado, investigate lightning, magnetic fields and whirlpools, or play with light, optics mirrors and reflections.

In Scotland, budding scientists should head for the Glasgow Science Centre (50 Pacific Quay, Glasgow G51 1EA, 0871 540 1000, www.glasgowsciencecentre.org). Make a parachute, take part in a K'Nex challenge, or prepare to be amazed by the spectacular demonstrations of Curious Chemistry. The Centre also incorporates a host of other attractions: the ScottishPower Planetarium, an IMAX cinema, the Science Show Theatre, Climate Change Theatre and 416-foot Glasgow Tower.

If you're looking for a local hands-on science experience, more than 80 science centres, museums and discovery centres are listed on Ecsite-uk, the UK Network of Science Centres and Museums (www.ecsite-uk.net).

# 811
## Visit the edge of England – the B3306 from St Ives to Land's End

Cornwall's beautiful wild west can be enjoyed in comfort on this 24-mile stretch of scenic road, with open, heathery moorland on your left and glimpses of craggy cliffs to the right. It's often a winding, single-lane track, so passengers benefit from the sweeping vistas more than drivers concentrating on hairpin bends – and the view upfront may include cows' backsides for several miles, as farms line the route. But the magical vistas of sparkling sea, rugged countryside and abandoned tin mines more than compensate.

The route is lined with prehistoric tombs and standing stones: three miles out of St Ives, in Zennor, take the public footpath through the gorse to Zennor Quoit Megalithic tomb – the views from the rocky hilltop stretch for miles. Lanyon Quoit (turn off the road about halfway between Morvah and Madron) is a marvellously atmospheric spot for a picnic, while at Men-an-Tol (turn left at Trevowhan) you can crawl through the centre of a huge, Polo-like stone. Other Neolithic remains include Chysauster Iron Age village, near New Mill, and Ballowall Barrow, close to St Just. Keep going south, past St Just – and don't miss the glorious beach at Sennen Cove before the short hop down to Land's End. Here the road widens and you'll meet more traffic, all heading for the car park and visitors' centre at the country's most westerly tip (www.cornwall-online.co.uk).

# 812
## Explore Urbis

Soaring above Manchester in a stunning glass building, Urbis describes itself as 'an exhibition centre of city life'. Drum 'n' bass, Reykjavik's street art and the legendary Hacienda club have all been the subject of past on-site exhibitions, while walking tours (£3 a pop) take visitors on to the city's streets; themes range from medieval Manchester to the story of Factory Records.
**Urbis** *Cathedral Gardens, Manchester M4 3BG (0161 605 8200/www.urbis.org.uk).*

# 813
## Join a green gym

Pounding the treadmill and lifting weights in pursuit of the body beautiful is generally a somewhat solitary endeavour – but there is a way to work out and contribute to the greater good. Renounce your costly gym membership and sign up for the green gym scheme (01302 388883, www.btcv.org.uk), run by the British Trust for Conservation Volunteers. Groups are dotted around the country, meeting at least once a week to take part in conservation work and gardening, led by a trained leader. After a warm-up session, you might find yourself toning up your thighs with allotment-digging, buffing your biceps with hedge-trimming, or improving your cardiovascular fitness with a spot of path-clearing. Working hard in the great outdoors brings a feeling of wellbeing that a session in the gym simply can't compete with – plus the warm glow that comes with doing a good deed.

**Time Out** 1000 Things to do in Britain **245**

# 814

## Join the Cloud Appreciation Society

Ever spent a summer's afternoon lying on your back, marvelling at the clouds? Why not join the Cloud Appreciation Society (www.cloudappreciation society.org), set up by the sky-gazing Gavin Pretor-Pinney? As the manifesto boldly declares, 'We believe that clouds are unjustly maligned, and that life would be immeasurably poorer without them.' For just £4, you'll receive a badge and membership certificate – and be able to submit your cloud-inspired photos, artwork and poetry for the edification and appreciation of like-minded souls.

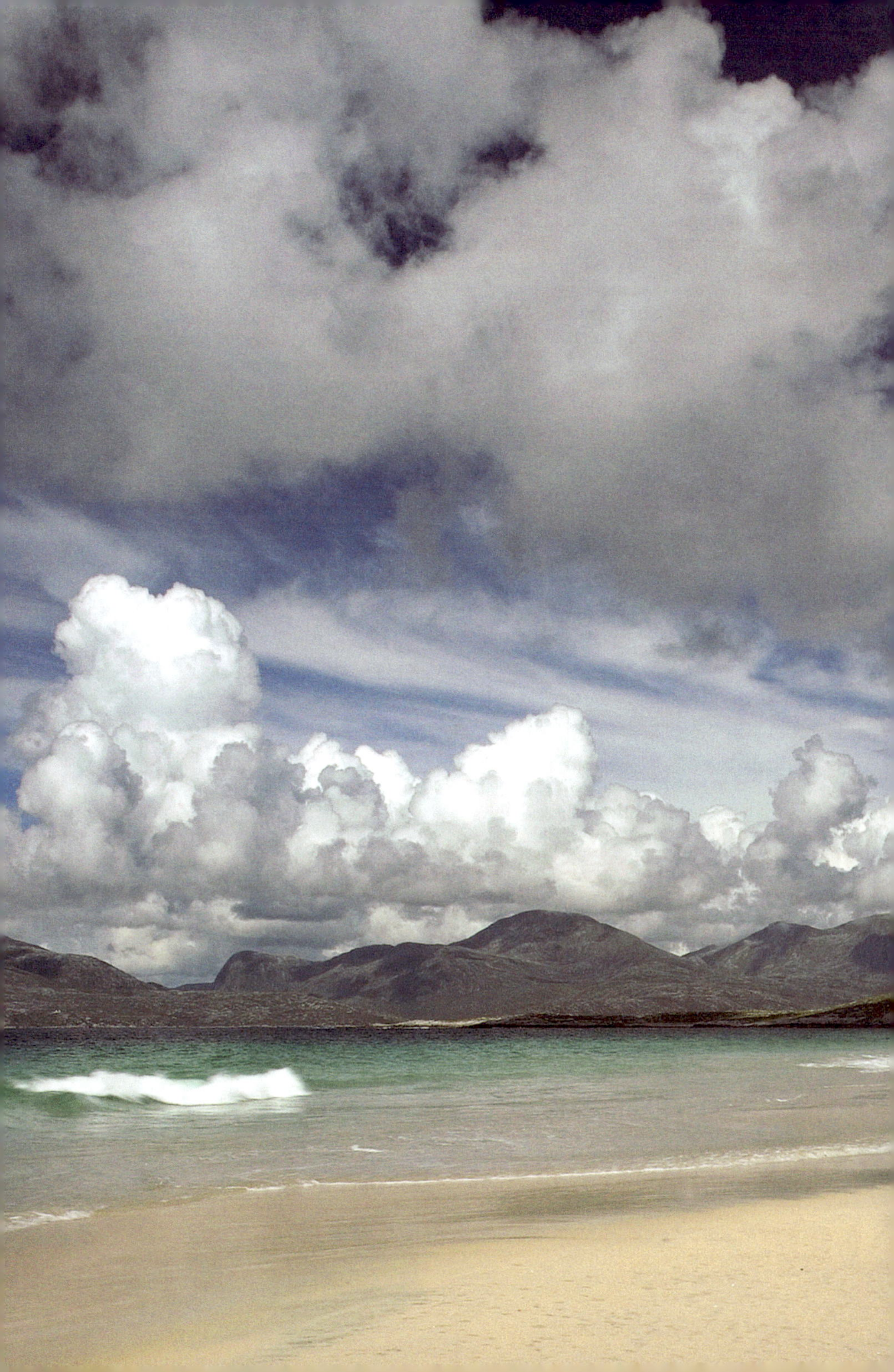

# 815 Visit the knight and his lady at Much Marcle

Medieval St Bartholomew's Church houses several impressive tombs, but the most romantic stands in the north-west corner. It's the 14th-century tomb of an unidentified knight and his lady; he's resplendent in his armour, while she's clad in a flowing gown (with, oddly, two dogs biting the hem). Perhaps the pair once sat under the ancient yew in the churchyard – thought to be over 1,500 years old, it has a seat inside the hollow trunk.
**St Bartholomew's Church** *Much Marcle, near Ledbury, Herefordshire HR8 2LY (01531 631531).*

# 816 Take a punt on the Grand National

Seeing sporting history in the making is cheaper than you'd think at the Grand National. While the sponsors' marquees and corporate areas in the towering stands rake in millions, it's still only £35 to pack into the Tattersalls and soak up the electric atmosphere of the parade ring and winners' enclosure, to take your place on Aintree Mound and cheer the knackered survivors home over the final fences.
**Aintree Racecourse** *Ormskirk Road, Aintree, Liverpool L9 5AS (0151 523 2600/ www.aintree.co.uk).*

# 817 Press your own apple juice at Middle Farm

Home to the National Collection of Cider and Perry, Middle Farm stocks over 100 varieties of apple-based tipple – including its own potent Pookhill cider. In autumn, visitors can bring a bag of their own apples and get them pressed for £2 a gallon: the cloudy, delicious juice is a world away from the shop-bought version.
**Middle Farm** *Firle, Lewes, East Sussex BN8 6LJ (01323 811411/www.middlefarm.com).*

# 818 Walk the causeway to St Michael's Mount

Though getting to this tiny Cornish island requires a boat when the tide is in, at low water you can cross the causeway from the mainland at Marazion on foot. Check the morning tide times and hit the beach just as it's turning; it feels quite magical to walk out into the sea, with the cobbled path gradually appearing before you (and there are fewer people around, marching like commuters up to the island). It's slippy, though, so no flip-flops.

Once there, explore the castle and check out the 18th-century tidal clock, which predicts the tides as well as telling the time, then take in the windswept but surprisingly lush gardens, set into a near-vertical cliff face on the island's southern edge. Elsewhere there's a medieval church and a tiny model of the island, made from the corks of champagne bottles that were served to the residents of the island in the 1930s; bizarre indeed. Opening times are seasonal, and admission to the castle and gardens is separate.
**St Michael's Mount** *Marazion, Cornwall TR17 0EF (01736 710507/www.stmichaelsmount.co.uk).*

# 819 Ogle the National Trust's largest art collection

Built in the 17th century and set in a Capability Brown landscaped park, Petworth House was immortalised in paintings by Turner. These days, it houses works by Gainsborough, Van Dyck, Titian, Bosch and Blake (among others), making up the National Trust's largest collection of pictures. There's a lot to take in, especially if you're also visiting the pleasure gardens, taking a peek at the servants' quarters or attending one of the open-air plays or concerts. The ten-minute Welcome to Petworth talk is a good general introduction to the house and grounds, before you choose what to focus on. Don't miss the Turner collection, 1592 Molyneux globe (the earliest English globe in existence) and 15th-century decorated vellum manuscript of the *Canterbury Tales*.
**Petworth House** *Petworth, West Sussex GU28 0AE (01798 342207/www.nationaltrust.org.uk).*

# 820
## Take a twilight tour of Sir John Soane's Museum

It's impossible to overestimate the legacy of Georgian architect Sir John – not just for his buildings, which include the Bank of England, but for the influence of his personal treasures, housed in Lincoln's Inn Fields and made public on his death in 1837. Ever since, this magnificently cluttered collection – an ancient Egyptian sarcophagus, Grecian sculptures, architectural fragments, Renaissance drawings – has acted as a connoisseur's guide to classical artistic and architectural taste; it's the original Design Museum, if you like. And nothing evokes its wonders quite as atmospherically as the candlelit tours that take place on the first Tuesday of every month.

**Sir John Soane's Museum** *13 Lincoln's Inn Fields, London WC2A 3BP (020 7405 2107/ www.soane.org).*

# 821
## Skim a stone at the world championships

It's an activity everyone fancies themselves adept at. Standing in front of a lake, selecting the perfect stone or pebble (the right mix of flat and weighty) and perfecting the best wrist-flick for maximum skim. Is there anything more satisfying than hitting a seven-plusser? We say: no. So do the pros who compete at the annual World Stone Skimming Championships. They gather every September on Easdale Island in Argyll to test their skimming arms. Show up to register at 11am, and be ready to skim by midday. Anyone can enter – but you can't select your own stones. These are pre-selected from the island's ample supplies of flat Easdale slate and then assigned to each contestant at random. The rules are simple. Each throw must achieve at least three skims and stay in a designated lane; points are awarded for the distance the stone travels rather than the number of bounces. Ready? Three, two, one – skim!

**World Stone Skimming Championships** *Easdale Isand, by Oban, Argyll PA34 4TB (www.stoneskimming.com).*

# 822-823
## Watch two 'hot' American sports – in Guildford

They like their sport with the temperature high in Surrey. Guildford Heat (01483 454005, www.guildfordheat.com) are one of the UK's leading basketball clubs, champions of the British Basketball League in 2007 and now facing the tougher challenges posed by Europe's leading sides in the ULEB Cup.

The Guildford Flames (01483 452244, www.guildfordflames.com), meanwhile, are a force to be reckoned with in ice hockey's English Premier League, skating off with the cup in 2007. Home for both clubs is the Guildford Spectrum leisure complex, where each has a loyal band of fans – and the Heat have a ten-strong troupe of glamorous girl dancers to spur them on to greater heights.

**Guildford Spectrum** *Parkway, Guildford, Surrey GU1 1UP (01483 443322/www.guildford spectrum.co.uk).*

**Guildford Heat**

# 824 *Pedal through the night on the Dunwich Dynamo*

**Ben Tobias** *hits the open road.*

It begins to rain as we reach London Fields, the start of the Dunwich Dynamo. The worsening weather is no surprise; the forecast predicted it with confidence, and sensibly most of our party have pulled out. My dad, however, was not to be put off. 'It'll probably spit a little bit, but in a refreshing way,' he assured us. Convinced by his optimism, we pack an extra layer and set off.

Undeterred by the weather, London's finest lycra has gathered for the event, and are busily putting on more clothes as the skies darken. Regulars at the nearby pub watch bemused as final checks are made to brakes, tyres and lights. With a final apprehensive glance up at the gathering clouds, we set off eastwards just before 9pm with 400 other cyclists, hoping to arrive in Dunwich, 124 miles away on the Suffolk coast, some time early the next morning.

Started in 1993, the Dynamo has become an annual institution. Legend has it that it began when a group of cycle couriers left London after work one evening and decided to keep on riding until they reached the sea. They arrived in Dunwich early the next day, and the Dynamo was born. The organisers boast that it's the only ride that gets shorter each year, as coastal erosion eats slowly away at the crumbling Dunwich shoreline.

After two hours of riding it's still raining heavily, with no sign of letting up. Perhaps the weatherman knows better than my dad after all. Crossing Essex, we pedal past various pubs, with boisterous drinkers gathered outside. They greet us in a variety of ways; some pull moonies, others throw stones, and we even get the occasional friendly shout of encouragement. But things quieten down as we get further away from London and turn down narrow, hedge-lined lanes, winding deeper and deeper into the countryside. We settle into a steady pace with a group of five or six other riders, each taking a turn at the front to face the full force of the weather. Despite the number of fancy bikes on show, there's a refreshing lack of talk about who has the lightest bike, clickiest gears or the most fluorescent lycra.

Safely through Essex, we count down the miles to the halfway stop. The village hall at Great Waldingfield opens for weary riders from 1am to 4am, and does a roaring trade in pasta salad, bananas, flapjacks and cups of sweet tea. We arrive at peak time, and the queue is snaking out of the door. Fortunately, my father, a veteran of the Dynamo (he claims to have done it a record 13 times), has come suitably prepared. From seemingly nowhere, he produces a packed lunch of cured ham, dark chocolate and a hipflask of single malt whisky. After squeezing as much water as possible out of our sodden gloves, shoes and jackets, we wolf it down.

By the time we return to our bikes, the rain has finally stopped. I check the route, and discover we're more than halfway. Things are looking up – but it's short lived. The rain starts again, and it's cold. Really cold. The small hours of Sunday morning are always the hardest: with tired legs, 50 miles still to go and no supplies left but half a squashed banana, the desire to fall asleep in the nearest ditch is almost overwhelming. I always thought Suffolk was flat, but now every incline feels like an Alpine climb. As the rain gets harder, I blindly follow the snaking procession of flashing red lights up ahead, leading the way to the sea.

As a new day begins, our flagging spirits lift. This is the best part of the Dynamo; the thing that makes it so different from other rides. The quiet whirring and clicking of wheels and gears is the only sound as we pass through small Suffolk villages, lifeless on a Sunday morning. The morning light reveals fields of haystacks and sleeping cattle, and we power along empty single-track lanes, revitalised by the sun's warmth. Then, at last, there's the unmistakable smell of the sea.

The ride ends rather unceremoniously in a gravel car park, beyond which lies the beach. The rain has stopped, and there's a hint of sunshine as we stagger off our bikes and into the Dunwich Café, which opened at 6am to cater for the hundreds of hungry cyclists turning up on its doorstep. After a reviving full English, we wander down to the sea to await the bus ride home.

It's a surreal sight: hundreds of cyclists, bikes and jerseys litter the beach, as rider after rider throws off their wet kit and finds the nearest comfortable pile of pebbles to curl up on. After a chilly doze, I announce firmly that I won't be doing the Dynamo next year if the weather is bad – I'm a fair weather rider from now on. But I've said that three years in a row now. And somehow, I just keep coming back for more.

*For further information on riding the Dynamo, visit www.londonschoolofcycling.co.uk.*

# 825-831
## Storm a castle

### Try a suit of armour out for size at Bodiam
A stunning example of a late medieval castle, Bodiam's imposing stone ramparts and towers rise from its moat in fairytale fashion – it's as if it's floating on the water. The interior is in ruins, but you can still climb the spiral staircases up to the battlements and scan the Sussex countryside for invaders. On selected dates in the school holidays, would-be valiant knights can try on a clanking suit of armour; call for details.
**Bodiam Castle** *Bodiam, Robertsbridge, East Sussex TN32 5UA (01580 830196/ www.nationaltrust.org.uk).*

### Look out for spooks at Chillingham Castle
The aptly named Chillingham claims to be Britain's most haunted castle – and peering into the dank depths of the oubliette, the 20-foot pit into which unfortunate prisoners were mercilessly hurled and left to die, it's not at all hard to believe. The castle's most famous ghost is the Blue Boy, who appears dressed in blue and surrounded by light, and who apparently emits unearthly screams; book a place on one of the evening ghost tours and see for yourself.
**Chillingham Castle** *Chillingham, Alnwick, Northumberland NE66 5NJ (01668 215359/ www.chillingham-castle.com).*

### Hear the clash of coconut shells on the ramparts at Doune
Cinematic history was made at this 14th-century Scottish castle when Cleese and company descended to film scenes from *Monty Python and the Holy Grail*. True devotees bring coconut shells to bang together in tribute to Lancelot and Patsy's unforgettable entrance. Don't worry if you've forgotten to bring your own; you can borrow a pair from the custodian.
**Doune Castle** *Doune, Stirlingshire SK16 6EA (01786 841742/www.historic-scotland.gov.uk).*

### Explore Dover's secret tunnels
Beneath Dover Castle lies a network of tunnels, parts of which date back to the Middle Ages. Expanded to form subterranean barracks during the Napoleonic War, they became the nerve centre for secret military operations during World War II and the Cold War. See the dimly lit underground hospital, then check out the atmospheric Command Centre, Telephone Exchange and Anti-Aircraft Operations Room.
**Dover Castle** *Castle Hill, Dover, Kent CT16 1HU (01304 211067/www.english-heritage.org.uk).*

### Honour the men of Harlech
One of Edward I's mighty 'iron ring' of castles, intended to prevent Welsh uprising, Harlech was built in the late 13th century. The Irish Sea once lapped at the rock on which the now land-locked castle stands – allowing vital supplies to be delivered during times of siege. During the War of the Roses, the castle withstood a seven-year siege – a feat immortalised in the Welsh anthem, 'Men of Harlech'.
**Harlech Castle** *Castle Square, Harlech, Gwynedd LL46 2YH (01766 780552/www.harlech.com).*

### See canine couture at Leeds
Set on two interconnected islands on the River Len in Kent, Leeds Castle is often described as England's loveliest castle. It's also home to one of its oddest museums: a collection of dog collars, spanning five centuries – from no-nonsense spiked iron bands to lavish velvet creations.
**Leeds Castle** *Maidstone, Kent ME17 1PL (01622 765400/www.leeds-castle.com).*

### Walk the ruins at Tintagel
Set on a windswept headland on Cornwall's Atlantic coast, castles don't come much more atmospheric than Tintagel. Legends swirl around the 13th-century castle – could it be King Arthur's birthplace? Scholars may scoff, but the ruins are gloriously romantic nonetheless.
**Tintagel Castle** *Tintagel Head, Cornwall PL34 0HE (01840 770328/www.english-heritage.org.uk).*

## 832 Chase a cheese in Gloucestershire

Every spring bank holiday, the fearless and foolhardy throw themselves down Cooper's Hill in Gloucestershire, in hot pursuit of a hunk of cheese (www.cheese-rolling.co.uk). The tradition might have originated from ancient fertility or harvest rituals, or with the Romans – no one's sure – but people have thrown a huge great wheel of cheese down this steep hill then hurtled down after it for hundreds of years. Not even World War II and food rationing stopped play: a wooden substitute, packed with a token piece of cheese, was used. In 1998, the event was banned over safety concerns – but die-hards still rolled an early morning cheese to keep the tradition unbroken. Cooper's Hill is no gentle giant; parts of it have a horribly steep gradient, the running surface is precipitously concave, and the runners' quarry, an 8lb Double Gloucester, can take off at up to 70 miles per hour.

Thankfully, there are 'catchers' waiting at the bottom of the hill to ensure safe landings for the runners who can't stop; it's impossible to remain on foot for the descent and injuries (usually minor) are almost always sustained – yet people enter year after year, abandoning all sense of personal safety. Festivities conclude with a free-for-all, with non-participants rolling down the infamous hill and children wallowing in the muddy mire at its base.

## 833 Attend the Anarchist Bookfair

Bookfairs might not be the sort of events ordinarily associated with anarchists, but then this isn't your typical literary gathering: the publishers, pamphleteers and pressure groups setting out their stalls are a Who's Who of the ideological underground. Established in 1983, London's event (www.anarchistbookfair.co.uk) is one of several anarchist bookfairs across the world – from Norwich to New York, Manchester to Montreal. Last year's fair, which took place at Queen Mary and Westfield College, featured film screenings and political performance art alongside a wealth of subversive literature, not to mention debates on such subjects as the struggle against Starbucks and resisting the 2012 London Olympics. There's also a quiz to test your knowledge of anti-authoritarianism through the ages – an education for anyone still clinging to the idea that all anarchists are either mohawk-sporting punks or shady, Molotov cocktail-wielding types from the pages of a Joseph Conrad novel.

## 834 Devour a real Bakewell pudding

Pudding, note, not 'tart'. You'll find the cake-like, shortcrust-pastry version on sale in supermarkets up and down the land, but for a proper pudding you'll have to go to the Derbyshire market town of Bakewell. This is supposedly where the much-loved dessert was accidentally invented in a local hostelry in the 1860s – though historic recipes suggest it was around long before that. Bakewell is a bit of a tourist trap these days, thanks to its location in the heart of the Peak District National Park, so there's no shortage of places purportedly selling the 'original' pud – including the Old Original Bakewell Pudding Shop on the Square (01629 812193) and Bloomers Original Bakewell Puddings on Water Street (01629 814844). It's markedly different from the tart; much rougher in look, with a puff pastry shell and a moist, squidgy, custard-like filling of eggs, sugar, butter and almonds on top of a layer of jam. Fans vow the taste's a revelation.

## 835 Tour a turbine in Norfolk

You'll need plenty of energy of your own to climb one of the wind turbines at Norfolk's Ecotech Centre. The 305-step hike up the spiral staircase, winding through the centre of the slender 15-foot-wide structure, is physically challenging and not for the claustrophobic. There are resting platforms along the way to catch your breath, and only one tour takes place at a time, so everyone's going in the same direction on the staircase. Once you've made it to the top, there are fantastic views over the surrounding countryside; on a clear day you can see Ely Cathedral, 26 miles away. Tours run three or four times a day in summer, less off-season, and it's advisable to book. The striking timber and glass Ecotech Centre houses a large exhibition space, lecture theatre and cinema; call for details of events.
**Ecotech Centre** *Turbine Way, Swaffham, Norfolk PE37 7HT (01760 726100/www.ecotech.org.uk/tourism.html).*

## 836 Keep your balance at Bolton Abbey

Back in the priory's heyday, the 57 stepping stones were the only way to cross the river without getting your habit wet. Today, the faint of heart and unsteady of step can take the bridge instead – an inviting prospect on wintery days, when the River Wharfe crashes below. In summer, when the water isn't so scary a prospect, you can cheat and walk part of the way in the river if you have a wobbly moment.
**Bolton Abbey** *Skipton, North Yorkshire BD23 6EX (Mon-Fri 01756 718009, Sat, Sun 01756 710663/www.boltonabbey.com).*

## 837 Rock out at Glasgow's Barrowland

You literally can't miss this legendary music venue – during World War II, its gigantic neon sign was temporarily taken down, as German bombers were using it to navigate by. Inside it's buzzing, as an up-for-it crowd regard it as their historical duty to go electrifyingly wild.
**Glasgow Barrowland** *244 Gallowgate, East End, Glasgow G4 0TT (0141 552 4601/www.glasgow-barrowland.com).*

## 838 Rediscover the Lost Gardens of Heligan

The gardens of the once-grand Heligan estate in Cornwall were 'lost' in the years after 1914, when the gardeners who kept the grounds in trim departed for war, never to return. Overgrown and neglected for more than 80 years, the gardens have been restored over the past decade to something of their former glory; the new leaseholders describe this effort as a tribute to the fallen gardeners. The gardens include a verdant subtropical jungle area and huge fruit and vegetable gardens, home to the Victorian pineapple pits – heated by an ingenious (if unsavoury) blend of rotting tree bark and horse manure.
**Lost Gardens of Heligan** *Pentewan, St Austell, Cornwall PL26 6EN (01726 845120/www.heligan.com).*

# 839
## Tread the divots at a polo match...

It's customary during breaks in play at a polo match at the Guards Club to walk around the playing area, replacing the turf dug up by the thundering horses' hooves. Then it's back to your binoculars to spot a few more celebs and minor royals in the VIP tents – or, if you're lucky enough to have privileged access yourself, to quaff another glass of champers in the company of faded rock stars, hedge fund managers and Argentinian professionals. The year's biggest occasion – both sporting and social – is the Cartier International in July, which attracts a host of top players from around the world; admission is £40 per car. Should you want to actually play at Guards, the joining fee is a mere £17,000, plus £5,450 per season. Oh, and £1 for a fixture list. Not all polo clubs are the preserve of the rich and famous, though: at Ham, the last surviving club in London, you can watch for just £10 per car and take a picnic.
**Guards Polo Club** *Smith's Lawn, Windsor Great Park, Egham, Surrey TW20 0HP (01784 434212/www.guardspoloclub.com).*
**Ham Polo Club** *Petersham Road, Richmond, Surrey TW10 7AH (020 8334 0000/www.hampoloclub.com).*

# 840
## ...or have a go yourself

If you fancy getting your hands on a mallet and playing a chukka or two, Ascot Park offers two-hour 'discover polo' sessions for beginners and non-riders (£95). Intensive day courses are also available, and include lessons on a mechanical wooden horse to improve your swing – not a bucking bronco, rest assured.
**Ascot Park Polo Club** *Windlesham Road, Chobham, Surrey GU24 8SN (01276 858545/www.polo.co.uk).*

# 841
## Go on pilgrimage to the Canterbury Tales

Chaucer's characters are alive and well and living in animatronic form in the Canterbury Tales attraction in – where else – Canterbury. We first meet the pilgrims at the Tabard Inn, where, clad in the requisite wimples and cloaks, they prepare for their journey to the tomb of 'hooly blisful martyr' Thomas à Becket, in Canterbury Cathedral. On the road we hear several of their lively tales, accompanied by suitable sounds, smells and special effects (the bum-out-of-the-window effect for the Miller's Tale is particularly popular with younger visitors), before finally reaching our destination: a reconstruction of the shrine of St Thomas.
**Canterbury Tales** *St Margaret's Church, St Margaret's Street, Canterbury, Kent CT1 2TG (01227 479227/www.canterburytales.org.uk).*

# 842
## Check out the Popemobile

For more than 20 years, the British Commerical Vehicle Museum has been inspiring would-be kings of the road with its collection of retro trucks, buses and vans as well as steam and fire engines. You can also have a gander at the Popemobile, used by John Paul II when he visited the UK in 1982.
**British Commercial Vehicle Museum** *King Street, Leyland, near Preston, Lancashire PR25 2LE (01772 451011/www.bcvm.co.uk).*

# 843
## Breakfast on a Craster kipper

This small hamlet on the coast of Northumberland is renowned across the world for its kippers, so where better to sit down and feast on the much-mocked delicacy? Produced by fish smokers L Robson & Sons (www.kipper.co.uk) over smouldering piles of oak sawdust, the kippers (actually smoked herring) are best served with toast and a wedge of lemon. Order a plate in the Craster Seafood Restaurant (Haven Hill, Craster, Alnwick, Northumberland NE66 3TR, 01665 576230).

# 844-849 *Go to market*

# Super markets

*Phil Harriss pays tribute to Britain's best street markets.*

Traditional markets are one of the unsung glories of Britain. There are still towns that are transformed on market day, becoming huge jamborees as local farmers, bargain-hunters and townsfolk head for the stalls. Pubs and cafés selling 'market day specials' fill with punters, for whom this is the main social event of the week. Often, the scene has been repeated weekly since the Middle Ages; markets helped bring the conurbations that surround them into existence, and a town's charter usually enshrines its right to hold a market. It's a pity, then, that so few town councils treasure their markets, often moving them off the traditional sites and on to grim, out-of-the-way car parks. And yet markets can flourish in the most unlovely of surroundings, producing a vivacious streetlife that offers an incomparable insight into the town you're exploring.

No councillor would dare suggest moving Swaffham's Saturday market from its town centre site. For the agricultural communities from neighbouring villages, the market remains a prime meeting place. Two fish stalls vie for custom, selling samphire in summer, Brancaster mussels in autumn and winter, and Cromer crabs most of the year. Look too for Mr Christie's cheese stall, where there are often supplies of Norfolk white lady, a brie-like cheese made from unpasteurised sheep's milk. At the eastern end of the market is the sprawling second-hand section: a splendid collection of junk, where for 30p you might snap up a naked Sindy doll or a 1950s back copy of *Geographical* magazine. If you managed to catch any of the Stephen Fry TV drama *Kingdom*, you might recognise Swaffham Market Place, with its distinctive Georgian Market Cross; much of the series was shot in the town.

The Home Counties, alas, aren't best blessed with street markets. Although street trading does exist, the affluent locals tend to look down on a humble costermonger singing paeans to his potatoes, preferring the more genteel interlocution found at farmers' markets. But there are exceptions, and one such is found at

**Swaffham Market**

**Barnstaple Pannier Market**

Thame, on the Oxfordshire–Buckinghamshire border. The town is set on a fine broad thoroughfare that comes into its own every Tuesday, when stalls take over the Upper Market Place car park. Come early to view the best of Chilly the Fish's catch, and to gaze at the waist-expanding cakes of the Women's Institute Country Market stall. Toys, trilbies, home-brew kit and fresh and cured pork are all up for grabs, and three stalls of fruit and veg compete for trade. Thame is one of the few places to incorporate a farmers' market within its general market, so come on the second Tuesday of the month and you'll also find local producers selling pork, beef, lamb, trout and pies.

Farmers' markets are nothing new; until industrialisation, most market traders were also food producers. There are a few pockets of England where the practice of local farmers bringing their produce to retail markets never died out, most notably the pannier markets of north Devon (named after the panniers in which the farmers' wives carried their goods). One of the best is at Barnstaple, housed in an iron-framed market hall built in 1855. Local, seasonal foods take pride of place on Tuesdays, Fridays and Saturdays, so in autumn you might see apple sellers with varieties that never make it on to supermarket shelves, and in spring, fresh asparagus. Wednesdays are for folk who love rifling through odds and ends loosely described as 'collectables', while local craftspeople make an appearance on Mondays and Thursdays.

Finding genuinely local produce is a highlight of visiting a market: an antidote to the drab uniformity of supermarkets' shelves. One of the stars of Bury Market in Greater Manchester is Chadwick's black pudding stall, where the bulbous delicacies are served hot straight from a steamer: fatty or lean, with or without a line of mustard. Among Bury's other 370 or so stalls – occupying a fish and meat hall, an indoor hall and outside in rather austere concrete surroundings – you'll also encounter several fruit and veg traders selling 'pot herbs' (the vegetables to make Lancashire hotpot). The loose-tongued chatter of local women out on the razzle adds to the entertainment.

Whereas Bury is a prime example of an urban market, Skipton, on the edge of the Yorkshire Dales, is the epitome of a country market town. More than 50 traders set up stall on either side of the town's High Street, selling all manner of household goods, leather belts, clothing (from lacy undies to no-nonsense windcheaters) and food. Don't miss the cheese stall, with its sterling display of North Country specimens: cotherstone and swaledale, as well as the world-famous wensleydale. Sweet confections can also be found at the market, perhaps including Lancastrian interlopers such as chorley cakes, eccles cakes and goosnargh cakes.

In the past, livestock trading was an essential part of a general market. Today, the two are usually separate, but in Melton Mowbray a livestock auction is one of the many attractions to hit the town every week. Although there's a smaller mart held on Friday, and a car boot sale on Sunday, Tuesday is when the entire town becomes a celebration of market trading in its multifarious forms. On the main site, off the Scalford Road, you'll find a succession of corrugated barns, some containing cows or sheep, another lined with food stalls, another packed with antiques sellers. Get there by 9.45am for the poultry, egg and game auction. The farmers' market occupies a series of spick and span lock-ups, while there are more food stalls on a pedestrianised street in the town centre. Don't leave without buying a Melton Mowbray pork pie and a hunk of stilton.

Part of the allure of a market is that it's never the same two weeks, or even two days, running,

so we can't guarantee that all the stalls we've mentioned above will be present at every market. In general, it's best to visit in the morning and in fine weather; traders tend to pack up early in rain. Likewise, certain times of the year are better than others. Local produce is abundant in the summer and autumn, less so in the lean months of January and February, but trading builds up to a climax in the weeks before Christmas. In full swing, with traders roaring, customers teeming and bargains enticing, markets create an excitement that superstores can't hope to emulate.

**Barnstaple Market** *The Pannier Market, Butchers Row, Barnstaple, Devon EX31 1SY (01271 379084/www.barnstaple panniermarket.co.uk). Open Crafts, collectibles & general goods 9am-4pm Mon, Apr-Christmas only. Local produce and general goods 9am-4pm Tue, Fri, Sat. Antiques, collectibles & book market 9am-4pm Wed. Crafts & general goods 9am-4pm Thur.*

**Bury Market** *Various sites, Bury Town Centre, Greater Manchester (www.burymarket.com). Open Main market, Market Parade & flea market 9am-4.30pm Wed, Fri; 9am-5pm Sat. Bury Market Hall 9am-5pm Mon-Sat. Bury Fish & Meat Hall 9am-5pm Mon, Wed-Sat; 9am-1pm Tue. Second-hand market 9am-4.30pm Thur.*

**Melton Mowbray Market** *Scalford Road, Melton Mowbray, Leicestershire LE13 1JY (01664 562971/www.meltonmowbray market.co.uk). Open General market 8am-4pm Tue. Farmers' market 8am-1.30pm Tue, Fri. Country Market (Gloucester House, Scalford Road) 9.15-11.30pm Tue (not Jan).*

**Skipton Market** *Market Setts, High Street, Skipton, North Yorkshire (01756 794357/ www.skiptonmarket.net). Open 9am-4pm Mon, Wed, Fri, Sat.*

**Swaffham Market** *Market Place, Swaffham, Norfolk. Open 9am-4pm Sat. For information, contact the Town Hall, 4 London Street, Swaffham, Norfolk PE37 7DQ (01760 722922).*

**Thame Market** *Upper High Street, Thame, Oxfordshire (01844 212833) Open 9am-4pm Tue. Farmers' market 2nd Tue of mth.*

# 850
## Make tracks to the Tank Museum

Tucked away in Dorset, on the edge of the New Forest, the scope and sheer size of the Tank Museum will come as a shock to anyone expecting a relatively parochial affair. The collection of over 300 armoured fighting vehicles from 26 countries is unrivalled anywhere in the world, and takes in many unique survivors of the World War I trenches, as well as recording a century of mechanised slaughter, right up to the state-of-art Challenger. A consistently human perspective gives welcome context to the industry of war: look down giant barrels, and share every tankie's fear of being boiled alive in a large tin can.
**Tank Museum** *Bovington, Dorset BH20 6JG (01929 405096/www.tankmuseum.co.uk).*

# 851-854
## Peer into a camera obscura

Translating as 'darkened chamber', this system of mirrors projects a periscope image of the outside world on to a white disc in the centre of a small, darkened room – reproducing the view in perfect miniature. Gadget-loving Victorian sightseers found peeping at the tiny panoramas enthralling; visit one of the surviving examples and judge for yourself. Bristol's camera obscura, housed in a former windmill, offers splendid views of Clifton Suspension Bridge (0117 975 0687, www.english-heritage.org.uk), while on the Isle of Man, the camera at Douglas (01624 686766) can be used to survey the surrounding headlands – or peek at unsuspecting bathers. The restored Victorian beauty at Eastbourne Pier (01323 410466) is also worth a gander, as is Edinburgh's gem at the top of the Royal Mile (0131 226 3709, www.camera-obscura.co.uk); while you're there, check out the powerful rooftop telescopes, which offer great city views.

# 855
## Buy vinyl at Beatin' Rhythm

This legendary Manchester record store stocks everything from '60s soul to rock 'n' roll – and carries the most extensive rare 45s section in the UK.
**Beatin' Rhythm** *42 Tib Street, Manchester M4 1LA (0161 834 7783/www.beatinrhythm.com).*

# 856
## Try out the 2010 Ryder Cup course

The Twenty Ten Course at Celtic Manor is the first to be built specifically for golf's biennial team showdown between Europe and the USA. Par is 71, but there are water hazards on half of the holes and the kind of risk-and-reward dilemmas that only the very best should even contemplate. A neat way to steal a march on the likes of Lee Westwood and Sergio Garcia is to book a package (£90-£150), which includes 18 holes on the Twenty Ten plus a two-course meal in the clubhouse.
**Celtic Manor Resort** *Coldra Woods, Usk Valley, Newport, South Wales NP18 1HQ (01633 413000/ www.celtic-manor.com).*

# 857
## See Margate's mysterious grotto

Discovered under a field in 1835 by a duckpond-digging local, the shell grotto remains an enigma to this day. A twisting, 70-foot-long passageway leads to a subterranean chamber, covered with intricate mosaics made from over four-and-a-half million laboriously glued-on shells – it's a bit like a *Blue Peter* project gone mad. First opened to the public in 1837, the grotto has bemused day-trippers ever since. Is it the meeting place of a secret sect, a pagan temple or simply a bizarre Regency folly? Sooty deposits from oil lamps used to light it in Victorian times mean that now it can't be carbon dated – so your guess is as good as anyone's.
**Shell Grotto** *Grotto Hill, Margate, Kent CT9 2BU (01843 220008/www.shellgrotto.co.uk).*

# 858
## Get retro at the Bakelite Museum

Housed in a disused water mill, this museum's collection of vintage plastic is the largest in Britain. Collectors will drool over the gorgeous art nouveau Bakelite picture frames and art deco jewellery, although the boisdurci desk sets might not be for everyone; this Belgian-invented material was made from pigs' blood. Curiosities include experimental plastic bicycles, scary-looking perming machines and hand grenades – and don't miss the 'hygienic, leakproof and vermin proof' coffin. In the summer months, retro picnics are held, complete with period clothes, Bakelite picnic sets, Spam sandwiches and a spot of bubbly; call for details.
**Bakelite Museum** *Orchard Mill, Williton, Somerset TA4 4NS (01984 632133/ www.bakelitemuseum.co.uk).*

# 859
## Admire a lovelorn artist's masterpiece

An ancient city, its domes and porticoes burnished by sunlight, stands by a harbour, overlooked by grey-blue mountains and a distant citadel. In the foreground, Neptune's crown and trident lie abandoned: a trail of damp footprints leading from the sea to the edge of the painting suggest that their owner has unexpectedly made an escape into the dining room at Plas Newydd, home to Rex Whistler's gloriously romantic masterpiece. Commissioned to paint the 58-foot panorama by the sixth Marquess of Anglesey in 1936, Whistler fell hopelessly in love with his patron's eldest daughter, Caroline. He even painted himself and Caroline as Romeo and Juliet (spot them on the picture's left-hand side) – but his passion was unrequited. Whistler was never to better his labour of love, dying in Normandy in 1944, aged 33. Now owned by the National Trust, Plas Newydd also houses an exhibition of Whistler's works and poignant love letters to his 'darling Caroline'.
**Plas Newydd** *Llanfairpwll, Anglesey LL61 6DQ (01248 714795/www.nationaltrust.org.uk).*

# 860
## Swim through Durdle Door

Seldom does Britain meet the sea with such rugged spectacle as at Durdle Door, a looming limestone arch on the Dorset coastline, close to Lulworth. The erosive processes that carved this unlikely monument have been at work since time immemorial – the name itself is over 1,000 years old, derived from the Old English 'thirl', meaning 'to pierce' – and will eventually lead the increasingly thin bridge section to collapse, leaving a towering coastal stack like the one at Ladram Bay in East Sussex. For now, however, a swim under this Jurassic proscenium is a genuinely sublime experience for both summer bathers and schools of friendly dolphins – the two spent one memorable afternoon playing together in August 2002. Less pleasant press coverage came in 2007, when a young man had to be airlifted to hospital after cliff-jumping over 60 feet from the top of the arch.

260 **Time Out** 1000 Things to do in Britain

# A few of my favourite things

# 861-867

## *Ekow Eshun, director of the ICA*

One of my favourite places in London is Cuts (39 Frith Street, London W1D 5LL, 020 7734 2171). I've been getting my hair cut there for about a dozen years, and it's become a part of my life. Lots of music and fashion people go there, and it's very sociable – you always end up meeting new people, or bumping into people you know. It's a real conduit of information too – some of it a little bit illicit, because that's the nature of Soho. They're all very hip, but it's the antithesis of a poncy hairdresser's: it's not over-fussy at all.
**I came across the Collection at Lincoln (Danes Terrace, Lincoln LN2 1LP, 01522 550990) a few years ago, when I was judging the Gulbenkian Prize. It was great: really intelligently put together. The permanent displays are fantastic, but there was also a temporary exhibition by Grayson Perry, who'd curated works from the collection and put in some of his own stuff. They managed to turn local history into something that alive, fascinating and fun.**
Pretty much my favourite shop in London is Start (menswear 59 Rivington Street, London EC2A 3QQ, 020 7739 3636; womenswear 42-44 Rivington Street, London EC2A 3BN, 020 7729 3334, www.start-london.com). They do various collections: Prada, Miu Miu and Comme, plus some less well-known European labels. The level of personal service is amazing; they suggest what might work for you cut-wise, colour-wise and shape-wise. I've never encountered anything like it. Their bespoke suits are narrower and more rakish than a traditional Saville Row suit – and cost less than a grand. My favourite one is a lightweight blue wool with a bright pink lining; when you open it up, there's a flash of colour and life.

Not many people know about the Wallace Collection (Hertford House, Manchester Square, London W1U 3BN, 0207 563 9500, www.wallacecollection.org), even though it's quite near Oxford Street and Selfridges. It's tucked away in an 18th-century townhouse, and is full of fantastic Dutch Old Masters. You can wander round in peace and spend hours looking at Rembrandts and Rubens. I love it there; the paintings – and portraits especially – are so full of human drama.
The Yorkshire Sculpture Park (West Bretton, Wakefield, West Yorkshire, WF4 4LG, 01924 832631, www.ysp.co.uk) blew me away. It's set in hundreds of acres of countryside and open fields, with pieces by Henry Moore, Elizabeth Frink, Antony Gormley and Barbara Hepworth; there's a happy discontinuity between the rural surrounds and the modernity of some of the sculptures. There's also a fantastic piece by James Turrell, the Deer Shelter. With his light installations, you sit in an enclosed space and look up at the sky; the walls of the space shift slightly with colour, but the main thing is that you simply sit and gaze at the sky. If you're there at sunset, you can watch the passage of time, from the vividness of daylight through to darkness.
**I've been going to Viet Hoa (70-72 Kingsland Road, London E2 8DP, 020 7729 8293), a Vietnamese restaurant on Kingsland Road, for years now. I always have pretty much the same thing; summer rolls to start, fried tilapi in fish sauce with mango, prawns with pickled greens, a goi salad... I go with my girlfriend and we always over-order, but normally find a way to eat everything. It's so fresh, and there's a fantastic mix of herbs and spices. There's nothing fancy about Viet Hoa, but it's incredibly friendly – the fantasy of what a local restaurant should be.**
Can I say the ICA (Institute of Contemporary Arts, The Mall, London SW1Y 5AH, 020 7930 3647, www.ica.org.uk)? A long time before it became its artistic director, I loved coming to the ICA – especially the bookshop. It's small, but it's like the Tardis; I go in there looking for one thing, then end up stumbling across all sorts of different stuff. The manager, Lena, has great taste, and there's so much strange and esoteric stuff in there. Philosophy, culture, memoir, politics, art... It stretches your brain in a very pleasurable way.

Time Out 1000 Things to do in Britain 261

## 868 Get vertigo in Matlock Bath

Running from the village of Matlock Bath, Britain's first Alpine-style cable car system soars over the Derwent River and across a rocky gorge to the summit of the Heights of Abraham – a hilly, 60-acre park, famed for its spectacular subterranean caverns and views over the Peak District. The cars were replaced with all-new models in 2004, providing a smoother ride and – with floor to ceiling windows – even better views. Gulp.
**Heights of Abraham** *Matlock Bath, Derbyshire DE4 3PD (01629 582365/www.heightsofabraham.com).*

## 869 Sink a pint at the Pandora Inn

With its flagstone floors, low beamed ceilings and thatched roof, it's not hard to believe that parts of this pub date back to the 13th century. Named after the ship that was sent to Tahiti to capture the mutineers of the *Bounty*, the Pandora is steeped in maritime history. Catch an aqua cab from Falmouth's Prince of Wales Pier (www.aquacab.co.uk), then sit back and enjoy the view as you quaff an ale in the sunset.
**Pandora Inn** *Restronguet Creek, Mylor Bridge, Falmouth, Cornwall TR11 5ST (01326 372678/ www.pandorainn.com).*

## 870 Celebrate children's literature

With storyteller sessions, dressing-up boxes and drop-in workshops, Seven Stories is an inspirational place for bibliophiles of all ages. The collections include original illustrations from the likes of *Ballet Shoes* and *Starring Tracy Beaker*, plus reams of manuscripts – Philip Pullman donated drafts from 14 of his books. There are Bookworm Babies sessions for tinies and storytime reads for under-fives; older kids (and adults) can meet authors and illustrators and discover how books are created.
**Seven Stories** *30 Lime Street, Newcastle-upon-Tyne NE1 2PQ (0845 271 0777/www.sevenstories.org.uk).*

## 871 Quaff cider with Rosie in Slad

The part of the world immortalised by Laurie Lee still retains an unspoilt air – the local nature reserves (three within Slad valley itself), picturesque setting and sleepy Cotswold village all combine to conjure up the epitome of a bygone era. There are more cars now than there were then, of course, not to mention more tourists, but the Woolpack Inn – Lee's local – still stands. The author's grave is in the nearby churchyard – stop for a moment of quiet reflection, gazing over a beautiful English landscape as he so often did, before heading inside for a pint of Uley Old Spot.
**Woolpack Inn** *Slad, Stroud, Gloucestershire GL6 7QA (01452 813429/www.woolpackslad.com).*

## 872 Explore the secret caves of the Hellfire Club

A series of hand-hewn chambers and passageways that stretch underground for nearly half a mile, these caves were once home to the 18th-century 'Brotherhood of St Francis of High Wycombe' – better known as the Hellfire Club. Rumours of wild debauchery, satanism and orgies swirled around its aristocratic members, whose motto was 'Do what thou wilt'. Yet for all the lurid speculation, the club's rakish founder, Sir Francis Dashwood, had a social conscience – he commissioned locals to dig out the caves to relieve unemployment after a poor harvest, then build the road from West Wycombe to High Wycombe with the excavated limestone. The murky underground chambers and winding tunnels, carved with spooky faces, are now open to explore (complete with unconvincing mannequins dressed up as Hellfire members).
**Hell Fire Caves** *Church Lane, West Wycombe, Buckinghamshire HP14 3AH (01494 533739/ www.hellfirecaves.co.uk).*

# 873 Kip in a vintage caravan

Deep in the woods of the North York Moors, La Rosa's 20-acre site is occupied by eight kitsch and colourful caravans. Each is kitted out according to a different retro theme; Vegas Vice pays tribute to Elvis, while La Rosa's opulent, mirror-bedecked interior is a homage to 1930s striptease star Gypsy Rose Lee. The whole site is run on low-tech lines and there's no electricity: three of the caravans are cosily heated by wood-burning stoves, while showers are candlelit affairs in a hay byre and toilet trips involve a compost loo in a converted shepherd's hut. 'Everything's reclaimed or recycled,' says owner Amanda Boorman. 'It's like a campsite run by the Wombles.' There's also a jauntily striped communal circus tent, where children can delve into the dressing-up box on rainy afternoons, and grown-ups natter and take afternoon tea from the charmingly mismatched rose-print crockery. During the day, spot deer in the North Yorkshire Moors National Park, ride the steam railway from Grosmont Station, or drive to nearby Whitby. In the evenings, sip spiced cider with your neighbours in front of one of the open fires. Caravanning doesn't get cooler than this – and all for just £26 a head.

**La Rosa** *Murk Esk Cottage, Goathland, Whitby, North Yorkshire YO22 5AS (07786 072866/ www.larosa.co.uk).*

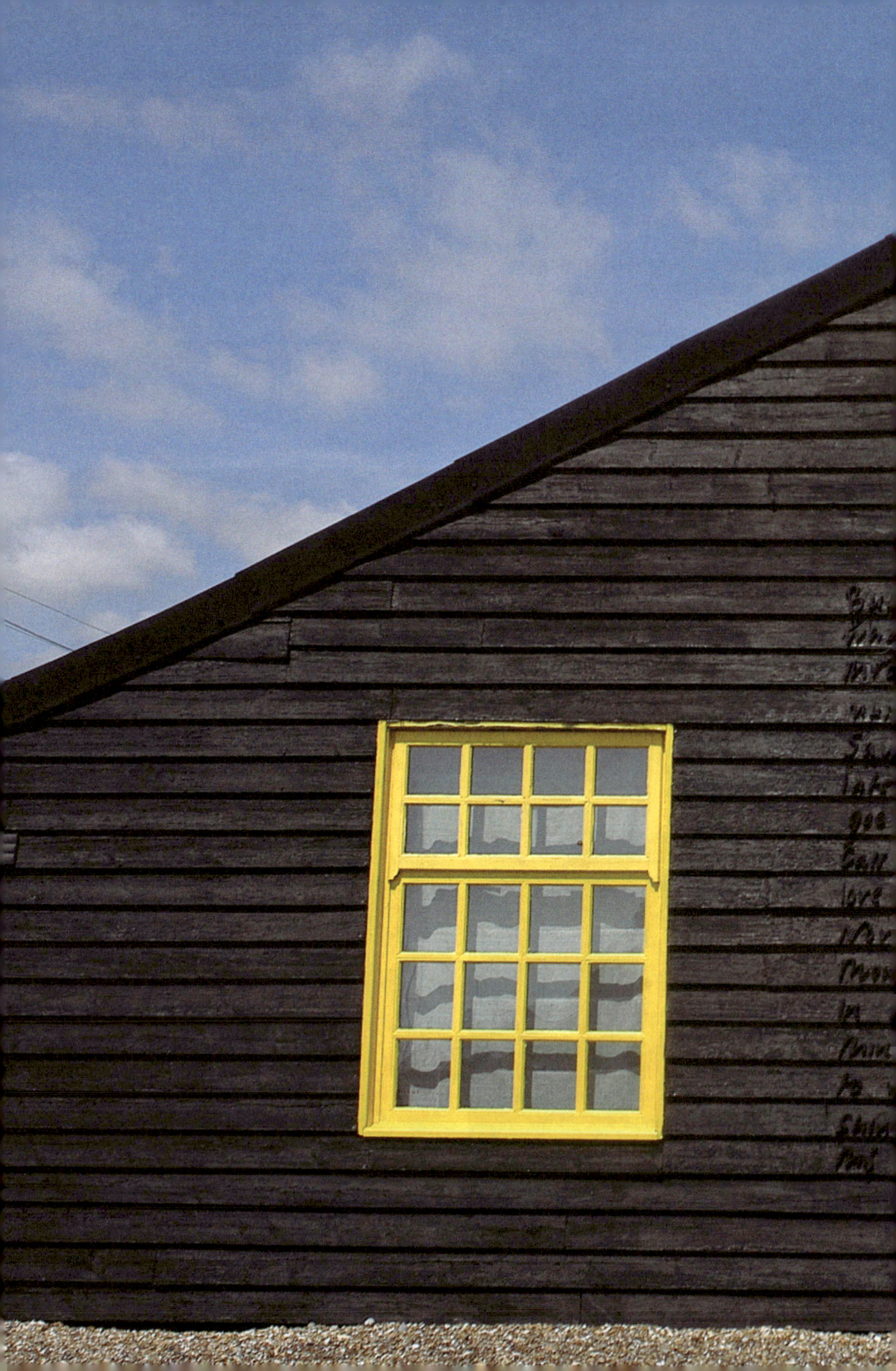

## 874

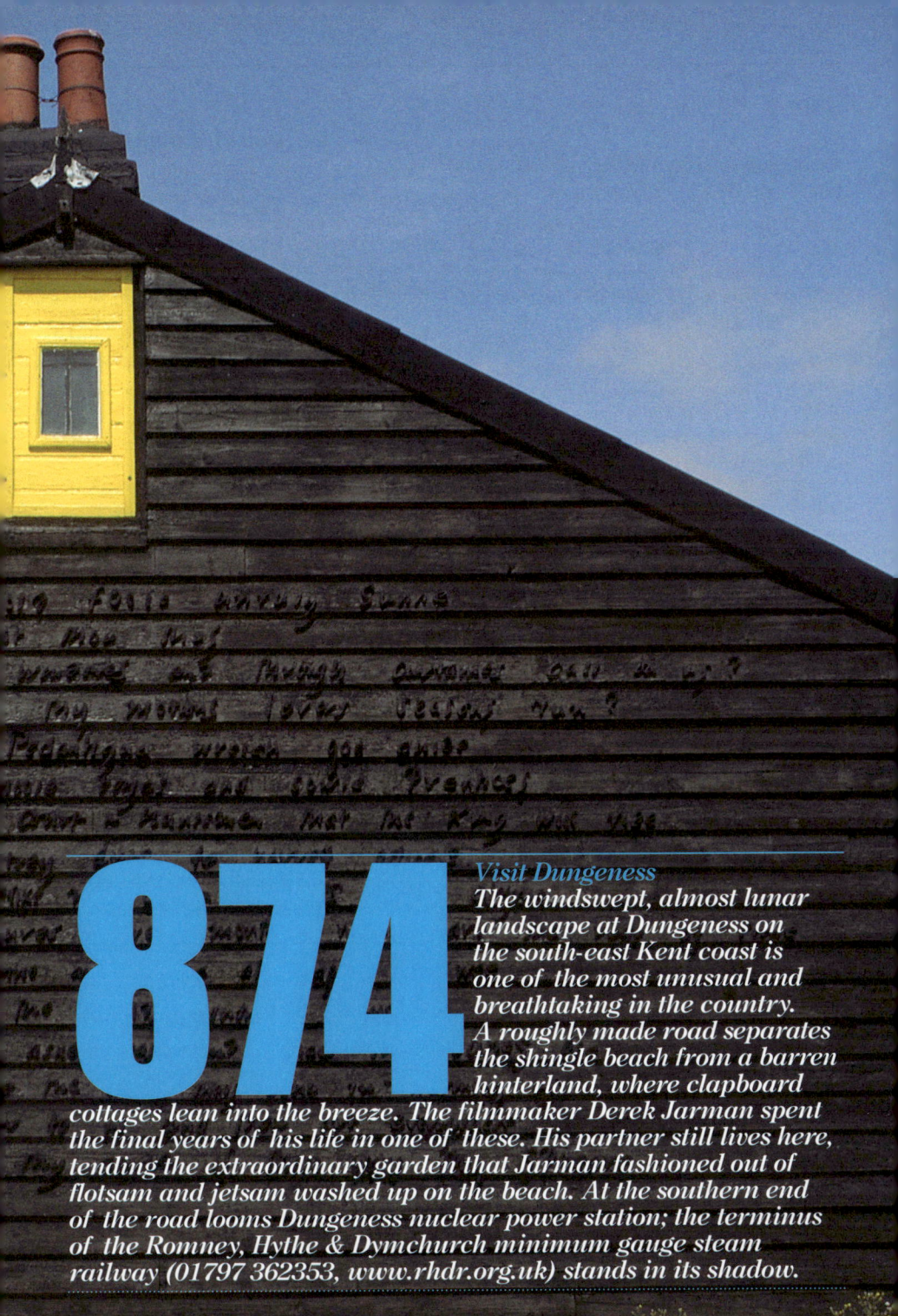

### Visit Dungeness

The windswept, almost lunar landscape at Dungeness on the south-east Kent coast is one of the most unusual and breathtaking in the country. A roughly made road separates the shingle beach from a barren hinterland, where clapboard cottages lean into the breeze. The filmmaker Derek Jarman spent the final years of his life in one of these. His partner still lives here, tending the extraordinary garden that Jarman fashioned out of flotsam and jetsam washed up on the beach. At the southern end of the road looms Dungeness nuclear power station; the terminus of the Romney, Hythe & Dymchurch minimum gauge steam railway (01797 362353, www.rhdr.org.uk) stands in its shadow.

# 875
## Test the 'whispering wa's' at the Hamilton Mausoleum

Just off Junction 6 of the M74 lies the Hamilton Mausoleum – the sole, lonely remains of the immense, fantastically grand palace that stood here from 1695 to 1921, until subsidence caused its collapse. The scale of the classical Victorian mausoleum, built by the tenth Duke of Hamilton, is awesome, with light pouring in through the cylindrical tower's glass-capped dome 131 feet above you. When the door slams behind you, you'll hear the longest-lasting echo of any building in the world. This bizarre acoustic anomaly also allows you to whisper sweet nothings to the wall (or 'wa') on one side of the building, and be heard by someone standing on the other side.

**Hamilton Mausoleum** *129 Muir Street, Hamilton, South Lanarkshire ML3 6BJ (01698 328232).*

# 876
## Make sloe gin

Adding sloe berries and sugar to a bottle of gin is alcoholic alchemy, creating wonderfully fruity, refreshing sloe gin – and it's simplicity itself. First you need to go fruit-picking, which shouldn't be too tricky: sloe berries grow on blackthorn bushes, which are found throughout the UK. Tradition has it that the berries shouldn't be picked until the 'first frost'; in practice, they're ripe and ready for picking in October and November.

You'll need a pound of sloes, a pint and three quarters of gin and eight ounces of caster sugar. Prick the sloes' skins and put them in a large, sterilised jar. Add the gin and the sugar, seal the jar tight and shake well. Store the jar in a cool, dark place and, during the first week, shake it every other day. Thereafter, give it a shake once a week. The sloe gin will be ready to drink after two months – although the longer you keep it, the more the flavour intensifies.

# 877
## Tour an Earthship...

The first Earthships were built in the US in the 1970s, the brainchild of Mike Reynolds. Made from tyres packed with earth, they generate their own solar power and collect rainwater via the roof; the idea is that they are self-sustaining, and anyone can build them. It's an intriguing concept that's caught on around the globe – and has now come to Britain. Visit www.earthship.co.uk for details of the Earthships in Fife and Brighton, both of which offer tours.

# 878-879
## ...or stare up at a Skyspace

A Skyspace is a small chamber containing a few seats and an aperture in the ceiling, through which the sky is visible. Artist James Turrell's idea is that visitors sit and gaze heavenwards in quiet contemplation as the sky is 'brought close' to them. The effect is extraordinary, especially at sunset. There are Skyspaces across the world, two notable ones being in Britain. At Cat Cairn in Kielder Forest in Northumberland (01434 250312, www.forestry.gov.uk), the Skyspace is a sleek, underground cylindrical chamber; the example at Yorkshire Sculpture Park (01924 832631, www.ysp.co.uk) is an adapted 19th-century deer shelter. Take a seat, look upwards, and prepare to be awed by the vivid, constantly shifting colours.

# 880
## Visit 'Brontë country'

Set on the edge of the Pennine moors, the village where the Brontë brood once lived is a tourist magnet. At its heart is their childhood home; now a museum, it has much of the original furniture still in place – including the sofa on which Emily died, aged 30. If the crowds get too much, escape for a walk on the wild and windswept moors.

**Brontë Parsonage Museum** *Church Street, Haworth, Keighley, West Yorkshire BD22 8DR (01535 642323/www.bronte.org.uk).*

## 881 Explore St David's – then adjourn for lunch

St David's is Britain's smallest city, thanks to its superb 12th-century cathedral – built on the site where St David's monastery stood in the sixth century. In medieval times this was a major place of pilgrimage, with two trips here considered the equivalent of one to Rome in terms of spiritual brownie points. Try to catch a service with one of the cathedral's three choirs in situ; otherwise, check out the finely carved Irish oak ceiling and misericords. Tours run in summer, led by volunteers: afterwards have lunch in the airy refectory, where the menu runs from top-notch sandwiches (Welsh black beef with horseradish, locally smoked salmon) to hearty home-made casseroles.

**St David's Cathedral** *The Close, St David's, Pembrokeshire SA62 6RH (01437 720199/ www.stdavidscathedral.org.uk).*

## 882 Stroll the gardens at Renishaw Hall

Sir George Sitwell (1860-1943) was an indefatigable gardener, as his eldest son Osbert drily observed: 'He abolished small hills, created lakes, and particularly liked to alter the levels at which full grown trees were standing. Two old yew trees in front of the dining-room window at Renishaw were regularly heightened and lowered; a process which I believe could have been shown to chart, like a thermometer, the temperature of his mood.' Divided by yew hedges, the gardens at Renishaw Hall (still owned by the Sitwell family) are a vision of classical Italianate splendour: the rose gardens, at their peak in early June, are gloriously romantic.

**Renishaw Hall** *Renishaw, Sheffield S21 3WB (01246 432310/www.renishaw-hall.co.uk).*

## 883 Go on a Neolithic pilgrimage along the Ridgeway

Britain's oldest road, the Ridgeway hugs the hilltops for 85 miles, meandering south through five counties to Salisbury Plain. Along the route are an impressive number of Neolithic sites, from Uffington's white horse and Avebury's stone circle to the ancient earthworks at Barbury, Liddington and Uffington. Also near Uffington is the atmospheric burial chamber of Wayland's Smithy. If Wiltshire's cluster of famous sites were Neolithic altars in Mother Nature's curvy cathedral, then the Ridgeway was our original Pilgrim's Way.

# 884-891
## Eat the freshest seafood money can buy

Delightfully ramshackle seaside buildings and spanking fresh seafood go together like buckets and spades. From the west of Scotland to the south coast of England, you'll find locally caught oysters, crabs and fish served in unremarkable-looking seashore shacks (many of the following are not open all year round, so call ahead to check first). Expect few frills but plenty of thrills from crustacea, molluscs and bivalves that come straight from the briny and taste like it too.

### Anchorstone Café
Overlooking the River Dart, this tiny eaterie has won itself an enviable reputation among in-the-know foodies. Lay claim to one of the outside tables, then feast on immaculately fresh seafood: the crab salad is highly recommended. Book well ahead, as locals flock here in summer. The nicest way to arrive is by catching a ferry upriver from Dartmouth quay; the journey takes about half an hour.
**Anchorstone Café** *Manor Street, Dittisham, Dartmouth, Devon TQ6 0EX (01803 722365).*

### Boathouse Restaurant & Crab Shed
Discover sandy, secluded Steephill Cove by boat or follow the footpath down. Here, the Wheeler brothers continue the centuries-old tradition of fishing for crab and lobster, and the more modern one of serving them in their rickety-looking restaurant – accompanied by wine, with raspberry brûlée to follow – or in

Wheeler's Crab Shed, where the crab pasties (£3.70) have a devoted following. You can also take crab and lobster home for tea. Book well ahead for the restaurant.
**Boathouse Restaurant & Crab Shed** *Steephill Cove, Ventnor, Isle of Wight PO38 1UG (Boathouse 01983 852747/Crab Shed 01983 852177/ www.theboathouse-steephillcove.co.uk).*

## Company Shed
An east coast legend, raising and serving some of the best oysters in the country. Scoff rocks all year round for 60p each, natives in season from 70p. The Shed also serves tiger prawns, razor clams and platters heaped with all sorts of seafood. And salad. That's it. Bring your own bread and butter and a bottle from the off-licence over the road, and be amazed at how little you have to shell out to eat so well.
**Company Shed** *129 Coast Road, West Mersea, Essex CO5 8PA (01206 382700).*

## Cookies Crab Shop
Smoked fish and fresh crab are the thing at this shop, close enough to the sea to glimpse crashing waves beyond the saltmarsh. Eat kipper and tomato soup, seafood sandwiches and platters inside a brick and flint outhouse or out in the garden. Prices, even for the Royal salad of crab, prawns, cockles and smoked fish, are a steal. Bring your own booze or drink the shop's tea – and save room for sticky toffee pudding with custard.
**Cookies Crab Shop** *The Green, Salthouse, near Holt, Norfolk NR25 7AJ (01263 740352/www. cookies.shopkeepers.co.uk).*

## Crab House Café & Oyster Farm
A typically English eccentricity, this little beachside shack is festooned with all manner of marine paraphernalia – fishing nets, ropes and rods; outside, the garden sports a boat planted with herbs. Don't be fooled into thinking this is a mere caff though; the food is decidedly superior. As the name suggests, oysters are raised locally in the Chesil Fleet. Order 'crab to crack' and tackle the magnificent creature with the tools provided. Or let the chefs do the hard work – turning locally caught fish into sensational dishes.
**Crab House Café & Oyster Farm** *Ferrymans Way, Portland Road, Wyke Regis, Dorset DT4 9YU (01305788867/www.crabhousecafe.co.uk).*

## Oyster Shack
Reached via a tidal track, this is no ordinary shack. The set-up may be simple but the cooking is smart, and you can shuck oysters straight from the River Avon, which flows off Dartmoor into the sea here. Have them au naturel, 'casino' (with bacon, peppers, lime and tabasco), or 'rockafella' (spinach, pernod, parmesan). Bring chilled white wine, and make it a good one to match fish dishes such as cajun sardines followed by turbot with anchovy, tomato and parsley salsa. Stick to fishcakes on a cheap date.
**Oyster Shack** *Stakes Hill, Bigbury, Devon TQ7 4BE (01548 810876/www.oystershack.co.uk).*

## Seafood Cabin
Brilliant and basic. Sit outdoors in the middle of nowhere and gaze across the Kilbrannan Sound to Arran, or inside in either a hut with a view or a shabby old kitchen without. It's glorified picnicking – with food brought to you. There are wholewheat rolls filled with crab straight off the boat, salmon served several ways, smoked fish over from Arran, langoustines and scallops. Home-made scones and chocolate or orange cake made with the Cabin's own hens' eggs round off a simply splendid, locally produced feast. The Cabin has its own liquor licence too, so no need to bring your own booze.
**Seafood Cabin** *Skipness Estate, Tarbert, Argyll PA29 6XU (01880 760 207).*

## Whitstable Oyster Fishery Co
In a roomy old oyster storage shed (Whitstable has been famous for its oyster beds for around 2000 years) situated right on the shingle beach, this shabby-chic, whitewashed restaurant is perennially popular. It's best known for its oysters, though the other seafood on the menu is also excellent. Rock oysters are available all year, or you can try Whitstable natives in season for twice the price. Smoked eel, razor clams, local seabass, panfried skate, roasted monkfish, lobster and crab from Dorset are yet more reasons for visiting. There's a white-leaning wine list to suit, and treacle tart with Jersey cream among the afters.
**Whitstable Oyster Fishery Co** *Royal Native Oyster Stores, The Horsebridge, Whitstable, Kent CT5 1BU (01227 276856/www.oysterfishery.co.uk).*

# A few of my favourite things

## 892-897
### Julie Verhoeven, fashion designer

Blackgang Chine (Ventnor, Isle of Wight PO38 2HN, 01983 730052, www.blackgangchine.com), carved out of the cliffs on the south coast of the Isle of Wight, is Britain's oldest theme park, and has a charm that reflects a gentler, kinder era. It's shabby but quaint, and filled with genteel British amusements like concrete dinosaurs poking out over hedges – I love the hall of mirrors and the Wild West set. It has heaps of fond memories for me.
**The stunning jetty at Lyme Regis** gives me flashbacks to *The French Lieutenant's Woman*, though it dates back much further than either John Fowles's novel or Karel Reisz's 1982 movie, in which it plays a major role. It's been there since the 13th century at least, when Edward I had it built to improve the harbour – and is actually called the Cobb. It's so dramatic and hazardous that it never fails to impress me, however many times I see it.

Icy cold whatever the weather, **Baggins Book Bazaar** (19 High Street, Rochester, Kent ME1 1PY, 01634 811651, www.bagginsbooks.co.uk) has a deceptively modest façade that disguises an endless stock of second-hand books. On its website it claims to be England's largest second-hand and rare bookshop, and seeing it, there's no reason to argue. Fantastic.
**The Air Hockey on Brighton Pier** (Madeira Drive, Brighton, East Sussex BN2 1TW, 01273 609361, www.brightonpier.co.uk) is fast, furious and fun for only 50p. I love the way people take it really seriously, but also fall about laughing while they're playing it. It's a quintessential seaside arcade game.
The **east cliff lift at Hastings** is another seaside favourite; it feels as if you're risking life and limb making the journey up the cliff in the charmingly shaky but faithful funicular railway. It's over 100 years old and is really pretty, with a mini-castle at its top and what looks like a little chapel at its base. The views from the top are fantastic too.
In London, the **Foot Tunnel at Greenwich** is a firm favourite. I love the scary journey under the Thames – it runs between Cutty Sark Gardens and Island Gardens – and the elegant lift that awaits you as a reward at either end. It's featured in lots of London films, and always makes me feel like I'm in a movie. It has a distorted *Clockwork Orange* feel to it.

## 898 Celebrate English wines

In the past decade, the amount of wine produced in England has grown threefold. English wine is on the up, and English Wine Week (www.englishwineweek.co.uk) is a celebration of this native viticulture. For a week in late May, vineyards up and down the country open to visitors, offering tours and tastings. England's largest vineyard, Denbies in Surrey, makes both red and white wine, cultivating a mixture of dornfelder, pinot noir, chardonnay and reichensteiner grapes. The soil on the North Downs is similar to that in Champagne, so sparkling wines are a speciality; in 2007, the vineyard was voted one of the top four sparkling wine producers in the world.
**Denbies Wine Estate** *London Road, Dorking, Surrey RH5 6AA (01306 876616/ www.denbiesvineyard.co.uk).*

## 899 Mix it up at the Burrell

Millionaire ship owner Sir William Burrell bequeathed over 9,000 artworks to Glasgow in 1944, but it wasn't until 1983 that the collection found its home. Set in the 350-acre Pollok Estate, the huge glass structure somehow manages to incorporate medieval arches and Renaissance doorways into its light, airy contours. The collection also offers a heady mix of time and place, with tapestries, ceramics, sculptures and stained glass from medieval Europe, works from ancient Egypt, Greece, Rome and China, sculptures by Epstein and Rodin, pieces by Degas and Cézanne and an impressive collection of Islamic art.
**Burrell Collection** *Pollok Country Park, 2060 Pollokshaws Road, Glasgow G43 1AT (0141 287 2550/www.glasgowmuseums.com).*

## 900-903
### Kayak through the Outer Hebrides

With their rugged scenery and deserted white sand beaches, the Outer Hebrides are a stunning setting for sea kayaking. The other big lure is the chance to get up close to the local wildlife: seals, otters, porpoises, dolphins, basking sharks and even the odd killer whale. At the end of a hard day's kayak-paddling, you really feel as if you've earned a big dinner and a shot of whisky. Companies offering supervised sea kayak tours in these parts include Adventure Hebrides (www.adventurehebrides.com), 58 Degrees North (www.canoehebrides.com), Wilderness Scotland (www.wilderness scotland.com) and Clearwater Paddling (www.clearwaterpaddling.com).

## 904
### Shed light on the Dark Ages at Sutton Hoo

In 1939, archaeologists unearthed the remains of an Anglo-Saxon burial ship in one of the grassy mounds at Sutton Hoo. It was packed with treasures, including a magnificent sword and exquisite, garnet-studded gold shoulder clasps. While the site's contents are now at the British Museum, you can take a guided tour around the atmospheric burial mounds and see a full-scale replica of the ship in the on-site visitors' centre.

**Sutton Hoo** *near Woodbridge, Suffolk IP12 3DJ (01394 389700/www.nationaltrust.org.uk).*

## 905
### Have a drink by the Shropshire Canal

In a remote corner of Staffordshire, on the Shropshire Union Canal, halfway between Telford and Stafford, stands the Anchor. The pretty beer garden fronts straight on to the canal, making it a favourite with those steering narrowboats down the 'Shroppie'. If you're passing, moor up and sup a glass of Weston's cider before clambering back on board.

**The Anchor** *Paggs Lane, High Offley, Staffordshire ST20 0NG (01785 284569).*

## 906
### Take in some culture on the south coast

Brighton's three-week annual shindig (www.brightonfestival.org) is England's largest arts festival, bringing a host of internationally renowned authors, actors, comedians and musicians to the city. In 2007, speakers included Lionel Shriver, Dave Eggers and Gordon Brown, while director Neil Bartlett's adventurous car-park production of Jean Genet's claustrophobic tale of intrigue, *The Maids*, was a dramatic highlight. The festival has its Fringe element too, often every bit as inventive and popular as the main event; last year saw an innovative use of beach hut space for one production. Crucially, the Festival also provides a showcase for creative Brightonians: local artists are put on display along with their artistic efforts in the Artists' Open Houses Trail, which sees many a boho Brightonian residence opened to the public.

# 907 *Explore Daphne du Maurier's Cornwall*

# Literary landscape

**Kate Mossman** *follows in her heroine's footsteps – and finds the Cornish scenery gloriously unchanged.*

A tour of Daphne du Maurier's Cornwall, the land that inspired *Rebecca, Jamaica Inn* and *Frenchman's Creek*, requires a few essentials. An OS map, an unlimited amount of sandwiches – and a ghoulish imagination.

In the climactic pages of *Jamaica Inn*, heroine Mary Yellan comes across a drawing by the Vicar of Altarnun, a village on Bodmin Moor. 'A caricature, grotesque as it was horrible. The people of the congregation were bonneted and shawled, but he had drawn sheep's heads upon their shoulders instead of human faces. The animal jaws gaped foolishly at the preacher with silly, vacant solemnity, and their hoofs were folded in prayer.'

Du Maurier's vicar was modelled on a real-life eccentric. The Reverend F Densham came to Warleggan (which lies off the A30, beyond the village of Mount) in 1931 – and his bizarre behaviour was soon driving the congregation away. Undeterred, he propped up cardboard images in the pews of his church to replace his recalcitrant flock.

Today, the 11th-century St Bartholomew's church (Warleggan, Cornwall PL30 4HB) is squat, dark and decidedly uneasy-looking. Densham himself appears in a photo on the church wall, gripping his canes and grinning in his shovel hat – and the church guidebook corroborates the 'cardboard congregation' story. 'They will all come to me in the end,' Densham is quoted as saying. 'I conduct their funerals.'

Du Maurier couldn't get enough of the story. She drove across the moors and crouched in the rectory bushes to get a glimpse of the unhappy clergyman, then ran away in fright. She recounts the story in *Vanishing Cornwall* – a humble, anorak-wearing book that lies somewhere between travelogue and fantasy, and functions as our guide.

Du Maurier combines her very precise local knowledge with a strange kind of romantic zeal. She leads you to places beyond the tourist trail that have, for centuries, been shrouded in Cornish legend. Dozmary Pool (drive through Warleggan, northwards on to the open moor,

Peatcutters, near Brown Willy

**Time Out** 1000 Things to do in Britain **273**

and follow the signs from Colliford Reservoir) is where the sword of Excalibur was thrown. As she writes in *Vanishing Cornwall*, 'Dozmary has many moods. It is still and limpid on a summer's day, tempting to the paddler, but once a whisper of a breeze ripples the surface the colour changes to a slatey grey, ominous and drear, and little wavelets splash the shore, pebbled with brown stones and peaty mud'. The surrounding moorland is equally desolate, and you'll feel as though no one has stood at the grey water's edge since Sir Bedivere himself.

The road from Dozmary Pool brings you to Jamaica Inn (Bolventor, Launceston, Cornwall PL15 7TS, 01566 86250, www.jamaicainn. co.uk). Du Maurier lamented that she changed the character of the place by writing the book ('As the author I am flattered, but as a one-time wanderer dismayed') – and today, Jamaica Inn is really only worth visiting if you want to see what can go wrong when Cornwall plays up to the tourists. The smell of gravy and disinfectant often fills the hall, while awkward, button-operated smuggler-mannequins tell tales in exaggerated West Country accents.

Du Maurier lived at the private country seat of Menabilly, two miles west of Fowey. She lost the lease in 1967, and never quite got over it: 'last night I dreamed I went to Manderlay again,' *Rebecca* famously begins, and Menabilly is thinly disguised. In Fowey itself, May brings the Daphne du Maurier Festival (01726 879500, www.dumaurierfestival.co.uk). It features a lively mix of literati, comedians and musicians, all doing their own thing against a backdrop of Du Maurier lectures delivered by the University of Exeter. You can even take a boat trip to have a cream tea with Du Maurier's son, Kit Browning.

The author honeymooned on her husband's dinghy around Frenchman's Creek, a short walk from Helford. The creek itself is a small tributary of the main estuary, and is very little to look at on its own (at low tide it's just mud). It's best seen as part of one of the many walking trails around the local area, taking in the beautiful Helford river.

The geographical contrast between the lush Helford estuary and the bleak moors of north Cornwall fascinated Du Maurier, who marvelled at its 'warm and soft climate, with its high hedges and tall protecting trees. Even the East wind was no hardship there, for the arm of the headland acted as a defence to those on land,

and it was only the river that ran turbulent and green, the wave-crests whipped with foam.'

Du Maurier set much of her fiction in the winter, when Cornwall is desperately, enticingly bleak. Loe Bar (near Helston) will get your eyes watering and your imagination racing. Reached via a coastal path from nearby Porthleven, it's a narrow strip of sand with Cornwall's largest natural freshwater lake lying serenely on your left, and the ocean thrashing 100 yards away on the other side.

> *"Last night I dreamed I went to Mandalay again," Rebecca famously begins, and Menabilly is thinly disguised.'*

Du Maurier learned to swim on Kennack Sands, east of Lizard Point, where she was haunted by the tale of a boy who drowned in nearby quicksands, the son of a local publisher. At Gunwalloe (at the eastern end of Loe Bar) experience the 'shifting sands' for yourself: a bank of gravel, sucked by the sea on either side. It's exhilarating, but the near-deserted beach is testament to the fact that only the most intrepid locals will take on the power of the sea at the Lizard Peninsula.

As the Lizard's coastal villages twinkle in the half-light, you're irresistibly reminded of the 'wreckers' with whom the novelist was obsessed – smugglers who planted false beacons on the cliffs, luring ships into the treacherous waters near St Keverne. As our heroine's wicked uncle Joss recounts in *Jamaica Inn*, 'I've killed men with my own hands, trampled them under water, beaten them with rocks… I see their white-green faces staring at me, with their eyes eaten by fish'. With Du Maurier's writing as your guide, and the wildest of landscapes at your disposal, it's easy to imagine you can see the glint of their lanterns on stormy nights.

## 908 Zoom around the Grand Prix Collection

Donington Park racing circuit is home to the largest collection of Grand Prix racing cars in the world, from the Lotus 18 in which Stirling Moss sped to victory in the 1961 Monaco Grand Prix to Nigel Mansell's mighty Williams FW14B. Filling five halls, the sleek, gleaming motors are a speed-fiend's dream – though the vast collection of drivers' helmets is probably best left to the real obsessives.
**Donington Grand Prix Collection** *Castle Donington, Derby DE74 2RP (01332 811027/ www.donington-park.co.uk).*

## 909 Walk across the Atlantic

Just south of Oban in Argyll, the Scottish mainland is separated from the island of Seil by a tiny sound, just a few metres across. Technically, this is part of the Atlantic Ocean – so when the modest, single span Clachan Bridge was built across it in the 18th century, it came to be known as the Bridge over the Atlantic. Once you've made your ocean-spanning stroll across, stop for a pint in the waterfront beer garden at the 18th-century Tigh an Truish Inn (01852 300242, www.tigh-an-truish.co.uk), which stands right by the old bridge in Seil.

## 910 See the bell-ringing swans of Wells

Adjoining the Gothic splendour of Wells Cathedral stands the magnificent medieval Bishop's Palace, long-time home to the Bishop of Bath and Wells. Providing a suitably grand setting, there's also a moat surrounding the palace on three sides, with regal swans gliding about as though they owned the place. That doesn't seem far from the truth when you discover that they have been trained to ring a bell hanging from the walls down to the water when they require feeding. It's a tradition that started in the 19th century and, to celebrate the 800th birthday of the palace in 2006, the Queen presented the current bishop with a new swan family (who presumably knew a good thing when they saw one).
**Bishop's Palace** *Wells, Somerset BA5 2PD (01749 678691).*

# 911 Explore Under the Pier

## Sedate Southwold is home to a very unusual amusements arcade, discovers **Elizabeth Winding**.

As the half-hour strikes on Southwold Pier, unwitting holidaymakers strolling past its weatherbeaten copper clock are treated to an extraordinary display. A pair of mechanised figures sit bolt-upright in the bath and spit water at each other, a neat row of red tulips rises from a window box to be watered and two boys loitering by a loo suddenly drop their shorts and have a wee – much to the delight of the open-mouthed children gathering round to gawp. A little further on, the traditional end-of-pier telescope has its own surprises in store: in place of the usual soporific sea views, there are oil slicks, shrieking swimmers being eaten by sharks and jetski-ing world leaders.

Both pieces are the handiwork of Tim Hunkin, who I'm meeting today for a tour of Under the Pier, his surreal amusements arcade (more of which later). A Cambridge-educated engineer, Hunkin admits he always had a penchant for off-the-wall, Heath Robinson-esque inventions. 'I discovered early on that I liked making things to make people laugh. My breakthrough was a burglar-catcher machine for my bedroom, using a pressure-sensitive mat and a photograph of Gladys Cooper; she beckoned the burglar towards her then hit him on the head with a hammer.' After Cambridge, Hunkin became a cartoonist for the *Observer*, then made the *Secret Life of Machines* series for Channel 4, which paved the way for several high-profile museum commissions, including the Science Museum's Secret Life of the Home gallery.

But Hunkin chafed under the constraints of working to museums' briefs. The idea of starting up an amusements arcade with his own coin-operated creations had always appealed, and in 2001 he decided to take the plunge. Housed in a wooden shed halfway along Southwold Pier, Under the Pier is a world away from conventional arcades. Rather than feeding change into penny falls and luridly-lit fruit machines, you can find your future in the Booth of Truth, experience an Instant Eclipse, submit a strand of hair to the Gene Forecaster 2000 for analysis, or sit in an armchair in front of a telly and be whisked away on a Micro Break – a three-minute 'virtual holiday'.

'In the early days, there were lots of bemused people. They were suspicious that it was somehow sinister – I thought I'd really got it wrong,' Hunkin admits. 'But all you need is for one person to start laughing, and the atmosphere's quite infectious.' These days, there are plenty of repeat visitors queuing to take a seat in the Expressive Photobooth (a contraption which tickles, tilts and surprises its occupants, then photographs the resulting expressions), or take the Mobility Masterclass ('Start training for the future today! Cross the motorway using the zimmer frame'). The interactive Doctor and Chiropractor automatons are also eternally popular: no visit's complete until you've surrendered your sock-clad foot to the latter's ministrations, or had a prescription scribbled by the Doctor (authentically illegible, of course).

Then there's the Art Expert, a stern-faced figure (with more than a passing resemblance to White Cube owner Jay Jopling), who wearily inclines his head to scrutinise the random objects visitors place before him. He then pronounces whether or not they are 'art' – and occasionally sticks a forked tongue out for good measure. Hunkin's own foray into the art world was short-lived; after exhibiting at the ICA in the 1980s, he realised it wasn't a milieu he felt at ease in. 'I like making things, but I don't really like all that... stuff that goes with the art world. I don't understand it, and I'm not interested in it. It seems so irrelevant.'

In truth, he says, he'd rather make people laugh. 'The arcade's not elitist, and it's so much more satisfying; the feedback is seeing people enjoying themselves. I make enough money to live, and it's tremendous fun.' At the far end of the arcade, wild shrieks and bangs are coming from the Expressive Photobooth. A slightly dishevelled, flushed-cheeked 60-something lady emerges, smoothing down her hair, blowing her nose and hooting with laughter as she rejoins her friends. 'Now that's an experience,' she says.

**Under the Pier** *Southwold Pier, North Parade, Southwold, Suffolk IP18 6BN (www.underthepier.com).*

# TEST YOUR NERVE

**Time Out** 1000 Things to do in Britain

# 912
## Make a poetic pilgrimage to Stoke Poges churchyard

It was in the Buckinghamshire village of Stoke Poges in 1750 that Thomas Gray composed the 'Elegy Written in a Country Churchyard', one of the most famous pieces of verse in the English language. If you want to make a pilgrimage to the site of the poem's composition, you'll need to head a couple of miles south of Stoke Poges itself to the Church of St Giles. In Gray's Field, next to the church, is a monument to the poet erected in the 19th century. An inscription on the church wall will help you locate the exact spot on which the 'Elegy' was written.
**Monument to Thomas Gray** *Church Lane, Stoke Poges, Buckinghamshire SL2 4NZ.*

# 913
## Take a tennis holiday

If your backhand is in need of attention (and whose isn't?) but you're keen to impress on the courts, then it might be worth taking a tennis holiday and honing your strokes with a qualified coach. Jonathan Markson commands a small army of them, whom he gathers together once a year for the Oxford Tennis Camp. Participants are given 30 hours coaching over six days, and are put up in university accommodation.

If that sounds a bit too monastic, a more luxurious getaway is the Windmill Hill Tennis and Golf Academy in Sussex, where guests stay in a Grade II-listed Georgian mansion. The coaching is just as intense, though, and includes video analysis and competitive matchplay.

Still more luxurious is Chewton Glen, a sumptuous country hotel and spa with top-of-the-range hard courts and a tennis professional who offers personalised coaching.
**Chewton Glen** *New Milton, Hampshire BH25 6QS (01425 275341/www.chewtonglen.com).*
**Jonathan Markson Oxford Tennis Camp** *(020 7603 2422/www.marksontennis.com).*
**Windmill Hill Tennis & Golf Academy** *Windmill Hill, East Sussex BN27 4RZ (0870 033 9997/ www.windmillhill.co.uk).*

# 914
## *Brave the waves in Tenby*

Each Boxing Day, a fearless bunch of bathers assemble at Tenby's North Beach on Wales's Pembrokeshire coast, and sprint into the waves (www.tenbyboxingdayswim.co.uk). Their only protection from the elements is a fancy dress costume (the theme changes from year to year), and the warm glow of knowing that they're raising funds for charity. There's no shortage of game volunteers: in 2007 over 500 shivering swimmers took the plunge, watched by crowds of sensibly clad spectators.

# 915
## Pay your respects at the Geddington Cross

When Eleanor of Castile died in 1290, her husband, King Edward I, was devastated. He ordered the construction of 12 magnificent monuments, marking each place that her body rested as it was carried from Nottinghamshire, where she died, to Westminster Abbey; the penultimate stopping-place was London's Charing Cross. Today, just three of the crosses survive: the best-preserved is the intricately carved, soaring hexagonal pillar in the village of Geddington, Northamptonshire.

# 916
## Search out Seldom Seen Farm

Aside from having one of the best names we've ever come across, this Leicestershire farm raises superlative-quality free-range geese. Fed on grass and own-grown corn, they're available from October to Christmas. The farm is also famed for its three-bird roast – a goose stuffed with a chicken, itself stuffed with a pheasant, layered with spiced pork and orange stuffing. The shop also sells fruit, chutneys, pickles, jams and cakes, and there's pick-your-own strawberries and raspberries.
**Seldom Seen Farm** *Billesdon, Leicestershire LE7 9FA (0116 259 6742/www.seldomseen farm.co.uk).*

# 917 Visit Bardsey Island

In the Middle Ages, the abbey on Bardsey Island was a magnet for pilgrims. Today, the abbey is in ruins and the visitors to this tiny island off the Llyn Peninsula in North Wales are more likely to be in search of peace and quiet than spiritual sustenance. That and the wildlife, which is abundant: Bardsey is a great spot for spotting seals, dolphins and porpoises. The trust that looks after the island (0845 811 2233, www.bardsey.org) rents out a handful of charmingly rustic cottages to visitors. Be warned: they don't have running water or electricity.

# 918 Be transported back to Dickensian times

Charles Dickens was particularly fond of the seaside resort of Broadstairs, which he declared 'one of the fresh and free-est little places in the world'. Since 1937 the town has held an annual knees-up devoted to the writer (www.broadstairsdickensfestival.co.uk), which sees the resort overrun with cheery enthusiasts, limbering up for the Victorian cricket match, attending an adaptation of one of the great man's novels at the Dickens House Museum (01843 861232, www.dickenshouse.co.uk) or simply strolling around town in full Victorian regalia. It can all come as rather a shock for uninitiated visitors, as crinoline-clad ladies rustle by, passing gentlemen politely doff their top hats, and stripey-suited bathers picnic on the sands.

# 919 Get a bird's-eye view of Britain

Find inspiration for an airborne adventure on the British Hang Gliding and Paragliding Association's website (www.bhpa.co.uk). Reaching 'Club Pilot' level generally requires nine to ten days' flying, plus an exam, but shorter taster courses are also on offer – though be warned: once you've experienced the thrill of being lifted by invisible air currents and drifting across a cloud-dotted sky, there's no going back.

# 920 Work the festival circuit with Oxfam

To guarantee you get into the biggest music festivals of the summer, while at the same time doing your bit for the future of mankind, become a festival volunteer for Oxfam (www.oxfam.org.uk/glastonbury). The charity sends teams to almost all the major festivals, including Glastonbury, Leeds and the Isle of Wight, pitching its marquee and serving fair trade coffee to weary festival goers. The volunteers' role is to chat to punters, and raise awareness of Oxfam's various campaigns.

Volunteers pay a refundable deposit of £155 and work a four-hour shift each day – leaving ample time to induge in the more familiar forms of festival behaviour. Oxfam also provides festival stewards at Glastonbury, in return for donations from the organisers; you work three eight-hour shifts over the festival's duration, and get to camp in a special fenced-off area – with its own all-important toilets and showers.

Competition for volunteering slots is fierce, with selection based on applicants' commitment to the cause. If you don't bag a place, consider applying to be a 'Green Volunteer' at Reading or Leeds, and promote the charity's iCount campaign against climate chaos.

# 921-926 Sample proper cider

Thanks to some clever marketing, growth in cider sales in Britain has been dramatic, up over 30 per cent between 2006 and 2007. Sadly, the market is dominated by fizzy keg cider. For the real thing (fermented, unpasteurised apple juice) you need to look further afield. Below is a list of places where you can buy direct from the producer; for a more comprehensive list, see the *Good Cider Guide* (Campaign for Real Ale, 2005, £10.99).

### Brain's Cider
*The Orchards, Edge Hills, Littledean, Gloucestershire GL14 3LQ (01594 822416/ 07887 678209).*
For over a century, Dave Brain's family has made cider and perry at this beautiful hilltop site by the Forest of Dean. Visits are by appointment only, so phone to arrange a sampling session in the venerable cider shed. Outside, sheep graze in the orchard, beneath Foxwhelps, Michelins and Yarlington Mills ripening on the branches.

### Burrow Hill Cider
*Pass Vale Farm, Burrow Hill, Kingsbury Episcopi, Martock, Somerset TA12 6BU (01460 240782/www.ciderbrandy.co.uk).*
Julian Temperley is a leading light among England's cider-makers, reviving the tradition of distilling cider to make cider brandy (the English version of Calvados). He also sells first-rate 'bottle conditioned' cider that's as fizzy as champagne, and cider straight from oak barrels. A visit here includes an orchard trail, where you can view Kingston Blacks and Brown Snouts awaiting the harvest. Call before visiting.

### Gwatkin Cider Co Ltd
*Moorhampton Farm, Abbey Dore, Herefordshire HR2 0AL (01981 550258).*
Denis Gwatkin formed his cider company in the early 1990s, and has since won several awards from the Campaign for Real Ale. He concentrates on producing single varietal ciders and perries, sold ready-bottled or draught in his farm shop. The shop also has stocks of lamb and beef (reared on the farm), wine and real ales. Gwatkin's drinks include Blakeney Red perry (named after a village in Gloucestershire) and ciders from Kingston Black and Yarlington Mill apples.

### Hartlands Cider & Perry
*Tirley Villa, Tirley, Gloucestershire GL19 4HA (01452 780480).*
Much of Dereck Hartland's farm, just off the B4213, is given over to the grazing of sheep, but next to the farmhouse is his beloved cider shed. In the yard, a large wooden-beamed cider press has pride of place, while inside a row of old oak barrels are filled with cider or perry. Bring your own bottles and you can buy a gallon for less than £6. Cider comes in dry, medium or sweet varieties, while the perry (still and dry) contains pears from the Moorcroft, Blakeney Red and Longhope trees. Dereck is happy to chew the cud as he pours you a glass full of his latest vintage.

### Haye Farm Cider
*Haye Farm, St Veep, Lerryn, Lostwithiel, Cornwall PL22 0PB (01208 872250).*
Renowned locally, the cider from Haye Farm is the genuine article: made entirely from the farm's apples (including many Cornish varieties), with nothing added. It can be bought in one- to five-litre containers. Trying before you buy is encouraged, making a trip to this out-of-the-way spot (find Lerryn, then take the St Veep road) well worth the effort.

### Perry's Cider
*Cider Mills, Dowlish Wake, Ilminster, Somerset TA19 0NY (01460 55195/www.perryscider.co.uk).*
Despite the name, this old family firm (run by the Perry family since 1923) sells only ciders – but the choice is wide. The visitors' centre includes a shop where cider can be bought from the barrel or ready bottled, and there's also a free-to-enter museum. Here you'll find collections of old cider-making and farming equipment, as well as the firm's two hydraulic presses, still used to make cider every autumn.

## 927 See the Bognor Birdman take flight

Each summer, men and their magnificent flying machines compete for a £25,000 prize by hurling themselves off a platform on Bognor pier; the furthest 'flight' over 100 metres wins the cash (www.birdman.org.uk). Many contestants take part as sponsored charity fundraisers, building elegant gliders and training all year round. Others knock up *Wacky Races*-style contraptions or make the leap dressed as Batman, flapping a bunch of balloons. Being Bognor, there's also plenty of beach-based revelry, with funfair rides and children's entertainment, plus anything from limbo-dancing under fiery poles to judo demonstrations taking place over the weekend.

## 928 Find out if the end is nigh at Knighton

Knighton's Spaceguard Centre was set up to keep a vigilant eye out for Near Earth Objects (NEOs) hurtling towards the earth. Despite – or perhaps because of – its warnings of death and destruction ('the impact of an asteroid or comet is now widely recognised as one of the most significant risks to human civilisation'), it has proved a hit with schoolchildren. Tours take visitors round the telescopes, planetarium and camera obscura; call for details of times.
**Spaceguard Centre** *Llanshay Lane, Knighton, Powys LD7 1LW (01547 520247/www.space guarduk.com).*

## 929 Take a working holiday with the National Trust

More than 100,000 people have taken a National Trust Working Holiday since the scheme began back in 1967 (0870 429 2429, www.national trust.org.uk). There are 450 options in over 100 locations throughout Britain, with projects including everything from planting trees and dry-stone walling to painting a lighthouse and stewarding at open-air concerts. Participants wax lyrical about learning new skills, making new friends, and the sense of satisfaction in helping to conserve Britain's heritage and countryside – they're clearly not exaggerating, as many of the holidays are full by February each year. You pay a fee for meals and basic accommodation and the NT throws in a year's free entry to its properties. Projects can last for up to ten days, but weekends start from £40; there are schemes for 16-18s and over-18s.

## 930 Stand atop Britain's highest mountain

Mostly, Ben Nevis has gale-force winds – not to mention rain and snow. Visibility is often so poor that you're lucky to see more than a few metres in front of your nose at the summit plateau, which tops out at 4,409 feet. Most visitors go up via the path known as the 'tourist route' – an unremittingly long slog from Glen Nevis, behind the small Lochaber town of Fort William. (The alternative route via the Carn Mor Dearg arête is for experienced climbers only).

But if you're lucky and time it right, on a clear day you can see everything from the Cairngorms to Ben Lawers in Perthshire, Ben Lomond down south, the peaks of Jura, Skye, Mull, and much, much more. For further details, plus vital safety information, visit www.visit-fortwilliam.co.uk.

## 931 Pitch your tent at Three Cliffs Bay

This clifftop campsite is justly famed for its magnificent views over sandy Three Cliffs Bay. The pitches on the field by the cliff's edge are somewhat sloping – but with views like that, who's complaining? (Plus there's a flatter back field for more cautious campers.) The beach is a short but slippery scramble down the cliff path; once you've made it safely down, you're rewarded by a picture-perfect, unspoilt stretch of sand: happily, limited car parking keeps the holidaymaking hordes away.
**Three Cliffs Bay** *Penmaen, Swansea SA3 2HB (01792 371218/www.threecliffsbay.com).*

## 932 Visit an open garden

A brilliantly simple idea, the National Garden Scheme (01483 211535, www.ngs.org.uk) sees privately owned and rarely seen gardens across the UK open their gates to the public for a few days (or possibly weeks) each year. Around 3,500 gardens are now listed in the *Yellow Book* – from urban affairs involving 'green roofs', terraces and hidden walled gardens to sprawling rural idylls. If you're inspired to open your own patch up to the nation, visit the website to download an information pack; a team of local volunteers will then come to look round, and assess whether it's worthy of inclusion. The book is updated with new locations annually; you can also search for gardens to visit online.

## 933 Swim with seals in Herne Bay

Operating out of Herne Bay in Kent, the *Wildlife* is a superb old-school passenger yacht that's now devoted to bird- and seal-watching forays (01227 366712, www.wildlifesailing.com). It's a two-hour trip to the seals' sandbanks, then a dingy trip ashore: when conditions are right, you can swim in the shallow water with the chummy, chubby pinnipeds.

## 934-938 Eat your greens

If you're still harbouring the notion that vegetarian food comprises joyless nut cutlets and limp salads, it's time to get out there and taste the reality. Dinner at Bristol's Café Maitreya (89 St Mark's Road, Easton, Bristol BS5 6HY, 0117 951 0100, www.cafemaitreya.co.uk) is a splendid way to start your voyage of discovery. The seasonal menu changes constantly, but might include such delights as rhubarb and sweet potato gratinée with griddled jerusalem artichoke, or a rich red onion, cider and saffron broth with halloumi croutons.

Inventive cooking in relaxed surrounds is also the hallmark at Brighton's Terre à Terre (71 East Street, Brighton, East Sussex BN1 1HQ, 01273 729051, www.terreaterre.co.uk), where the globally inspired menu encompasses everything from blue cheese soufflé with watercress cream to fragrant aubergine jungle curry.

Opened in 1989, London's the Gate (51 Queen Caroline Street, London W6 9QL, 020 8748 6932, www.thegate.tv) is another accomplished old-timer. Set in an airy, stripped-down attic above a pretty courtyard, its menu is a delight. Dishes are simple and fresh (leek and trompette tart, parsnip risotto with dolcelatte and parmesan), letting the tastes and textures shine through.

Further north, the Waiting Room (9 Station Road, Eaglescliffe, Stockton-on-Tees, Cleveland TS16 OBU, 01642 780465, www.the-waiting-room.co.uk) serves up wholesome, generously portioned fare: think puy lentil shepherd's pie, or baked mushroom rarebit. On Sundays, the chaotic camaraderie of the Waiting for Sunday music sessions keeps the back room jumping.

Any whistlestop tour of Britain's best veggie eateries should also include David Bann (56-58 St Mary's Street, Edinburgh EH1 1SX (0131 556 5888, www.davidbann.com). Book a table in the elegant, understated dining room and take your pick from a delightfully varied menu: aromatic spiced tofu fritters or butternut squash ravioli with home-made curd cheese to start, perhaps, followed by pancake-wrapped dosa with banana chutney or a creamy mushroom and tarragon crêpe with beetroot and radish salad. And that's just a taster of what's out there.

# 939
## Explore ingenious Cragside

Victorian industrialist Sir William George Armstrong wasn't a man to do things by halves – so when he decided to build a new pad in Northumberland, he wanted something spectacular. The result was the 170-room Cragside, dubbed 'the palace of a modern magician'. Packed with ingenious gadgets and newfangled technology, it was the first house in the world to be lit by electricity, using hydro-electric power. The Shah of Persia and the King of Siam both came to behold its marvels – though the crowning glory was a visit from the Prince and Princess of Wales (history, alas, doesn't record whether the royal pair braved a dip in the Turkish baths, or were impressed by the kitchen's water-powered rotating spit). Once you've admired the mansion, check out the sprawling rock garden (Britain's largest) and soaring Douglas Fir (England's tallest). Those Victorians knew how to show off in style.

**Cragside** *Rothbury, Morpeth, Northumberland NE65 7PX (01669 620333/www.nationaltrust.org.uk).*

# 940
## Take a pew in St Margaret's

In the complex of Edinburgh Castle stands St Margaret's Chapel, built in the early 12th century by Scotland's King David I in memory of his English mother, Queen Margaret (later canonised for her good works). Still in excellent nick for something approximately 900 years old, the small Norman-style structure is the oldest building still in use in the city. Most visitors are tourists who have come to see the ever-popular castle in its entirety, but the chapel still hosts the odd wedding – although you can't fit many guests inside (there's room for just 25 people). Simple and affecting, it's quite a contrast to the more swashbuckling attractions to be found elsewhere at the castle complex, built on a rock that has been home to some sort of fortification since the Bronze Age.

**St Margaret's Chapel** *Edinburgh Castle, Edinburgh EH1 2NG (0131 225 9846/ www.historic-scotland.gov.uk).*

# 941
## See Maggi Hambling's scallop at Aldeburgh

The Suffolk seaside town of Aldeburgh has become synonymous with Benjamin Britten and his creative and personal partner Peter Pears, who lived here for decades. The house in which Britten wrote many of his best-loved works is now open to the public (www.brittenpears.org), but perhaps a better way to capture the essence of Britten's relationship with Aldeburgh is by listening to his opera *Peter Grimes*. Britten wrote the work as a tribute to 'the perpetual struggle of men and women whose livelihood depends on the sea'. A line from the opera, 'I hear those voices that will not be drowned', is pierced around the edge of Maggi Hambling's memorial to Britten, a stark, 13-foot high steel scallop on Aldeburgh Beach. Stop for a moment in quiet contemplation – and try to decide whether the controversial sculpture is an eyesore on the shingle beach, or a fitting tribute to the great composer.

# 942

### Plant a tree
Go green and become a member of the Woodland Trust (www.woodland-trust.org.uk), an organisation that campaigns to conserve and restore native woodlands. For a tenner you can buy a personal tree dedication (choose from 20 Trust-owned woods throughout the UK), or for £90 think big and sponsor a numbered plot in a Woodland Creation site. Either would make a great green gift, but with the latter your recipients can visit and picnic among 'their' trees.

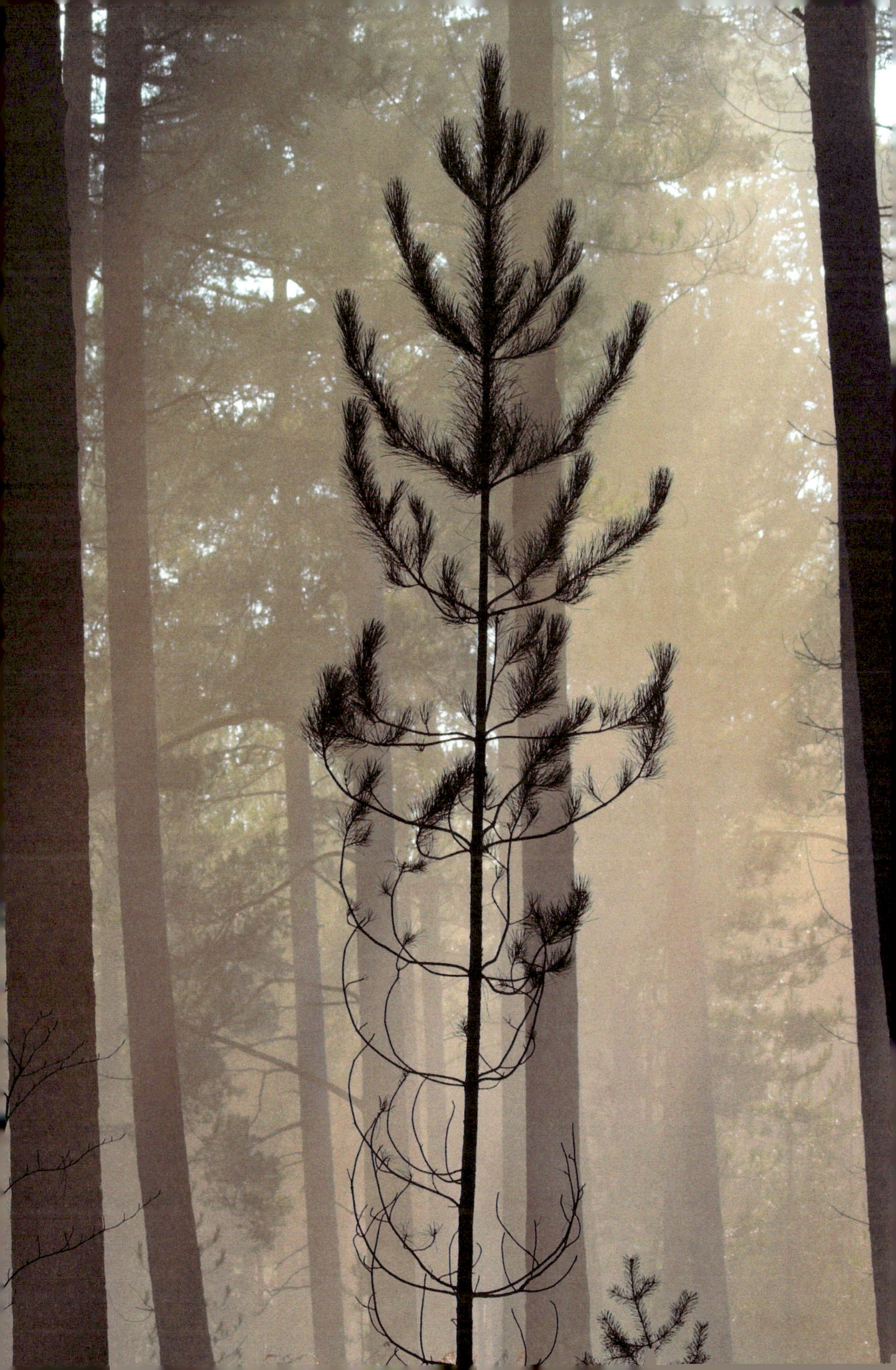

# 943
## Remember the war poets at Craiglockhart

Famously the meeting place of World War I poets Siegfried Sassoon and Wilfred Owen, as described in Pat Barker's novel *Regeneration*, Craiglockhart was a military psychiatric hospital for the treatment of shell-shocked officers from 1916 to 1919. The hospital's enlightened regime – the responsibility of Dr William Rivers and his colleague Dr Arthur Brock – eschewed electric shock treatment, or an approach that viewed patients as either mad or cowardly. Instead the doctors used talking therapies, encouraging the officers to open up about their horrific experiences on the front. Brock also persuaded Owen to edit the hospital magazine, *The Hydra*, to which Sassoon contributed. Now part of Napier University, Craiglockhart is home to the War Poets Collection, with first editions, letters, photographs and memorabilia, plus copies of *The Hydra*.
**War Poets Collection** *Craighouse Library, Napier University, Edinburgh EH10 5LG (0131 455 6021/ www2.napier.ac.uk/warpoets).*

# 944
## Ponder the wall paintings at Stoke Dry church

The attractive oddities of St Andrew's in Stoke Dry are disproportionate to both its size and the tiny Rutland village in which it stands. Most striking of all are the arrow-wielding warriors pictured in the *Martyrdom of St Edmund* wall painting – quite clearly Native Americans, even if, inexplicably, the 14th-century work predates the supposed 'discovery' of America. Then there's the cartoonish Norman art on the chancel columns, including a group of yobs yanking an angel down from heaven. Above the porch is a tiny parvis, allegedly where Everard Digby hatched the Gunpowder Plot – and where, long ago, a vicar is said to have starved a suspected witch to death. Eyebrook Reservoir, overlooked by the church, was used to practise the 'Dambusters' raid.
**St Andrew's Church** *Main Street, Stoke Dry, Rutland LE15 9JG (01572 822717).*

# 945
## Camp out on the Thames in a skiff

The idea of navigating the Thames in an antiquated, round-bottomed rowing boat might sound alarming at first, but bear with us: it's the *upper* stretches of the Thames, where tranquillity reigns and the route is lined with idyllic waterside boozers. The boats in question are also things of beauty: a fleet of seven 100-year-old skiffs, stars of the annual Swan Upping swan census held on the river (not to mention *Shakespeare in Love* and *Harry Potter and the Goblet of Fire*). Everything you could possibly need is on board – sculls (oars), mooring spikes, a stove and cooking equipment, crockery, sleeping and rowing mats and, best of all, a wet-weather cover that enables your boat to double up as a three-berth tent. All in all, it's a Jerome K Jerome fan's dream come true.
**Thames Skiff Hire** *64 Carlton Road, Walton-on-Thames, Surrey KT12 2DG (01932 232433/ www.skiffhire.com).*

# 946
## Have a pint in Britain's smallest pub

There clearly wasn't room to swing a cat in the tiny Nutshell pub – there's one hanging from the ceiling. This timber-framed former pawnbrokers on the medieval thoroughfare of the Traverse in Bury St Edmunds measures just 15 by seven feet, enough for an average nightly clientele of 20. 'We also get a few tourists in summer,' says landlord Jack Burton. 'They pick up on us from the *Guinness Book of Records*.' Although the Nutshell doesn't do food – there's not the elbow room – it can offer a fine pint of Greene King, brewed in town. And the cat? 'It was bricked up by builders hundreds of years ago,' says Jack. The pub's other curiosities include a human leg and an eel trap – so mind your step.
**Nutshell** *17 The Traverse, Bury St Edmunds, Suffolk IP33 1BJ (01284 764867).*

## 947 Learn about the British Empire...

Find out about Britain's 500-year imperial past at this modern museum, housed in Isambard Kingdom Brunel's imposing Temple Meads station. Interactive exhibits, films and photos guide you through the history of the British Empire, from the early days of private trading empires like the East India Company, through muscular Victorian imperialism, to how and why it all came crashing down. Children can learn Morse code and dress up in period clothes; they can also sample exotic spices – which may or may not go down so well.
**British Empire & Commonwealth Museum**
*Clock Tower Yard, Temple Meads, Bristol BS1 6QH (0117 925 4980/www.empiremuseum.co.uk).*

## 948 ...then download the Slave Trade Tour

Continue your discovery of Bristol's slave trade connections on foot by downloading a special walking tour of the city to your MP3 player (http://visitbristol.co.uk). Starting at College Green and finishing up at the harbourside Ostrich pub, the route guides you around six key historic sites. Among them is 7 Great George Street; now a museum, it was once home to John Pinney, who amassed a vast fortune from his Caribbean sugar plantations and was one of Bristol's foremost slave trade advocates. In contrast is the stop on Broad Street, where the medieval Guild Hall once stood. It was here, in 1788, that the first open meeting calling for the trade's abolition took place.

## 949 Peek inside Queen Mary's doll's house

As befits a doll's house made for a queen, this is a truly palatial residence. The house itself was designed by the most eminent architect of the day, Sir Edwin Lutyens, who decided it should become a showcase for British craftsmanship. Miniature working lifts were installed, along with hot and cold running water and flushing toilets in the five bathrooms; even the tiny gramaphone could be played. The detail is astonishing – from the tiny tin of Colman's Mustard in the pantry to the diminutive silver cutlery, made by Garrard; in the walnut-clad library, the books were commissioned from the likes of Thomas Hardy and Rudyard Kipling. It's a superb small-scale vignette of a 1920s household – albeit an exceedingly rich one.
**Windsor Castle** *Windsor, Berkshire SL4 1NJ (020 7766 7304/www.royal.gov.uk).*

# 950
## Discover Moore

Moore's instantly recognisable abstract bronzes grace sculpture parks, public areas and museums around the world. At Perry Green in Hertfordshire you can see the largest of his works, including the 29-foot-long *Large Reclining Figure*. Guided tours of the gardens, studio and galleries run during the week; at weekends, visitors are allowed to wander around unaccompanied. If you book ahead, you can also take a tour of Hoglands, the 16th-century farmhouse Moore and his wife Irina inhabited for over 40 years; its rooms are dotted with their personal effects, with the ground floor carefully recreated as it was in the 1970s. Note that the entire site is only open from April to late October, and admission is strictly by appointment only.
**Henry Moore Foundation** *Dane Tree House, Perry Green, Much Hadham, Hertfordshire SG10 6EE (01279 843333/www.henry-moore-fdn.co.uk).*

# 951
## Cross the ley lines at Glastonbury

Whether you believe in ley lines – defined by the *Oxford English Dictionary* as 'supposed straight lines connecting three or more prehistoric or ancient sites, sometimes regarded as the line of a former track, and associated by some with lines of energy and other paranormal phenomena' – or not, Glastonbury is the ley line equivalent of Clapham Junction, as well as the honorary spiritual capital of Somerset. You can pick up a map of the ley lines radiating from the ancient Isle of Avalon from one of the town's numerous new age shops; alternatively, follow the spiral 'maze' (probably medieval farming terraces) to the top of Glastonbury tor, yet another reputed birthplace of King Arthur, and look for points on the ley line that runs through the heart of the hill; to the south-east you may be able to pick out Cadbury camp, site of the mythical Camelot.
**Glastonbury Tourist Information Centre** *9 High Street, Glastonbury, Somerset BA6 9DP (01458 832954/www.glastonburytic.co.uk).*

# 952-954
## Attend a folk festival

The British folk revival of the 1950s and '60s has left a lasting and substantial legacy: folk festivals are now as much a fixture on the summer circuit as rock-oriented behemoths like Glastonbury and Reading. Two of the most alluring are the long-established Sidmouth (01395 578627, www.sidmouthfolkweek.co.uk) and Broadstairs Folk Weeks (01843 604080, www.broadstairsfolkweek.org.uk), both taking place in August in genteelly charming seaside surrounds. At both festivals the emphasis is on traditional folk styles – so expect lots of fiddles and reels.

Contemporary folk music isn't all cable-knit sweaters and real ale, however. Today, the term covers a dizzying range of musical styles – a diversity that is reflected each year in the bill at the mighty Cambridge Folk Festival (www.cambridgefolkfestival.co.uk). In 2007, the line-up included artists as diverse as Joan Baez and Toots & the Maytals, Nanci Griffith and the Ukelele Orchestra of Great Britain, who closed their set with a rousing rendition of the Sex Pistols' 'Anarchy in the UK'.

# 955
## Freecycle your junk

Freecycle is about giving and receiving – and saving several tonnes of unwanted goods from landfill sites. Sign up at www.freecycle.org with your local group (there are now around 300 in the UK), then post up details of any bits and pieces you no longer want or need (anything goes, from books and toys to three-piece suites, fridges, pianos and digeridoos). Once you've successfully donated something to someone else (the onus is on the receiver to come and pick up the item from you), you can start reaping the rewards of a whole new world of free second-hand goodies yourself. Ebay is so early naughties.

# 956-957
## Ride the Wheels

When you're booking your ticket for the London Eye (0870 990 8883, www.londoneye.com), it's easy to snigger at the conceit of calling a single rotation a 'flight'. But 30 minutes later, having glided seemingly effortlessly 443 feet into the air, it all makes perfect sense, with views that stretch some 25 miles across London and down the Thames to the sea.

Meanwhile, the former Manchester Wheel has now relocated to the National Railway Museum in York, and become the Yorkshire Wheel (0844 8153139, www.nrm.org.uk). It offers a pigeon's-eye view of the centre of York, the River Ouse and York Minster from 177 feet up – the same height as the great Gothic cathedral. Best of all, though, is the plush VIP gondola, with its walnut interior, leather seats, cocktail cabinet and telephone. Now that's what we call high class.

# 958
## See podium prodigies

Besides having splendidly wild and windswept landscapes, Orkney is also a somewhat surprising hub for top classical music talent. Peter Maxwell-Davies, the eccentric Master of the Queen's Music, hails from the area and is responsible for founding the St Magnus Festival, Orkney's annual arts shindig (01856 871445, www.stmagnusfestival.com). Despite its remote location, the festival has attracted an impressive selection of A-list classical musicians in past years, including Vladimir Ashkenazy, André Previn, Evelyn Glennie, Joanna MacGregor and Steven Isserlis. It also runs the concurrent Orkney Conducting Course, an intensive ten-day boot camp for young conductors. The participants hail from around the world and represent some of the best young conducting talent, so it's a great chance to watch some exceptional musicians wielding their batons.

# 959
## Cross the Atlantic in Bath

Since 1961, Bath's stately Georgian Claverton Manor has been occupied territory. Set up by two collectors, one American, the other English, the invading forces at the American Museum in Britain are strictly cultural and artistic, allowing visitors to step into 15 period rooms, apparently belonging to New Orleans madames, Protestant Shakers and other decorative-minded settlers. The only museum dedicated to Americana outside the States, other highlights include some joyously garish quilts and innocent folk art, as well as an American Heritage Exhibition, with touchscreen exhibits on slavery and Native American culture. Outside, there are American trees in the arboretum, American 'erbs in the Colonial Herb Garden and a re-creation of George Washington's garden at Mount Vernon.
**American Museum in Britain** *Claverton Manor, Bath BA2 7BD (01225 460503/www.american museum.org).*

# 960 Laugh your socks off at Britain's finest comedy clubs

# Joking aside...

*...deciding where to see the best stand-up is a serious business. Malcolm Hay consults Britain's top comedians.*

Live comedy can flourish almost anywhere. It's gone on in the strangest of settings: shops, launderettes, public toilets, in a ramshackle auditorium constructed on the sidecar of a motorbike – even among valuable exhibits on display at the Museum of London. Successful comedy shows spring from a subtle and elusive compound of the comedian's performance, the atmosphere of the place where it happens, and an audience's reactions – and the venue plays a crucial part in creating an exciting gig.

It's no surprise, then, that comics tend to develop an attachment to particular locations. Sometimes (predictably) they're the scenes of past triumphs. For Jack Dee, that's London's Comedy Store (0844 847 1728, www.thecomedystore.co.uk). 'It's where I first stepped on stage to do stand-up over 20 years ago, and it's still my first choice of club to drop into to try out new material,' he says. 'I never walk down those steps without feeling a mixture of trepidation and excitement.' Satirical stand-up Andy Parsons is also partial to performing at the Store. 'It's 400 seats, which is big by comedy club standards, but it feels incredibly intimate from the stage. It's usually always open seven nights a week, with a range of different shows.' Above all, he says, the Store attracts a knowledgeable audience. 'It's not all hen nights only interested in dancing to "It's raining men, hallelujah".'

The Comedy Store is rare in being a dedicated space for stand-up; shows often take place in pubs and bars. A few hundred yards from the Comedy Store, for instance, the thriving Comedy Camp (020 7734 3342, www.comedycamp.co.uk) is held every Tuesday night in the basement of Bar Code, a straight-friendly gay Soho watering hole. London-based Australian stand-up Sarah Kendall is a big fan of the venue, largely thanks to the audiences it attracts. 'They're smart, they've got loads of energy, and they're there to have a good time. They give a performer enough support to take some risks.

I think that's why a lot of big name acts often do unannounced gigs there.'

Elsewhere in central London, the half-dozen-strong group of 99 Clubs (www.the99club.co.uk), set up over the past couple of years by comedian Jim Woroniecki, gains strong support from Anglo-Iranian stand-up Shappi Khorsandi. 'If you haven't been to live comedy before, the intimacy of these clubs will excite you as much as the cheap-as-chips entrance fee. The aim isn't to make a great profit; they're intended to keep alive the glorious tradition of stand-up in its most raw, spit-and-sawdust form.'

In the London suburbs it's often the oldest clubs, run by experienced promoters, that find most favour with comics. In Crouch End, Peter Grahame's Downstairs at the King's Head (020 8340 1028, www.downstairsatthekingshead.com) has been in business for almost as long as the Comedy Store. Award-winning stand-up Zoe Lyons sums up its appeal: 'Low ceilings, chairs packed in, a sound booth that doubles up as a cramped green room, a couple of dodgy-looking lights pointed at a flat stage – the space screams comedy! Now that the smoking ban has come in, there's the additional advantage of being able to breathe in there.' Lee Mack also approves of the claustrophobic surrounds. 'A low ceiling is always good for comedy because the sound of the laughs bounces off it,' he argues. 'It's so low at the King's Head, I've seen a bloke doing his act with his head tilted to one side.'

Veteran comic and compere Arthur Smith prefers the long-established Banana Cabaret at the Bedford in Balham (020 8682 8940, www.bananacabaret.co.uk), close to where he lives. 'With its circular auditorium and a gallery above, it's unusual for a pub venue. I can remember when there'd be a line of prostitutes standing on Bedford Hill. They're long gone – it's a lot more salubrious now.'

Smith (together with a large bunch of leading comics) also has a huge affection for east London's refurbished Hackney Empire (020 8985 2424, www.hackneyempire.co.uk), built in 1901 as a music hall. Charlie Chaplin, WC Fields, Marie Lloyd and Stan Laurel are among the great acts who've played there. 'It's seen troubled times,' Smith observes. 'For 23 years it was used as a bingo hall. Now it's closely associated with the new movement in comedy.' Jo Brand reckons 'the Empire has showbiz leaking out of its walls', while Russell Brand loves 'its history, its opulence, its splendour – that Frank Matcham geezer was clearly a very great genius'.

> **'The Glasgow Stand is bigger and more raucous than the Stand in Edinburgh. But if you don't like insult humour, what are you doing in Scotland?'**

Theatre architect Matcham (who died in 1920 from blood poisoning, bizarrely brought on by excessive trimming of his fingernails) left a legacy of 20 surviving buildings, which have made it to the present day more or less intact. Several appear on comedians' lists of ideal venues. Sean Hughes goes for the beautifully-restored Gaiety Theatre (01624 694555, www.villagaiety.com), located on the seafront in Douglas on the Isle of Man, while Julian Clary cites 'that gilded fairy palace' Buxton Opera House (0845 127 2190, www.buxtonoperahouse.org.uk), and Blackpool Grand Theatre (01253 290190, www.blackpoolgrand.co.uk). 'They were built to house Variety shows,' Clary explains. 'They have a very different feel from other theatres.'

Northern England provides another popular choice in the shape of the Leeds City Varieties (0845 644 1881), chosen by Hughes, Ed Byrne and Al Murray (the Pub Landlord). The Varieties started life as a music hall back in 1865, when it was known as Thornton's Fashionable Lounge. Byrne likes the place so much that he decided to record the DVD of his stand-up show there, while Murray thinks that being or performing there 'is like taking a trip back in time'. Hughes believes it's immeasurably superior to the 'drab council halls' that he sometimes plays on tour. 'Though I wish people wouldn't keep banging on about how the "Good Old Days" TV series was filmed there. That really was a crap programme.'

Razor-sharp stand-up and BBC Radio 4 comic Jo Caulfield is a big fan of the Comedy Zone in Worcester. 'On a small side street that looks like a perfect location for the latest BBC period drama is a small sign for the Marrs Bar (01905 613336). Behind this tasteful exterior is a fantastically vibrant and exciting music venue that, once a month for the last six years, has been running a comedy night. It's perfect for comedy; it has that grungy, intimate feel that all great comedy rooms must aim for. The audience here is so enthusiastic that comedians don't want to leave the stage. You feel slightly like you've joined a cult, but it's a cult of drinking and laughter, so I'm happy to sign up.'

In Scotland, the famous Stand Comedy Clubs (www.thestand.co.uk) in Glasgow and Edinburgh also get Caulfield's vote. 'They both have a brilliant atmosphere. The Glasgow club is bigger and more raucous – but if you don't like insult humour, what are you doing in Scotland?' Meanwhile, super-energetic young stand-up Russell Kane (recently nominated for an If.comedy Best Newcomer Award) sings the praises of 'the smallest purpose-built club in the whole of Europe': the Mull Theatre (01688 302673, www.mulltheatre.com) in Tobermory on the Isle of Mull (head north-west from Glasgow to Oban and take the ferry). 'It's a tiny cube of an edifice,' he rhapsodises. 'A tiny bar with about five cans of Coke and four beers. A tiny ticket office with an old lady squeezed inside. A tiny stage. Forty seats. Brilliant. Tiny, weird and brilliant.'

If.comedy Award winner for 2007 Brendon Burns plumps for Wales, making Cardiff's Glee Club (www.glee.co.uk) his first choice; 'Splendidly run. The Glee Club in Birmingham is good too.' Rhod Gilbert, himself a Welshman, draws on specialist local knowledge to put the principality's Popty Ping Comedy Night at Café Europa (029 2066 7776) in his top spot. 'The Europa is one of the UK's best-kept comedy secrets. It's all farmhouse kitchen tables, battered old couches and shelves stacked high with books. "Popty Ping" is Welsh for "microwave". Not many people know that. Seriously, it means "oven ping". Not many people know that either.'

Wales is home to another popular choice, the Llangollen Fringe Festival (01978 860600, www.llangollenfringe.co.uk). 'For a couple of nights a year this small, picturesque town in North Wales turns its town hall into a comedy venue,' says Zoe Lyons. 'I've performed there twice, and both times the atmosphere has been fantastic. I think it's fair to say that for most of the year there's not a great deal going on in Llangollen, so the locals have really got behind the event, and it's a brilliant thing to be part of. People travel from all over North Wales and neighbouring England to attend the shows. The organisers are so passionate about the events, and work very hard to pack out the venue. Performers and punters alike delight in the community spirit.'

Seaside towns don't seem to be hugely popular as comedy venues (unless you're a fan of Roy 'Chubby' Brown), but Lyons sings the praises of Brighton's diminutive Marlborough Theatre (07782 278521, www.marlborough theatre.co.uk). 'Brighton is a town that practically crackles with creativity. Everywhere you look there's a kid with a guitar strapped to their back on their way to a jam session, or someone knocking up wind chimes out of recycled beer cans and a bicycle wheel, so it's no surprise that stand-up has taken off in a big way, with plenty of smaller venues now hosting comedy nights. The Marlborough is a super little venue: a tiny 50-seater theatre above a bar of the same name, with a proper stage and lighting. It has a music hall feel about it, and is a great place to catch preview shows from some of the circuit's hottest acts before they go to Edinburgh'. Lyons also praises the club's annual fringe festival (www.brightoncomedy

> '*Seaside towns don't seem to be hugely popular as comedy venues, but Brighton's Marlborough Theatre is a great place to catch hot preview shows before they go to Edinburgh.*'

fringe.co.uk), which runs alongside the main Brighton Comedy Festival in October. It offers the chance to see top comedians at bargain prices, with no ticket costing more than £6.

Last but not least, Jo Brand makes a case for college comedy gigs – 'always a bit anarchic' – and singles out Durham University (0191 334 2000), where she's enjoyed some spirited heckling in the past, for particular praise.

In the end, perhaps, there's no absolute logic to why certain places become hotbeds of great comedy, while others fall by the wayside. Take the Bearcat Club, held in the Turk's Head pub (020 8891 1852, www.bearcatcomedy.co.uk) out on the edge of London in Twickenham since 1984. 'It's run by two great gentlemen of comedy, James Punnett and Graham Limmer,' says one of its devotees, stand-up and actor Omid Djalili. 'There's a great atmosphere, together with a no-nonsense, sit-down-and-laugh policy.' Another Bearcat admirer, Sean Hughes, puts the case more bluntly. 'The stage is awful. The dressing room is an old kitchen that sometimes smells of chip fat. In terms of facilities, it's got nothing going for it. Yet there's something magical about the place. I always look forward to playing there.' He pauses, then laughs out loud. 'It's a mystery.'

# 961
## Admire George Bernard Shaw's revolving writing hut

Shaw's Corner in Hertfordshire was where the celebrated playwright lived from 1906 until his death in 1950; he wrote *Pygmalion* here, in a revolving hut at the bottom of the garden. Built on circular tracks that allowed the huts to swivel to follow the light, these were all the rage in the early 1900s (and long overdue a revival, in our book). Shaw's was kitted out with a heater and phone connection to the house, where his staff could turn away visitors by truthfully telling them, 'Mr Shaw is out.' Sadly, following a break-in, visitors are not currently permitted to enter the hut or see it take a turn. Shaw's typewriter was stolen by the thieves, although many of his other personal effects, including his Oscar and Nobel Prize, are on display in the main house. Phone for details of open-air performances of Shaw's plays in June and July. **Shaw's Corner** *Ayot St Lawrence, near Welwyn, Hertfordshire AL6 9BX (01438 820307/www.nationaltrust.org.uk).*

# 962
## Bring home the mackerel in Brighton

Fishing for mackerel may not be quite so prestigious an activity as casting your fly in search of wild salmon in Speyside, but there's a down-to-earth, democratic quality to it that makes it hugely appealing nonetheless. As long as you get lucky with the shoals, it's hard not to catch something on your line, with its multiple hooks and a lead weight on the end – you don't even need bait. Brighton is a particularly popular spot; Watertours (07958 246414, www.watertours.co.uk) is one of several operators in the Marina that will take groups of ten out for an hour or so for around £12 per person. You can bring your catch home, and bake it in foil with a slice of lemon for tea.

# 963
## Be inspired by the Big Draw

Each October, the Campaign for Drawing attempts to coax out the nation's latent artistic abilities with its ever-growing Big Draw event (www.campaignfordrawing.org). Special events encouraging everyone to get drawing run in galleries, museums, shopping centres and community centres across the land. It's not just paper and pencil creations, either: past works have involved leaves, sand and vapour trails.

# 964
## Picnic on Brownsea Island

Enid Blyton's love of Dorset led her to holiday in the county thrice yearly for two decades, and her *Famous Five* characters consequently got up to all sorts of adventures round these parts. In *Five Have a Mystery to Solve*, the action centres around spooky Whispering Island, home to a ruined castle. Locals reckon the island to be Brownsea; in Blyton's day, the reclusive Mrs Bonham-Christie owned it, banning visitors and living in splendid isolation while nature took over all around her. Brownsea remains a haven for wildlife: its woodland is one of the few places in the country where native red squirrels have survived. Adventure-seeking children still abound too; scout and guide pack holidays have taken place on the island ever since 1907, when Baden-Powell ran his first scout camp here.

Public access is limited on the island's Dorset Wildlife Trust-run northern portion but there are accessible beaches to the south. The ferry (01929 462583, www.brownseaislandferries.com) will drop you off on the south-eastern edge of the island, with Brownsea Castle on your left (closed to the public, alas). If, unlike the Five, you've forgotten to bring lashings of ginger beer and other picnic supplies, there's a handy National Trust-run café. The visitors' centre (01202 707744, www.nationaltrust.org.uk) runs events for children during the summer holidays, and if you fancy a spot of alfresco theatre, productions take place in a picturesque clearing (www.brownsea-theatre.co.uk).

## 965 Pray for snow in the Pennines

Unlikely as it sounds, Cumbria has its very own ski slope (01228 561634, www.thepriceofcheese.com): Yad Moss, seven miles south of Alston. It's volunteer-run, and facilities are simple but sufficient: a new lodge with loos and picnic tables, a 1,837-foot-long button tow lift and a piste groomer, which ensures that when the white stuff does fall, it's evenly spread over the hillside. At £14 a day for non-members, it's a terrific bargain when conditions are right: check the online snow report and webcam for the latest.

## 966 Drop by the Royal Opera House

Even if you're not attending a performance at the Royal Opera House, it's well worth dropping by its Covent Garden premises. Up until around 3.30pm, there's open access to the magnificent Paul Hamlyn Hall and the Amphitheatre Café Bar, with its terrace overlooking the piazza; on Mondays, there's a free lunchtime concert at 1pm. Excellent backstage tours (£9) run three times a day, sometimes peeking in on Royal Ballet dancers in classes or rehearsals.
**Royal Opera House** *Bow Street, London WC2E 9DD (020 7304 4000/www.royalopera.org).*

## 967 Seek out the Hidden Gardens of Glasgow

The derelict site of a former tram depot and boilerhouse in the Pollokshields area of Glasgow became a stunning new public garden in 2003, thanks to an inspired collaboration between landscape architects, artists and the local community. The garden is designed to reflect the area's ethnic diversity, with native and exotic trees planted next to each other to highlight their similarities. A central open area is dominated by a gingko tree, planted on top of three stones from the summit of Mount Sinai – significant in Islam, Christianity and Judaism. Art installations include a tranquil water feature and a series of sandstone markers inscribed with poems, adding to the garden's atmosphere of quiet contemplation. Check the website for details of up-and-coming events.
**Hidden Gardens** *Tramway, 25 Albert Drive, Glasgow G41 2PE (0141 433 2722/www.thehiddengardens.org.uk).*

# 968-977 Listen to evensong

One of the loveliest experiences in British cathedral cities is evensong when the choir is in residence. Perhaps the descending sun is shedding its rays through the great west window on to the altar in the east; or the day's heat is ebbing away, dissipated by the cool stone; or it is already dark and the congregation is huddling in overcoats while the choir sings some warming Tallis or a dissonant modern composer who will test the sight-reading skills of the singers. Daily evensong, usually at around 5.30pm, also has the added bonus (in some people's eyes) of being shorter than Sunday Eucharist or Mass.

Britain is the undisputed world leader in the production of cathedral, abbey and chapel choirs. There are over 50 currently in existence, typically consisting of 30 male singers; boys with unbroken voices on the top line, the men behind them. Most are attached to schools and many date back centuries, to a time when they doubled up as acting companies that supplied boys to play female parts.

The most famous choir is that of King's College Cambridge (01223 331100, www.kings.cam.ac.uk). They are busy all year round, but are ubiquitous at Christmas, with their CDs entertaining shoppers and the Christmas Eve carol service which, as well as *Once in Royal David's City*, also traditionally includes a fiendishly difficult new carol by a leading composer.

At Cambridge, however, some claim that St John's College Choir (01223 338600, www.joh.cam.ac.uk), singing in its more intimate chapel, is superior to King's. Others say that neither is as fine as that of Christ Church Cathedral Oxford (01865 276155, www.chch.ox.ac.uk), where voices are softened by the building's yellow Cotswold stone. Others believe that Wells Cathedral Choir (01749 674483, www.wellscathedral.org.uk) is the best, having developed into one of just a handful of specialist music schools in the country.

Rehearsing and sight-reading daily, the singers become skilled musicians and are often in demand at local music festivals. Indeed, such events may have sprung up around them as has happened at Worcester, Gloucester and Hereford with the annual Three Choirs Festival (01905 616200, www.3choirs.org).

For centuries, cathedral choirs were open only to men and boys. In 1991, however, Salisbury Cathedral (www.salisburycathedral.org.uk) introduced the first girls' choir, which operated separately from the boys', alternating services between them. No one was struck by a celestial thunderbolt, and other cathedrals followed suit.

St Paul's cathedral choir (020 7236 4128, www.stpauls.co.uk) has nearly 50 singers and dates from the 11th century (the oldest of the capital's choirs). In fact, 200 years ago, it sparked a revival that has led to the current golden age. A certain Miss Maria Hackett is famous in the annals of cathedral music for her pestering of the St Paul's choirmaster for an improvement in the slave-labour conditions endured by the choristers. Now the financial benefits of becoming a chorister are considerable, and can include free or reduced-price education as well as recording fees.

The only London choir to admit girls is tiny Southwark Cathedral (020 7367 6700, www.southwark.anglican.org), in the middle of Borough Market. Although they rarely sing together, the girls and boys share responsibility for the cathedral music.

All the cathedral choirs in Britain are Anglican except one; London's Catholic Westminster Cathedral (020 7798 9055, www.westminstercathedral.org.uk), whose choir is provided by the Westminster Cathedral Choir School. Westminster Abbey (020 7222 5152, www.westminster-abbey.org) also has a top-class choir, plus the added responsibility for singing at coronations and royal funerals. To sit in the Gothic hulk of such an ancient edifice while the choir's voices echo round the masonry is to connect with history and the ghosts of past generations. To some, indeed, this is all that worship is.

# 978
## Take afternoon tea at Claridge's...

The elegant foyer and reading room at Claridge's are the perfect setting for sampling this most English of pleasures. The hotel has more than 30 varieties of tea to choose from, and even makes its own tea-infused jam. Your £31 gets you dainty finger sandwiches, french pastries and raisin and apple scones with thick clotted cream – though you may as well go the whole hog and spend an extra eight quid on the champagne tea, which comes with a glass of Laurent Perrier. Afternoon tea is served between 3pm and 5.30pm: reservations are advised, especially on weekends, when you may have to book up to two months in advance.
**Claridge's** *Brook Street, London W1K 4HR (020 7409 6307/www.claridgeshotellondon.com).*

# 979-981
## ...or sample the brews at a less traditional London teahouse

Postcard Teas (9 Dering Street, London W1S 1AG, 020 7629 3654, www.postcardteas.com) was founded by tea obsessive Timothy d'Offay, after a life-changing cuppa in Taipei. The experience prompted him to start selling teas sourced directly from small producers in East Asia and elsewhere – first at a stall in Borough Market, and now at his central London shoebox. Take a seat at the tasting table, which seats up to six at a time, and for £1.50 you can try a pot of any tea in stock – including the unique Coffee Blossom Tea and the spicy, cinnamon-infused garam assam chai. Other London haunts for the tea-potty include the cosy Tea Box in Richmond (7 Paradise Road, London TW9 1RX, 020 8940 3521), which stocks around 40 different teas, and east London's chic Tea Smith (6 Lamb Street, London E1 6EA, 020 7247 1333, www.teasmith.co.uk), which also serves great cakes.

# 982
## Catch a performance in The Shed

Near the market town of Malton on the edge of the Yorkshire moors, The Shed is one of the few venues in the country with a location as inspiring as its programme of live music and performance art. The latter's affinity with the surreal end of the creative spectrum is largely thanks to the boundless imagination of its creator, Simon Thackray, whose ideas are often too large to be limited to his makeshift stage: in 2004, for example, he had jazz saxophonist Lol Coxhill touring North Yorkshire market towns in a skip; a year earlier, improvising trombonist Alan Tomlinson did likewise in a fish and chip van, serenading customers as they queued for battered cod. Other weird and wonderful outings have involved everything from knitted Elvis wigs to rowing down the river in oversized Yorkshire puddings, although there's plenty making more conventional use of the 100-capacity Shed's candlelit interior – from the live comedy of Stewart Lee and the spoken word poetry of regular collaborator Ian McMillan to all manner of world, classical, jazz, blues and folk music.
**The Shed** *Brawby, Malton, North Yorkshire YO17 6PY (01653 668494/www.theshed.co.uk).*

# 983
## Investigate Conan Doyle

Stephen Fry's mellifluous tones and Arthur Conan Doyle's Sherlock Holmes stories were made for each other. So it was no surprise when Portsmouth City Museum asked the actor to be the voice of the interactive displays in their new exhibition on Sir Arthur Conan Doyle, opened in 2007. Conan Doyle worked as a doctor in Portsmouth in the 1880s – and it was during a quiet spell at his practice that he began writing the stories that would make his fortune. The impressive collection of first editions, letters and memorabilia was left to the city by Conan Doyle expert Richard Lancelyn Green in 2004.
**Portsmouth City Museum** *Museum Road, Portsmouth PO1 2LJ (023 9282 7261/ www.portsmouthmuseums.co.uk).*

# 984-993 Hit the beach

Hugh Graham *rolls up his trousers and heads off to explore the great British seaside.*

## Build a castle at Bamburgh

The Northumberland coast is one of Britain's best-kept secrets, with its long, often deserted beaches, dotted with magnificent castles. There is Dunstanburgh, a 14th-century ruin looming majestically over the sea near Alnwick, itself home to a storied medieval castle. Another gem is Lindisfarne Castle, a romantic 16th-century affair perched on Holy Island, with Lutyens-designed interiors. But the real showpiece is Bamburgh. A dramatic Norman stronghold overlooking the sea, it is one of England's most photographed castles. In front of it lies a beauty of a beach, sprawling for three golden miles and backed by shapely dunes and rare plants. And yet it's often empty: the bracing North Sea winds have blown away the hordes. Still, Bamburgh has a loyal following among beach purists, historians, kite-fliers and bird lovers: the Farne Islands host colonies of puffins and Arctic and common tern, not to mention seals galore.

## Be charmed by Barafundle Bay

On a sleepy stretch of Pembrokeshire coast, this little jewel is like the setting for a Welsh fairytale. The approach is through a dark forest, past a storybook village and cosy tearoom, then across verdant fields. The final touch is a stone arch and sweeping staircase down to the beach; a fanciful entry to an otherworldly place. The golden sands emit a glow even in overcast weather, while the forested path on the far side of the beach is a rich canvas for a child's imagination; you can see why *Country Life* magazine voted Barafundle the best beach in Britain for a picnic. The sheltered position, tucked behind a headland, may also have had something to do with it: the waters are gentle, the bathing is safe and you won't get sand blowing into your sandwiches here. Children can play on the dunes among the rabbits – or scour the shore for mermaids, fairies and dragons. They're out there somewhere.

## Stretch your legs at Holkham

For long, contemplative walks, Holkham in Norfolk offers mile upon mile of white sand, surrounded by giant swathes of sea and sky. But the scenery is by no means monotonous: the beach is backed by a majestic stretch of pine woods and dunes, while the adjacent fields and marshland are sprinkled with migrating birds. A couple of miles east, a jaunty row of beach huts at Wells-next-the-Sea lends a splash of colour to the muted palette. Behind the beach, the stately Holkham Hall (01328 710227, www.holkham.co.uk) – a Palladian extravaganza – adds a touch of class (indeed, the Queen has been known to walk her corgis on this beach while staying at Sandringham). The lack of public transport keeps away the hoi polloi; the solitude only adds to the sense of vastness. The vistas disappear when the fog rolls in from the North Sea, but even on a grey day, Holkham's desolation has its charms. On sunny days, the beach comes alive with swimmers and kite-flyers – though sunbathers would be advised to bring a windbreak.

## Fall in love at Kynance Cove

Could Kynance Cove be Britain's most romantic beach? Tucked away near the end of Cornwall's Lizard Peninsula, at the end of a lonely hillside path, it's certainly far from the madding crowd. The dazzling colours – Aegean blues, pinkish sands and shimmering serpentine rock – have lured artists, poets and lovers through the centuries: William Holman Hunt, the Pre-Raphaelite painter, used to come here for inspiration, as did Lord Tennyson. The coves, caves and rockpools call to mind a summer holiday with the Famous Five, but when the sun is shining you could almost be in Bermuda. Though the azure seas and crimson sunsets cry out for marriage proposals and declarations of undying love, in high summer it's a popular destination for families (Prince Albert started

Kynance Cove

Sandwood Bay

Rhossili Bay

the trend when he brought his children here on holiday in 1846). That said, take care when swimming (the currents can be tricky; stick to the pools) and beware of the tides. It's easy to get stranded on one of the rocks at high tide, when the beach all but disappears.

## *Be swept away by Luskentyre*
On the right day, and with a good camera, the far north of Scotland could double for the South Pacific. Harris, in the Outer Hebrides, is fringed with beaches of jaw-dropping beauty and tropical colours. The star of the show is Luskentyre, measuring one mile across and about two miles long at low tide, bathed in shimmering channels of water in myriad shades of blue. Seilebost and Rosamol, the neighbouring hamlets, are similarly blessed with silvery surf, lapis lazuli seas and sand that looks like icing sugar. Ancient green mountains complete the postcard fantasy. If you drive south on the A859 past Seilebost, and look back across the inlet, this is the best vantage point for the money shot. Though the photographs could pass for Bora Bora, any tropical fantasies will be rudely interrupted when you put your feet into the sea and feel the icy blast of the North Atlantic.

## *Soak up the view at Rhossili Bay*
There are beaches for walking and talking. There are beaches for swimming and surfing. And then there are beaches for sitting and staring. Rhossili Bay is made for the latter: this is the landscape of the sublime. The Gower Peninsula, in the south-west corner of Wales, was the first area in Britain to be designated an Area of Outstanding Natural Beauty, and it's not difficult to see why. The beach gives new meaning to the word sweeping (it's about three miles long and, at low tide, seems about three miles wide); the dunes are mountainous; the downs behind are majestic and windswept; and the thundering surf is relentless. The scene from the hills above could compete with the world's great coastal vistas: Highway 1 in California, say, or Australia's Great Ocean Road. On a breezy day the wind might whip you raw, but you can always seek shelter in the Worm's Head Hotel (01792 390512, www.thewormshead.co.uk), perched right on the edge of the cliff – and soak up the view, along with a welcome pint.

## *Get spooked at Sandwood Bay*
Sandwood Bay, on the north-west tip of Scotland, is on the edge of nowhere. Britain's most remote beach, it's south of a place called Cape Wrath, which sets the ominous tone. It takes two hours to walk there, along a lonely path through bleak moors near the sleepy hamlet of Blairmore. But the two miles of empty beach are utterly magnificent. Completely unsheltered, its white sands and jagged rocks are pummelled by the relentless North Atlantic waves (the odd daredevil surfer takes their life in their hands). The combination of romance and rocks is soul stirring, and Am Buachaille, the eerie, sci-fi sea stack, adds to the *sturm und drang*. Behind the dunes, a ruined cottage overlooks desolate Sandwood Loch. It has its own resident ghost, apparently, as does the beach: a bearded sailor of Armada vintage, who wanders the sands in a forlorn fashion. Mermaids have been spotted here too. Maybe it's the shipwrecks along this fearsome coast that produce all the spooks. But chances are, the only thing that will haunt you at Sandwood is its fierce beauty.

**West Wittering**

## Do the dunes at Saunton Sands

Framed by craggy, gorse-covered headlands, set on the north Devonshire coast, Saunton's three miles of pale gilt sand seem to go on forever; the big skies, salty breeze, pounding Atlantic swell and fine white mist add to the sense of grandeur. This cinematic quality has lured many filmmakers: David Niven is washed up on the beach in the 1946 Powell and Pressburger classic, *A Matter of Life and Death*; it doubled for Normandy in the 1982 Pink Floyd film *The Wall;* and Robbie Williams filmed his 'Angels' video here. But the biggest talking point is Braunton Burrows, the largest sand dunes in Britain. The view from the top is beloved of photographers, while children love sliding down the massive mounds. A UNESCO-designated area of Outstanding Natural Diversity, the dunes' interior hosts over 500 species of plants and birdlife galore. Back on the beach, surfers (board and body) tackle the rollers (stay away from the south end of the beach, where the currents are treacherous) and walkers while away the hours – and rack up the miles.

## Go naked at Studland

Less than three hours from London, but worlds away in spirit, Dorset's Studland beach is the stuff of desert island fantasy – and naked beauty. The relaxed vibe at the nudist beach is like another country altogether. Wide, sweeping and seemingly deserted, with a gentle surf and streaks of turquoise sea, this natural wonder possesses a sensual beauty that is particularly conducive to stripping off. The rustling grasses provide a soothing soundtrack and the dunes afford some privacy for bashful types, though shyness is uncommon in these parts. The north end of the beach is particularly popular with gay men, who pose atop the dunes like nude statues – it is called Studland, after all; heterosexuals congregate a little further south, but show no signs of timidity either, enthusiastically rubbing sun cream on all the right places. By Middle Beach, families cover up and the crowds come out for watersports, sun loungers and sustenance at the National Trust-run café.

## Take the family (and the barbecue) to West Wittering

A sandy haven on the pebbly Sussex coast, West Wittering is picnic heaven – and just two hours away from London. Kids can splash safely here: the sands are gently shelving, there are shallow, sun-warmed tidal pools and pounding breakers don't exist at this Blue Flag favourite. Sheltered by the Isle of Wight and the South Downs, West Wittering basks in its own benign microclimate, though cups of hot cocoa from the café take the edge off the winter chill. The café, a shop and some takeaway hatches are the sole concessions to commercialism, but most families bring a picnic or spark up the barbecue. On a summer's day, the main stretch of sand can get busy, but West Wittering is a tale of two beaches: East Head, at the western end, is a peaceful sand and shingle spit of splendid isolation. The shore glitters with treasures from the sea – pearl-lined slipper limpet shells and razor clams – and is backed by undulating dunes, where skylarks hover and tiny lizards scuttle away at your approach. Wandering among them, you could be the last person on earth – until a small child puffs over the horizon, playing hide-and-seek.

# 994 Climb Stanage Edge

A two-and-a-half-mile stretch of gritstone crags, set amid the rolling hills of the Peak District, Stanage Edge is legendary among the climbing community (www.rockfax.com). Its walls, buttresses, boulders, slabs and fissures offer a multitude of routes to climbers – it would take years to scale them all. The rocky contours afford quality climbs for every ability, from beginners-level routes such as Grotto Slab to seriously challenging ascents like Suicide Wall, the Left Unconquerable and Calvary. Even in the worst weather, climbers head here to test their mettle; on more clement days, the High Neb area tends to be the least crowded.

# 995 See skulls in Hythe

Perched on a hillside in the small coastal town of Hythe is the parish church of St Leonard's – a fine 11th-century affair, with an unusual attraction for macabre-minded sightseers. Its alternative name ('the church with the bones') gives some clue as to what awaits in its crypt: Britain's largest ossuary. Here, some 2,000 medieval skulls are neatly stacked on shelves, along with 8,000 thighbones; instead of storing entire skeletons, a skull and thighbone were considered enough to ensure resurrection.
**St Leonard's Church** *Hythe, Kent CT21 5DN (01303 263739/www.stleonardschurchhythekent.org).*

# 996 Cosy up in a Romany caravan

This traditional Romany caravan now has a permanent home, in a wildflower meadow near Llangrannog in West Wales. Built in 1924, it has a wood-burning stove and is just big enough for two (01239 851410, www.under thethatch.co.uk); best of all, you get exclusive use of the tranquil meadow. As well as the caravan, there's a cabin with a shower room, kitchen and wooden veranda; sitting out here on a balmy summer evening is heavenly.

## 997 Tread carefully in Alnwick's Poison Garden

Approach Alnwick's Poison Garden with caution: some plants here are so poisonous they're kept behind metal bars. Intrepid visitors tour the flame-shaped beds, while guides explain which plants cause skin irritations, sickness and hallucinations – and which was said to make you fly (henbane). Cocaine, opium poppies and magic mushrooms grow alongside the innocuous-looking Nux Vomica, or strychnine tree – a nasty bit of work that even a suicidal Cleopatra rejected; while fast acting, ingesting its seeds causes agonising seizures, without loss of consciousness. Thankfully, not all of Alnwick's botanical areas are so beastly. There are delightful rose and ornamental gardens, spectacular fountains, twisting paths of rustling bamboo in the labyrinth and a truly fantastical treehouse with rope bridges and walkways. Harry Potter fans might also enjoy a visit to nearby Alnwick Castle, where the Quidditch scenes in the first two films were shot.
**Alnwick Garden** *Denwick Lane, Alnwick, Northumberland NE66 1YU (01665 511350/ www.alnwickgarden.com).*

## 998 Watch the Kirkwall Ba'

Football wasn't always the preserve of multi-millionaire players, running around on perfectly manicured pitches in lightweight kit and fancy boots. In medieval times, the beautiful game involved an inflated animal bladder and two teams (hopefully of roughly equal numbers), and was really just a licence to riot, as each side tried to get the ball to the opposite 'goal' – often just their opponents' end of town. At Kirkwall in Orkney, this riotous street mêlée survives (01856 872856, www.visitorkney.com). On both Christmas Day and New Year's Day, the Ba' (short for 'ball') is played out by two teams – Uppies and Doonies – whose allegiance is traditionally determined by the end of town they come from. A couple of hundred players join the ruck, and chaos reigns in Kirkwall's winding streets: spectators are advised to keep well back.

## 999 Take the Sausage Trail in Ludlow

Launched in 1995, Ludlow's famed food festival eschews bland, industrially produced food and celebrates the finest free-range and organic fare. Especially popular is the Sausage Trail; tickets (£3.50) are limited, and sold on a first-come-first-served basis at the ticket office by the castle entrance. Devotees start queuing as early as 5.30am so they can visit each of the town's five butchers to sample their secret-recipe sausages. Tasting notes are written on the voting forms and marks out of ten allocated: judging takes place at 4pm on Saturday, and the best banger is officially announced on Sunday. Don't worry if you can't snag a ticket; the sausages then go on sale for the rest of the year.
**Ludlow Marches Food & Drink Festival** *Buttercross, Ludlow, Shropshire SY8 1AW (01584 873957/www.foodfestival.co.uk).*

## 1000 Make tracks out of here

You've explored the loveliest corners of Britain, sampled its finest food, swum in its rivers and lidos, basked on its beaches, danced until dawn in its clubs and admired its art collections, castles, gardens and museums. It's probably just about time for a change of scene. Pack your bags, unearth your passport and head to London's St Pancras station – the sleek, shiny home of Eurostar's new terminal (0870 518 6186, www.eurostar.com). Before you go, drop by the station's glamorous champagne bar (Europe's longest) for a much-deserved drink. We'd suggest investing in a bottle of sparkling British wine (Balfour Brut Rosé, from the Hush Heath vineyard in Kent, £56) or perhaps a more extravagant bottle of Pol Roger Cuvée Sir Winston Churchill 1998 (£150). Then take your seat, and head to pastures new.

# Advertisers' index

Please refer to relevant sections for addresses and / or telephone numbers

**When you have run out of things to do, why not visit......................**

| | |
|---|---|
| Carbon Neutral | 24 |
| londontown.com | IBC |
| Trees for Cities | 74 |

## Sights & Museums

| | |
|---|---|
| Battersea Park Zoo | 24 |
| Brunel's SS Great Britain | 78 |
| Jane Austen's House Museum | 6 |
| Roald Dahl Museum and Story Centre | 24 |
| Somerset House | IFC |
| Sussex Past | 78 |
| Think Tank Birmingham Science Museum | 6 |

## Activities

| | |
|---|---|
| Bodyflight | 46 |
| Wetland Centre | 14 |

## Arts & Entertainment

| | |
|---|---|
| Comedy Store | 18 |
| Imax Cinema | 6 |
| Wellcome Collection | 34 |

## Eating, Drinking & Nightlife

| | |
|---|---|
| Gordon's Wine Bar | 24 |
| Leffe | 54 |
| Wagamama | 8 |

# County index

In addition to counties, major cities are also indexed.

## Channel Islands
Herm 241
Jersey 28, 66, 125, 164, 212
Sark 241

## England
**Bedfordshire** 142
　Bedford 206-207
　Clapham 47
　Sandy 179
　Whipsnade 161, 184
**Berkshire** 198
　Bray 94
　Cookham 110
　Lambourn 66
　Uffington 84, 145
　Windsor 39, 47, 287
**Bristol** 16, 23, 90, 93, 114, 122, 126, 161, 177, 186, 219, 224, 244, 259, 282, 287
**Buckinghamshire**
　Beaconsfield 96-99
　Bletchley Park 117
　Great Missenden 19
　Milton Keynes 55, 60
　Stoke Poges 278
　Stowe 218
　West Wycombe 262
**Cambridgeshire** 200, 288
　Cambridge 61, 86, 104, 182, 229, 296
　Duxford 105
　Sawston 48
　Wisbech 27
**Cheshire** 198
　Anderton 53
　Chester 90, 100, 161
　Delamare Forest 103
　Hack Green 60
　Knutsford 177
　Tatton Park 138
**Cornwall** 110, 245
　Bodmin Moor 178, 272-274
　Boscastle 52
　Bude 212
　Eden Project 90, 201
　Falmouth 36, 102, 262
　Fowey 94, 274
　Gweek 147
　Heligan estate 254
　Land's End 75, 245
　Lizard Peninsula 75, 160, 274, 298-300
　Newlyn 25
　Newquay 15, 212
　Padstow 94, 194
　Pendennis Castle 106

Penzance 25, 44, 104, 213
Port Eliot 42-43
Port Quin 156
Porthcurno 107
Redruth 83
St Ives 73, 245
St Michael's Mount 248
St Veep 280
Saltash 225
Sennen Cove 211-212
Tintagel 252
Truro 160
**Cumbria** 15, 102, 225
　Ambleside 209
　Appleby 95
　Cartmel 29
　Dalemain 116
　Egremont 165
　Grasmere 12, 202
　Great Langdale 83
　Honister 55
　Kendal 218
　Keswick 60
　Long Meg 59
　Old Tebay 49
　Silecroft 101
　Windermere 192, 236
　Yad Moss 295
**Derbyshire** 20-22
　Bakewell 158, 253
　Buxton 47, 292
　Castle Donington 275
　Castleton 142
　Chatsworth 36, 201
　Chesterfield 120
　Eyam 44
　Hartington Hall 232
　Ilam 170
　Kinder Scout 220
　Matlock Bath 262
　Stanage Edge 302
　Swadlincote 205
**Devon** 124, 142, 185, 232
　Abbotsham 197
　Barnstaple 185, 257, 258
　Bigbury 269
　Braunton Burrows 156
　Buckfastleigh 203
　Buckland Monachorum 190
　Burgh Island 182
　Combe Martin 219
　Croyde 211, 212
　Dartmoor 62-64, 104, 172
　Deeper Marsh 236
　Dittisham 268
　Dunkeswell 214
　Exeter 90, 143, 185, 232
　Ilfracombe 177, 202
　Lifton 55
　Lundy Island 117
　Marwood 190
　Newton Abbot 107
　Plymouth 39, 104, 232
　Salcombe 196

Saunton Sands 301
Sidmouth 208, 288
Topsham 184
Totnes 102
Whimple 184
Woolacombe 211, 212
**Dorset** 26
　Abbotsbury 188
　Abbotsham 197
　Bockhampton 83, 84
　Bournemouth 113
　Bovington 259
　Bridport 157
　Brownsea Island 294
　Buckland Newton 53
　Cerne Abbas 145
　Durdle Door 260
　East Holton 233
　Great Torrington 192
　Kimmeridge 33
　Lyme Regis 12, 26, 215, 270
　Studland 301
　Sturminster Newton 157
　Tyneham 105
　Wareham 169, 184
　Wyke Regis 268
**Durham, County**
　Billingham 126
　Durham 229, 293
　Seaham 119
　Stockton-on-Tees 282
**Essex**
　Brentwood 60
　Colchester 116
　Elmstead Market 192
　Ingatestone 48
　Leigh-on-Sea 103
　Mersea Island 103
　Saffron Walden 37
　West Horndon 148-149
　West Mersea 268
　Wickham Bishop 193
**Gloucestershire** 138
　Barnsley 118
　Cheltenham 40, 41, 44, 94, 104
　Colesbourne 190
　Cowley 118
　Cooper's Hill 253
　Daylesford 214
　Gloucester 126, 296
　Hidcote Bartrim 228
　Kelmscott 194
　Little Dean 280
　Newent 132-135
　Northleach 168
　Ozleworth 170
　Sezincote 159
　Slad 262
　Slimbridge 136, 222
　Snowshill 177
　Toddington 44
　Westonbirt 146

Time Out 1000 Things to do in Britain 305

| | | |
|---|---|---|
| **Greater Manchester** | | |
| Bolton | | 158 |
| Bury | | 258 |
| Manchester | 16, 32, 55, 66, 87, 90, 93, 109, 150, 229, 244, 245, 259 | |
| Stockport | | 56 |
| Wigan | | 72 |
| **Hampshire** | | 144, 198, 225 |
| Beaulieu | | 79 |
| Brockenhurst | | 116 |
| Burghclere | | 110 |
| Chawton | | 44 |
| Hambledon | | 156 |
| Isle of Wight | 45, 49, 65, 95, 106, 115, 159, 198, 199, 268, 270, 279 | |
| Liphook | | 26 |
| Marwell | | 57 |
| Mottisfont | | 83 |
| New Milton | | 119, 278 |
| Portsmouth | 100, 122, 221, 297 | |
| Winchester | | 160, 178 |
| **Herefordshire** | | 180, 198, 200 |
| Abbey Dore | | 280 |
| Credenhill | | 56 |
| Hereford | | 296 |
| Kilpeck | | 209 |
| Much Marcle | | 248 |
| **Hertfordshire** | | |
| Ayot St Lawrence | | 294 |
| Berkhampsted | | 168 |
| Chandler's Cross | | 119 |
| Much Hadham | | 288 |
| Royston | | 137 |
| Tring | | 13 |
| **Isle of Man** | 156, 204, 259, 292 | |
| **Isles of Scilly** | | 100, 147 |
| St Martin's | | 228 |
| St Mary's | | 44, 147 |
| Tresco | | 44, 83 |
| **Kent** | | |
| Biddenden | | 136 |
| Birchington | | 67 |
| Broadstairs | | 157, 279, 288 |
| Canterbury | | 182, 255 |
| Dover | | 106, 252 |
| Dungeness | | 193, 264-265 |
| Faversham | | 220 |
| Goudhurst | | 136 |
| Greatstone-on-Sea | | 136 |
| Herne Bay | | 282 |
| Hever | | 37 |
| Hythe | | 302 |
| Leeds Castle | | 37, 252 |
| Littlestone-on-Sea | | 136 |
| Lympne | | 127 |
| Margate | | 259 |
| Rochester | | 270 |
| Scotney Castle | | 48 |
| Sevenoaks | | 130, 136, 218 |
| Strood | | 35 |
| Tudeley | | 139 |
| Whitstable | 164, 177, 182, 237, 269 | |
| **Lancashire** | | 126 |
| Blackpool | 113, 140-141, 163, 292 | |
| Carnforth | | 243 |
| Lancaster | | 66 |
| Preston | | 48, 230 |
| Rawtenstall | | 59 |
| **Leicestershire** | | 144 |
| Billesdon | | 278 |
| Coalville | | 84, 278 |
| Hallaton & Medbourne | | 106 |
| Husbands Bosworth | | 29 |
| Leicester | | 19, 44 |
| Melton Mowbray | | 258 |
| **Lincolnshire** | | |
| Alkborough | | 37 |
| Donna Nook | | 147 |
| Folkingham | | 173 |
| Lincoln | 19, 100, 144, 228, 261 | |
| Skegness | | 163 |
| Stamford | | 237 |
| Waddington | | 102 |
| **London** | 19, 109, 112-114, 126, 131, 136, 158, 189, 205, 214-215, 218, 242, 250, 253, 261, 290-292 | |
| Barnes & Mortlake | | 115,170 |
| Billingsgate | | 75 |
| Bloomsbury | | 32, 86 |
| Borough Market | | 56 |
| Brockwell Park | | 104 |
| Camden Passage | | 188 |
| Chelsea | | 110, 118, 124, 238 |
| Chinatown | | 87 |
| City | | 56 |
| Chiswick | | 181 |
| Clapham | | 196 |
| Clerkenwell | | 32 |
| Columbia Road | | 196 |
| Covent Garden | | 32, 90, 142 |
| Crystal Palace | | 36 |
| Eastcheap | | 100 |
| Euston Road | | 150 |
| Forest Hill | | 225 |
| Greenwich | | 19, 270 |
| Hammersmith | | 16, 136, 282 |
| Hampstead | | 32, 104 |
| Highbury | | 230 |
| Highgate | | 32, 170 |
| Holborn | | 86, 145 |
| Holland Park | | 232 |
| Hoxton | | 80-82 |
| Hyde Park | | 50, 131 |
| Islington | | 32 |
| Kensington | 15, 131, 169, 189, 244 | |
| Knightsbridge | | 119, 136 |
| Lincoln's Inn Fields | | 12, 136, 249 |
| London Zoo | | 161 |
| Maida Vale | | 181 |
| Marylebone | | 56, 174-176 |
| Mayfair | | 297 |
| Millennium Footbridge | | 66 |
| Paddington Basin | | 150 |
| Piccadilly Circus | | 84 |
| Regent's Park | | 55, 159 |
| Richmond | | 297 |
| St Pancras | | 303 |
| St Paul's Cathedral | | 296 |
| Smithfield | | 222 |
| Soho | | 56, 238 |
| South Kensington | | 90 |
| Southbank | 16, 107, 131, 289 | |
| Southwark/Borough Market | 174, 196, 296 | |
| Spitalfields | | 35, 297 |
| St John's Wood | | 230 |
| Thames, River | | 110 |
| Tower Bridge | | 69, 224 |
| Trafalgar Square | | 131, 138 |
| Wapping | | 181 |
| West Kensington | | 139 |
| Westminster | | 53, 296 |
| White City | | 202 |
| Wimbledon | | 231 |
| **Merseyside** | | 143 |
| Crosby Beach | | 128-129 |
| Formby | | 202 |
| Liverpool | 19, 48, 60, 75, 87, 112, 143, 158, 220, 248 | |
| New Brighton | | 122 |
| St Helens | | 72 |
| Southport | | 157 |
| **Middlesex** | | |
| Southall | | 197 |
| Twickenham | | 230, 293 |
| Wembley | | 231 |
| **Norfolk** | | 172 |
| Bewilderwood | | 88-89 |
| Blakeney | | 147 |
| Cley-next-the-Sea | | 130 |
| East Ruston | | 193 |
| Great Yarmouth | | 163 |
| Hemsby | | 23 |
| Holkham | | 298 |
| King's Lynn | | 42 |
| Norwich | | 65, 90, 221 |
| Oxburgh | | 48 |
| Salthouse | | 268 |
| Swaffham | | 254, 256, 258 |
| Walsingham | | 241 |
| Wells-Next-the-Sea | | 84, 298 |
| **Northamptonshire** | | 200 |
| Ashton | | 85 |
| Coton | | 193 |
| Geddington | | 278 |
| Kelmarsh Hall | | 216 |
| Podington | | 73 |
| Rushton | | 67 |
| Salcey Forest | | 120 |
| Silverstone | | 17 |
| **Northumberland** | | |
| Alnwick | 84, 106, 252, 298, 303 | |
| Bamburgh | | 298 |
| Belsay Hall | | 106 |
| Craster | | 84, 255 |
| Dunstanburgh | | 84, 298 |
| Farne Islands | | 147 |
| Hadrian's Wall | | 126 |
| Kielder Forest | | 188, 266 |
| Lindisfarne (Holy Island) | 166-167, 298 | |
| Rothbury | | 283 |
| **Nottinghamshire** | | 26 |
| Blyth | | 190 |
| Hucknall Torkard | | 122 |
| Laxton | | 137 |
| Newstead Abbey | | 240 |
| Nottingham | 16, 114, 139, 238 | |
| Ravenshead | | 243 |
| **Oxfordshire** | | |
| Blenheim Palace | | 35, 36 |
| Faringdon | | 67 |
| Garsington | | 57 |
| Great Milton | | 94 |
| Henley on Thames | | 231 |
| Hook Norton | | 66 |
| Oxford | 61, 85, 86, 125, 130, 136, 181, 240, 278, 296 | |
| Stoke Row | | 159 |
| Thame | | 257, 258 |
| **Rutland** | | |
| Egleton | | 172 |

| | |
|---|---|
| Stoke Dry | 286 |
| **Shropshire** | |
| Bridgnorth | 177 |
| Hawkstone Park | 66 |
| Ironbridge | 59 |
| Ludlow | 303 |
| Much Wenlock | 146 |
| Stiperstones | 45 |
| **Somerset** | |
| Babington | 118 |
| Bath | 70, 126, 144, 183, 232, 289 |
| Clevedon | 123 |
| Coleridge Way | 130 |
| Dunster | 170 |
| Exmoor | 165 |
| Faulkland | 220 |
| Glastonbury | 198, 279, 288 |
| Kingsbury Episcopi | 280 |
| Minehead | 198 |
| Stoney Littleton | 127 |
| Wells | 275, 296 |
| Williton | 260 |
| Wookey Hole | 37 |
| **Staffordshire** | |
| Alrewas | 172 |
| Alton Towers | 163 |
| Drayton Manor | 162, 163 |
| Fordhouses | 48 |
| High Offley | 271 |
| Lichfield | 100, 127 |
| Mow Cop | 67 |
| **Suffolk** | |
| Aldeburgh | 87, 283 |
| Bury St Edmunds | 286 |
| Dunwich | 250-251 |
| Marlesford | 196 |
| Orford | 121 |
| Orwell Bridge | 196 |
| Southwold | 43, 197, 199-200, 276-277 |
| Sutton Hoo | 271 |
| Thorpeness | 67 |
| Walberswick | 240 |
| Yoxford | 196 |
| **Surrey** | |
| Bagshot | 119 |
| Bisley | 57 |
| Carshalton | 184 |
| Chobham | 255 |
| Cobham | 178 |
| Compton | 189 |
| Denbies vineyard | 270 |
| Egham | 255 |
| Guildford | 104, 249 |
| Hampton Court | 36 |
| Kew | 93 |
| Painshill Park | 67 |
| Redhill | 171 |
| Richmond-upon-Thames | 255, 297 |
| Runnymede | 168 |
| Surbiton | 139 |
| Thorpe Park | 162, 163 |
| Walton-on-Thames | 286 |
| Wisley | 107 |
| **Sussex, East** | |
| Ashdown Forest | 23, 26 |
| Bexhill-on-Sea | 125 |
| Bodiam | 252 |
| Brighton | 32, 104, 109, 114, 116, 158, 159, 164, 266, 270, 271, 282, 293, 294 |
| Camber Sands | 136, 198 |

| | |
|---|---|
| Charleston Firle | 151 |
| Eastbourne | 139, 178, 259 |
| Firle | 248 |
| Hastings | 17, 136, 156, 177, 270 |
| Lewes | 104 |
| Northiam | 192 |
| Sheffield Park | 101 |
| Windmill Hill | 278 |
| **Sussex, West** | 83 |
| Ardingly | 15 |
| Bognor Regis | 281 |
| Chichester | 19, 139 |
| Fishbourne | 79 |
| Goodwood Estate | 117, 221 |
| Littlehampton | 150 |
| Lower Beeding | 159 |
| Petworth | 248 |
| Shoreham-by-Sea | 145 |
| Singleton | 170 |
| West Dean | 193 |
| West Wittering | 301 |
| **Tyne & Wear** | |
| Gateshead | 185 |
| Newcastle-upon-Tyne | 16, 90, 150, 262 |
| South Shields | 237 |
| Sunderland | 122, 208 |
| Whitley Bay | 126 |
| **Warwickshire** | |
| Compton Verney | 178 |
| Coughton Court | 48 |
| Leamington Spa | 76 |
| Ryton | 193 |
| Warwick | 90, 173 |
| **West Midlands** | |
| Baddesley Clinton | 48 |
| Dudley | 161 |
| Birmingham | 19, 32, 114, 139, 151, 168, 238, 244, 292-293 |
| Solihull | 143 |
| Walsall | 52 |
| **Wiltshire** | |
| Avebury | 17, 83, 267 |
| Bradford on Avon | 209 |
| Devizes | 25 |
| Longleat | 37, 100 |
| Ridgeway | 267 |
| Salisbury | 173, 296 |
| Salisbury Plain | 105 |
| Stourhead Estate | 67 |
| **Worcestershire** | |
| Bretforton | 83 |
| Broadway | 110 |
| Droitwich | 104 |
| Harvington | 48 |
| Stoke Heath | 72 |
| Worcester | 292, 296 |
| **Yorkshire, East Riding of** | 60 |
| Hull | 126, 224 |
| Withersea | 60 |
| **Yorkshire, North** | 152-155 |
| Bolton Abbey | 254 |
| Brimham Rocks | 49 |
| Coverham | 208 |
| Dalby Forest | 25 |
| Dent Station | 202 |
| Goathland | 263 |
| Halifax | 67 |
| Harrogate | 37, 48, 52 |
| Haworth | 125 |
| Helmsley | 214 |
| Keighley & Worth | 125 |

| | |
|---|---|
| Malton | 297 |
| Mount Grace Priory | 106 |
| North Stainley | 163 |
| Richmond | 84 |
| Robin Hood's Bay | 173 |
| Scarborough | 69, 111, 212 |
| Skipton | 258 |
| Whitby | 238 |
| York | 60, 90, 100, 225, 228, 289 |
| **Yorkshire, South** | |
| Sheffield | 16, 112, 170, 222, 244, 267 |
| **Yorkshire, West** | |
| Bradford | 32, 72, 233 |
| Halifax | 164 |
| Huddersfield | 122 104 |
| Leeds | 23, 55, 72, 90, 94, 142, 238, 279, 292 |
| Saltair | 182 |
| West Bretton | 171, 261, 266 |

## Scotland

| | |
|---|---|
| Aberdeen City | 86 |
| Aberdeenshire | 104 |
| **Argyll & Bute** | |
| Dalmally | 130 |
| Easdale Island | 249 |
| Seil | 275 |
| Tarbert | 269 |
| **Ayrshire** | |
| Dumfries House | 218 |
| **Dumfries & Galloway** | |
| Langholm | 213 |
| Port Logan | 190-192 |
| **Dundee City** | 224, 240 |
| **East Lothian** | |
| East Fortune airfield | 178 |
| **Edinburgh, City of** | 12, 16, 32, 33, 40-41, 47, 52, 73, 77, 83, 86, 90, 103, 105, 119, 120, 136, 173, 224, 238, 259, 282, 283, 286, 292 |
| **Falkirk** | 53 |
| **Fife** 266 | |
| East Neuk | 126 |
| St Andrews | 29, 86 |
| Troywood | 60 |
| **Glasgow, City of** 16, 55, 66, 83, 86, 101, 115, 143, 165, 201, 219, 231, 244, 254, 270, 292, 295 | |
| **Highland** | 87, 228 |
| Ben Nevis | 195, 281 |
| Cairngorm Mountains | 171, 195 |
| Kinlochleven | 26 |
| Loch Garten | 233 |
| Loch Lochy | 236 |
| Loch Ness | 234-236 |
| Loch Oich | 236 |
| Sandwood Bay | 300-301 |
| Tain | 144 |
| **Inverness-shire** | |
| Aonach Mor | 106 |
| Aviemore | 215 |
| Culloden Moor | 222 |
| Inverness | 113, 208 |
| **Lanarkshire, North** | |
| Carfin | 188 |

**Time Out** 1000 Things to do in Britain **307**

| | |
|---|---|
| **Lanarkshire, South** | |
| Dunsryre | 233 |
| Hamilton | 266 |
| Wanlockhead | 72 |
| **Midlothian** | |
| Roslin | 232 |
| **Morayshire** | |
| Findhorn | 215 |
| Pluscarden Abbey | 205 |
| **Orkney Islands** | 177, 185 |
| Kirkwall | 289, 303 |
| Lamb Holm | 79 |
| Scapa Flow | 145 |
| Skara Brae | 160 |
| **Perthshire & Kinross** | 69, 200 |
| **Ross-shire** | |
| Achiltibuie | 94 |
| **Shetland Islands** | 177 |
| Lerwick | 168 |
| **Stirlingshire** | |
| Aberfoyle | 170 |
| Doune | 252 |
| Dunmore Park | 173 |
| **Western Isles (Hebrides)** | 271 |
| Barra | 157 |
| Eigg | 120 |
| Harris | 300 |
| Monach Isles | 147 |
| Mull | 292 |
| Skye | 123, 208, 224, 236 |
| Tiree | 13, 56 |

| | |
|---|---|
| **Powys** | 199 |
| Brecon Beacons | 243 |
| Hay-on-Wye | 40 |
| Knighton | 281 |
| Llangoed Hall | 218 |
| Llanwrtyd Wells | 39 |
| Machynlleth | 68 |
| **South Wales** | 43 |
| Celtic Manor | 259 |
| Dunraven Bay | 12 |
| Mountain Ash | 72 |
| **Swansea** | |
| Llangennith | 212 |
| Rhossili Bay | 300 |
| Three Cliffs Bay | 282 |
| **Torfaen** | |
| Blaenafon | 116 |

# Wales

| | |
|---|---|
| **Anglesey** | 260 |
| **Cardiff** | 16, 59, 86, 90, 292-293 |
| **Cardiganshire** | |
| Aberystwyth | 26 |
| Llangrannog | 302 |
| New Quay | 160 |
| **Carmarthenshire** | |
| Laugharne | 43 |
| Llanarthne | 193 |
| **Conwy** | |
| Llandudno | 106 |
| **Denbighshire** | |
| Llangollen | 293 |
| River Dee | 137 |
| **Glamorgan** | 200 |
| Senghenydd | 72 |
| Ystrad | 72 |
| **Gwent** | |
| Tredegar | 72 |
| **Gwynedd** | |
| Abersoch | 35 |
| Bardsey Island | 279 |
| Harlech | 252 |
| Penrhos | 35 |
| Porthor | 120 |
| Portmeirion | 52 |
| **Monmouthshire** | |
| Abergavenny | 94 |
| Tintern Abbey | 194 |
| **Pembrokeshire** | 173, 212 |
| Barafundle Bay | 298 |
| Canaston Bridge | 163 |
| Ramsey Island | 147 |
| St David's | 267 |
| Tenby | 278 |

# Thematic index

Note: number refers to page, not list entry.

## A

**accommodation**
- ancient B&B 136
- camper vans 142
- fisherman's huts 164
- for fishing enthusiasts 55
- for football fanatics 158
- hotel bars with views 131
- lighthouses 223
- luxurious hostels 232
- monastic 84, 106
- spas 118-119
- stunning hotels 182, 218
- unusual holiday lets 67, 106, 117, 156, 173, 202, 223, 279
- vegetarian hotel 12
- vintage caravans 95, 263, 302
- windmill guesthouse 130
- see also camping

**activities, unusual**
- air guitar championship 157
- bodyflight 47
- bog snorkelling 39
- Bognor Birdman flights 281
- bottle-kicking 106
- caving 20-22
- chaos paintball 29
- cheese-rolling 253
- conker championships 85
- digger driving 35
- green gym scheme 245
- gurning contest 165
- hound trailing 102
- indoor bungee jump 244
- letterboxing 172
- panning for gold 72
- Poohsticks 23
- world stone skimming championships 249
- White Air festival 115
- woodland adventures 88-89, 103, 120, 169, 226-227, 303
- zorbing 83
- see also sport (participation)

**animals**
- badgers 53
- bats 170
- butterflies 206
- donkeys 208
- livestock auction 258
- llama trekking 26
- red squirrels 188, 202, 294
- in Scottish wilderness 171
- sheep races 197
- stuffed 13, 67, 93, 225
- trail hounds 102
- see also equestrian pursuits; fish & marine life; zoos & wildlife parks

**archaeology & ancient sites**
- barrows & tombs 17, 105, 127, 245, 267, 271
- Cerne Abbas giant 145
- clapper bridge 165
- Cornish sites 245
- fossils 26
- Ridgeway sites 267
- Roman remains 79, 126, 183
- Skara Brae 160
- stone circles 17, 59
- white horses 17, 84, 145, 267

**architecture & buildings**
- art deco 125, 131, 145, 182
- art nouveau 143
- Arts and Crafts 189, 194
- Blackpool Tower 140
- British Museum 145
- cathedrals 127, 139, 267, 275
- environmentally-friendly 68, 266
- follies 66, 67, 110, 173
- glasshouses 107, 193
- Heatherwick, Thomas 148-150
- historic buildings, museums of 72, 170
- Houses of Parliament 53
- Indian style 159
- Italianate 52, 79, 232
- Matcham theatres 292
- modern 218, 221, 233, 242, 270
- open days 205
- opulent toilets 158
- Turkish baths 37
- see also houses, historic & stately

**art & artists**
- Art Car Boot Fair 35
- artists' homes & haunts 110, 151, 189, 260, 300
- Big Draw, the 294
- church art 66, 110, 139, 189, 209, 232, 286
- galleries 25, 52, 93, 110, 115, 131, 182, 185, 189, 221, 261, 270
- installations 123, 200, 225, 237, 295
- murals 100, 110
- open houses trail 271
- Secret Sale 169
- in stately homes 151, 178, 248, 260
- see also sculpture

**aviation**
- air shows 102, 105
- beach landings 157
- fly classic planes 105
- helicopter trips 44, 102
- historic airport, Shoreham 145
- museums 105, 178

## B

**bakeries**
- best 214-215, 228
- clangers 179
- German 52
- gingerbread 202
- organic 17, 214

**beauty & grooming**
- hairdresser 261
- Miss Transgender pageant 164
- see also fashion; spas

**birdwatching**
- Big Garden Birdwatch 123
- birds of prey 132-135, 233
- nightingales 172
- seabirds 282, 298, 301
- starlings 222
- swans 188, 275
- water fowl 136

**boats & ships**
- aqueduct 137
- Anglo-Saxon burial 271
- burning 168
- ferries 13, 121, 143, 199, 241, 268, 292, 294
- fishing trips 294
- historic 100, 102, 219, 240
- punting 61
- RIB tours 110
- river-bugging 69
- rowing museum 231
- sea kayaking 271
- tall ship adventures 179
- Thames skiffs 286
- wildlife trips 147, 160, 298
- wrecks 117, 145, 301

**bridges & river crossings**
- aqueduct 137
- clapper bridge 165
- iron 59
- mathematical 182
- millennium 66
- over the Atlantic 275
- spectacular 196, 224
- stepping stones 254

## C

**camping**
- camper vans 142
- clifftop site 282
- wild 62-64

**canals**
- beer garden 271
- boat lifts 53
- locks 25

**cars & driving**
- custom car & VW festival 15
- museums 79, 275
- racing (participation) 17, 73
- scenic coastal route 245
- vintage racing cars 221, 275
- vintage rally 158

**castles**
- bats 170
- best 252
- holiday lets 106, 117
- ice rink 90
- on islands 166, 248
- knight schools & armour 205, 252
- in Northumberland 84, 298, 303
- royal 287

Time Out 1000 Things to do in Britain 309

**cathedrals**
   architecture & art   127, 139, 267, 275
   choirs   296
   necropolis   101
   tree cathedral   184
**charity**
   events   23, 123, 278, 281
   festival volunteers   279
   shops   12, 136
**cheese**
   British   144
   Cheese Society Café   19, 144
   market stalls   256, 258
   rolling   253
**children's attractions**
   aquariums   140, 225
   farm activities   33, 197
   fencing lessons   33
   Forbidden Corner   208
   glass-making sessions   208
   Jurassic Walk   140
   kite-flying   122, 298
   knight schools & armour   205, 252
   mazes   37
   Midnight Ramble, Kew   93
   model village   96-99
   Museum for Children, the   164
   Poohsticks   23
   Punch & Judy   106
   Queen Mary's doll's house   287
   rollercoasters   162-163
   science museums   244
   Shambala festival   200
   storytelling   19, 262
   *see also* circuses; fairground attractions; ice-cream; puppet shows; seaside & beaches; space; theme parks; zoos & wildlife parks
**chocolate**
   award-winning   188
   tasting sessions & school   33
**churches & chapels**
   art & sculpture   66, 110, 139, 189, 209, 232, 286
   choirs   296
   churchyards   32, 194, 278
   historic chapels   232, 283
   Italian chapel   79
   mystery plays   100
   ossuary   302
   tombs   122, 248
   unusual spires   120, 127
   *see also* cathedrals; religious & spiritual sites
**circuses**
   Blackpool Tower   140
   classes, circus skills   80-82, 140
   Insect Circus   30-31
**classes & courses**
   bakery   228
   butchery   174-176
   chocolate   33
   circus skills   80-82, 140
   clay shooting   57
   conducting   289
   crafts   102
   dance   73
   falconry   134-135
   flying   145
   gardening   52
   glasscraft   208

   hang gliding & paragliding   279
   motor racing   17
   music   102
   playwriting   238
   polo   255
   sculpture   171
   seafood preparation   75
   surfing   210-212
   tennis   278
   wild food & bushcraft   152-155
**climbing**
   Ben Nevis   281
   ice wall   26
   rocks   49, 302
   trees   110
   *see also* caving
**comedy**
   best venues   290-293, 297
   festivals   199-200, 293
   improvised   84
   silent   23
**cricket**
   at sea   49
   home of   156
   local derby   126
   Lords tour & MCC Museum   230
**cultural events**
   animation festival   233
   Brighton Festival   271
   Dartington Hall   102
   East Neuk   126
   gay   60
   literary festivals   40-43, 151, 168, 279
   Liverpool 2008   75
   street theatre festival   160
   *see also* music; theatre
**cycling**
   Channel Islands   241
   Dunwich Dynamo   250-251
   Manchester Velodrome   93
   mountain bike trails   25, 65,106
   National Trails   116, 178, 182, 185, 194

# D

**dance**
   classes   73
   contemporary   32, 65
   events   75
   venues   32
**disabled access**
   purpose-built exhibition space   233
   trails with wheelchair access   65, 171, 233
**drink**
   breweries & tours   66, 103, 107, 184
   Britain's strongest ale   184
   cider & apple juice   220, 248, 280
   gin distillery   39
   malthouse   107
   perry   248, 280
   sarsaparilla   59
   sloe gin   266
   Temperance Bar   59
   vineyards   103, 270

# E

**ecology & environment**
   alternative technology centre   68
   beach cleaning   10
   fix my street scheme   13
   freecycle scheme   288
   green buildings   68, 266
   green gym scheme   245
   marine reserves   33, 117
   nature reserves   121, 147, 171, 172, 206
   tree dedications   284
   wildlife conservation   28, 117
   wind turbines   23, 254
**engineering feats**
   bridges   59, 66, 137, 182, 224
   boat lifts   53
   canal locks   25
   funicular railways   177, 270
   hydro-electric station   130
   Papplewick's Victorian pumping station   243
   railway   232
   sea tractor   182
   steam-powered brewery   66
**equestrian pursuits**
   beach-riding   101
   Grand National   248
   harness racing   95
   horse fair   95
   National Trails   65, 178
   polo   255
   racing stables   66
   three-day eventing   237

# F

**fairground attractions**
   amusement arcades   270, 276-277
   rollercoasters   162-163
   steam fair   26
   vintage slot machines   116
**farms**
   apple & cider specialists   220, 248, 280
   badger watching   53
   brewery   184
   free-range geese   278
   lavender fields   184
   Open Farm Sunday scheme   33
   sheep   197
   snail   56
   vegetables   203
**fashion**
   museum   70-71
   shops   261
**festivals**
   ballooning   186
   Burns Night   242
   Chinese New Year   87, 229
   Christmas events   90, 146, 168, 278, 296, 303
   Earl of Rone   219
   Easter events   66, 106
   food   65, 83, 116, 303
   Gothic   239
   kite flying   122
   May Day & Beltane celebrations   47, 125, 177, 194
   religious   125
   *see also* cultural events; music

## film & cinemas
- animation festival 233
- film locations 84, 125,159, 204, 232, 243, 252, 270, 301, 303
- independent cinemas 16, 102
- James Bond gadgets 79
- old cinemas 32, 117, 151
- silent movies 23

## fish & marine life
- aquariums 140, 225
- crabbing 240
- dolphins, whales & seals 147, 160, 177, 271, 279, 282, 298
- fishing holidays 55
- herring festival 23
- kippers 204, 255
- mackerel fishing 294
- marine reserves 33, 117
- market stalls 256, 257
- oysters 103, 237, 268-269
- preparing 75
- restaurants & cafés 56, 94, 196, 242, 255
- seafood shacks 103, 268-269

## food
- apples 220
- asparagus 83
- Bakewell pudding 253
- black butter 164
- black pudding 258
- cheeses 144
- cheese rolling 253
- Cheese Society Café 19, 144
- chocolate 33, 188
- clangers 179
- Cornish pasties 160, 228
- cream teas 124
- festivals 65, 83, 116, 303
- fish 23, 204, 255
- foraging for 152-155, 172
- free-range geese 278
- garlic festival 65
- gingerbread 202
- herring festival 23
- marmalade 116
- organic vegetables 203
- oysters 103, 237, 268-269
- pudding night 209
- samphire 172
- sausages 303
- seafood shacks, the best 103, 268-269
- shops 17, 52, 56, 278
- snails 56
- see also bakeries; markets; drink; restaurants & cafés; teas

## football
- American 222
- hotel with a view 158
- the original game 303
- stadium tours & museums 230-231

## G

### gardens & gardening
- Arts and Crafts 228
- bats 170
- best 190-193
- botanic 85, 93, 124, 190, 193
- Capability Brown 178, 248
- Chatsworth 201
- community 295
- Derek Jarman's 193, 264-265
- Eden Project 90, 201
- exotic 159
- follies 67
- glasshouses 107, 193, 201
- Gothic 66, 208
- green gym scheme 245
- island 248
- Italianate 170, 267
- lavender 184
- lawnmower museum 157
- lost & restored 65, 254
- mazes 36-37
- memorial 137
- open days 282
- organic 68, 193
- plant market 196
- poets' 233, 240
- poisonous plants 303
- political 218
- rock 283
- roses 83, 267, 303
- sculpture 73, 171, 189, 193, 288
- seed collections 15, 179
- snowdrops 190
- subtropical 196, 254
- topiary 192, 218
- vegetables 52, 193

### gay scene
- beach 301
- clubs & bars 113, 290
- Homotopia 60
- Pride festivals 108-109

### ghostly & macabre places
- abandoned villages 105, 156
- eerie nature reserve 121
- ghosts 182, 252, 300-301
- gruesome museums 12, 142, 173
- Hell Fire Caves 262
- Museum of Witchcraft 52
- ossuary 302
- seaside tales 274
- shipwrecks 117, 145, 301
- Whitby & its Goths 239
- see also graves & graveyards

### golf
- academy 278
- courses 29, 259

### graves & graveyards
- atmospheric cemeteries 32, 101, 229
- barrows 17, 105, 127
- Burton, Sir Richards's tomb 115
- Byron's grave 122
- knight's tomb 248
- magnificent mausoleums 39, 115, 266
- plague village 44
- Sutton Hoo 271

## H

### holidays
- fishing 55
- swimming 100
- tennis 278
- working 281
- see also accommodation; camping; seaside & beaches

### hotels
- see accomodation

### houses, historic & stately
- art collections 151, 178, 248, 260
- Arts and Crafts 194
- Beatles' 220
- eccentric collections 177, 196
- 18th-century 178, 218
- follies 67
- gardens 83, 201,218, 228
- literary homes 44, 84, 125, 130, 184, 294
- mazes 36-37
- Palladian 298
- priest holes 48
- romantic 12
- Victorian new technology 283
- Tudor 136, 218
- as youth hostels 232

## I

### ice-cream
- parlours 111, 157
- traditional 158
- van for hire 158

### ice skating
- fen-skating 27
- outdoor rinks 90

### islands
- Bardsey 279
- Brownsea 294
- Burgh 182
- car-free 241
- Herm 241
- Isle of Man 156, 204, 259, 292
- Isles of Scilly 44, 83, 100, 147, 228
- Isle of Wight see by county index, p307
- Jersey 28, 66, 125 164, 212
- Lindisfarne 166, 298
- Lundy 117
- Sark 241
- St Helier's Day Pilgrimage 125
- St Michael's Mount 248
- Scottish 13, 56, 120, 123, 147, 157, 208, 224, 236, 249, 271, 275, 292, 300
- seals & birdlife 147, 298

## K

### knights
- jousting 200
- schools & armour 205, 252
- Templars 137
- tomb 248

## L

### lectures
- public 86
- see also classes & courses

### literature & books
- anarchist bookfairs 253
- authors' homes & haunts 44, 84, 125, 130, 168, 184, 240, 262, 266, 272-274, 279, 294
- bookcrossing 151

**Time Out** 1000 Things to do in Britain 311

| | | |
|---|---|---|
| bookshops | 12, 131, 181, 270 | |
| Canterbury Tales | 255 | |
| children's festivals | 262 40-43, 151, 168, 279 | |
| Inklings tour | 181 | |
| libraries | 26, 120, 130, 145, 218, 238, 286 | |
| museums | 44, 266, 279, 297 | |
| playwriting courses | 238 | |
| poetry & poets | 120, 122, 130, 233, 240, 242, 278, 286, 297, 300 | |
| Rebustours | 136 | |

**living history**
- battle re-enactments 156, 216-217
- Mass Observation project 122

# M

**markets**
- antiques 196
- Borough 174, 196, 296
- farmers' 257-258
- flowers 196
- street 256-258
- Sturminster Newton 157
- Women's Institute 157, 257

**mazes**
- best 36-37
- Glastonbury 288
- maize 225

**memorials & monuments**
- Benjamin Britten 283
- Byron 122
- Byron's dog 240
- Eleanor crosses 278
- Fire of London 218
- Heroes' Wall 189
- Holocaust 137
- JF Kennedy 168
- TE Lawrence 184
- Thomas Gray 278
- World War I 110, 172

**militaria & war history**
- American war memorabilia 105, 229
- art 110
- battle re-enactments 156, 216-217
- code-breaking centre 117
- communications tower 178
- Culloden 222
- Dambusters location 286
- medieval war machines 173
- museums 60, 105, 115, 229, 259, 286
- tanks 259
- wartime bunkers & tunnels 60, 252
- weapons test site 121
- World War I hospital 286

**motorcycles & scooters**
- museum 143
- scooter rally 45
- speedway 59
- TT races 156, 204

**museums**
- Americana 105, 229, 289
- aviation 105, 178
- Bakelite 260

| | | |
|---|---|---|
| British Empire | 287 | |
| cars | 79, 275 | |
| children's | 164 | |
| commercial vehicles | 255 | |
| computers | 117 | |
| dog collars | 252 | |
| eclectic & eccentric | 136, 225, 240, 249 | |
| fashion | 70-71 | |
| fish-curing | 204 | |
| historic buildings | 72, 170 | |
| Holocaust | 137 | |
| lawnmowers | 157 | |
| literature | 44, 266, 279, 297 | |
| Manchester city life | 245 | |
| maritime history | 102, 178, 219 | |
| media | 32, 233 | |
| medicine & health | 12, 37, 44, 142, 173 | |
| militaria | 60, 105, 115, 229, 259, 286 | |
| mining | 72, 116 | |
| motorcycles | 143 | |
| musical boxes & automata | 168 | |
| natural history | 13, 93 | |
| Oriental | 229 | |
| pencils | 60 | |
| railways | 228 | |
| Romans | 126 | |
| science & industry | 59, 196, 244 | |
| slavery | 287 | |
| sports | 230-231 | |
| telephone kiosks | 72 | |
| witchcraft | 52 | |

**music**
- air guitar 157
- amateur singing concerts 29
- Britten's home 283
- chamber music 138
- church choirs 296
- classical music festivals 15, 87, 126, 289
- conducting course 289
- contemporary music festival 122
- country music 83
- folk festivals 199, 200, 288
- goth-rock 239
- Hallé birthday celebrations 229
- inspiring venues 83, 254, 297
- jazz festival 243
- Liverpool 2008 events 75
- opera 47, 57, 209
- pipe band championship 201
- record store 259
- rock, pop & dance festivals 198-200, 279
- sea shanties 75
- Smiths tour 55
- special combined events 15, 35, 43, 115
- summer festivals 107, 209, 279

**myths & legends**
- Arthurian 178, 252, 274, 288
- Chesterfield church spire 120
- Devil's Chair 45
- Earl of Rone 219
- Isle of Tiree 13
- Lincoln imp 228

| | | |
|---|---|---|
| Long Meg | 59 | |
| masonic murder | 232 | |
| Ringing Stone | 13 | |

# N

**natural wonders**
- ancient rock formations 13, 45, 49, 260
- caverns 142
- clouds 246-247
- ley lines 288
- Northern Lights 185, 188

**night-time pursuits**
- art installations 123
- best clubs 112-114
- candelit tours 249
- Dunwich Dynamo 250-251
- Kew Midnight Ramble 93
- overnight safari 127

# P

**politics**
- anarchist bookfairs 253
- garden 218
- Houses of Parliament 53
- petitions 220
- Speakers' Corner 50-51

**pubs & bars**
- canalside 271
- comedy venues 290, 291, 293
- historic inns 27, 136, 182, 204, 220, 229, 232, 262, 275, 286
- historic wine bar 142
- Ramsay gastropubs 181
- rupees accepted 197
- serving asparagus 83
- smallest 286
- temperance 59
- with views 131

**puppet shows**
- Punch & Judy 106
- Russian 219

# R

**railways**
- Devon coastal line 232
- disused trackways 182, 185
- funicular 177, 270
- museum 228
- Scottish scenic lines 87, 208
- sleeper trains 12, 195
- station refreshments 243, 303
- stay in a station 202
- steam trains 26, 44, 101, 125, 263, 264
- Tarka Line 185

**religious & spiritual sites**
- Buddhist 60, 180, 213
- Catholic shrines 188, 241
- Glastonbury Tor 288
- monasteries, abbeys & priories 84, 106, 166, 188, 194, 205, 240, 279
- *see also* cathedrals; churches & chapels; solitude & contemplation

**restaurants & cafés**
- afternoon teas 297
- architecture 150, 218

| | |
|---|---|
| in art galleries | 131, 182, 185, 242 |
| breakfasts | 16, 255 |
| British | 181, 222, 242 |
| Buddhist | 213 |
| cheese | 19, 144 |
| fish & seafood | 56, 94, 103, 196, 242, 255, 268-269 |
| French | 94 |
| haute cuisine | 29, 94 |
| healthy motorway food | 49 |
| ice-cream parlours | 111, 157, 158 |
| Italian | 56 |
| Mediterranean | 136 |
| memorable cafés | 182, 193, 196, 215, 243 |
| organic vegetables | 203 |
| pie & mash | 69 |
| puddings | 209 |
| Punjabi | 197 |
| Ramsay gastropubs | 181 |
| student-run | 168 |
| vegetarian | 12, 213, 282 |
| Vietnamese | 261 |
| with views | 131, 185 |
| *see also* teas | |

**rugby league**
| | |
|---|---|
| local derby | 126 |
| northern leagues | 72 |

**rugby union**
| | |
|---|---|
| local derby | 126 |
| stadium tour & museum | 230 |
| Welsh matches | 72 |

## S

**sculpture**
| | |
|---|---|
| chainsaw | 138 |
| Heatherwick, Thomas | 148-150 |
| in natural settings | 117, 128-129, 171, 189, 193, 194, 201, 225, 261, 288 |
| public | 237 |
| sculptors' studios | 73, 288 |

**seaside & beaches**
| | |
|---|---|
| ancient jetty | 270 |
| beach airport | 157 |
| beach cleaning | 10 |
| beach huts | 197, 298 |
| Bognor Birdman event | 281 |
| clubbing scene | 114 |
| coastal walks | 75, 84, 202 |
| donkey rides | 23 |
| historic pier | 123 |
| horse riding | 101 |
| macabre history | 274 |
| melancholy resorts | 136 |
| nudist beach | 301 |
| open-air theatre | 107 |
| Punch & Judy | 106 |
| rugged scenery | 260 |
| samphire | 172 |
| sand dunes | 136, 156, 298, 300, 301 |
| sculpture | 128-129 |
| seafood shacks | 103, 268-269 |
| state-of-the-art café | 150 |
| surfing beaches | 210-212, 301 |
| traditional resorts | 125, 157 |
| tunnels & tidal pools | 202 |
| unspoilt beaches | 12, 13, 282, 298-301 |

| | |
|---|---|
| volleyball | 164 |
| whistling sands | 120 |

**shops**
| | |
|---|---|
| books | 12, 131, 181, 270 |
| butchers | 56, 174-176 |
| charity | 12, 136 |
| chocolate | 202 |
| crafts | 12 |
| fashion | 261 |
| food | 17, 52, 56, 278 |
| interior design | 165 |
| records | 259 |
| vintage | 136 |
| *see also* bakeries | |

**snorkelling**
| | |
|---|---|
| bog | 39 |
| on Lundy island | 117 |
| trail | 33 |

**solitude & contemplation**
| | |
|---|---|
| hidden garden | 295 |
| Faith House | 233 |
| monastic guesthouse | 84 |
| peaceful wild places | 121, 279 |
| retreats | 180, 205 |
| Skyspaces | 266 |
| tree cathedral | 184 |

**space, outer**
| | |
|---|---|
| interactive centre | 44 |
| planetariums | 19, 244 |
| stargazing events | 188 |
| watching for NEOs | 281 |

**spas**
| | |
|---|---|
| best | 118-119, 183, 278 |
| Turkish baths & Pump Room | 37 |

**sport (participation)**
| | |
|---|---|
| clay shooting | 57 |
| coasteering | 173 |
| fencing | 23 |
| field archery | 226-227 |
| golf | 29, 259, 278 |
| hang gliding & paragliding association | 279 |
| ice skating | 27, 90 |
| indoor snowsports | 55, 205 |
| lacrosse (men's) | 56 |
| marathons | 83 |
| motor racing | 17, 73 |
| mountainboarding | 171 |
| orienteering | 137, 172 |
| outdoor snowsports | 106, 195, 295 |
| White Air festival | 115 |
| *see also* activities, unusual; climbing; cricket; cycling; equestrian pursuits; football; snorkelling; swimming; tennis; watersports | |

**sports events (spectator)**
| | |
|---|---|
| American football | 222 |
| basketball | 249 |
| equestrian events | 237, 248, 255 |
| Highland games | 228 |
| ice hockey | 126, 249 |
| local derby matches | 126 |
| motorcycle races | 59, 156, 204 |
| original modern Olympics | 146 |
| rugby league | 72, 126 |
| rugby union | 72, 126, 230 |
| stadium tours & museums | 230-231 |

| | |
|---|---|
| Tenby Boxing Day Swim | 278 |
| volleyball | 126, 164 |
| *see also* cricket | |

**subterranean mysteries**
| | |
|---|---|
| caves | 20-22, 37, 137, 142, 208, 262 |
| city aqueducts | 143 |
| cliff tunnels | 202 |
| foot tunnel | 270 |
| grottos | 66, 67, 188, 259 |
| hydro-electric station | 130 |
| mines | 55, 116, 142, 213 |
| underground Skyspace | 266 |
| wartime bunkers & tunnels | 60, 252 |

**swimming**
| | |
|---|---|
| around the Scilly Isles | 100 |
| Boxing Day | 278 |
| lidos | 104 |
| with seals | 282 |
| tidal pool | 202 |
| under Durdle Door | 260 |
| wild | 234-236 |

## T

**teas**
| | |
|---|---|
| afternoon tea | 297 |
| cream tea | 124 |
| Potting Shed Tea Room | 215 |
| Tibetan tea rooms | 213 |

**television**
| | |
|---|---|
| BBC tour | 202 |
| nostalgic children's | 32 |
| programme locations | 52, 256, 292 |

**tennis**
| | |
|---|---|
| holidays | 278 |
| real | 76 |
| tournaments | 139 |
| Wimbledon Lawn Tennis Museum & tour | 231 |

**theatre**
| | |
|---|---|
| Alan Ayckbourn | 69 |
| Brighton Festival | 271 |
| comedy venues | 292, 293 |
| mystery plays | 100 |
| old theatres | 32, 84 |
| open air | 55, 107, 294 |
| street | 160 |

**theme parks**
| | |
|---|---|
| Alton Towers | 163 |
| Bewilderwood | 88-89 |
| Blackgang Chine | 270 |
| Diggerland | 35 |
| Drayton Manor Theme Park | 162 |
| Legoland | 47 |
| Lightwater Valley | 163 |
| Oakwood Theme Park | 163 |
| Thorpe Park | 162 |

**toilets**
| | |
|---|---|
| compost | 68 |
| famous | 159 |

**transport**
| | |
|---|---|
| aviation museum | 105, 178 |
| cable car | 262 |
| camper vans | 142 |
| cliff railways & funiculars | 177, 270 |
| commercial vehicles museum | 255 |
| motorcycle museum | 143 |
| Routemaster buses | 19 |

Time Out 1000 Things to do in Britain **313**

scooter rally 45
sea tractor 182
tandems 116
*see also* canals, cars & driving; cycling; railways

## V

**views**
  from bars & restaurants 131, 616
  from big wheels 26, 288
  from cable cars 262
  camera obscura panoramas 259
  from hills & mountains 103, 192, 281, 282
  from towers 131, 140, 178, 190, 221, 223
  from wind turbines 254

**villages**
  abandoned 105, 156
  model 96-99
  plague 44
  prehistoric 160, 245
  quirky architecture 52
  Victorian 182

## W

**walks**
  Ben Nevis 281
  coastal 75, 84, 202
  Coleridge Way 130
  disused railway lines 182, 185
  Kinder Scout 220
  with llamas 26
  Ministry of Defence land 105
  National Trails 65, 126, 178
  Northumberland 84, 188
  Ridgeway 267
  South Downs Way 178
  slavery tour 287
  Tarka Trail 185
  in Wainwright's footsteps 15
  woodland 84, 169, 178, 182, 188, 298

**watersports**
  coasteering 173
  diving 145
  river-bugging 69
  sea kayaking 271
  snorkelling 33, 39, 117
  surfing 138, 210-212, 301
  wakeboarding 35

**wildlife**
  *see* animals; birdwatching; ecology & environment; fish & marine life; zoos & wildlife parks.

**woods, forests & trees**
  activities & adventures 88-89, 103, 169, 226-227, 303
  arboretums 136, 146, 172
  autumn leaves 146
  bluebells 165
  caravans 263
  conservation 284, 294
  cycle trail 25
  food foraging 152-155
  plant a tree 384
  sculpture 117
  star-gazing 188
  tallest tree 283

tree cathedral 184
tree climbing 110
treetop walkway 120
walks 84, 169, 178, 182, 298

## Z

**zoos & wildlife parks**
  bats 170
  conservation 28
  donkeys 208
  giraffes at eye level 57
  ice rinks 90
  'keeper for a day' schemes 161
  monkeys 169
  overnight safari 127
  penguins' parade 77
  rare cats 116
  red squirrels 202

# A-Z index

Note: number refers to page, not list entry.

## A

| | |
|---|---|
| Abbotsbury Swannery | 188 |
| Acclimbatize | 20-22 |
| Adopt-a- Beach scheme | 10 |
| Adventure Hebrides | 271 |
| Aintree Racecourse | 248 |
| Air Guitar Championship | 157 |
| Air Hockey | 270 |
| Airstream caravans | 95 |
| Aldeburgh Festival | 87 |
| Alexander McQueen | 136 |
| All Saints Church | 139 |
| All Tomorrow's Parties | 198 |
| Alnwick Garden | 303 |
| Alton Towers | 163 |
| American Museum in Britain | 289 |
| Anarchist Bookfair | 253 |
| Anchor, The | 271 |
| Anchorstone Café | 268 |
| Anderton Boat Lift | 53 |
| Another Place | 128-129 |
| Anthony's | 94 |
| Antiques Market, Yoxford | 196 |
| Appleby Tourist Information Centre | 95 |
| Arsenal Museum & Tour | 230 |
| Art Car Boot Fair | 35 |
| Artists' Open Houses Trail | 271 |
| Artois Championships | 139 |
| Arundell Arms Hotel | 55 |
| Ascot Park Polo Club | 255 |
| Ashdown Forest Centre | 23 |
| Ashdown Forest Llama Park | 26 |
| Ashmolean Museum | 240 |
| Asparagus Festival | 83 |
| Atmospheric Railway Inn | 232 |
| Atrium | 168 |
| Audio Brighton | 114 |
| Avebury stone circle | 17, 267 |
| Avoncroft Museum of Historic Buildings | 72 |

## B

| | |
|---|---|
| B of the Bang | 150 |
| Babington House | 118 |
| Baddesley Clinton | 48 |
| Baggins Book Bazaar | 270 |
| Bailey, Liam | 96-99 |
| Bakelite Museum | 260 |
| Ballowall Barrow | 245 |
| Baltic Centre for Contemporary Art | 185 |
| Bamburgh Castle | 298 |
| Banana Cabaret | 291 |
| Bar Code | 290 |
| Barbara Hepworth Museum & Sculpture Garden | 73 |
| Barfly | 112 |
| Barnards Farm | 148 |
| Barnsley House | 118 |
| Barnstaple Market | 257, 258 |
| Barra Airport | 157 |
| Bat Conservation Trust | 170 |
| Bath Rugby Club | 126 |
| Battle of Hastings | 156 |
| BBC Television Centre | 202 |
| Bearcat Club | 293 |
| Beatin' Rhythm | 259 |
| Beatles, The | 220 |
| Bedbug | 113 |
| Bedford Butterfly Park | 206-207 |
| Bedford Pub | 291 |
| Bedgebury Pinetum | 136 |
| Bekonscot Model Village | 96-99 |
| Bell, Vanessa | 151 |
| Belsay Hall | 106 |
| Beltane Festival, Edinburgh | 47 |
| Ben Cruachan | 130 |
| Bentley's | 242 |
| Bestival | 198 |
| Beth Chatto Gardens | 191, 192-193 |
| Beth Shalom Holocaust Centre | 137 |
| Bewilderwood | 88-89 |
| BFI *see* British Film Institute | |
| Big Blue | 212 |
| Big Chill | 198 |
| Big Draw | 294 |
| Big Garden Birdwatch | 123 |
| Big Pit National Coal Museum | 116 |
| Big Sheep | 197 |
| Billingham Bombers | 126 |
| Billingsgate Market & Seafood Training School | 75 |
| Birmingham Hippodrome | 32 |
| Birmingham Museum of Science & Discovery | 244 |
| Birmingham Rep | 238 |
| Bishop's Palace | 275 |
| Black Friars Distillery | 39 |
| Blackgang Chine | 270 |
| Blackpool Grand Theatre | 292 |
| Blackpool Pleasure Beach | 63 |
| Blackpool Tower | 140-141 |
| Blackwell Bookshop | 181 |
| Blakeney National Nature Reserve | 147 |
| Bleigiessen | 150 |
| Blenheim Palace | 35, 36 |
| Bletchley Park National Codes Centre | 117 |
| Blewetts Bakery | 160 |
| Bliss Day Spa | 118 |
| Blissfields | 198 |
| Bloomers Original Bakewell Puddings | 253 |
| Blue Carpet | 150 |
| Bluebell Railway | 101 |
| Blyton, Enid | 294 |
| Boathouse Restaurant & Crab Shed | 268 |
| Boatman's Association | 147 |
| Bodiam Castle | 252 |
| Bodleian Library | 130 |
| Bodyflight | 47 |
| Bog snorkelling | 39 |
| Bognor Birdman festival | 281 |
| Boisdale | 242 |
| Bolton Abbey | 254 |
| Bookshop, Lyme Regis | 12 |
| Borough Market | 174, 196, 296 |
| Bradford Animation Festival | 233 |
| Bradford Bulls RLFC | 72 |
| Braemar Gathering | 228 |
| Brain's Cider | 280 |
| Braunton Burrows | 156 |
| Brecon Jazz Festival | 243 |
| Bridgnorth Cliff Railway | 177 |
| Brief Encounter | 243 |
| Brighton Festival | 271 |
| Brimham Rocks | 49 |
| Bristol International Balloon Fiesta | 186 |
| Bristol Rugby Club | 126 |
| Bristol Zoo | 90, 161 |
| Bristol's City Museum & Art Gallery | 93 |
| BritBowl | 222 |
| British Cheese Festival | 144 |
| British Commercial Vehicle Museum | 255 |
| British Empire & Commonwealth Museum | 287 |
| British Film Institute | 16 |
| British Hang Gliding & Paragliding Association (BHPA) | 279 |
| British International Ltd | 44 |
| British Lawnmower Museum | 157 |
| British Library | 218 |
| British Museum | 145 |
| British Open Crabbing Championship | 240 |
| British Orienteering | 137 |
| British Surfing Association | 211 |
| British Trust for Conservation Volunteers (BCTV) | 245 |
| Britten, Benjamin | 283 |
| Broadhalfpenny Down cricket pitch | 156 |
| Broadstairs Folk Week | 288 |
| Broadway cinema | 16 |
| Broadway Tower | 110 |
| Brockwell Lido | 104 |
| Brogdale Farm | 220 |
| Brontë Parsonage Museum | 266 |
| Brownsea Theatre | 294 |
| Brunel, Isambard Kingdom | 219, 224, 232, 287 |
| Burgh Island Hotel | 182 |
| Burghley Horse Trials | 237 |
| Burns Night | 242 |
| Burrell Collection | 270 |
| Burrow Hill Cider | 280 |
| Burton, Sir Richard | 115 |
| Bury Market | 258 |
| Butlins holiday camps | 198 |
| Buxton Festival | 47 |
| Buxton Opera House | 292 |
| Byron, Lord | 122, 240 |

## C

| | |
|---|---|
| C2C cycle route | 194 |
| Caen Hill locks | 25 |
| Café Europa | 293 |
| Café Maitreya | 282 |
| Cairngorms National Park | 171, 195 |
| Caledonian Sleeper train | 12, 195 |
| Cally Gardens | 192 |
| Cambridge, University of | 86, 229, 296 |
| Cambridge Folk Festival | 288 |
| Camera obscura | 259 |
| Campaign for Drawing | 294 |
| Canteen | 242 |
| Canterbury Tales | 255 |
| Cardiff University | 86 |
| Cardiff Winter Wonderland | 90 |
| Carfin Lourdes Grotto | 188 |
| Cargo | 114 |
| Carisbrooke Castle | 106 |
| Carnforth Station | 243 |
| Carshalton Lavender | 184 |
| Cartier International Polo Tournament | 255 |
| Cass Sculpture Foundation | 117 |
| Celtic Manor Resort | 259 |
| Centre for Alternative Technology (CAT) | 68 |

Time Out 1000 Things to do in Britain 315

| | |
|---|---|
| Cerne Abbas giant | 145 |
| Chagall, Marc | 139 |
| Chagford swimming pool | 104 |
| Chalice, MV | 147 |
| Champignon Sauvage | 94 |
| Chaos Paintball | 29 |
| Chapter Arts Centre | 16 |
| Charleston House & Festival | 151 |
| Chatley Heath Semaphore Tower | 178 |
| Chatsworth | 36, 201 |
| Cheese Rolling | 253 |
| Cheese Society | 19, 144 |
| Chelsea Physic Garden | 124 |
| Cheltenham Festival | 40, 41 |
| Cherwell Boat House | 61 |
| Chester Zoo | 90, 161 |
| Chewton Glen | 119, 278 |
| Chibuku | 112 |
| Chichester Cathedral | 139 |
| Chillingham Castle | 252 |
| Chinese New Year | 87, 229 |
| Cholmondeleys | 65 |
| Christ Church Cathedral choir | 296 |
| Chysauster Iron Age village | 245 |
| Cinnamon Twist | 214 |
| Circus Space | 80-82 |
| Clachan Bridge | 275 |
| Claridge's | 297 |
| Clearwater Paddling | 271 |
| Clevedon Pier | 123 |
| Cley Windmill | 130 |
| Clifton Suspension Bridge | 224 |
| Cloud Appreciation Society | 246-247 |
| Clouds Hill | 184 |
| Coco | 33 |
| Colchester Zoo | 116 |
| Coleridge Way | 130 |
| Colesbourne Park | 190 |
| Collection, The | 261 |
| Colston Bassett Dairy | 144 |
| Columbia Road Flower Market | 196 |
| Comedy Camp | 291 |
| Comedy Store | 84, 290 |
| Comedy Zone | 292 |
| Commissions North | 237 |
| Common Loaf | 214 |
| Company Shed | 268 |
| Compton Verney House Trust | 178 |
| Concorde | 178 |
| Concorde 2 club | 114 |
| Conversation Piece | 237 |
| Cookies Crab Shop | 268 |
| Cornerhouse cinema | 16 |
| Cornwall Tourist Board | 75 |
| Coton Manor Garden | 191, 192, 193 |
| Coughton Court | 48 |
| Couple | 237 |
| Cowal Highland Gathering | 228 |
| Cowley Manor | 118 |
| Crab & Winkle Way | 182 |
| Crab House Café & Oyster Farm | 268 |
| Cragside | 283 |
| Crank Club | 113 |
| Craster Seafood Restaurant | 255 |
| Creamfields | 198 |
| Credenhill Snail Farm | 56 |
| Creek Inn | 204 |
| Cruachan Visitor Centre | 130 |
| Crystal Palace Park | 36 |
| Culloden Moor battlefield & visitor's centre | 222 |
| Cumberland Pencil Company Museum | 60 |
| Cuts | 261 |
| Cycleexperience | 116 |

## D

| | |
|---|---|
| Dahl, Roald | 19 |
| Dalby Forest cycle trails | 25 |
| Dancebase | 73 |

| | |
|---|---|
| Dartington Hall | 102 |
| Dart's Farm | 184 |
| David Bann | 282 |
| David Marshall Lodge | 170 |
| Daylesford Organic | 214 |
| De La Warr Pavilion | 125 |
| Denbies vineyard | 270 |
| Dent Station | 202 |
| Devil's Chair | 45 |
| Devonshire, The | 181 |
| DFS Classic | 139 |
| Dickens Festival, Broadstairs | 279 |
| Dickens House Museum | 279 |
| Diggerland | 35 |
| Discovery, RSS | 240 |
| Diverse | 136 |
| Don Valley Stadium | 222 |
| Donington Park & Grand Prix Collection | 275 |
| Donkey Sanctuary | 208 |
| Doors Open Days | 205 |
| Doune Castle | 252 |
| Dover Castle | 106, 205, 252 |
| Downland Cycles | 182 |
| Downstairs at the King's Head | 291 |
| Dozmary Pool | 178, 272, 274 |
| Drayton Manor Theme Park | 162, 163 |
| Droitwich Spa Lido | 104 |
| Du Maurier, Daphne | 272-274 |
| Duchy Marathon | 83 |
| Dudley Zoo | 161 |
| Duke of York's Picturehouse | 32 |
| Dumfries House | 218 |
| Dunmore Park | 173 |
| Dunraven House | 12 |
| Dunstanburgh Castle | 84, 298 |
| Dunster Castle | 170 |
| Dunwich Dynamo | 250-251 |
| Durdle Door | 260 |
| Durham University | 229, 296 |
| Durrell Wildlife Conservation Trust | 28 |

## E

| | |
|---|---|
| Eagle, The | 229 |
| Earl of Rone festival | 219 |
| Earthships | 266 |
| East Beach Café | 150 |
| East Neuk Festival | 126 |
| East Ruston Old Vicarage | 193 |
| Eastbourne International Open | 139 |
| Eastbourne Pier | 259 |
| Ecotech Centre | 254 |
| Ecsite-uk | 244 |
| Eden Project | 90, 201 |
| Edgbaston Priory Club | 139 |
| Edinburgh Castle | 283 |
| Edinburgh Festival | 40-41 |
| Edinburgh Festival Theatre | 32 |
| Edinburgh Marathon | 83 |
| Edinburgh Winter Wonderland | 90 |
| Edinburgh Zoo | 77 |
| Egremont Crab Fair | 165 |
| Eleanor crosses | 278 |
| Electric Cinema | 151 |
| L'Enclume Restaurant & Rooms | 29 |
| End, The | 112 |
| English Open Chainsaw Carving Competition | 138 |
| English Wine Week | 270 |
| Eureka! The Museum for Children | 164 |
| Eurostar | 303 |
| Exchange, The | 25 |
| Exeter Castle | 90 |
| Exeter Underground Passages | 143 |
| Exmoor National Park | 165 |
| Explore-at-Bristol | 244 |
| Eyam Museum | 44 |

## F

| | |
|---|---|
| Fabric | 112, 113 |
| Faith House | 233 |
| Falkirk Wheel | 53 |
| Falko | 52 |
| Fantasy Island | 163 |
| Faringdon Tower | 67 |
| Farm Café | 196 |
| Fashion Museum | 70-71 |
| Fat Duck | 94 |
| Featherstonehaughs | 65 |
| Festival of History | 216 |
| Festival of Marmalade | 116 |
| 5th View | 131 |
| 58 Degrees North | 271 |
| Filmhouse, Edinburgh | 16 |
| Financial Times HQ | 242 |
| Fine Cheese Company | 144 |
| Fishbourne Roman Palace | 79 |
| Fitzpatrick's | 59 |
| FixMyStreet scheme | 13 |
| Flour Station | 214-215 |
| Flying Fish Tours | 110 |
| Forbidden Corner | 208 |
| Formby Point Red Squirrel Reserve | 202 |
| Forth Road Bridge | 224 |
| Forum, Norwich | 90 |
| Foster, Norman | 105, 145, 193, 221 |
| Franklins | 242 |
| Frederick's of Chesterfield | 158 |
| Freecycle scheme | 288 |
| Frogmore House | 39 |

## G

| | |
|---|---|
| Gaiety Theatre | 292 |
| Garden House | 190, 191 |
| Garden Organic | 193 |
| Garlic Festival | 65 |
| Garsington Opera | 57 |
| Gastro | 196 |
| Gate restaurant | 282 |
| Gatecrasher | 114 |
| Geevor Tin Mine | 213 |
| Gifford Lectures | 86 |
| Ginger Pig | 56, 174-176 |
| Glade Festival | 198 |
| Glasgow Barrowland | 254 |
| Glasgow Necropolis | 101 |
| Glasgow Film Theatre | 16 |
| Glasgow School of Art | 143 |
| Glasgow Science Centre | 244 |
| Glassy Junction | 197 |
| Glastonbury Festival | 198, 279 |
| Glastonbury Tourist Information Centre | 288 |
| Glee Clubs | 292-293 |
| Glen Chantry | 193 |
| Glendurgan Garden | 36 |
| Gloucester Rugby Club | 126 |
| Gloucestershire-Warwickshire Steam Railway | 44 |
| Go Ape | 103 |
| Goodwood Revival Meeting | 221 |
| Gordon's Wine Bar | 142 |
| Gormley, Anthony | 128-129 |
| Gothic Weekend, Whitby | 239 |
| Graham Greene Festival | 168 |
| Grand National | 248 |
| Grand Ole Opry | 83 |
| Grasmere Gingerbread Shop | 202 |
| Gray, Thomas | 278 |
| Great Britain, SS | 219 |
| Great Dixter | 191, 192, 193 |
| Great Langdale Marathon | 83 |
| Green Man Festival | 43, 199 |
| Greenwich Foot Tunnel | 270 |
| Grove, The | 119 |
| Guardian Hay Festival | 40, 43 |

**316 Time Out** 1000 Things to do in Britain

| | |
|---|---|
| Guards Polo Club | 255 |
| Guildford Flames | 249 |
| Guildford Heat | 249 |
| Guildford Lido | 104 |
| Guildford Spectrum | 249 |
| Gunn's Bakery | 179 |
| Gwatkin Cider Co Ltd | 280 |

## H

| | |
|---|---|
| Hack Green Nuclear Bunker | 60 |
| Hackney Empire | 292 |
| Hadrian's Wall | 126 |
| Hallé Orchestra | 229 |
| Ham Polo Club | 255 |
| Hamilton Mausoleum | 266 |
| Hammersmith Town Hall vintage sales | 136 |
| Hampden Park Tour | 231 |
| Hampstead Churchyard | 32 |
| Hampton Court Palace | 36 |
| Harbour Bar | 111 |
| Harbour Lights tearoom | 204 |
| Hardy's Cottage | 84 |
| Harlech Castle | 252 |
| Harlow Carr, RHS Garden | 52 |
| Harrogate Turkish Baths | 37 |
| Hartington Hall | 232 |
| Hartlands Cider & Perry | 280 |
| Harvey Nichols | 136 |
| Harvington Hall | 48 |
| Hat Fair | 160 |
| Hawkstone Park | 66 |
| Haye Farm Cider | 280 |
| Heatherwick, Thomas | 148-150 |
| Heaven | 113 |
| Heights of Abraham | 262 |
| Hell Fire Caves | 262 |
| Henry Moore Foundation | 288 |
| Hepworth, Barbara | 73, 261 |
| Herbal | 114 |
| Heritage Open Days | 205 |
| Heritage Seed Library | 179 |
| Heroes Wall | 189 |
| Hever Palace | 37 |
| Hidcote Manor Garden | 228 |
| Hidden Gardens | 295 |
| Highgate Cemetery | 32 |
| Highgate Wood | 170 |
| Highland Fine Cheeses | 144 |
| Hilton, London | 131 |
| Hockney, David | 182 |
| Hodsock Priory | 190 |
| Holehird Gardens | 192 |
| Holkham Hall | 298 |
| Holland Park hostel | 232 |
| Hollycombe Steam Fair | 26 |
| Holmpton, RAF | 60 |
| Holocaust Centre | 137 |
| Holton Lee | 233 |
| Homotopia | 60 |
| Honister Slate Mine | 55 |
| Hook Norton Brewery | 66 |
| Horniman Museum | 225 |
| Hotel Continental, Whitstable | 164 |
| House in the Clouds | 67 |
| Houses of Parliament | 53 |
| Huddersfield Contemporary Music Festival | 122 |
| Hull rugby league clubs | 126 |
| Humber Bridge | 224 |
| Hunkin, Tim | 276-277 |
| Hunterian Museum | 12 |

## I

| | |
|---|---|
| I Camisa & Son | 56 |
| ICA *see* Institute of Contemporary Arts | |
| Ice Cube | 90 |
| Ice Factor, Lochaber | 26 |

| | |
|---|---|
| Ice Factor, York | 90 |
| Iford Manor | 209 |
| Ightham Mote | 218 |
| Ilam Park | 170 |
| Ilkley Pool & Lido | 104 |
| Imperial War Museum, Duxford | 105 |
| Ingatestone Hall | 48 |
| Inklings tour | 181 |
| Insect Circus & Museum | 30-31 |
| Institute of Contemporary Arts | 261 |
| Island Sailing Club | 49 |
| Island Sea Safaris | 147 |
| Isle of Man | 204 |
| Isle of Skye Bridge | 224 |
| Isle of Tiree | 13 |
| Isle of Wight Festival | 199, 279 |
| Italian Chapel | 79 |

## J

| | |
|---|---|
| Jamaica Inn | 272, 274 |
| James, Edward | 193 |
| Jane Austen's House Museum | 44 |
| Jarman, Derek | 193, 264-265 |
| Jazz Café | 114 |
| Jesus Green Pool | 104 |
| Jonathan Markson Oxford Tennis Camp | 278 |
| Jubilee Pool | 104 |
| Judges Bakery | 17 |
| Julian's Bower | 37 |
| Jurassic Coast | 26, 33 |

## K

| | |
|---|---|
| Kagyu Samye Ling Monastery & Tibetan Centre | 213 |
| Keighley & Worth Valley Railway | 125 |
| Keith Harding's World of Mechanical Music | 168 |
| Kelmarsh Hall | 216 |
| Kelmscott Manor | 194 |
| Kelvedon Hatch Secret Nuclear Bunker | 60 |
| Kelvingrove Art Gallery & Museum | 115 |
| Kennedy memorial | 168 |
| Kennet & Avon Canal | 25 |
| Kensington Gardens | 189 |
| Kew Gardens *see* Royal Botanic Gardens | |
| Kielder Forest | 188, 266 |
| Kimmeridge Bay Snorkelling Trail | 33 |
| King Alfred's Tower | 67 |
| King's College Cambridge | 296 |
| King's Lynn festivals | 42 |
| Kite Society & kite festivals | 122 |
| Knight Schools | 205 |
| Knights Templar | 137 |
| Knole | 130, 136 |

## L

| | |
|---|---|
| Lakeland Maze | 225 |
| Lakeside Arts Centre | 238 |
| Lalique, René | 66 |
| Lamb & Flag Inn | 27 |
| Lancashire County Cricket Club | 126 |
| Lancrigg Country House | 12 |
| Landmark Trust | 173 |
| Lanyon Quoit | 245 |
| Latitude Festival | 43, 199-200 |
| Laugharne Festival | 43 |
| Lawrence, TE | 184 |
| Leamington Tennis Court Club | 76 |
| Leeds Castle | 37, 252 |
| Leeds City Varieties | 292 |
| Leeds Rhinos RLFC | 72 |
| Legoland Windsor Park | 47 |

| | |
|---|---|
| Leonardslee Gardens | 159 |
| Lepard, Dan | 214-215 |
| Levens Hall | 218 |
| Liberty | 136 |
| Lichfield Cathedral | 127 |
| Lightwater Valley | 163 |
| Linbury Studio Theatre | 32 |
| Lincoln Cathedral | 228 |
| Lindisfarne Castle | 166-167, 298 |
| Lindsay House | 242 |
| Little Sparta | 233 |
| Lizard Pasty Shop | 160 |
| Llangoed Hall | 218 |
| Llangollen Fringe Festival | 293 |
| Lloyd, Christopher | 192 |
| Logan Botanical Gardens | 190 |
| Lola's On Ice | 158 |
| London Docklands Volleyball | 126 |
| London Eye | 289 |
| London School of Economics & Political Science | 86 |
| London to Brighton Vintage Car Rally | 158 |
| London Zoo | 161 |
| Long Meg | 59 |
| Longleat | 37, 100 |
| Longshore Herring Festival | 23 |
| Lord's Tour | 230 |
| Lost Gardens of Heligan | 254 |
| Lowry, The | 32 |
| Lucy's On a Plate | 209 |
| Ludlow Marches Food & Drink Festival | 303 |
| Lundy Shore Office | 117 |
| Lyburn Farm | 144 |

## M

| | |
|---|---|
| Mackintosh, Charles Rennie | 143 |
| MacLeans | 56 |
| Madhu's | 197 |
| Madingley American Cemetery | 229 |
| Magdalen Tower | 125 |
| Magna Science Adventure Centre | 244 |
| Malory Volleyball Club | 126 |
| Manchester United Museum & Tour | 230 |
| Mandarin Oriental | 119 |
| Manoir aux Quat' Saisons | 94 |
| Manze, M | 69 |
| La Mare Vineyards | 164 |
| Marina Villa Hotel | 94 |
| Marine Conservation Society | 10 |
| Marlborough Theatre | 293 |
| Marrs Bar | 292 |
| Marwell Zoological Park | 57 |
| Marwood Hill Gardens | 190 |
| Mass Observation project | 122 |
| Mathematical Bridge | 182 |
| May Day festivals | 47, 125, 177, 194 |
| MCC Museum | 230 |
| Mechanical Memories Museum | 116 |
| Mega Maze | 225 |
| Melton Mowbray Market | 258 |
| Men-an-Tol | 245 |
| Mersea Island Vineyard | 103 |
| Mersey Ferries | 143 |
| Middle Farm | 248 |
| Mighty Oak Tree Climbing Company | 110 |
| Millennium bridges | 66 |
| Millennium Seed Bank | 15 |
| Millennium Stadium | 59 |
| Minack Theatre | 107 |
| Ministry of Defence | 105, 121 |
| Miss Transgender | 164 |
| Mitre, The | 204 |
| Momentum Festival | 238 |
| Monkey World | 169 |
| Monty Python | 252 |
| Monument | 218 |

**Time Out** 1000 Things to do in Britain **317**

| | | | | | | | |
|---|---|---|---|---|---|---|---|
| Moore's Traditional Museum | 204 | One Spa | 119 | Rebustours | 136 |
| Morris, William | 194 | Open Farm Sunday | 33 | Regent's Park | 55, 159 |
| Moseley Old Hall | 48 | Open House Weekend | 205 | Renishaw Hall | 170, 267 |
| Motion | 113 | Orford Ness National | | Repository for | |
| Mottisfont Abbey Garden, | | Nature Reserve | 121 | Distressed Gentlefolk | 12 |
| House & Estate | 83 | Oriental Museum | 229 | Restaurant Nathan Outlaw | 94 |
| Morelli's | 157 | Orwell Bridge | 196 | Ridgeway | 267 |
| Mount Grace Priory | 106 | Osborne Bros | 103 | Ringing Stone | 13 |
| Mount Saint Bernard Abbey | 84 | Osborne House | 159 | Ripley Castle | 48 |
| Mountain Ash RFC | 72 | Osprey Centre | 233 | River & Rowing Museum | 231 |
| Mow Cop castle | 67 | Outdoor Swimming Society | 234-236 | Riverford Farm | 203 |
| Mudeford Spit beach huts | 197 | Outer Reef Surf School | 212 | Riverside Studios | 16 |
| Mull Theatre | 292 | Overbecks Museum & Garden | 196 | Rivington | 242 |
| Murthwaite Green Trekking Centre | 101 | Owen, Nicholas | 48 | Roald Dahl Museum | |
| Museum of Lead Mining | 72 | Oxfam | 136, 279 | & Story Centre | 19 |
| Museum of Rugby | 230 | Oxford, University of | 85, 86 | Roast | 242 |
| Museum of Science & Industry | 244 | Oyster Shack | 268-269 | Rolling Bridge | 150 |
| Museum of Witchcraft | 52 | | | Romney, Hythe & | |
| mystery plays | 100 | ***P*** | | Dymchurch Railway | 264 |
| | | | | La Rosa campsite | 263 |
| ***N*** | | Paddington Basin | 150 | Rosemoor Garden | 192 |
| | | Painshill Park | 67 | Rosslyn Chapel | 232 |
| Nae Limits | 69 | Pandora Inn | 262 | Round of Gras | 83 |
| Narrow, The | 181 | Papageno | 136 | Routemaster buses | 19 |
| National Birds of Prey Centre | 132-135 | Papplewick Pumping Station | 243 | Royal Armouries | 23 |
| National Botanic | | Parliament Hill | 104 | Royal Botanic Gardens, Kew | 93 |
| Garden of Wales | 193 | Paul A Young Fine Chocolates | 188 | Royal College of Art Secret Sale | 169 |
| National Clay Shooting Centre | 57 | Paxton & Whitfield | 144 | Royal College of | |
| National Collection of Cider & Perry | 248 | Peace Pagoda | 60 | Surgeons of Edinburgh | 173 |
| National Cycling Centre | 93 | Pells Pool | 104 | Royal Court Theatre | 238 |
| National Dining Rooms | 242 | Pendennis Castle | 106, 205 | Royal Festival Hall | 107, 131 |
| National Field Archery Society | 226-227 | Pennyhill Park | 119 | Royal Garden Hotel | 131 |
| National Football Museum | 230 | Petworth House | 248 | Royal Horticultural Society | 52, 107,192 |
| National Fruit Collection | 220 | Philharmonic Dining Rooms | 158 | Royal Observatory | 19 |
| National Gallery | 242 | Philpot Museum | 26 | Royal Opera House | 32, 291 |
| National Garden Scheme | 282 | Phoenix Bakery | 215 | Royal Pavilion, Brighton | 159 |
| National Glass Centre | 208 | Physical Energy | 189 | Royal Pump Room Museum | 37 |
| National Malus Collection | 148-149 | Pilchard Inn | 182 | Royal Scotsman | 87 |
| National Maritime | | Pitt Rivers Museum | 136 | Royal Scottish Pipe Band | |
| Museum, Cornwall | 102 | PJ's Surf Shop | 212 | Association | 201 |
| National Media Museum | 32, 233 | Place, The | 32 | Royal Society for the | |
| National Memorial Arboretum | 172 | Plantation Garden | 65 | Protection of Birds | 123, 147, 233 |
| National Monument, Edinburgh | 103 | Plas Newydd | 260 | Royal Southern Yacht Club | 49 |
| National Motor Museum | 79 | Plastic People | 114 | Royston Cave | 137 |
| National Motorcycle Museum | 143 | Players of St Peter | 100 | RSPB *see* Royal Society | |
| National Museum of Flight | 178 | Pleasure Beach, Great Yarmouth | 163 | for the Protection of Birds | |
| National Portrait Gallery | 189 | Plug | 112 | Rules | 242 |
| National Railway Museum | 228, 289 | Pluscarden Abbey | 205 | Run to the Sun | 15 |
| National Seal Sanctuary | 147 | Plymouth Gin | 39 | Run What Ya Brung | 73 |
| National Space Centre | 19, 44 | Poohsticks | 23 | Rushton Triangular Lodge | 67 |
| National Surfing Centre | 211, 212 | Port Eliot Literary Festival | 42-43 | Rutland Water Nature Reserve | 172 |
| National Trails | 65, 126, 178 | Port Lympne Wild Animal Park | 127 | | |
| National Trust Working Holidays | 281 | Port Quin | 156 | ***S*** | |
| Natural History Museum, London | 90 | Portmeirion | 52 | | |
| Natural History Museum at Tring | 13 | Portobello Road Market | 136 | Sadler's Wells | 32 |
| NCS Surfboards | 212 | Portsmouth City Museum | 297 | Saffron Walden Common | 37 |
| Neal's Yard Dairy | 144 | Portsmouth Historic Dockyard | 100 | Sainsbury Centre for Visual Arts | 221 |
| Neolithic Marathon | 83 | Postcard Teas | 297 | St Andrew's Church | 286 |
| Nevis Range Mountain Experience | 106 | Postman's Park | 189 | St Andrews Links Trust | 29 |
| New Art Gallery Walsall | 52 | Potting Shed Tea Room | 215 | St Bartholomew's Church, | |
| New Asian Tandoori Centre | 197 | Pride festivals | 108-109 | Much Marcle | 248 |
| New Quay Boat Trips | 160 | Priory Farm | 171 | St Bartholomew's Church, | |
| Newark Park | 170 | Promenade Concerts, BBC | 15 | Warleggan | 272 |
| Newlyn Art Gallery | 25 | Prospect Cottage | 193 | St Clement, Eastcheap | 100 |
| Newstead Abbey | 240 | Punch & Judy | 106 | St David's Cathedral | 267 |
| 99 Clubs | 291 | Purbeck Marine Wildlife Reserve | 33 | St Giles, Church of | 278 |
| Northern Lights | 185, 188 | Purple Mountain Bike Centre | 25 | St Helier's Day Pilgrimage | 125 |
| Nottingham Open | 139 | | | St John restaurant | 222 |
| Nutshell | 286 | ***Q*** | | St John's College Choir | 296 |
| NVA | 123 | | | St Leonard's Church | 302 |
| | | Quality Chop House | 242 | St Magnus Festival | 289 |
| ***O*** | | Queen's Club | 139 | St Margaret's Chapel | 283 |
| | | Queen Mary's dollshouse | 287 | St Martin in the Fields church | 138 |
| Oakwood Theme Park | 163 | Quex House & Gardens | 67 | St Martin's Bakery | 228 |
| O'Connors Campers | 142 | | | St Mary and All Saints church | 120 |
| O'Hanlon's Brewery | 184 | | | St Mary & St David, | |
| Old Henley Farm | 53 | ***R*** | | Parish Church of | 209 |
| Old Original Bakewell Pudding Shop | 253 | | | St Mary Magdalene Church, | |
| Olympic Games | 57, 93, 146 | Ramsay, Gordon | 181 | Hucknall Torkard | 122 |
| On Ice | 90 | Rankin, Ian | 136 | St Mary Magdalen's | |
| | | | | RC Church, Mortlake | 115 |

| | | | | | |
|---|---|---|---|---|---|
| St Matthew's Church | 66 | Stein, Rick | 94, 194 | Turnmills | 113 |
| St Michael's Mount | 248 | Stephen Joseph Theatre | 69 | Twentieth Century Society | 242 |
| St Pancras station | 303 | Steyning Stinger Marathon | 83 | Twickenham Stadium Tour | 230 |
| St Paul's Cathedral choir | 296 | Stockport Lacrosse Club | 56 | TYF Adventure | 173 |
| Saints RLFC | 72 | Stoke Row wellhead | 159 | | |
| Salcey Forest treetop walk | 120 | Stonehaven Pool | 104 | | |
| Salisbury Cathedral choirs | 296 | Stonehenge | 17 | | |

## U

| | | | |
|---|---|---|---|
| Saltaire village | 182 | Stoney Littleton Long Barrow | 127 |
| Saltdean Lido | 104 | Stowe House | 218 | Uffington White Horse | 84, 145, 267 |
| Salts Mill | 182 | Sturminster Newton market | 157 | Under the Pier | 276-277 |
| Samlesbury Hall | 48 | Summer Isles Hotel | 94 | University College London | 86 |
| Sandford Parks | 104 | Surbiton Trophy | 139 | University College of | |
| Sandham Memorial Chapel | 110 | Surfer's Paradise | 212 | Food, Birmingham | 168 |
| Santa Pod Raceway | 73 | Surgeons Hall Museum | 173 | Up-Helly-Aa | 168 |
| Sausage trail, Ludlow | 303 | Surrey Hills Llamas | 26 | Urbis | 245 |
| Sawston Hall | 48 | Sutton Hoo | 271 | | |
| Scapa Scuba | 145 | Swadlincote Ski & | | | |
| Scarborough Surf School | 212 | Snowboard Centre | 205 |

## V

| | | | |
|---|---|---|---|
| Science Museum | 244 | Swaffham Market | 256, 258 |
| Scotney Castle | 48 | Swan House | 136 | VFM Scoot | 45 |
| Scotrail | 12, 208 | Sweeting's | 56, 242 | Vertigo 42 bar | 131 |
| Scottish Football Museum | 231 | Swimtrek | 100 | Victory, HMS | 100 |
| Scottish Poetry Library | 120 | Syndicate | 113 | Viet Hoa | 261 |
| Screen on the Green | 32 | | | Vindolanda & the Roman | |
| Scudamore's | 61 | | | Army Museum | 126 |
| Sea Watch Foundation | 177 |

## T

| | | | | Vintage Vacations | 95 |
|---|---|---|---|---|---|
| Seafood Cabin | 269 | | | Vipassana Centre | 180 |
| Seafood Restaurant, Rick Stein's | 94 | T in the Park | 200 | Virginia | 136 |
| Seaham Hall | 119 | Tall Ship Adventures | 179 | Volleyball England | 164 |
| Secret Garden Party | 200 | Tank Museum | 259 | Voyages of Discovery | 147 |
| Seldom Seen Farm | 278 | Tapestry Goes West | 200 | | |
| Senghenydd RFC | 72 | Tarka Line & Tarka Trail | 185 | | |
| Sequoia | 119 | Tarr Steps | 165 |

## W

| | | | | | |
|---|---|---|---|---|---|
| Serenity Spa | 119 | Taste the Wild | 152-155 | | |
| Seven Stories | 262 | Tate Britain | 189 | Waddington Air Show | 102 |
| Severn Bore | 138 | Tate Modern | 131 | Wainhouse's Tower | 67 |
| Severnwye Llama Trekking | 26 | Tatton Park Country Show | 138 | Wainwright, Alfred | 15 |
| Sezincote | 159 | Tay Road Bridge | 224 | Waiting Room | 282 |
| Shambala Festival | 200 | Tea Box | 297 | Wakehurst Place | 15 |
| Sharmanka Kinetic | | Tea Smith | 297 | Wakestock | 35 |
| Gallery & Theatre | 219 | Tebay Services | 49 | Wallace Collection | 261 |
| Shaw's Corner | 294 | Teignworthy Brewery | 107 | Walnut Tree Inn | 94 |
| Shed, The | 297 | Telford, Thomas | 137 | Walsingham RC National Shrine | 241 |
| Shell Grotto | 259 | Tenby Boxing Day Swim | 278 | War Poets Collection | 286 |
| Shoreham Airport | 145 | Tenth Bar | 131 | Warrington, The | 181 |
| Shot at Dawn Memorial | 172 | Terre à Terre | 282 | Warwick Castle | 90, 173 |
| Showroom, Sheffield | 16 | Thackray Museum | 142 | Watershed Media Centre | 16, 23 |
| Side Cinema | 16 | Thame Market | 257, 258 | Watersplash | 212 |
| Sidmouth Folk Week | 288 | Thames Skiff Hire | 286 | Waterstone's, Piccadilly | 131 |
| Silecroft Beach | 101 | Theatre Royal, Richmond | 84 | Watertours | 294 |
| Silverstone Circuit | 17 | Theatre Writing Partnership | 238 | Watts, George Frederick | 189 |
| Singlive UK | 29 | Thekla | 114 | Watts Gallery & Chapel | 189 |
| Sir John Soane's Museum | 136, 249 | Thermae Bath Spa | 183 | Wayland's Smithy | 267 |
| Sitwell family | 267 | Thinktank | 19, 244 | WC Rowe | 160 |
| Skara Brae | 160 | Thomas Hardy's ale | 184 | Weald & Downland | |
| Skipton Market | 258 | Thorpe Park | 162, 163 | Open Air Museum | 170 |
| Skylon | 131 | Thousand Island Expeditions | 147 | Wellcome Trust | 150 |
| Skyspace | 266 | Three Chimneys | 136 | Wells Cathedral Choir | 296 |
| Slapstick Silent Comedy Festival | 23 | Three Choirs Festival | 296 | Welsh Surfing Federation | |
| Slave Trade Tour | 287 | 333 Club | 114 | Surf School | 212 |
| Smeaton Farm | 225 | Tigh an Truish Inn | 275 | Wembley Stadium Tour | 231 |
| Smiths | 55 | Times Square ice rink | 90 | West Dean Gardens | 193 |
| Snail Trail | 142 | Timorous Beasties | 165 | West Kennett Long Barrow | 17 |
| Snowshill Manor | 177 | Tinside Lido | 104 | West Yorkshire Playhouse | 238 |
| Soho Theatre | 238 | Tintagel Castle | 178, 252 | Westminster Abbey choir | 296 |
| Sole Bay Fish Company | 240 | Tiree | 13 | Westminster Cathedral choir | 296 |
| Somerset House | 90, 91 | Tintern Abbey | 194 | Westonbirt, the | |
| South Downs Planetarium | 19 | Top Floor at Smiths | 242 | National Arboretum | 146 |
| South Downs Way | 178 | Tower Bridge | 224 | Whale and Dolphin | |
| Southwark Cathedral choir | 296 | Tower 42 building | 131 | Conservation Society | 177 |
| Spaceguard Centre | 281 | Tower of London | 90 | Whipsnade Tree Cathedral | 184 |
| Speakers' Corner | 50-51 | Town Mill Bakery | 215 | Whipsnade Wild Animal Park | 161 |
| Speedway World Championship | 59 | Trafalgar Roof Garden | 131 | Whistler, Rex | 260 |
| Speedwell Cavern | 142 | Traverse Theatre | 238 | Whitby Gothic Weekend | 239 |
| Speke Hall | 48 | Tredegar RFC | 72 | White Air festival | 115 |
| Spencer, Stanley | 110 | Tresco Marathon | 83 | White Swan | 84 |
| Spinnaker Tower | 221 | Trinity House | 223 | Whites hotel | 158 |
| Stand Comedy Clubs | 292 | Tru Thoughts | 114 | Whitley Warriors | 126 |
| Standon Calling | 200 | TT races | 156, 204 | Whitstable Oyster Festival | 237 |
| Stanley Spencer Gallery | 110 | Tucker's Grave Inn | 220 | Whitstable Oyster | |
| Start | 261 | Tuckers Maltings | 107 | Fishery Company | 269 |
| | | Turk's Head | 293 | Whitstable Regatta | 237 |

**Time Out** 1000 Things to do in Britain **319**

| | |
|---|---|
| Wigan Warriors RLFC | 72 |
| Wild Britain | 206-207 |
| Wilderness Scotland | 271 |
| Wildfowl & Wetlands Trust, Slimbridge | 136, 222 |
| Wilton's | 242 |
| Wimbledon Lawn Tennis Museum & Tour | 231 |
| Windmill Hill Tennis & Golf Academy | 278 |
| Windows | 131 |
| Windsor Castle | 287 |
| Wisley, RHS Garden | 107 |
| Wolseley | 218 |
| Women's Institute | 116, 157, 257 |
| Woodland Trust | 284 |
| Wookey Hole Caves | 37 |
| Woolpack Inn | 262 |
| World Bog Snorkelling Championships | 39 |
| World Conker Championships | 85 |
| World Museum | 19 |
| World Pipe Band Championship | 201 |
| World Stone Skimming Championships | 249 |
| Worm's Head Hotel | 300 |
| Wright Brothers | 196 |
| WWT London Wetland Centre | 170 |
| Yorkshire Sculpture Park (YSP) | 171, 261, 266 |
| Yorkshire Wheel | 289 |
| Youth Hostel Association | 232 |
| Ystrad Rhondda RFC | 72 |

# Z

| | |
|---|---|
| Zennor Quoit | 245 |
| Zorb South UK | 83 |

# X

| | |
|---|---|
| Xscape | 55 |

# Y

| | |
|---|---|
| Yardbird | 114 |
| York Cold War Bunker | 60 |
| York Maze | 225 |
| Yorkshire County Cricket Club | 126 |

# Picture credits

**Photography by** pages 5, 186, 187 Bristol Balloon Fiestas Ltd; 5, 225 Tony West; 5, 7, 264, 265, 299 (top left), 300, 301 Britta Jaschinski; 7, 53, 238 Olivia Rutherford; 7, 81, 226, 227 Heloise Bergman; 9, 39, 137 Crown Copyright (2007) Visit Wales; 9 Alnwick Gardens; 9, 81, 260 Andrew Blackenbury; 10, 11, 246, 247 Alistair Keddie; 13 National History Museum;15, 33 Rob Greig; 21, 22 Hiromi Mori; 25 Ian Kingsnorth; 28 Durrell/Gregory Guida; 30, 31, 277 Nick Butcher; 35 Nick Cunard; 36 Longleat Enterprises Ltd; 41 Robert Haines/Alamy; 42, 43 Justin Williams; 47 Stewart Turkington; 49 Chris Thomas 2007; 50, 51 Oliver Knight; 57 Tristram Kenton/Lebrecht Music; 59 Andrew Stanney; 63, 64 Maisie Tomlinson; 65 Lea Anderson; 67, 205, 216, 217 English Heritage Photo Library; 68 CAT; 69 Active Focus Productions; 70, 71 Fashion Museum, Bath & North East Somerset Council; 73 Bowness, Hepworth Estate/Bob Berry; 75 Rogan Macdonald; 77 Alan R Thomson@rzss;79 www.visitorkney.com; 86 UCL; 87 Orient-Express Hotels, Trains & Cruises; 88, 89 Keiron Tovell; 91 Courtesy of Somerset House Trust/Hayes Davidson; 93 gargantuaphotos.com; 97, 98, 99 Liam Bailey; 101 Iain Masterton/Alamy; 102 Dartington Hall Trust; 104 Nick Dawe/Arcaid.co.uk; 108, 109, 139, 213, 219 Getty Images; 111 Roger Scruton; 117 Bryan Kneale; 117 Sally Matthews; 121 Loop Images/Paul Knight; 123 Euan Myles, 2005; 124 Chelsea Physic Garden; 125 Alan Galley/Alamy; 127 The Aspinall Foundation; 128, 129 images provided by The Mersey Partnership; 133, 134, 135 Jamie Harris; 144 Cephas Picture Library/Alamy; 146 Hugh Angus; 147 Billy Shiel's Boat Trips; 148, 149 Rick Guest; 150 Andy Stagg/VIEW; 151 Courtesy of The Charleston Trust; 153, 154, 155 Rachel Ragg; 157 Martin Parr/Magnum Photos; 159 The Royal Pavilion & Museums, Brighton & Hove; 162 Courtesy of Pleasure Beach, Blackpool; 166 Don Brownlow; 171 Jonty Wilde; 173 The Landmark Trust; 175, 176 Charlie Pinder; 181 Ming Tang Evans; 183 Matt Cardy; 189 Watts Gallery, Compton; 191, 193 Jonathan Buckley; 196 Ben Murphy; 197 Nadia Isakova/Alamy; 199 David Hoffman Photo Library/Alamy; 203 Martin Ellis; 204 Peter Jordan/Alamy; ; 206, 207 Bedford Butterfly Park; 211 John Wormald; 213 Jim Allan/Alamy; 221 John Colley; 224 Britainonview/Lee Beel; 230 Paula Glassman; 233 Helene Binet; 235 D. Tyler 2007; 241 Chapel Studios; 243 Universal Pictures/Photofest; 244 Magna Science Adventure Centre; 245 Elizabeth Blanchet; 249 Alan Bone; 253 Cotswold Photo Library/Alamy; 257 AA World Travel Library/Alamy; 267 Jason Gallier/Alamy; 273 Courtesy of Chris Bond_cornovia.org.uk; 275 The Bishop's Palace, Wells; 281 James de Bounevialle/Alamy; 283 Sam Robbins; 284, 285 Adam Burton; 287 Royal Collection © 2007, Her Majesty Queen Elizabeth II; 289 Abigail Lelliott; 295 Clementine Sandison; 299 James Gordon (top right); 299 Andrew Kneath (bottom).

The following images were provided by the featured establishments/artists: pages 3, 5, 7, 12, 17, 23, 27, 42, 43, 66, 95, 103, 105, 107, 115, 118, 119, 120, 131, 143, 165, 169, 185, 199, 200, 201, 208, 214, 215, 223, 229, 231, 237, 254, 257, 261, 263, 271, 279, 302, 304.

**Illustrations by Ian Keltie** 45, 85, 61, 113, 141, 161, 179, 195, 209, 239, 250, 251, 268.